This belongs to
David Cross

The Buchenwald Report

Bericht über das
Konzentrationslager Buchenwald bei Weimar

Prepared by a special intelligence team from the
Psychological Warfare Division, SHAEF:

Albert G. Rosenberg

Max M. Kimenthal

Richard Akselrad

Alfred H. Sampson

Ernest S. Biberfeld

Assisted by a committee of Buchenwald prisoners:

Eugen Kogon

Joseph Berman

Herbert Froebess

Valentin Gelber

Lionel Guierre

Stefan Heymann

Ernst Holzer

Jan Robert

Ferdinand Römhild

Karl Stockmar

~

April–May 1945

The Buchenwald Report

Translated, edited, and
with an introduction by

David A. Hackett

Foreword by
FREDERICK A. PRAEGER

WESTVIEW PRESS
Boulder • San Francisco • Oxford

English translation and additional material copyright © 1995 by Westview Press, Inc.

The Buchenwald Report is a translation of *Bericht über das Konzentrationslager Buchenwald bei Weimar,* prepared in April and May of 1945 by a special intelligence team from the Psychological Warfare Division, SHAEF, assisted by a committee of Buchenwald prisoners.

Published in 1995 in the United States of America by Westview Press, Inc., 5500 Central Avenue, Boulder, Colorado 80301-2877, and in the United Kingdom by Westview Press, 12 Hid's Copse Road, Cumnor Hill, Oxford OX2 9JJ

Library of Congress Cataloging-in-Publication Data
The Buchenwald report / translated and edited by David A. Hackett.
    p.   cm.
    Original report was produced by the Intelligence Team of the
Psychological Warfare Division of the Supreme Headquarters of the
Allied Forces.
    Includes bibliographical references (p.) and index.
    ISBN 0-8133-1777-0
    1. Buchenwald (Germany : Concentration camp)—History—Sources.
2. Holocaust, Jewish (1939–1945)—Germany—Personal narratives.
I. Hackett, David A.   II. Allied Forces. Supreme Headquarters.
Psychological Warfare Division. Intelligence Team.
D805.G3E7746   1995
940.53'1743226—dc20
                                                                    94-39714
                                                                    CIP

Printed and bound in the United States of America

 The paper used in this publication meets the requirements
of the American National Standard for Permanence of Paper
for Printed Library Materials z39.48-1984.

10   9   8   7   6   5   4   3   2

To the twenty-eight members of the Rosenberg family
who died in the Nazi Holocaust

PROFESSOR EDMUND N. AND MRS. LENORE CAHN
who saved the life of the compiler of this report and

ALBERT G. ROSENBERG
who compiled the report, preserved it, and
shared it with the world

Contents

In memoriam

FREDERICK A. PRAEGER

1915–1994

Publisher, athlete, survivor, and dreamer of dreams

Foreword

Because of history's many ironies, the Buchenwald concentration camp and the Buchenwald Report have been intimately and continuously connected to my life. Even now, when I am almost eighty years old, this connection continues to exist as a clear, contoured, and vivid part of my life, entering for brief or longer periods and sometimes appearing in dreams. These memories are usually reawakened in me on such occasions as watching Steven Spielberg's remarkable film *Schindler's List.*

My father, Dr. Max Praeger, a Viennese publisher and bookseller, was a prisoner in Buchenwald from autumn 1939 to spring 1945, in what were to be the last years of his life. I myself had narrowly escaped arrest, and probable internment in Buchenwald, at least three times before leaving Austria for Paris. But it was clear that France was not going to be a safe haven for much longer, and so I came to the United States. There I held numerous jobs—lens grinder, soda jerk, gas station attendant—before joining the army. Eventually I found myself, in that final spring of the war, as an intelligence officer attached to the Sixth Armored Division of George S. Patton's Third Army, which had raced across France and had entered Germany. Having thought of my father throughout four campaigns in Western Europe, including the Battle of the Bulge, and having to some extent experienced these campaigns and battles as a race for his life, I had remained quite optimistic about his fate. One day in my jeep, early in April 1945, I encountered a column of concentration camp inmates in their striped uniforms who had run away from their guards and who told us that they had left Buchenwald two days before. When I inquired whether anybody knew my father, one of the prisoners identified himself as a member of the same work detail as my father. This man (whose name, sadly, I soon forgot in the swirl of events) had been my father's partner on a large two-man saw of the type used in the logging work in the forests near Buchenwald. For two years they had shared the hardships of prison labor. He also told me that my father had been sent to Auschwitz and certain death. For so long I had dreamed of finding him alive; now I learned that I had just missed saving him. My informant reported that my father had been obsessed with the idea of my finding him and that his dream had been to see me again in an American uniform.

Buchenwald was liberated on April 11, 1945, by a reconnaissance battalion of the Sixth Armored. The next day, April 12, as this unit had moved on in the direction of Czechoslovakia and the other U.S. troops that were to take over the camp had not yet arrived, I was the only American in Buchenwald. I took the opportunity to talk with some of the inmates. When I asked about my father, a certain Herr Herzog, the barracks chief and another friend of my father, showed me the bare wooden bunk my father had shared with a dozen other men and described to me his fate and his last hours in the camp. My father had got into an altercation with a Communist trusty in the breakfast line and had been struck on the head with a coffee ladle. The wound became inflamed and affected his one good eye. Under the circumstances this meant the cattle car and subsequent gassing at Auschwitz. I was too shaken to stay in Buchenwald for long and face the realities of what remained of life in what must have been a hell on earth; I left later that same day.

This did not end my personal connection with Buchenwald. With one exception, all of the members of Albert Rosenberg's SHAEF psychological warfare team who had organized the preparation of this report ended up in Wiesbaden after the war. There they were put in charge of the Information Control Division offices for the province of Hesse, in central Germany. When I later moved from General Lucius D. Clay's Berlin headquarters to Wiesbaden to take over the intelligence branch, I inherited the members of this team as a part of the Military Government Control Division for which I was to be responsible. And so by a quirk of fate we all became colleagues and friends. This was especially true in the case of Albert Rosenberg and Richard Akselrad. Akselrad not only hailed from my native Vienna but had also been for many years the number two man in one of my father's bookstores in the Rotenturmstrasse.

Moreover, I later came to know Eugen Kogon, author of *The Theory and Practice of Hell,* whom some of the Buchenwald inmates had succeeded in hiding from the SS during the last days before liberation and who had contributed what were in historical and analytical terms the most important parts of this report. He became my best friend, and I spent innumerable hours discussing the SS organization and how it functioned in this particular environment.

I'm very grateful that through David Hackett's scholarship *The Buchenwald Report* finally appears in English, not only as a tribute to the many prisoners of Buchenwald but also particularly as a memorial to Eugen Kogon, his indomitable courage, and his work. Kogon must be counted as one of the great historians and sociologists of the twentieth century.

The publication of this book also memorializes my father's suffering and death, and perhaps even gives them some meaning.

Frederick A. Praeger
March 23, 1994

Preface

THE WORK TRANSLATED in this volume is one of the most significant documentary discoveries from the World War II period. Although parts have appeared before in other forms, this is the first time the Buchenwald Report has been published in its entirety in any language since the information was recorded in April 1945. Its existence has been well known to scholars for many years, as Eugen Kogon credited it as the principal source of his classic work *The Theory and Practice of Hell*, first published in German in 1946 and in English in 1950. But the report itself was never published, and many scholars assumed that it had been lost.

One of the original carbon copies of the report was kept by Albert G. Rosenberg, the U.S. Army officer who headed the intelligence team responsible for interviewing prisoners at Buchenwald. In 1983, during a dinner with publisher Frederick A. Praeger, he mentioned the report. Mr. Praeger had copies sent to several major archives in the United States and abroad. In 1987, Mr. Rosenberg, then a professor of social work at the University of Texas at El Paso, offered his original copy of the manuscript to me, a colleague at the university who specialized in German history. I initially planned to use the report as the basis of an article discussing the historical role this manuscript played in the earliest efforts to document the Holocaust.

After some preliminary work along these lines, I decided to tackle the laborious task of translating the entire manuscript. During the first stage I transcribed, collated, and restored the organization of the original German-language text, contained on 400 yellowed, brittle, and blurry sheets of carbon copy paper. Next, I created a rough translation of the German, a task made more difficult by the prisoner slang and National Socialist jargon and terminology in the text and the imperfect command of German of at least some of the inmates who gave testimony. The final stage has been the revision of the text, the preparation of the scholarly apparatus, and the cross-referencing of the report to a wide variety of postwar publications.

As editor and translator, I realize that I owe a great debt of thanks to many institutions and individuals. I am especially grateful to Albert G. Rosenberg for making the manuscript available to me in the first place and for his consistent support and confidence in me during the lengthy period of its preparation. I thank Frederick A. Praeger, founder and longtime publisher of Westview Press; Peter W. Kracht, senior editor; and Shena Redmond, project editor, for their constant support, sound advice, and helpful criticism. I also thank Alice Colwell, copy editor, whose linguistic and grammatical skills helped me untangle many complicated German sentences.

In conducting the research for the scholarly documentation, I visited many institutions. I extend special thanks to the archivists at the National Archives in Washington, D.C., and Suitland, Maryland, for their assistance in making their collections accessible. I also received much help at the archives of Gedenkstätte Buchenwald in Weimar, Germany; in particular I must thank Sabine Stein for allowing me to draw upon her thorough knowledge of the Buchenwald materials. Financial support and course-release time were made possible by the Faculty Development Fund of the College of Liberal Arts at the University of Texas at El Paso. My trip to Germany was funded in part by a grant from the German Fulbright Commission for participation in their German studies seminar.

The library of the University of Texas at El Paso provided valuable material from its S.L.A. Marshall Military Collection and Ravel Judaica Collection. Its interlibrary loan department proved efficient in tracking down any number of obscure sources. I also made extensive use of the New Mexico State University Library, Zimmermann Library at the University of New Mexico, and Hayden Library of Arizona State University. Friends and colleagues who loaned valuable research materials include David Kittermann, Margaret Eskew, Peter de Wetter, and Albert G. Rosenberg, whose "magic closet" yielded far more than the original manuscript. Like all authors, I owe much to the numerous scholars who have worked on these topics before me, and I have tried to express my gratitude by acknowledging their work in the annotations and bibliography.

I owe a number of personal debts to those whose influence is more indirect. Friendships with Holocaust survivors have increased my understanding of this era; among these friends are Frank Oppenheimer, the late Dr. Frederick Bornstein, Al and Edith Eger, and Henry Kellen. Other friends and colleagues who have shared their knowledge of this period with me include Albert Schwartz, Z. Anthony Kruszewski, and Ilse Irwin. My professors at the University of Wisconsin—T. S. Hamerow, Robert L. Koehl, and George L. Mosse—gave me inspiration that has sustained me throughout my career. Colleagues in the Department of History at the University of Texas at El Paso have also been encouraging and supportive. Students who have helped in the preparation of the manuscript include Barbara Balian, Angelica Gonzalez, Nancy Nemeth Jesurun, and Maria Valenzuela.

Finally, I thank my family for their forbearance during my months of intensive work on the manuscript. My wife, Anne Hackett, has suffered through the numerous crises with patience and given me good advice; my children, Mary Elizabeth, Michael, and Caroline, have put up with an often absent or absentminded father. It is largely to them—and to all the young people of the next generation—that I dedicate this book, in hopes that it will make a contribution toward creating a more humane world.

David A. Hackett
El Paso, Texas

The Buchenwald Report

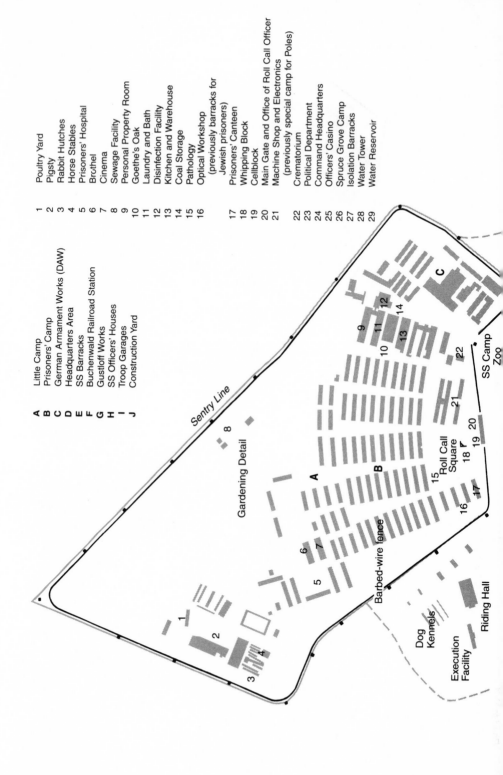

A Little Camp
B Prisoners' Camp
C German Armament Works (DAW)
D Headquarters Area
E SS Barracks
F Buchenwald Railroad Station
G Gustloff Works
H SS Officers' Houses
I Troop Garages
J Construction Yard

1   Poultry Yard
2   Pigsty
3   Rabbit Hutches
4   Horse Stables
5   Prisoners' Hospital
6   Brothel
7   Cinema
8   Sewage Facility
9   Personal Property Room
10 Goethe's Oak
11 Laundry and Bath
12 Disinfection Facility
13 Kitchen and Warehouse
14 Coal Storage
15 Pathology
16 Optical Workshop
    (previously barracks for
    Jewish prisoners)
17 Prisoners' Canteen
18 Whipping Block
19 Cellblock
20 Main Gate and Office of Roll Call Officer
21 Machine Shop and Electronics
    (previously special camp for Poles)
22 Crematorium
23 Political Department
24 Command Headquarters
25 Officers' Casino
26 Spruce Grove Camp
27 Isolation Barracks
28 Water Tower
29 Water Reservoir

Sentry Line

Gardening Detail

Roll Call Square

Barbed-wire Fence

Dog Kennels

Execution Facility

Riding Hall

SS Camp Zoo

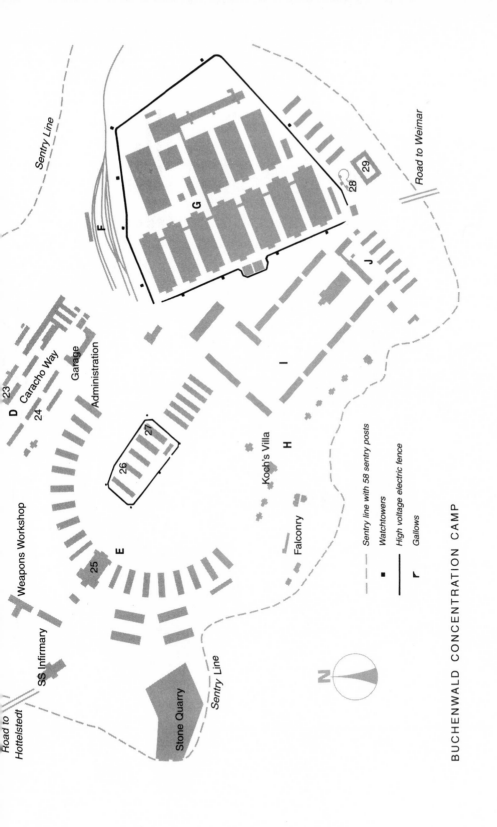

Road to Hottelstedt

SS Infirmary

Weapons Workshop

25

E

Stone Quarry

Sentry Line

D 23

Caracho Way

24

Garage

Administration

26

27

Koch's Villa

Falconry

H

I

J

F

G

28

29

Sentry Line

Road to Weimar

N

- - - - Sentry line with 58 sentry posts

■ Watchtowers

—— High voltage electric fence

⌐ Gallows

BUCHENWALD CONCENTRATION CAMP

Introduction
Documenting the Nazi Camps: The Case of the Buchenwald Report

B UCHENWALD HAD the distinction of being the first major concentration camp to fall into the hands of the Western Allies while it still had a full population of prisoners. The U.S. Army had earlier discovered an abandoned Nazi camp at Natzweiler, France, near the end of 1944; the Soviets had come upon abandoned and partially destroyed camps at Maidanek in July 1944 and later at Auschwitz, Poland, in January 1945. On April 5, the U.S. Army, however, found fresh evidence of atrocities on a large scale when they overran recently abandoned camps at Ohrdruf and Nordhausen-Dora. But these discoveries had not fully prepared Allied troops and their commanders for the sight of the sprawling camp at Buchenwald near Weimar in central Germany, which they reached on April 11, 1945.[1] It held 21,000 starving and ragged prisoners and was complete with crematoriums, execution rooms, and a hospital used for medical experiments on prisoners.

Four days later, on April 15, the British Army stumbled on Bergen-Belsen near Hannover, finding an even larger number of prisoners, most of whom were dying from starvation as well as typhus and typhoid. Later, U.S. troops would also discover Dachau near Munich (April 29) and Mauthausen near Linz, Austria (May 8). The Soviet Army liberated Sachsenhausen (April 22) and Ravensbrück (April 30) north of Berlin and Theresienstadt north of Prague (May 8). It gradually became clear that reports of atrocities made earlier in the war were neither isolated incidents nor exaggerations for propaganda purposes like those made against Germany in World War I but prima facie evidence of the brutality and inhumanity inherent in the Nazi system.

The comprehensive report and collection of statements from prisoners at Buchenwald was compiled by an intelligence team from the Psychological Warfare Division of the U.S. Army soon after the liberation of the camp. The Buchenwald Report stands as a unique document because in no other case were prisoners of a Nazi concentration camp systematically interviewed *while still in camp,* immediately after liberation. The report was an attempt to document the history, organization, and life of the camp in its entirety. Made with the active collaboration of 104 prisoners who contributed 168 reports, it was a collective effort. It represents the views of people of many nationalities rather than the perspective of any single individual, as do most later memoirs and oral histories. Unfortunately, this unusual report was never published in its original form, and even the survival of the manuscript has been in doubt until recently.

The existence of such a document has long been known to scholars and students who have read Eugen Kogon's classic book on the Nazi concentration camps, *The Theory and Practice of Hell*. The introduction to the American edition states:

> On April 16, 1945, five days after the first American armored units had arrived, an Intelligence Team from the Psychological Warfare Division visited the Buchenwald concentration camp. Its mission was to study the situation and to prepare a comprehensive report for the Supreme Headquarters Allied Expeditionary Forces (SHAEF). The report was to show how a German concentration camp was organized, what role was assigned to it in the Nazi State and what happened to those who were sent to the camps by the Gestapo and detained there by the SS.

The translator described the report itself as follows:

> The first report comprised some 400 typewritten pages, single-spaced. There was a main report of 125 pages which Kogon himself had dictated, and approximately 150 statements from individual prisoners, who by virtue of their experience had been asked to give their views on various facts, incidents, persons and phases.[2]

The fate of the document on which Kogon based his book long remained a mystery to scholars in the field. But at least one copy of the original report Kogon used survived.[3] It comes from a duplicate set of carbon copies kept by the U.S. Army officer who headed the military interrogation team, Second Lieutenant (later Captain) Albert G. Rosenberg, who gave it to me. It is now published in its entirety for the first time in this Westview Press edition.

It is only fitting that this report should finally appear in English, as that was always the intention of the team who collected the material. They originally planned for the report to come out in 1945 so that the world could make its own judgments about what had occurred in Nazi concentration camps. But the initial goal of translating the report was apparently abandoned under the pressure of more urgent problems at the end of the war. Instead, the document appeared in a quite different form, a completely rewritten version (in German) under the signature of one of the principal authors of the report, Eugen Kogon. His book was first published in early 1946 in Munich as a slim volume aimed at a German audience.[4]

In the pages that follow, the prisoners of Buchenwald speak in their own voices of the suffering that took place there. They tell of events so recent, so painful, so deeply engraved in their memories that they cannot speak without strong emotions. Portions of the manuscript relate occurrences in the measured tones of the scholar and bureaucrat, but statements of the individual prisoners in Part Two are far more emotional. The inmates speak eloquently of the sufferings of Jews, political prisoners, homosexuals, Jehovah's Witnesses, clergymen, Poles, Russian prisoners of war, slave workers who labored outside the camps, and women and children. They report not only of Buchenwald itself but of the vast network of Nazi concentration camps within which prisoners were constantly being transferred. The statements contain occasional inconsistencies, minor errors, strongly held opinions, and at times ideological cant, but an overall picture of the Nazi concentration camp system clearly emerges.

A vast flood of later historiography has further confirmed the alarming testimony first recorded in this report in May 1945. Perhaps if it had been published in 1945, as intended, the Buchenwald Report would have been, in the words of Deborah Lipstadt, "beyond belief." Now, two generations later, we have learned from the testimonies of many thousands of survivors that it is all too true.

The Liberation and Its Aftermath

Easter Sunday, April 1, 1945, was a special day for the prisoners of Buchenwald concentration camp.[5] The news that U.S. tanks had penetrated the Fulda gap and were approaching the vicinity of Eisenach (about 40 miles west of Weimar) was an "Easter present," the prisoners said. It meant that liberation should only be a matter of days. The prisoners vowed to stiffen their resistance to SS commands and to prepare for a possible armed showdown with the SS if they attempted to destroy the camp before withdrawing (see Part One, XIII, and Part Two, Chapter Ten, §149).* There was tremendous tension in the air because the inmates knew that at Auschwitz the Nazis had evacuated all the prisoners capable of walking and believed that they had murdered the sick prisoners who remained and destroyed the camp. (In fact, the Russian troops arrived quickly enough to rescue the sick, and much of Auschwitz had remained standing.) It was feared that the same scenario would be played out at Buchenwald. Prisoners had secretly smuggled arms into camp beginning with the August 1944 air raid, and an underground military unit had gradually been created. But the prisoners knew that their lightly armed units were no match for the heavily armed SS guards. Armed resistance by the prisoners would have to be a last resort.

The prisoners' worst fears seemed to be borne out by the sequence of events in the next few days. A top secret work detail was assigned the task of digging large trenches, probably for mass graves, which a few days later were filled in again. On April 4 all Jews in camp were ordered to report for roll call, an order that met with mass resistance—not a single person appeared. During the night many Jews "submerged," changing names, numbers, and blocks. The next day came a tip that the remaining twenty Englishmen and two Americans would be killed; some of them were able to survive by submerging. On the same day information about an order for the arrest of forty-six camp leaders (among them Eugen Kogon) was leaked, and they, too, submerged. Not one of them was found by the SS. Finally, camp leaders developed a daring plan to prevent the evacuations the SS had

---

*Cross-references to the text of the Buchenwald Report are indicated by part, chapter, and section numbers.

scheduled. On April 8 Kogon was smuggled out of camp in order to post a letter to Camp Commandant SS Colonel Hermann Pister that purported to come from an English paratroop officer, Major James McLeod, who had landed near Weimar. It warned the commandant against "death transports" like those that had come from Ohrdruf, threatening Allied reprisals against the people of Thuringia if Buchenwald were evacuated (Part One, XIII).

Meanwhile the Nazis had begun the evacuations despite the passive resistance of prisoners, who refused to appear for roll calls after April 5. Nazi guards had to enter the camps and forcibly gather together the prisoners. On April 6 more than 3,000 Jews left Buchenwald on foot; the following day more than 14,000 were supposed to leave, but fewer than half that number were gathered. The entire camp was supposed to be emptied on April 8, but the McLeod letter caused the commandant to hesitate. On April 9, 4,880 prisoners were sent on transport and a day later 9,280. Pister's commanding officer, SS General Prince Josias zu Waldeck-Pyrmont, came to Weimar in a fit of anger and ordered the camp commander to evacuate the camp completely. But by then it was too late. The SS men were already packing for their own flight.

As the front rapidly approached the camp on the Ettersberg, the Nazis made a last-ditch effort to cover up their atrocities. The prisoners in the camp jail were murdered during the night of April 10, and the surviving inmate orderly was assigned to clean up the bloodstains (Part Two, Chapter Five, §58). In the execution room adjoining the crematorium, they removed the meat hooks used for hanging bodies, cemented in the holes, and covered up the blood-spattered walls with a fresh coat of white paint. In their haste, however, they did not completely finish the job of hiding the evidence: After liberation, an American medical officer reported seeing four hooks still in the wall and partially filled holes for forty-four more, as well as a bloodstained club.[6]

The long-awaited liberation finally arrived on Wednesday, April 11 (see Main Report and Part Two, Chapter Eleven, §151). The day began quietly, but within a few hours the sounds of combat could be heard at a distance. At 10:15 A.M. Camp Commandant Pister summoned Senior Camp Inmate Hans Eiden and stated that the camp would be turned over to his control. This reassured the prisoners somewhat, although some knew that the commandant had ordered dive bombers from a nearby airfield to destroy the camp, an order the German airbase commander apparently rejected. By noon the loudspeaker ordered SS men to report to their stations outside the camp, sentries still remaining in the guard towers at the perimeter of the camp. By 2:10 P.M. the first U.S. tanks rolled by on the road outside the camp. The tanks were from the Reconnaissance Battalion, Sixth Armored Division, of General Patton's Third U.S. Army. Around 3:00 the sentries began to abandon their posts and run into the nearby woods. A few minutes later, the prisoner militia and camp police, who had been hiding with their weapons, took over the guard towers and main gate. (Today the camp's clocks are still set at 3:15 P.M. to commemorate the exact moment of liberation.) Soon the armed prisoner militia began scouring the woods in search of escaping SS men, many of whom had already changed into civilian clothes. By the end of the day, seventy-six former SS guards had been taken prisoner. A state of confusion prevailed: When the Weimar police president called the camp after 6:00 P.M. to issue an order to the SS to finish off the remaining prisoners in the camp, an inmate answered the telephone.[7]

The courageous actions of the prisoner militia on the afternoon of April 11 would eventually lead to the postwar myth of the prisoners' "self-liberation" of Buchenwald. There is of course some truth to this legend; the prisoners' actions are well documented. But in later East German literature, their part took on enormous importance, whereas the role of the U.S. military in the camp's liberation was ignored or denigrated. (See the section, "The Published Literature," below.)

The first two Americans to enter Buchenwald on April 11 were probably Egon W. Fleck, a civilian, and First Lieutenant Edward A. Tenenbaum, intelligence officers assigned to the Publicity and Psychological Warfare unit of the Twelfth Army Group Headquarters (under General Omar N. Bradley). According to their report, they first became aware of the liberation of the camp when their jeep encountered a unit of armed prisoners, still in their striped uniforms, marching down the road. They reported the startling sight as follows:

> [We] turned a corner onto a main highway, and saw thousands of ragged, hungry-looking men, marching in orderly formations, marching East. These men were armed and had leaders at their sides. Some platoons carried German rifles. Some platoons had panzerfausts on their shoulders. Some carried "potato masher" hand grenades. They laughed and waved wildly as they walked. … These were the inmates of Buchenwald, walking out to war as tanks swept by at 25 miles an hour.[8]

The units the two Americans encountered were the "shock troops," or prisoner militia, of which the Buchenwald prisoner leadership was so proud.

It was about 5:30 P.M. when the jeep with the two Americans pulled into the camp. They reported that the 21,000 prisoners "cheered at the sight of an American uniform, rushed out to shake hands, and threw valuable binoculars from their slave workshops." The intelligence officers met "the Camp Commandant, a German inmate," and later the camp leadership and council (the International Camp Committee). They were provided with beds for the night in Block 50, the experimental typhus laboratory.

The next morning, April 12, they were "awakened by a brass band, which serenaded them until they appeared at the windows, to be cheered by several thousand inmates." Later they witnessed an enormous parade, part of the camp's first "freedom roll call." Lieutenant Tenenbaum briefly greeted the prisoners in what one prisoner called "American German."[9] The officers stayed long enough to gather material for an eighteen-page preliminary report that included a short history of the camp and an analysis of camp organization, particularly stressing the role of the Communist-dominated inmate leadership. They could not help being impressed that "instead of a heap of corpses, or a disorderly mob of starving, leaderless men, the Americans found a disciplined and efficient organization in Buchenwald."[10]

For much of that day (Thursday, April 12), Buchenwald lay becalmed after the storm of combat that had swept past it. General George S. Patton's Third Army moved rapidly through Weimar, striking southeast into Saxony in the direction of Zwickau before eventually turning south into Czechoslovakia. The army's goal was to complete an encircling movement around Nazi-held Bavaria, alleged to be the last-ditch Alpine redoubt of the Hitler regime. About the same time, the newly conquered area around Weimar was officially transferred to the jurisdiction of General Courtney H. Hodges's First Army.

During this brief hiatus, another jeep brought U.S. intelligence officers to the camp. Its ranking officer was Captain Peter de Wetter, a German-speaking officer from the G-2 Section (counterintelligence) assigned to the headquarters of Hodges's First Army.[11] De Wetter found the camp eerily quiet, with neither German nor American troops present, and thousands of starving and sick prisoners milling about or sitting calmly in the sun. He was startled by the sight of a prisoner lying in the gutter, mumbling incoherently to himself, oblivious to his surroundings—one of those in a catatonic state near death who were dubbed "Muslims" in camp slang. He was also shown the crematorium, where stacks of emaciated corpses were still to be seen, along with a partially burned body on the grate and a mound of human ashes beside it. Using an amateur camera, de Wetter took a number of pictures of the incredible scenes, probably the earliest of many such photographs.

For the prisoners, the following day, Friday the thirteenth, would turn out to be lucky, "a red-letter day for the surviving inmates."[12] It was on that day that U.S. troops arrived in force to take control of the camp, bringing food, medical supplies, and other urgent necessities. Also on that day top-ranking American generals came to view the camp: General Dwight D. Eisenhower, supreme commander, accompanied by Generals Bradley and Patton. Their visits would touch off a major effort to publicize the atrocities found at Buchenwald, one that would occupy much of the next month.

The immediate tasks of the new American commandant, Major L. C. Schmuhl, were to feed thousands of starving prisoners, provide medical treatment for the most urgent cases, bury the dead, and restore sanitary conditions. The latter was especially problematic, because the last act of the withdrawing SS troops had been to destroy the pumps that provided the camp's water supply. Without water pressure, the camp's sewage system soon backed up, producing a powerful stench that the liberating troops and later visitors long remembered. An American medical officer who arrived in the camp on April 17, Captain Robert Dinolt, reported, "I saw people defecating all over the place. I saw urine splashing around the barracks, in the bunks."[13]

Epidemics of typhus and dysentery were an ever present threat to all concentration camps. The U.S. Army Medical Corps prevented a massive outbreak by quickly launching a decontamination campaign using DDT. At that point sixty-two cases of typhus had already been diagnosed but were isolated in a hospital ward.[14] American engineers finally restored Buchenwald's water supply on April 20, after the camp had gone nine days without water. Even then the sewage system was blocked, so the American commandant requisitioned ex-Nazis to haul excrement away until the sewer lines could flow again.

The 120th Evacuation Hospital, Semimobile, was rushed to the scene to care for the sick and dying. Commanded by Colonel W. E. Williams, it was a large unit, with twenty-one medical officers, 207 enlisted men, and forty nurses. It arrived in the Buchenwald area on the evening of April 15, but was not set up and ready to begin operations until two days later, when Captain Dinolt toured the camp to assess its needs. He estimated that about half the camp's surviving population (8,000 to 10,000 inmates) needed medical attention, "and among this group at least half were in such poor condition that their survival would be doubtful, unless medical care was given soon."[15] The majority of these prisoners were in the Little Camp, where conditions had been the worst in the final weeks. The American mobile hospital stayed in the area just over a week, during which they were able to reduce the death rate from 150 per day to about twenty per day. On April 25, conditions having been stabilized, the unit moved on to its next assignment.

Starvation was the most serious problem facing the camp at the end. In early 1945 the already inadequate camp rations had been cut still further. (See Part Two, Chapter Three, §25). It was estimated that in the final days of the camp, prisoners in the larger camp received 600 to 700 calories a day, whereas those in the Little Camp received only 500 a day.[16] At liberation thousands of prisoners were severely emaciated, many weighing less than half their normal body weight. The inmate who guided Brigadier General Eric F. Wood on his tour of the camp, French general René L'Hôpital, weighed only ninety-five pounds instead of his normal 175 pounds. Another American officer was guided by a Czech man, the former owner of a Prague hotel, who weighed 110 pounds compared to a normal 185 pounds.[17]

Indeed, these prisoners had lost all resemblance to individual human beings. Fleck and Tenenbaum reported meeting "an old man, dirty, bearded, one eye blind, [who] totters up and introduces himself as a French general." It was probably L'Hôpital, mentioned above, but the first group of American officers was clearly skeptical. They commented later in the report, in regard to the prisoners of the Little Camp, "They are brutalized, unpleasant to look on. It is easy to adopt the Nazi theory that they are subhuman, for many have in fact been deprived of their humanity."[18]

Feeding the prisoners became the most urgent task of the occupying American forces. Soon after liberation, abundant quantities of food, requisitioned from nearby Weimar, were made available to the camp inmates. But on receiving the food, the severely malnourished prisoners developed gastrointestinal problems, and many died. Major General Warren F. Draper, chief of the Public Health Branch, reported after his visit that "the intake is now controlled" to make sure no prisoner received too much food. In the worst cases of malnutrition, prisoners were fed intravenously in the hospital or were given a mixture of diluted cereal, milk, and sugar in amounts that were gradually increased.[19]

On April 16, 1945, a count of the camp population showed a total of 20,000, about 1,000 fewer inmates than were counted on the day of liberation. The U.S. Army's breakdown of the surviving camp population by nationality showed the following figures:[20]

French	2,900
Polish	3,800
Hungarians	1,240
Yugoslavs	570
Russians	4,380
Dutch	324
Belgians	622
Austrians	550
Italians	242
Czechs	2,105
Germans	1,800
Dutch [Luxemburgers?]	260
Anti-Franco Spanish and miscellaneous	1,207
	20,000

The report stated that the number of Jews, who were included in the nationality groups above, was 4,000. The same report also estimated the number of children in the camp at about 1,000. Later, more accurate figures put the number of children at about 850.[21]

Allied visitors to Buchenwald after liberation considered the presence of children to be one of the most disturbing aspects of the camp. The children, all boys, ranged in age from three and a half to seventeen years (Part Two, Chapter Nine, §118). Most were Jewish, and a high percentage were orphans. Many had seen their parents murdered before their eyes. An intelligence report commented on their plight: "During their years in concentration camp, they have received no schooling, have read no children's books, have seen no movies, have enjoyed none of the normal sport of children." The Polish children in particular did not want to return to their homeland because "there is a general fear that anti-Semitism has not yet been finally stamped out in Poland." Because many had no known relatives, a large number of children remained in camp after other prisoners had been released. Later a United Nations relief team visited the camp to make arrangements to move the 350 remaining children to Switzerland. The transfer was completed by the end of June.[22]

A week after liberation, life in camp had begun to reach some semblance of normality. From April 16 to May 16, 1945, the camp Information Bureau put out a daily newspaper, which was hung on bulletin boards around the camp. At first it was called *Lagerbericht* (Camp report) then *Nachrichten* (The news). In the beginning the newsletter printed some of the personal experiences of individual prisoners, several of which were included in the Buchenwald Report. Later it covered events outside the camp as well.

There were other signs of a return to normality in camp life: A mass memorial service was held on April 19 to commemorate the 51,000 prisoners who had died at Buchenwald and to honor President Franklin D. Roosevelt, who had died on April 12 and whom the former prisoners hailed as a liberator and a great fighter against fascism. In the same ceremony the inmates swore to destroy fascism, an act that the East Germans later mythologized. The first Jewish religious service at Buchenwald took place on April 20. Several hundred of the surviving Jewish prisoners took part in the services conducted by a U.S. Army chaplain, Rabbi Herschel Schacter.[23]

A few days later, the camp changed hands again and a new American commandant, Captain Ball, took over. On April 24 Ball told the International Camp Committee that his task was to work toward the quickest possible return of the prisoners to their homelands. He added to his staff five liaison officers representing the Soviet Union, Poland, Czechoslovakia, the Netherlands, and Yugoslavia. The West Europeans were to be repatriated first, since conditions were more normal there; the situation for the East Europeans was still unclear. The French government had agreed to provide temporary quarters to repatriated Spaniards and Italians. On May 2 Ball ordered the International Camp Committee to end its activities, stating that they had fulfilled the tasks they had set for themselves, work for which he expressed his thanks.[24] His order to disband the committee came, perhaps not coincidentally, the day after the Communist camp leadership had organized a massive May Day celebration along socialist lines.

By early May the now officially renamed Buchenwald Displaced Persons Center was slowly beginning to dissolve itself. Before the end of April, the French, Belgian, and Luxemburgian contingents had already left the camp. On V-E Day the Dutch left, followed by the Norwegians and the Czechs. An American Review Commission was processing papers for German and Austrian prisoners. By mid-May, they, too, began to be released as rapidly as possible. Political questions delayed the release of Poles and Russians, but by early June many of them were being repatriated as well. Although information on the camp is scarce for the last weeks of American control, it appears fairly certain that by the time U.S. forces turned the area over to the Soviets (July 4, 1945), the camp was nearly empty.

Publicizing Atrocity

In the first three weeks after its discovery, Buchenwald was exposed to the full glare of modern publicity in all its forms. Perhaps because it was the first major camp to be liberated, it received more attention than any other. Reporters and photographers from major American and British magazines and newspapers toured its barracks and interviewed prisoners. Delegations from the U.S. Congress and British Parliament visited, followed by selected groups of prominent newspaper editors, clergymen, and trade union leaders. British and American officers and soldiers passed through the camp in the early weeks, both in the line of duty and as curious observers. At least four different U.S. Army units served at Buchenwald at various times. The Third U.S. Army overran the camp, then control passed to units of the First, the Ninth, and finally the Seventh U.S. Armies.[25]

The decision to make Buchenwald the center of a major publicity effort to document German atrocities came from the highest level of the U.S. and British governments: General Dwight D. Eisenhower, SHAEF commander; General George C. Marshall, army chief of staff; President Harry S Truman; and Prime Minister

Winston Churchill. But it is clear that Eisenhower was the essential catalyst in organizing the publicity barrage. Prompted by reports of atrocities and discoveries of Third Reich treasures in Thuringia, Eisenhower left his headquarters at Reims on April 11 to see General Hodges at the Twelfth Army Group Headquarters in Wiesbaden. The following day Eisenhower, accompanied by Generals Patton and Bradley, made a brief visit to the underground salt mine at Merkers (Thuringia), in which the government of the Third Reich had hidden large amounts of gold, foreign currency, and art treasures. Eisenhower's entourage also toured the small concentration camp at Ohrdruf, near Gotha. He was so moved by this first impression of German atrocities that he wrote General Marshall from Reims on April 15:

> But the most interesting—although horrible—sight that I encountered during the trip was a visit to a German internment camp near Gotha. The things I saw beggar description. ... The visual evidence and the verbal testimony of starvation, cruelty and bestiality were so overpowering as to leave me a bit sick. In one room, where [there] were piled up twenty or thirty naked men, killed by starvation, George Patton would not even enter. He said he would get sick if he did so. I made the visit deliberately, in order to be in a position to give *first hand* evidence of these things if ever, in the future, there develops a tendency to charge these allegations merely to "propaganda."[26]

On April 13, less than forty-eight hours after its liberation, Eisenhower, along with Bradley and Patton, toured Buchenwald camp. That evening in Marburg he discussed Ohrdruf, Buchenwald, and Nordhausen-Dora with Hodges and Bradley in the presence of his son, Captain John Eisenhower. "The only speck of optimism I can see," he said, "is that I really don't think that the bulk of the Germans knew what was going on." After relating that Patton had told him that the mayor of Gotha and his wife had committed suicide after seeing Ohrdruf, he added, "Maybe there is hope after all." Captain John Eisenhower left by jeep the next day to make his own visit to Weimar and Buchenwald.[27]

Eisenhower was still so disturbed by what he had seen that the atrocities again became the major topic of conversation when he met Prime Minister Churchill in London a few days later. Eisenhower spent a long evening with Churchill discussing the state of the war and visited him the next morning at the annex to 10 Downing Street (the War Rooms). Eisenhower promised to send photos of the camps to Churchill, who apparently shared his outrage. He urged Churchill to send a group of members of Parliament and journalists to tour the camps at once. An American delegation, Eisenhower feared, "might be too late to see the full horrors, whereas an English delegation, being so much closer, could get there on time." On April 19 General Walter Bedell Smith relayed a report to Churchill through Lord Ismay that "the German concentration camps which have recently been overrun by the Allied armies are even indescribably more horrible than those about which General Eisenhower spoke to you yesterday."[28]

With fresh reports appearing about British discoveries at Bergen-Belsen, all London was talking about German atrocities. John Colville, Churchill's private secretary, wrote in his diary, "The papers are full of [reports], with stomach-turning photographs, consequent on the Allied armies overrunning Buchenwald and other German concentration camps. Proof is now supplied that the stories of the last ten years have not been just propaganda, as were many of the last war's atrocity stories."[29]

On the day after Eisenhower's visit, April 19, Churchill delivered a short but moving speech to Parliament in reply to a member's question. E. P. Smith had asked whether steps would be taken to maintain "the captured prison camp of Buchenwald as a memorial to German methods." Although refusing to commit himself to specific steps, Churchill stated:

> No words can express the horror which is felt by His Majesty's Government at the proofs of these frightful crimes now daily coming into view. ...
> I have this morning received an informal message from General Eisenhower saying that the new discoveries, particularly at Weimar, far surpass anything previously exposed. He invites me to send a body of Members of Parliament at once to his Headquarters in order that they may themselves have ocular and first-hand proof of these atrocities.[30]

Calling the matter one of "urgency," he arranged for the appointment of a special team of ten members of Parliament "for this extremely unpleasant but none the less necessary duty" of investigating the camp.

A carefully balanced delegation of four Conservatives, three Labour members, one Liberal, one Liberal National, and one Independent left London within twenty-four hours. Among them were one woman and one Jewish member; two of the ten were from the House of Lords. The delegation arrived at Eisenhower's SHAEF Headquarters in Reims the evening of April 20. The next morning the group flew on military Dakotas (DC-3s) into Weimar and reached Buchenwald at 11 A.M. on Saturday, April 21, just ten days after liberation.[31] The committee's brief, factual report, published by His Majesty's Stationery Office in May 1945, concluded

> that a policy of steady starvation and inhuman brutality was carried out at Buchenwald for a long period of time; and that such camps as this mark the lowest point of degradation to which humanity has yet descended. The memory of what we saw and heard at Buchenwald will haunt us ineffaceably for many years.[32]

Meanwhile, on April 19, Eisenhower also cabled Marshall in Washington to arrange for a visit of a U.S. congressional delegation. In his telegram he stated:

> We continue to uncover German concentration camps for political prisoners in which conditions of indescribable horror prevail. I have visited one of these myself and I assure you that whatever has been printed on them to date has been understatement. If you would see any advantage in asking about a dozen leaders of Congress and a dozen prominent editors to make a short visit to this theater in a couple of C-54's, I will arrange to have them conducted to one of these places where the evidence of bestiality and cruelty is so overpowering as to leave no doubt in their minds about the normal practices of the Germans in these camps.[33]

Eisenhower's telegram was carried by staff officers to the Speaker of the House and the majority leader of the Senate the next day. A delegation was quickly assembled that would be prepared to leave on Sunday, April 22. It included six senators and six representatives, divided equally between majority (Democrats) and minority (Republicans). Among the most prominent members of the delegation were Senators Alben W. Barkley (D.–Ky.) and Leverett Saltonstall (R.–Mass.) and Congressman R. Ewing Thomason (D.–Tex.). The delegation arrived in Paris on April 23 and left for Weimar the next morning. (Interest in Congress was high enough that a second, unofficial group was sent a few days later.) The delegation was accompanied by General John M. Weir, Colonel Robert H. Thompson, Colonel John A. Hall, and a group of photographers.[34] The congressional committee also visited the camp at Nordhausen-Dora and toured Dachau on May 2, just forty-eight hours after its liberation. In their sixteen-page official report, the members expressed a belief

> that out of [the horror of the camps] justice will emerge and that through the sickening spectacle which we have witnessed of the degradation to which human beings have been subjected will come ultimately a firmer realization that men of all nations and tongues must resist encroachments of every theory and every ideology that debases mankind.[35]

Eighteen prominent U.S. newspaper publishers and editors arrived in Buchenwald April 25 and later met with Eisenhower at his headquarters in Reims to compare notes on their visits to the "hell camps." Eisenhower reportedly said that "he hoped every American newspaper would print the story of German bestiality in detail."[36] The leaders of the journalists' group, Julius Ochs Adler, Malcolm Bingay, and Stanley High, asked that the following telegram be sent to Secretary of War Henry L. Stinson: "It is the unanimous judgment of the delegation of magazine and newspaper editors sent here to investigate conditions of German prison camps that the reports of atrocities committed upon war prisoners, political prisoners and civilians have not been exaggerated."[37]

In quick succession a delegation of seven U.S. labor leaders and a group of U.S. clergymen toured the camp.[38] At that point even Eisenhower finally became somewhat annoyed at the frequent visits by prominent personalities. He cabled General Marshall on May 4, 1945, that a telegram indicating his concurrence to a visit of "preachers" had been "garbled." He added,

> If the War Department believes that any additional groups should come, arrangements should be made at an early date. We have just uncovered another camp [Dachau] in the south. My own belief is that if America is not now convinced, in view of the disinterested witnesses we have already brought over, it would be almost hopeless to convince them through bringing anyone else.[39]

British and American groups were not the only ones to visit the camps. At Eisenhower's invitation a group from the United Nations War Crimes Commission went to Buchenwald on April 26 and 27. The thirteen-member commission, chaired by Lord Wright of Great Britain, included representatives of twelve different nations: Australia, Belgium, Canada, China, Czechoslovakia, France, Greece, India, the Netherlands, Poland, the United Kingdom, and the United States. A few days earlier a special French mission headed by General Paul Jean-Roger Kaeppelin had arrived; its members included two former inmates of Buchenwald: Colonel Henri Frédéric Manhes and Marcel Paul, a prominent French Communist leader.[40]

General Bradley finally put a stop to continuous official visits with a cable to European theater headquarters on May 9:

> Buchenwald concentration has been cleaned up, the sick segregated and burials completed to such an extent that very little evidence of atrocities remains.
>
> This negatives any educational value of having various groups visit the camp to secure first hand information of German atrocities. In fact, many feel quite skeptical that previous conditions actually existed.
>
> Suggest that further visits [to] this camp be discontinued.[41]

About this time virtually all visits to camps, official or otherwise, were curtailed. Dachau was placed under quarantine on May 10, 1945, because of a serious typhus epidemic, and only a minimum number of official visitors were allowed in. An order from Twelfth Army Group Headquarters of May 14 discouraged any further visits, "especially when made by distinguished persons," because they delayed the work of cleaning up the camps. Only medical teams or other technical experts would be permitted to come.[42]

In addition to the official delegations to Buchenwald, many well-known war correspondents and photographers visited the camp after liberation. Percy Knauth and photographer Margaret Bourke-White arrived in the camp on April 15. Bourke-White's famous photographs of shocking camp scenes appeared in *Life* magazine and in a book about her travels through a destroyed Germany, *Dear Fatherland*. Edward R. Murrow delivered an emotional, firsthand report from the camp on the CBS radio network. After describing the liberated camp and recounting the stories of a Czech physician and a French professor, Murrow said, "I pray you to believe what I have said about Buchenwald. I reported what I saw and heard, but only part of it. For most of it, I have no words."[43]

Meyer Levin, then representing a small Jewish press agency, the Overseas News Service, also toured Buchenwald. In his postwar memoir he retold in detail the story of a Polish Jew named Mordecai Striegler whom he met at the camp;[44] this was almost certainly the Motek Strigler who wrote the report on the burnings at Skarzisko Kamienna (Part Two, Chapter Twelve, §161). By the time a Signal Corps film crew headed by Billy Wilder arrived to make a documentary, conditions at the camp were no longer as severe as they had been at liberation.

The Allies were making similar efforts through the Psychological Warfare Division (PWD) of SHAEF to spread among the German population knowledge of Nazi atrocities. For the most part, the Allies failed to evoke a response. Photographs of Buchenwald concentration camp posted at the town hall in Lippstadt seemed to draw little reaction. An American intelligence report said of the silent observers: "None seemed to doubt the authenticity of the scenes portrayed, but

their attitude seemed detached, not responsible, and dissociated from the perpetrators of the crime."[45]

The British Office of War Information printed 50,000 copies of a magazine-
sized illustrated booklet for distribution in German towns and among German
soldiers in Allied prisoner of war camps. A compilation of large black-and-white
photographs of Buchenwald and Bergen-Belsen with only short passages of German-language text, it, too, met with near disinterest. An intelligence officer who
discussed the booklet with a group of German POWs found that most "at least
pretended to be horrified by the facts revealed in the pamphlets though the terms
they used had a certain ring of superficiality about them." The German prisoners
claimed to have no knowledge of the camps, although the intelligence officer
noted that many of them slipped by using the word *berüchtigt* (notorious) when
referring to the camps. Some of the prisoners criticized the photographs of piles
of bodies because they did not clearly show the cause of death; according to the
officer, "the consequences of the Allied air raids had completely inured the mass
of the German people to sights of this kind," the Germans tending to compare
their own sufferings with those of the camp inmates. They did not explicitly
blame the Allies for the air raids but blamed the Nazis for both types of suffering.
The analysis concluded: "The logical deduction [is] that the people in the camps
and the great mass of Germans were both in the same position of being innocent
victims of Nazi aggression and that sympathy is deserved in equal measure by
each class."[46]

The Allied intelligence officers found German claims not to know about concentration camps or atrocities puzzling. Another PWD report said that "most
Germans claim, of course, that they know little or nothing about what went on in
such camps as Buchenwald or Ohrdruf or Auschwitz." The report continued that
no German living near Gotha or Weimar "could fail to have a fairly clear picture
of the general proceedings at Buchenwald or Ohrdruf." Stories about the camps
from camp guards and prisoners on work details were widespread in these areas.
One intelligence officer argued that the Germans were lying to themselves as
much as to the Allied officers: "The secret of blissful ignorance lies in the mental
block which most Germans seem to have set up, to exclude from their daily consciousness knowledge of this sort. But however deeply buried in the minds of individuals, a certain essential knowledge of what happened remains."[47] The analysis ended by saying that the big question was not "that the Germans must be told,
but with what purpose and to what end they are to be told."[48]

While Buchenwald was in the short-term glare of publicity from media around
the world, several U.S. Army intelligence teams arrived with long-range tasks.
One was the special team of interpreters from PWD-SHAEF commanded by
Lieutenant Rosenberg, whose report is translated in this volume. Their task was
to create a detailed report that would serve overall intelligence needs by including
an in-depth analysis of the inner workings of Buchenwald and, by extension, of
the entire Nazi concentration camp system.

A separate team of interrogators commanded by Lieutenant Colonel Raymond
C. Givens and assigned to the War Crimes Branch of the Third U.S. Army arrived

about the same time.[49] Its mission was more narrowly defined: It was to provide detailed evidence of Nazi war crimes that could be used in trials. It established itself in the Hotel Elefant in the center of Weimar and worked independently from the PWD team. In the course of its activities, it took depositions from 177 prisoners of fourteen nationalities. Each prisoner was sworn in, signed an oath in the prisoner's language when appropriate, then gave testimony with the help of interpreters. These individual statements, transcribed into English (different from the ones translated here), became the principal documentary evidence for the U.S. prosecution case at the Buchenwald camp guards trial at Dachau in 1946–1947.

It seems fairly clear in retrospect that Buchenwald received more publicity than the other camps for largely accidental reasons. First, it was the first large camp the Allied forces discovered. Second, with more than three weeks before V-E Day, most prisoners had to be kept in camp for a time before they could safely return to their homes. Third, in other large camps like Dachau and Bergen-Belsen, the medical situation was even more serious than it had been in Buchenwald, and all but the most urgent official visits to those camps were strongly discouraged. Buchenwald thus came to stand for all the camps, a surrogate for all the seventy-seven installations with more than 335,000 surviving prisoners that the Allies liberated in 1945.[50]

Origins of the Report

A few days after the liberation of the camp, on April 16, 1945, a special intelligence team from the PWD-SHAEF in Paris arrived to begin interviewing the prisoners. The special intelligence detail commanded by Lieutenant Rosenberg had just been assigned to new duties two weeks earlier.[51] Its commander had been born into a well-to-do German Jewish family in Göttingen and had attended the University of Göttingen before emigrating to the United States in 1938. In addition to Rosenberg, the team consisted of four German-speaking enlisted men: Max M. Kimenthal, Alfred K. Sampson, Richard Akselrad, and Ernest S. Biberfeld. It had begun its intelligence work by interrogating captured Nazi prisoners in the area around Frankfurt. Its greatest success had been the interrogation of Prince August Wilhelm of Prussia, popularly known as "Auwi," one of the last kaiser's sons who had become a high-ranking Nazi. A few days afterward the team was ordered to Weimar.

The PWD team worked in a climate of immediate need to document the atrocities and horrors. Time was limited because of pressure to release prisoners to their home countries as soon as possible, as well as the impending transfer of the camp and the region around it to Soviet authorities.

Information about the writing of the Buchenwald Report is somewhat sketchy. Less than a week after the arrival of the PWD team, Kogon and nine other ex-prisoners were installed in a crowded room in one of the Nazi camp administration offices outside the Buchenwald gate. The ex-prisoner clerks included four Germans, two Austrians, and one each from France, Czechoslovakia, the Netherlands, and Latvia, the latter individuals serving primarily as translators. In addition to Kogon the team consisted of Joseph Berman, Herbert Froebess, Valentin Gelber, Lionel Guierre, Stefan Heymann, Ernst Holzer, Jan Robert, Ferdinand Römhild, and Karl Stockmar.[52]

The selection of Kogon to lead the prisoner team was fortunate. His keen intellect, outstanding academic training, deep intuitive insights, and wide-ranging contacts within the camp made him the ideal man for the job. Furthermore, he lacked the strong ideological and nationalist biases that marked many of the other camp leaders. A brief sketch of his life illustrates some of these unique qualities.

At the end of the war in 1945, Kogon was a forty-two-year-old Austrian citizen, a former journalist with a doctorate in economics.[53] He was born on February 2, 1903, in Munich, where his father was an imperial Russian consular official. Kogon was educated in Bavaria in Catholic schools run by Benedictine and Dominican monks.[54] After World War I he studied sociology and economics at the universities of Munich and Florence, completing a doctorate in economics under the influential conservative economist Othmar Spann in Vienna.[55] In the late 1920s and early 1930s, he served as deputy chief editor of *Schönere Zukunft* (Better future), the leading Austrian Catholic weekly, and was an adviser to the Christlichen Gewerkschaften, the Christian trade union movement in Austria.

From 1934 to 1938 he had served as chief administrator for the estates of Prince Philipp Josias Kohary of the house of Saxe-Coburg-Gotha in Vienna and Budapest. This position had involved frequent travels throughout Europe, including Germany, where as early as 1937 he was arrested twice by the Nazis. His travels enabled him to make comparisons between countries, turning "the conservative Catholic into an unrelenting opponent of Hitler."[56] As an advocate of Austrian independence and an opponent of the Austrian Nazis, he was on the first blacklist prepared by the Gestapo. He was arrested in Vienna on March 12, 1938, the day of the Nazi occupation of Austria. After more than a year in various Gestapo prisons, he was transferred to Buchenwald in September 1939.[57]

During the seven years he spent in the camp, he lived through, if he did not actually witness, most of the events described in the Buchenwald Report. In 1942 he became active in the illegal opposition in the camp. Three times his name appeared on death lists, starting in 1943, but each time he escaped execution with the help of friendly prisoners.[58] In the latter years of the camp, Kogon worked as one of the privileged prisoners (*Kommandierten*) as a clerk in the prisoner hospital. He served as private secretary to Dr. Erwin Ding-Schuler, the camp doctor, starting in April 1943.[59] In this post he acquired detailed knowledge of the medical experiments conducted on prisoners. As one of the more knowledgeable prisoners, he was placed on the list of forty-six "antifascists" to be executed in April 1945 before evacuation of the camp.

The conditions under which the report was written were extremely difficult. But after surviving years of camp life, the men on the team barely noticed any hardship. In a note to Lieutenant Rosenberg dated April 24, 1945, Kogon requested cigarettes and cartons of food, since "we are nine strong men who need to be fed." Other than that, he asked only for a few reams of typing paper. The workroom was so crowded, however, that Kogon complained that they were stepping on each other's toes. Sometime later the team moved to more spacious and comfortable quarters in Weimar in a requisitioned villa that had once belonged to Baldur von Schirach, onetime leader of the Hitler Youth and later the wartime mayor of Vienna.

In addition to the team of clerks and translators who worked directly under Kogon at the camp office and the Schirach villa, there were any number of official informants representing the inmate leadership and the committees formed by the different nationalities in the camp. (A lengthy list of names in the Afterword gives some indication of who they were.) From the national committees there were three English, five French, three Dutch, one Czech, two Poles, one Russian, and one Ukrainian. The Western Europeans, like the English officers Captain Christopher Burney and Wing Commander Forest Yeo-Thomas and the more prominent French prisoners, were there partly to offset the strong influence of the Communists among the remaining twelve representatives of the German and Austrian camp leadership. Handwritten notes next to these names indicate that eight were Communists, two were Social Democrats, one was a nonpartisan socialist, and one was a Franciscan monk.[60]

In the preface to the first edition of his own book (1946), Kogon gave a detailed description of the origins of the camp report.[61] Kogon dictated the 125-page Main Report (Part One) himself. His closest collaborators were the socialist author Ferdinand Römhild, the Social Democrat Heinz Baumeister from Dortmund, and the journalist Stefan Heymann, an "orthodox Communist." He also frequently discussed the text with Dr. Werner Hilpert, a prominent lawyer from Leipzig and former leader of the Saxony Catholic Center party, and Franz Hackel, a nonpartisan "left radical" author from Prague. All of them, except for Heymann, were longtime friends of his from the camp; all had been in camp at least five years and had "risen from below" to leadership positions under difficult conditions. With Heymann Kogon maintained good personal relations, but a certain atmosphere of mistrust nevertheless prevailed because Kogon said Heymann had originally been skillfully assigned to him by the camp's Communist leadership to maintain contact and keep Kogon under the control of the KPD.

Kogon said that a first draft of the entire report was read to the fifteen-member prisoner committee in early May. Only the last two chapters of the individual reports (Chapters Eleven and Twelve) were missing. The committee "approved its contents as relevant and objective." At some point the Western representatives (the English, French, and Dutch prisoners) had a draft of the report read to them, although it was probably only Kogon's Main Report (Part One), not the individual reports. The committee vouched for the accuracy of the contents.

A second, independent effort to document the camp's history came from the camp's Communist leadership. Its organizer was the Austrian Communist engineer Gustav Wegerer. Kogon called him "a good friend of mine, to whom I owe much, like many other non-Communist comrades."[62] Wegerer led the effort to create a "camp chronicle," which was organized through the camp Information Bureau. A number of individual reports on particular themes were commissioned. The camp newspaper, which the Information Bureau published in the

weeks after liberation, put out repeated calls for experienced journalists to participate in this project, the first coming as early as April 21.[63] The Information Bureau also shared in the efforts of Kogon's team. With Kogon's approval, Heymann
gave the Information Bureau a carbon copy of every report that Heymann had
edited. Some of these reports, such as the one on medical experiments in Dachau,
later appeared verbatim in East German publications. Indeed, the degree of duplication appears to be very high: Of the approximately 120 individual reports
(*Erlebnisberichte*) in the Buchenwald archives, about 70 percent appear to be substantially similar to the ones the Kogon team collected.[64]

The full text of the report organized by Rosenberg and Kogon was completed in
just four work weeks, April 16 through May 11. Although some details about the
period of composition are known, less is known about its later fate. A
semimonthly progress report of PWD dated June 7, 1945, listed among its current
projects "translation of a 400 page Intelligence Report on Buchenwald Camp with
a view to the requirements of PWD Media Section."[65] It seems unlikely that the
translation into English was completed, as the report is absent from a lengthy list
of supporting evidence presented at the Buchenwald camp guards trial.[66]

Kogon stated that one copy of the finished report went to PWD-SHAEF headquarters in Paris (later moved to Bad Homburg) and another to the headquarters
of the Twelfth Army Group at Bad Nauheim. The report was probably later forwarded to the War Crimes Commission in Wiesbaden. It apparently served as
supporting evidence for the International Military Tribunal at Nuremberg and
the U.S. trials of concentration camp guards at Dachau. Several of those trials
dealt with guards at Buchenwald. Portions of the report were probably used as
supporting evidence at those trials. Buchenwald trial records at the National Archives include a four-page, typed, German-language summary of atrocities at Buchenwald that appears to have come from Chapter Three of the Buchenwald Report.[67] But without the connecting sinew that the entire text of the report offers,
the individual statements must have seemed to the military lawyers to be anec-
dotal and unsubstantiated evidence.

In the long run, it was Kogon who would be the principal user of the information in the report. At the suggestion of the British PWD civilian officer Richard
Crossman (later a famous Labour party politician), Kogon was commissioned to
turn out a German-language book based on the report's information. A secret
PWD cable shows that he was flown out from Paris to Frankfurt on June 15 when
PWD headquarters was relocated to Bad Homburg.[68] A few weeks later Kogon
settled in the Frankfurt suburb of Oberursel, where he completely rewrote the
manuscript between June 15 and December 15, 1945.

The result, he claimed in the 1946 edition, was "a new manuscript." Although
he occasionally made use of "his original manuscript," the "style was completely
altered." He adopted a tone of "calm objectivity" and avoided "polemics," "as difficult as that was at times."[69] Kogon thoroughly reworked the main report and
added relevant bits of evidence from the individual reports, reproducing other
portions verbatim.

In the years since 1945, the original official copies of the manuscript were lost or buried somewhere in U.S. government archives. A complete original, once kept by the U.S. Army at PWD headquarters in Bad Homburg, then at its War Crimes Center in Wiesbaden, has yet to be located. In the 1950s noted scholars Daniel Lerner and Saul Padover, both of whom had served in PWD, tried to locate the original manuscript. At that time most of the documents related to it were still classified, and Lerner and Padover were unsuccessful in their attempts.[70] Perhaps the simple fact that it was never translated into English prevented this document from becoming better known at the time.

It also seems likely that increasing cold war tensions contributed to the burial of the original version of the report in bureaucratic obscurity. By 1946–1947 the prominent role of Communist camp leaders in administering the camp increasingly attracted the attention of U.S. war crimes investigators, who put some of the Buchenwald kapos on arrest lists. No doubt the Communists' influence at Buchenwald would have led many U.S. investigators to treat the report with some suspicion. In any case, the Buchenwald Report never surfaced again, until the present publication.

The Published Literature

An enormous quantity of material has appeared on the Third Reich, the SS, concentration camps, and the Holocaust. It would be impossible to evaluate that vast literature here, but in the following pages I give a brief account of the most pertinent works dealing primarily with Buchenwald. This discussion focuses on the early literature documenting the camps, most of which was published before 1960. (For further research and reading, see the Selected Bibliography at the end of the text.)

The first serious scholarly account of Nazi concentration camps to appear anywhere was Kogon's version of the Buchenwald Report (mentioned above), published as *Der SS-Staat* in 1946. The first edition was a small paperback volume of 339 pages, printed on newsprint and published in small numbers by an obscure Munich publisher under a license from the U.S. military government. In 1949 a major West German publisher came out with a revised edition in hardcover library format. The only editorial change was a new concluding chapter that reflected the emergence of the cold war and the evolving international situation. This revised edition was translated into English by Heinz Norden in 1950 and published in Great Britain and the United States as *The Theory and Practice of Hell*. It was also translated into French as *L'Enfer organisé* (1947) and Spanish as *Sociología de los campos de concentración* (1965).[71]

After it had been in print for over two decades, Kogon prepared a substantially revised second edition in 1974. For this edition, Kogon went back to the original 1945 report and drew still more material from it, primarily for examples to support his general themes. He also replaced the final chapter with his 1946 essay reflecting on the issue of German guilt.[72]

A close examination of the Kogon book confirms his account of how he used the material. Although paragraph-length excerpts from the original U.S. Army report appear in the published account, for the most part the report is paraphrased and serves as supporting evidence. For example, the story of the fate of a Jew named Hamber is clearly based on the report in Chapter Three, §39.[73] The grim story of prisoners who were buried alive is taken from Chapter Four, §54. Some of the longest excerpts are from the reports on other camps in Chapter Twelve. Kogon uses three paragraphs from Dr. Ludwig Fleck's account of the Lemberg ghetto, but the original report is three times this long (Chapter Twelve, §162).[74] The longest such excerpt is Vladimir Blumenfeld's account of the Warsaw ghetto uprising, Chapter Twelve, §164, the only case in which virtually an entire report is reproduced.[75] It is typical of Kogon's methodology that the lengthy excerpts are mainly from reports of *other* camps, not of Buchenwald. I estimate that no more than 10 percent of the Buchenwald reports have ever been published, even in excerpted form.

In addition to his enormous success in writing a book that became a classic in historical and political literature, Kogon managed to play an active part in numerous aspects of West German intellectual and political life after the war.[76] From 1951 to 1968 he pursued an active academic career as professor of political science at the Technical University of Darmstadt. From 1946 to 1985 he was copublisher of the monthly review *Frankfurter Hefte*, which he founded with his close friend Walter Dirks. With Dirks he also helped establish the Christian Democratic Union (CDU), which he left in the early 1950s to become an independent. In his later years he increasingly leaned toward the Social Democratic party (SPD). He became an early supporter of the movement toward European federalism by joining the European Union, of which he later became international president. In the early 1960s Kogon made a brief attempt to reach a still broader audience as cohost of a popular television newsmagazine.

In his later years, though he developed something of a reputation as an "angry old man" for his outspoken stands on many of Germany's most controversial issues, he was recognized with many prizes and honors: the Buber-Rosenzweig Award for Christian Jewish Cooperation (1980), the J. H. Merck Award of the city of Darmstadt, and the chairmanship of the Martin Niemöller Foundation. He died at the age of eighty-four on December 24, 1987, at his home in Falkenstein/Taunus near Frankfurt. At the time of his death, over 300,000 copies of *Der SS-Staat* had been sold in Germany alone; many more were sold in translation throughout the world.

His book will no doubt be a lasting legacy. As the first major study, it directly and indirectly influenced all later literature on Nazism, the SS, concentration camps, and the Holocaust. It is still one of the most frequently cited works in the field. Hannah Arendt drew heavily from Kogon's published work and other accounts of Buchenwald by Bruno Bettelheim and David Rousset for her influential book *The Origins of Totalitarianism* (1951, 1958).[77] In the 1960s the German scholars Helmut Krausnick, Hans Buchheim, Martin Broszat, and Hans-Adolf Jacobsen produced a new study, *Anatomy of the SS State* (1965, English edition

1968). In that work Broszat referred to Kogon's "masterly book" and drew on it in part for his own account. More recently, Konnilyn G. Feig, author of *Hitler's Death Camps: The Sanity of Madness* (1981), mentioned the report of "a military team" and Kogon's role in it but gave no indication that she saw the report in the archives at Buchenwald.[78]

Had Kogon never published his book, ample documentation of the events at Buchenwald would still have been available even in the early years. In 1946 three well-known accounts of life in the camp, all by former inmates, appeared independently of Kogon's report. In his short book *The Dungeon Democracy*, Christopher Burney described the camp's organization, the daily life of the prisoners, and the behavior of the various nationalities in camp. The most interesting chapter is an account of the last days of the camp, which is very similar to the version in Kogon's report. (Burney used the actual names of the Nazis in his book but protected the identities of the prisoners by giving them fictional names. Kogon, a man for whom Burney had great praise, is called Emil Kallman; Heinz Baumeister is Heinrich Bilder.)

More literary and philosophical is *L'Univers concentrationnaire* by the Frenchman David Rousset, which first appeared in English as *The Other Kingdom* in 1947. Rousset arrived at Buchenwald near the end of the war, after having been in several other camps. Rousset's account is surrealistic; to him the camp was the realm of the absurd. He presents life in the camp as proceeding by rules so different from the real world that it was more like another world. The anger that many prisoners felt for the Communist-dominated prisoner leadership also comes out rather strongly in his book. The German Ernst Wiechert's *Totenwald* (published in English as *The Forest of the Dead* in 1947) is a work of fiction. Like Elie Wiesel and Jorge Semprun, Wiechert based his novel on his own experiences. Although Wiechert does not mention Buchenwald by name, many clues besides the title point to the identity of the camp, including the real name of one of the most brutal SS sergeants there.

At least a dozen other accounts of Buchenwald, mostly in German, appeared in Western Europe in the first three years after the war. Most, however, were published in small numbers by obscure publishers; few were translated into English; and they generally failed to attract much attention. Because they are the accounts of individuals, these works lack the breadth of Kogon's classic or other major works mentioned here.

In the same period a number of works were published in East Germany, the most important of which were created by the International Camp Committee. The earliest was a small paperback booklet titled *KL Bu*, published in Erfurt in 1946; a larger, hardcover edition appeared in 1949. As mentioned above, the individual reports in these works overlapped to a large extent with the report Kogon's team prepared. A completely separate account written by a group of Communist former inmates was published in Leipzig in 1945 under the title *Das War Buchenwald* (That was Buchenwald). Another account was that of Udo Dietmar, *Häftling X* (Prisoner X), which appeared the following year. A strong ideological bias pervaded all these works, most of which ignored or downplayed the racial and nationalist aspects of Nazi policies in the camp. The definitive East German work, also sometimes linked to the International Camp Committee, was by Walter Bartel. Published in 1960, *Buchenwald: Mahnung und Verpflichtung* (Buchenwald: warning and duty) drew from all of the previous East German accounts and some Western ones, as well as from documents in East German government archives. Although it was a work of solid scholarship, it, too, reflected a Communist bias.

Conclusion

Percy Knauth, one of the correspondents who visited Buchenwald in April 1945, suggested that a "tower of Buchenwald" be built on the Ettersberg where the Bismarck Tower stood, to commemorate the victims of the concentration camp. He suggested that the monument become a

> place where people come to meditate on concentration camps and what they mean. If we do that, remembering every year as we remember Christ who died on a cross that was not unlike Buchenwald's famous Tree, then the 51,000 dead of Buchenwald will surely have proved stronger than those who sought to live the proposition that all men are not created equal on this earth.[79]

Knauth was not alone in seeing a similarity between the Nazi practice of hanging prisoners from trees and the crucifixion of Christ. In the novel *Night* Elie Wiesel invoked the same image in an emotionally powerful scene that told of the hanging of a young boy in front of the prisoners in the camp.[80] A tower *was* built on that exact site a decade later by the new government of East Germany. It was called the *Mahnmal,* or monument of admonition. Enclosing the tower was an avenue of stone tablets dedicated to the nations whose prisoners were held in the camp. In front was a stone circle that held an eternal flame and a statue of a group of defiant prisoners raising their fists in rebellion against their oppressors.

By the late 1950s the *Mahnmal* and the museum at Buchenwald camp had become a regular destination for East German youth groups and school classes. What they learned there was badly distorted history: that the camp had been used mostly to imprison heroic antifascists, socialists, and Communists who had opposed fascism and capitalism. The racial and nationalistic basis of Nazi persecution was ignored; the fate of Jews went unmentioned. The Soviet Union, students were told, had liberated their nation from Hitler's dictatorship; the United States played no part in this version of history. A direct link was drawn between the Communists who were active in the International Camp Committee and the leaders of the East German regime.

With the collapse of communism and the unification of Germany, the role of the Buchenwald monument in providing a historical basis for the legitimacy of the East German regime came to an end. Quarrels arose about which aspects of Buchenwald's past the museum should portray, many demanding that the museum tell of the prisoners held there by the Soviets from 1945 to 1950 in the so-called Second Camp.

The time may have come for all of us "to meditate on concentration camps and what they mean," as Knauth suggested. Readers of this book and of other books on the Holocaust and related themes can scarcely reflect on the material without raising some difficult and disturbing questions about humanity in general and about our collective experience in the twentieth century. It is probably impossible to draw any lessons about which everyone will agree, but it is less difficult to identify some key issues around which the controversies revolve.

Perhaps the most painful issue this book raises is the issue of German guilt, and with it the issue of collective guilt. The reader of these pages will certainly see the prisoners' anger toward Germans and toward Nazis in particular. Germany was, of course, the birthplace of the ideology that had caused the prisoners so much suffering, and German military power had spread it throughout Europe. Yet everywhere in Europe the Nazis found collaborators willing to do their bidding. But there was another Germany, the Germany of those famous earlier citizens of Weimar—Johann Wolfgang von Goethe and Friedrich Schiller. Still another Germany was represented by the supporters of the republic named after Weimar, especially the Social Democrats, Democrats, and Center politicians, many of whom ended up in Nazi concentration camps.

At times readers should remind themselves that there were "good" Germans, too, decent citizens like the SS corporal who smuggled mail out for the prisoners (and smuggled Kogon out in a crate) and the SS doctor who immediately chose to serve on the eastern front rather than serve as a concentration camp doctor. There was a German gendarme in Poland, partly Jewish himself, who smuggled messages for Jewish prisoners in a secret work detail. Often individual Germans, even among the SS, gave prisoners timely tips about forthcoming actions (mass round-ups of certain categories of prisoners), saving many lives. Finally, of course, there were the Germans *in* the camp who had taken courageous stands of conscience, those like Pastor Paul Schneider, numerous unnamed Catholic clerics, and the stoic Jehovah's Witnesses. Thoughts similar to these may have kept Kogon from condemning Germany in his works, despite the suffering he had endured in the camp. He remained an optimist throughout his life, convinced that people can learn from experience and that we can avoid horrors of this type in the future.

If facile explanations based on German culture are unsatisfactory, then how is the behavior of the guards in the camp to be explained? In part, this phenomenon is about the power of ideology to distort human behavior. A growing body of scholarly literature shows that the racial doctrine of National Socialism was at its very core, not a secondary issue or a by-product of its foreign policy. Well before 1939, the Nazi campaign against the Jews was cast in the terminology of war, a rhetorical war that became real with German military victories in the East. It has also become clear that Nazi propaganda was extremely successful in spreading its racial ideology among the population. Propaganda was, as one scholar put it, "the war that Hitler won."[81]

The men who ran the concentration camps were probably not, for the most part, psychopathic killers. But as Christopher Browning wrote, "War, and especially race war, leads to brutalization, which leads to atrocity."[82] The camp guards were probably ordinary men who, influenced by the ideology of Nazism and following orders from above, carried out their duties of killing with great efficiency. For them, the victims had long since ceased to be human and the act of killing had become a matter of routine. Browning wrote of a different Nazi unit: "Once the killing began, ... the horrors of the initial encounter eventually became routine, and the killing became easier. In this sense, brutalization was not the cause but the effect of these men's behavior."[83]

In the broadest sense, then, the Buchenwald Report is about the abuse of power—the power of one group of humans over another, of one individual over another. It is about too much power, the power of life and death, given too freely and exercised too freely by too many individuals. At Buchenwald the famous adage of that great nineteenth-century British historian Lord Acton was demonstrated once again: "Power corrupts, and absolute power corrupts absolutely."[84]

The temptation to abuse power, to oppress and enslave those human beings seen as "the other," as less human and less worthy of life, is a universal and recurring one, as events in many parts of the world show today. We therefore must not allow ourselves to forget what happened at Buchenwald and the other concentration camps. The only real weapon we have is the weapon of memory. As Milan Kundera put it, "The struggle of man against power is the struggle of memory against forgetting."[85]

Main Report

Report on Buchenwald Concentration Camp at Weimar

I Buchenwald Concentration Camp

An attempt will be made in the following to provide an objective and comprehensive report on Buchenwald concentration camp near Weimar in Thuringia. Its origins, significance, internal organization, development, and end will be described. Buchenwald concentration camp will be viewed as a part of those institutions created by the SS to suppress and eliminate all activity by the opposition.

The report is based on documentary sources, reliable testimony, and biographical accounts of longtime inmates. Not only because of their work assignments but also because of their character and intellect, they could provide a clear picture of the camp and its complex relationships.

As only German prisoners were to be found in Buchenwald until well into 1939, the best informers accordingly came out of their ranks. However, this report was written with the cooperation of reliable spokesmen from all nations, to exclude the danger of a one-sided presentation.

The report cannot possibly give a completely exhaustive picture of the reality of the camp. Although it must relate horrible events, it is more than just a compilation of atrocities by the SS. It is evidence of the system of fascist terror and its methods, with Buchenwald as an example.[1] Especially striking and typical individual cases appear in Part Two, which is made up of brief representative statements.[2]

II The SS and Concentration Camps

The SS was founded by Heinrich Himmler as an order for the development and protection of the German racial system of rule. All that stood in the way of this

---

1. Eugen Kogon stressed the idea of an organized system of terror in the famous book he based on this report, *Der SS-Staat* (Munich: Karl Alber Verlag, 1946, and later editions), published in English as *The Theory and Practice of Hell*, trans. Heinz Norden (New York: Farrar, Straus and Cudahy, 1950). Cross-references given in notes are to recent paperback editions, indicated by *SSS* (Munich: Heyne, 1989) and *TPH* (New York: Berkley, 1980).

2. Cross-references to individual reports in Part Two are given in brackets. They are indicated by the chapter number and a section symbol followed by an arabic numeral, for example, [§99].

ideology, or could possibly stand in its way, was ruthlessly suppressed. The instruments for this were the Gestapo and the concentration camp, both in the hands of the SS.

The supreme principle of this terror was that it is better to put ten innocent people behind barbed wire than to leave a single actual opponent in freedom. Everything opposed to or inconsistent with National Socialist rule and its theory of state had to be removed. This meant primarily political opponents, to which Jews were automatically counted, along with criminals, elements regarded as anti-social, homosexuals, and Gypsies. Jehovah's Witnesses were included because they rejected the military ideology and principles of the state. Also included were personalities from the major religious denominations regarded as hostile or dangerous by National Socialism. The goal and practice of the concentration camp was to isolate, degrade, and decimate these groups while simultaneously creating a deterrent effect on the National Socialist German racial community. In this manner cheap SS-owned slave workers were created who could be subjected to the unlimited despotism of this new "ruling class" in remote, unobserved locations. For the SS, that was both a pleasant and profitable by-product of this system.

III Numbers and Types of Concentration Camps in Germany

The earliest concentration camps after the Nazi seizure of power [in 1933] were not representative of the type that later developed. In many locations camps were immediately built that were still under the control of the SA [*Sturmabteilung*, or Storm Troopers]. The largest among them were Dachau near Munich and the Judicial Moor camps in Emsland. In the events that followed the breaking of the SA's power on June 30, 1934 [the Blood Purge], many smaller camps such as Sachsenburg, Lichtenburg, and Bad Sulza were gradually dissolved. Their inmates were transported to large, newly founded concentration camps under the exclusive control of the SS. Most notable until recently have been Dachau; Sachsenhausen near Berlin; Buchenwald near Weimar; Flossenbürg near Weiden in Bavaria; Mauthausen near Linz, Austria; Neuengamme near Hamburg; and Ravensbrück in Mecklenburg, a women's concentration camp.

All these camps eventually established many subsidiary camps, so that whole regions of the countryside were interspersed with these terror institutions of the SS. After 1939 the spread of National Socialism throughout Europe brought with it a true "concentration camp founding boom."[3] The infamous camps Auschwitz, Lublin [Maidanek], Riga, Stutthof near Danzig, Natzweiler in the Vosges Mountains, Gross-Rosen in the Lausitz, Bergen-Belsen near Hannover, and many smaller ones were built.

---

3. This is probably an ironic reference to the "founders' epoch" (*Gründerzeit*), which led to the creation of many large business enterprises after Bismarck's unification of Germany in 1871.

After 1940–1941 the concentration camps were divided into three categories. Category I (work camps) represented the mildest form. Category II meant harsher living and working conditions. In Category III were the "death factories" [*Knochenmühlen,* literally, bone mills]. Counted in the last group, for example, were Auschwitz, Lublin, Gross-Rosen, Mauthausen, and Natzweiler. Dachau was Category I (which anyone who knows about conditions in Dachau would regard with a certain black humor). Buchenwald was at first Category II, then Category I.

The intention, though never fully achieved, was to place in camps of Category III all criminals, homosexuals, Jews, and political prisoners who seemed especially dangerous, of whatever nationality.[4] This was prevented, however, by verdicts of the local Gestapo authorities on various individual prisoners and was also thwarted by camp administrations. They were often no longer willing to give up valuable workers or ignored orders that did not suit them. Finally, it proved useful to mix prisoner categories in all camps, according to the principle of divide and rule, to prevent political prisoners from consolidating power.

The significance of individual categories of prisoners in concentration camps must be outlined briefly. Between political prisoners and criminals, a constant struggle for power took place—at times open, at times underground—leading to different results in various camps. Antisocials and homosexuals played a subordinate role in this regard. Since antisocials leaned toward the criminals, the politicals regarded them with a certain amount of suspicion. Jehovah's Witnesses, with their patient expectation of the end of the world, were regarded by both the SS and the prisoners as loyal and obedient workers. Their numbers provided primarily skilled craftsmen, orderlies, and domestic servants [*Kalfaktoren*]. Even from the National Socialist standpoint, it was especially scandalous to tear families of Jehovah's Witnesses apart, take their children from them, and lock them up in men's and women's concentration camps.

From the beginning, Jews were special targets of the SS will to annihilate [*Vernichtungswillen*]. Some achieved an extraordinary significance in the camps. Because they lived under the constant pressure of immediate or eventual liquidation, they often had to seek refuge in the lowest positions. They frequently served as lightning rods for the bad tempers of the SS, so that the other camp inmates got off more easily. For this reason especially close personal ties arose between Jewish and non-Jewish political prisoners, which found expression in countless acts of solidarity. This solidarity and almost improbable good luck are why many Jews who were delivered to the concentration camp in the early years survived at all.

---

4. Nearly all concentration camp prisoners were being held under "protective custody" (*Schutzhaft*) provisions. As early as February 28, 1933, an emergency decree allowed the Gestapo to imprison for indefinite periods persons deemed dangerous to the state. They were not permitted a trial or access to the court system. A more detailed and comprehensive set of regulations in April 1934 further expanded police powers in this area, thus making possible the concentration camp system described in this report. See Helmut Krausnick et al., *Anatomy of the SS State* (New York: Walker and Company, 1968), 400–420.

Another basic observation should be made regarding the political prisoners. The red triangle was hardly a certain indicator that the wearer belonged to the antifascist opposition.[5] Without a doubt the majority belonged to parties opposed to National Socialism or were nonpartisan individuals with similar views. In addition, there were among the reds some people who had belonged to the NSDAP and were imprisoned for some type of party offense. There were also Wehrmacht soldiers who were sent to concentration camps for stealing from comrades, for serious cases of failure to obey orders, or for desertion. Soldiers of the [French] Foreign Legion who had returned or were brought back were also assigned to the reds. Occasionally assigned to this category were those who had violated German currency laws, had listened to illegal radio broadcasts, or were constant complainers. Some had fallen under the wheels of the Gestapo because of purely personal denunciations. With such a conglomeration of types wearing the red triangle, the already difficult conditions were of course further aggravated. A general atmosphere of distrust among the prisoners was significantly heightened.

Non-Germans who arrived after the beginning of the war were usually marked as politicals. Not only this situation but language and nationality differences as well as the lack of camp experience among the foreigners brought about frequent and often painful difficulties. It was not always possible to resolve them satisfactorily.

External identification of prisoners consisted of sequential numbers and a colored triangle on the left chest and the right pants leg. Red stood for politicals, whereas second offenders, the so-called recidivists, had a stripe of the same color above the point. Green was for criminals, purple for Jehovah's Witnesses, black for antisocials, and pink for homosexuals. At times brown was used for the Gypsies and antisocials rounded up in certain "actions."[6] Jews always wore a yellow triangle under their red, green, black, purple, or other marking, thus forming a six-pointed star. The so-called race defilers (violators of the Nuremberg racial laws) wore a black-outlined triangle superimposed over the yellow or green triangle.

Foreigners had the initial letter of their nationality printed on the triangle—for example, a *T* for the Czechs [*Tschechen*] and an *F* for the French. Some German political protective custody prisoners were brought to the concentration camp for alleged unreliability as "action prisoners." Their numbers were written across the

---

5. The term *red* in the concentration camp meant any type of political prisoner, as the context shows, even though in the early days most were from the German Social Democratic party (SPD) and the Communist party of Germany (KPD). During the war virtually all foreigners, such as the French and Dutch, were classified as red, as were increasing numbers of the German conservative opposition to Hitler.

6. "Actions" were organized roundups by the Gestapo of particular categories of people destined for the concentration camps. They were often designated with colorful secret code names. See the glossary in Martin Weinmann, ed., *Das nationalsozialistische Lagersystem* (Frankfurt: Zweitausendeins, 1990), ix.

triangle, whereas numbers were usually placed under the triangle by a width of two fingers.

Similarly, after the beginning of the war, prisoners were delivered as "war criminals," marked by a K [*Kriegsverbrecher*] printed on the triangle. They were immediately placed in the punishment company, in a special "K Company" created for them. The reasons for their incarceration were often insignificant. It sometimes came to pass that prisoners who had been in the camp a long time were also assigned to the K Company. "Labor disciplinary prisoners" [*Arbeitserziehungshäftlinge*] received an A on the black triangle. They were generally in camp for just a few weeks to scare them after they had been reported to the Gestapo by factory leaders for a labor offense or insufficient productivity. Members of the punishment companies had a black, dollar-sized dot between the bottom of the triangle and the number. Escape suspects had a target sewn or painted on their chests and backs.

The green triangles were the "BV prisoners" [*Befristete Vorbeugungshäftlinge*], "limited preventive detention prisoners" (from which came *Berufsverbrecher*, "professional criminal," their general title in camp). They had already served their sentences for criminal activities but had been delivered by the Reich Criminal Police to the concentration camp via the Gestapo for preventive purposes. In contrast to the BV prisoners were criminals still serving sentences, among them many serving life sentences, who were brought into the concentration camps after 1943. They were distinguished by the letter S (an abbreviation for "security prisoner") on the green triangle.

Out of this abundance of designations could arise a real rainbow of markings. For example, there was a Jewish Jehovah's Witness who was a "race defiler" with an escapee mark and a punishment company designation.

The relative numerical strength of these different categories varied greatly. There were predominantly red and predominantly green camps at the outbreak of the war, before the red triangle became the absolutely predominant color. Dachau, Buchenwald, and Sachsenhausen were for a long time—the two first named, up to the present—red-dominated camps; Mauthausen, Flossenbürg, Gross-Rosen, and Neuengamme were green dominated.

It should be emphasized that markings as such were no absolute guarantee that the wearer had certain qualities or truly belonged to that group. For example, among the greens there were many useful people, whereas many reds really should have worn a green triangle. Occasionally remarkings were in fact carried out more or less correctly.

No reliable information on the total number of persons delivered into the concentration camp is yet available. Even a rough count would be made extraordinarily difficult by the constantly changing population. Without a doubt millions went through the concentration camps in the twelve-year reign of National Socialism. The average population, that is, the number of prisoners in the camps at any given point, probably hardly passed the million mark, since the large base camps like Dachau, Buchenwald, and Sachsenhausen, with their subsidiary camps, seldom counted more than 100,000 inmates each. A further clue is

Himmler's order to the Reich SS and police medical officer in March 1945, made available to us by SS Major Dr. [Erwin] Schuler of Weimar-Buchenwald. According to this document, of the remaining 600,000 concentration camp inmates, the 120,000 who could no longer work were to be immediately brought into a "better state of health." The chief public health officer, SS Brigadier General Professor [Joachim] Mrugowsky of Berlin, was quickly sent to the infamous transit camp Bergen-Belsen near Hannover to direct an eight-day cleansing action. At this point the concentration camps at Auschwitz, Lublin, Riga, Stutthof, Gross-Rosen, Natzweiler, and several smaller ones had already been liberated or evacuated. Therefore the population figure of about 1 million would probably not be far off the mark.

IV The Concentration Camp at Buchenwald

Buchenwald concentration camp was founded by the SS on July 19, 1937, with 149 prisoners from Sachsenburg concentration camp.[7] For this purpose the SS obtained a sizable forest area located 5 miles north of Weimar on the Ettersberg Mountain.[8] It was purchased from the Princely Domain Administration of Thurn and Taxis under conditions about which little is known. The selection of the site was symbolic in a higher sense: Weimar is the German national cultural monument, formerly the city of the German classicists, who through their works gave German emotional and intellectual life its highest expression. Buchenwald (as it was later named; originally it was called Ettersberg) is in a natural forest area. It is a monument to the new German sensibilities. Thus a new set of connections was created: the sentimentally preserved museum culture of Weimar versus the uninhibited brutal desire for power of Buchenwald.

At the top of the 1,578-foot-high mountain, the first three barracks for the SS were built.[9] From Lichtenburg and Sachsenburg concentration camps, three further transports came with 600 prisoners each (political, criminal, Jehovah's Witnesses). During that summer they took part in clearing the forest from the foggy north slope. The so-called Goethe Oak, known throughout the region, was piously preserved as the camp center, whereas the no less famous Schottmann's Linden fell victim to the ax. Wooden barracks in rows of five were built and surrounded with barbed wire. The last row, which stood outside the fence, was as-

---

7. Sachsenburg was located in an old castle in Frankenberg, Saxony, near Chemnitz. It was a former teacher training institute and later became a Nazi party training school for women leaders.

8. Weimar was and is famous for museums devoted to its most famous residents: Johann Wolfgang von Goethe and Friedrich Schiller, as well as to Franz Liszt and Friedrich Nietzsche. The library of Grand Duchess Anna Amalia is maintained as a monument to eighteenth-century classicism.

9. Buchenwald is located on a heavily wooded mountain, the Ettersberg (altitude 1,578 feet), that rises high above the city of Weimar (836 feet). The railroad station, from which the prisoners had to march at double time, is at the base of the slope, about 80 feet above the heart of the city.

signed to the SS guards. At their head stood three top SS officers: SS Major [Karl] Koch, camp commandant; SS Major [Arthur] Rödl, recipient of the Blood Order, first deputy commandant; and SS Captain Weissenborn, second deputy commandant. Koch had begun his infamous career as a master sergeant in the Moor camps. Like Weissenborn, who had previously been a prison guard, he possessed a peculiar preference for the greens. Rödl had come along in the move from Sachsenburg. Weissenborn was best characterized by the graffiti that even the SS wrote on bulletin boards and barracks: "God in his scorn created SS Captain Weissenborn" ["Gott erschuf in seinem Zorn den Hauptsturmführer Weissenborn"].

The prisoners' living and working conditions were the worst imaginable. Work lasted from the first glimmer of morning light until twilight, at times longer. There was a one-hour break at midday, from twelve to one, that was mostly filled by two roll calls. Every day four roll calls took place. The first was in the morning before moving out to work, the second at midday on return, the third midday at moving out, the fourth in the evening after work. Almost no time remained for meals and bodily care. Sanitary conditions were inadequate beyond description; in particular the camp suffered from a constant shortage of water. Between blocks ran a primitive water main into which holes had been bored, allowing a trickle of water that could be caught. For a long time toilets consisted of open latrines. Materials for the building of the barracks were supplied by the SS.

The work of the prisoners was made more difficult by a considerable shortage of tools and by deliberate tormenting on the part of the SS. For example, after trees were felled, the deep-lying, broad roots of the beeches [*Buchen*] had to be laboriously removed by hoes and hands, whereas the loose roots of the cedars were blown up. Blows and taunts were an important part of the daily routine. As premiums for shooting prisoners during so-called escape attempts, guards were offered special leaves, salary bonuses, or rapid promotion. SS guards thus devoted themselves to the following type of provocation: The cap of a prisoner would be snatched from his head because it was allegedly dirty. With the words "Go fetch your filthy cap and show it to me clean tomorrow!" the cap would be thrown past the sentries who stood around the work detail. If the prisoner innocently ran after it, he was shot down for "attempted escape."

This foundation period continued into the year 1939. In spring 1938 the camp still comprised only about 2,500 prisoners, who had to accomplish an immense amount of work. They were engaged in clearing forest; grading and building roads outside the camp; building barracks, military quarters, officers' houses, a motor pool garage, and a concrete road to Weimar. They also made excavations for the laying of cables, were engaged in stone quarrying, laid water and sewer mains, and built workshops. In the early months of 1938, the camp was surrounded by an electrically charged barbed wire fence. By then it consisted of thirty-four wooden barracks and the first row of stone buildings, along with a kitchen and laundry. It was rare for prisoners to be chased into the electric fence. More often, desperate prisoners committed suicide by running into it deliberately.

At the end of April 1938, deliveries of the so-called antisocials began by the thousands. Among them the first shipment of 500 Jews was brought in June. They were packed into the sheep barn; two months later, 150 of them were dead. Soon after that the remainder were moved to wooden barracks because of a report on English radio by a released Jew who had emigrated. In September 1938 around 2,000 Jews, predominantly Austrian political prisoners, came from Dachau. Around 450 Austrian preventive detention prisoners came at the same time. Among them were many prominent personalities—for example, the former Austrian attorney general and minister of justice, Freiherr von Winterstein; other high governmental officials; military officers; professors; and authors. The total population of the camp then comprised between 7,000 and 8,000 men.

The organization of the camp had the following framework: At the top on the SS side was Commandant Koch with his adjutants; among them were the deputy commandants, including those previously named (Rödl and Weissenborn). The administrative officer was SS Captain Weichseldörfer. Liaison to the camp was created by the establishment of the important position of roll call officer, through whom all details of the camp were routed. The roll call officer during this time was SS Master Sergeant [Heinrich] Hackmann.[10] He came from Osnabrück, was the cleverest among the SS officers, but was brutal and had a "cynical humor." He was generally known in camp by the nickname "Jonny." He went away in 1939 for a few months of training and returned as SS first lieutenant and adjutant to Koch. After serving in 1940 as SS captain and for a short time holding the post of second deputy commandant, he was transferred to Lublin and was later arrested in connection with the Koch trial [Chapter Eleven, §155]. He was twice sentenced to death by an SS court. In April 1945 he was still alive and was evacuated by the Gestapo.

Representing the Gestapo in camp was the political department, which was independent of the camp command [Chapter One, §5]. The relationship between the two authorities was often strained because the camp administration considered itself an extraterritorial power that would not allow any form of interference in its operations. It wanted to be the sole beneficiary of the permanent, enormous system of corruption within the camp and sought to prevent the threat of any sort of outside rival. The delivery and release of prisoners from and to the Gestapo went through the political department. Its director was SS First Lieutenant Frerichs, who was mainly a figurehead, with the actual work accomplished by Detective Inspector [Hubert] Leclaire. Leclaire, despite his name, played a very dark role.

---

10. Heinrich Hackmann was one of the thirty-one persons tried at the Buchenwald camp guards trial at Dachau (April to August 1947), known as *United States v. Prince Josias zu Waldeck et al.* He was sentenced to death by hanging, which was commuted to life imprisonment. National Archives (NA), Record Group (RG) 338, case 000-50-9, box 426, "Review and Recommendations of the Deputy Judge Advocate for War Crimes, 16 November 1947," 54–55, 94–95.

One could say that many a prisoner came close to a heart attack when he was suddenly summoned to Leclaire over the loudspeaker. For example, the Austrian lieutenant colonel [Franz] Heckenast suffered a heart attack one day because he was no longer able to stand the stress of hearing his name called on the loudspeaker for the nth time. Interrogations in the political department were not just a form of psychological torture what with the mysterious terror that always surrounded this Gestapo institution (often comrades failed to return from it and disappeared without a trace).[11] Interrogations were also almost always accompanied by severe abuse. Leclaire seldom missed an opportunity to beat prisoners with his own fists or to bring about ingenious forms of torture. In 1939 he was transferred to the Gestapo in Weimar.

His successor, Detective Inspector [Walter] Serno, took over administration of the department and remained in that position until the end of the camp. Serno did not personally abuse prisoners, as far as is known. He was extraordinarily dumb, but he was not entirely impervious to certain humanitarian reflections. He was mainly interested in his love affairs and a life of gluttony and intemperance. Under him the political department lost none of the paralyzing terror that emanated from it.

SS control over the camp itself was exercised by the block officers, who were all carefully chosen terrorists and sadists, with a few minor exceptions who felt unhappy in the midst of this band of robbers. Each of them had a block under his control, over which he could exercise unlimited rule, even though he was formally responsible to the camp administration. There were never any restrictions placed in their way; on the contrary, they constantly received instructions to handle the prisoners harshly. Block officers lived outside the camp, but they could enter the blocks at any time of day or night. They often spent hours in the midst of the prisoners, either alone or in groups, while those in their presence scarcely dared to breathe. Most infamous were Sergeants [Hubert] Abraham, Adam, Kubitz, [Helmut] Roscher, Uhlemann, [Emil] Pleissner, and Schmidt.[12] There was also the notorious sadist Zöllner, known by the nickname "Aunt Anna," who was later charged with pederasty and hanged himself in the cellblock. From their ranks as well came the "Hangman of Buchenwald," Sergeant [Martin] Sommer, who for years was in charge of the camp jail. When he entered the camp with the black

---

11. The word *comrade* appears frequently throughout the manuscript and is probably meant more to convey the atmosphere of genuine solidarity in camp than leftist political beliefs, although that distinction becomes vaguer in the later chapters. In any case the German term that appears in the report is *Kamerad,* the same word soldiers used in the trenches in World War I, whereas a party comrade was called *Genosse* or *Parteigenosse,* terms absent from the manuscript. On feelings of solidarity among prisoners, see Terrence Des Pres, *The Survivor: An Anatomy of Life in the Death Camps* (New York: Oxford University Press, 1976), 199f.

12. Roscher was tried at the Buchenwald camp guards trial and sentenced to hanging, which was commuted to life. Pleissner was also sentenced to hanging, but it is not known if the sentence was carried out. NA, RG 338, case 000-50-9, box 426, "Review," 77–78, 80–81, 94–95.

gloves that he always wore, a wave of terror went through the ranks of the prisoners. Sergeant Warnstädt, later the executioner in the crematorium, was also a block officer at that time.

Equal in rank to the block officers were the SS officers who supervised the work details. They, too, had unrestricted authority over life and death.

The camp's entire system of labor, its control and organization, lay under the authority of the labor service officer, above whom, much later, a labor assignment officer was placed to meet the demands of the war. The negative side for the prisoners was that the labor service officer could transfer any prisoner named by a work detail officer, block officer, or other authority, to a place where the work conditions could cost him his health and his life. He could also transfer any prisoner who, often for the most trivial reasons, caught his attention while on patrol. Furthermore, the labor service officer, and later the labor assignment officer, determined the composition of the transports designated to build new subsidiary camps elsewhere or for other external work details. These transports were especially feared; more will be said about them later. SS Captain [Albert] Schwarz, who led the labor assignment after 1941, was a fanatical hater of Jews.[13]

The SS was basically divided into three parts: Section I—commandant and adjutants, Section II—headquarters staff (administration), and Section III—camp officers. The block officers and later the work detail officers as well were placed under Section III. They were originally subordinated to the guard battalion. After 1939 the troops of the Waffen SS stationed at Buchenwald were independent of the camp; their strength grew over time, especially during the war, until they reached two standards, that is, 6,000 men. The prisoners also built barracks for them. When the original concentration camp guard no longer sufficed, a concentration camp reinforcement of four companies (up to 500 men) was transferred to Buchenwald. This unit provided the guards for the sentry line and those who later occupied the watchtowers erected in the camp. The towers were equipped with machine guns and searchlights. The concentration camp reinforcement was merged into the SS Death's-Head Corps Buchenwald. This guard battalion was at first composed entirely of Germans, but in the course of time it included all sorts of foreign nationals, among them especially large numbers of Croatians and Ukrainians. In general they shot only on orders and showed the prisoners no particularly hostile attitude. With the progressive disintegration of the SS, many of them were guilty of breaches of discipline favoring the prisoners, which kept the SS court busy in the latter years.

In 1943 a canine patrol was attached to the guard battalion, its bloodhounds and wolfhounds specially trained to attack men in striped clothing. The dogs were stationed outside the sentry line (for example, during the building of the railroad and similar details), and they caused many serious injuries.

---

13. Schwarz was tried at the Buchenwald camp guards trial and sentenced to hanging. The sentence was commuted to life. NA, RG 338, case 000-50-9, box 426, "Review," 85–86, 94–95.

The first commandant of the SS Guard Battalion Buchenwald was SS First Lieutenant Kröger. He, like his successor, SS Second Lieutenant Büscher, did not enter into any special relations with the prisoners. Their interests were mainly in "organizing trips" as far away as Holland and purely external things like military pomp. Under Büscher the guard battalion military band above all gained importance, constantly practicing along the main camp street to prepare for parades and similar ceremonies. In spring 1942 SS Captain [Otto] Förschner took over leadership of the guard battalion. His conduct toward the prisoners was always above reproach. When he later became commandant of the Dora camp at Nordhausen, he distinguished himself from the rest of the SS administration through his understanding of the prisoners' situation.[14]

In 1943 he was replaced by SS First Lieutenant [Guido] Reimer, under whom the situation basically changed for the worse.[15] Reimer came from the Sudetenland, the son of a teacher in Trautenau. As a corporal, he had already attracted attention for his capricious brutality toward the prisoners. He had moved rapidly up the promotion ladder by his enthusiastic "bicycling" (obsequious ambition characterized by the maxim "Bow to those above, step on those below"). One of his first measures as commandant of the guard battalion was to order the guards to fire upon prisoners as soon as they were within five paces of the sentry line; until then shots had been fired only when the prisoner had crossed the sentry line. (In the subsequent investigation the prisoner had to be found lying with his head in the direction of escape, with a fatal shot in the back.) In training sessions for the guards that took place twice a day, he constantly stirred up the troops against the prisoners. Reimer remained commandant of the guard battalion until it was taken over by former Wehrmacht officers in fall 1944. He went from Buchenwald to Dora concentration camp.

Internal organization on the prisoners' side looked as follows: At the top stood the senior camp inmate [*Lagerälteste*], who was chosen by the SS.[16] Over time it became possible for nominations for this important function to be made by the prisoners and then confirmed. In the beginning there was only one senior camp inmate; later, with the expansion of the camp, the number grew to three (designated LA I, LA II, LA III). The senior camp inmate's duty was to be the official representative of the camp with whom the SS would deal when they had any sort of order to give. This task was extremely difficult and dangerous. To take it on re-

---

14. Förschner was executed by an American tribunal in May 1946 for his role as commandant at Dora. Konnilyn G. Feig, *Hitler's Death Camps: The Sanity of Madness* (New York: Holmes and Meier, 1981), 456.

15. Tried at the Buchenwald camp guards trial, Reimer was sentenced to hanging. His sentence was commuted to life in 1947 and remitted in 1950. NA, RG 338, case 000-50-9, box 426, "Review," 78–80, 94–95; appeals, box 460.

16. The term *Lagerälteste* dates back at least to World War I, when the head inmates in German prisoner of war camps in Russia were identified by this title.

quired a great deal of courage as well as a sense of responsibility. The wrong man in this post was a disaster for the camp.

Especially at first the SS placed the most emphasis on having a senior camp inmate who was pliable and could be used against the camp. The first of this sort was a professional criminal appropriately named Hubert Richter [literally, judge], who before his arrival had been a member of the SA at one of the Emsland camps. He was an unscrupulous tool of the SS and was himself capable of unbelievable brutality. A saying referred to him: "We are no longer in the land of poets and philosophers [*Dichter und Denker*] but in the land of judges and executioners [*Richter und Henker*]!" He acted out this maxim all too well. Because of an attempted escape by two greens that he had fearfully tried to cover up, he was removed as senior camp inmate at the end of 1937. He received a whipping, was sent to the cellblock, and was released from there.

After an interval of half a year, he was again senior camp inmate for newly arrived blacks [antisocials]. He tyrannized over them in an indescribable manner. In spring 1939 he was again placed in the cellblock on account of a corruption scandal and met a gruesome end at the hands of the SS itself. After Richter the function of senior camp inmate remained a special right of the "politicals" (with one very bitter exception that will be discussed later), as the SS administration had learned that any other arrangement would create conditions that could cost them their necks.

Corresponding to the SS roll call officer on the prisoners' side was the camp records office. It was only sporadically under the supervision of an SS man and was run entirely by prisoners. The office administered the entire internal administration of the camp—the card file, assignment to blocks, preparation for roll call, allocation of food, and other similar tasks. Its significance for the camp was enormous; its accomplishments were absolutely positive. It is no exaggeration to say that over the years, with the help of the camp records office, literally thousands of comrades were saved from death, protected from serious damage to their health, and brought into positions where they could effectively work in the interests of the prisoners.

Relationships with the labor service officer and the labor assignment officer were handled on the prisoners' side by the so-called labor records office. It contained occupational information card files for the population of the camp. Its importance grew tremendously over the years, since the labor assignment officer was no longer able to put together transports for external work details by himself. Here, too, there was a central power position with much positive or negative influence that could be exercised on behalf of the prisoners. Hundreds of valuable people could be saved only with help from the labor records office, in part by secretly striking them off the lists of death transports, in part by smuggling them into external work details when their lives were in danger inside the camp. Many comrades, however, were brought into situations where they suffered serious harm or death because of dark machinations and intrigues inside or outside the camp. The tasks the labor records office had to manage—it could happen that the office had to organize transports of thousands of prisoners in the space of two hours—were thankless and difficult. Some comrades therein performed enormous services.

Heading the individual housing blocks on the prisoners' side were the senior block inmates, who were nominated by the senior camp inmate and confirmed by the camp administration. They were responsible to the block officers for everything that happened in the block. The senior block inmate selected for each dormitory wing two or three so-called room attendants to support him; they had to be confirmed by the senior camp inmate. The room attendants were responsible for maintaining order in the block and getting the rations; they themselves distributed the food.

Under the prevailing circumstances, this institution was both necessary and on the whole useful. But it should not be forgotten that the power involved in these positions was at times badly misused by those elements in camp with weak characters. Senior block inmates and room attendants often stood under considerable pressure from the SS, but the enticements of corruption and tyranny over fellow prisoners were too much for many, whether it was a question of reds, greens, blacks, or other colors. Even in Jewish blocks such reprehensible situations were not altogether rare.

The psychological situation is to some degree evident to anyone who knows human nature and understands how it is to be crowded together with hundreds of the oppressed of the most varied sorts and qualities, for years at a time, often under scarcely bearable conditions. In the final analysis, it is the National Socialist system that should be blamed for the problems emphasized here. Nevertheless, the forces of order in the camp succeeded over the years in ending some of the principal evils. For example, Buchenwald concentration camp distinguished itself more and more from other camps through a more equitable distribution of food rations.

Similar conditions existed for the appointment of the kapos, prisoners who directed work details and were responsible to the SS work detail officers, who appointed them through the labor service officer. Kapos had foremen at their sides. Only in unavoidable cases did the SS fill the kapo positions with skilled workers. Especially in the beginning, it was usually a role for more robust natures, at first primarily former SA men, Foreign Legionnaires, and professional criminals— those who knew how to use a whip, which they often enough got to feel for themselves at the hands of the SS. In several work details, especially in the building, tunneling, sewage, and stone quarry details, the ordinary prisoner frequently had no other means of staying alive, or at least of maintaining somewhat bearable conditions, than bribery. At times it reached unimaginable proportions. Extortion acted as a worthy accompaniment.

A few shining examples stand out from the many depraved characters who functioned as kapos. There were a number of older prisoners who, insofar as they remained alive, served as models of purity, humanity, and personal courage from beginning to end. Here we must name Robert Siewert from Chemnitz and Baptist Feilen.

The senior camp inmate, the senior block inmates, the kapos, and the foremen were distinguished from the camp officers by black armbands with white lettering that they wore on their left arms.

V The Drone Existence of the SS

The SS did everything possible to use the existing unpaid labor force to the maximum extent, exploiting it for the SS and its egoistic ruling instincts. This went so far that the most valuable skilled workers were denied release on threadbare pretexts and the arrest and delivery of other workers was instigated. In the final days, this tendency led toward deliberate sabotage of the German war effort in that large-scale release actions were repeatedly delayed or undermined. The sadism of the SS, combined with its softness and taste for luxury, had become habitual.

The camp had to create a series of enterprises for the SS administration's demands for luxuries; existing enterprises constantly had to perform special tasks for the same purpose. Among the special facilities created, the following should be named:

Sculpture Studio.   Assigned to it were architects, wood and stone sculptors, woodcarvers, stonemasons, gold- and silversmiths, painters, potters, and graphic artists who were employed exclusively for the needs of the SS. They provided artistic interior decorations for the dwellings of the SS officers, made the countless gifts that members of the clique gave one another, and created the decorative façade of the camp, behind which misery spread. For the porcelain painters, a special and very expensive kiln was erected. The materials and tools put at the disposal of the sculpture studio were of the very highest quality. In SS circles far beyond Buchenwald, the Viking ships it made became a much-sought-after specialty. In 1941 potters went to the German Earth and Stone Works at Berlstedt near Buchenwald, a branch of the Berlin SS enterprise. Porcelain painters went to the SS porcelain manufacturing enterprise at Allach in Bavaria.

Genealogical Research.   The new rulers, whose origins were mostly of a rather dark nature, almost all had the ambition to acquire long lines of ancestors and gleaming coats of arms. The SS gathered together a staff, largely of former Czech officials, who were assigned the task of creating tables of ancestors, family trees, racial passes, and family chronicles.[17] They worked in cooperation with the Registration Office [*Standesamt*] created in Buchenwald. The coat of arms of the Himmler guard was designed by prisoners and registered in the Heraldry Office

---

17. A racial pass (*Ahnenpass*) was a document used to prove Aryan (non-Jewish) descent, a requirement for membership in the SS as well as for important political posts in the Third Reich.

[*Sippenamt*] in Berlin. The second deputy commandant, SS Major Schobert, who was appointed in 1940, had a six-foot-high family tree painted.[18] He donated it to the city of Würzburg, where it was put on display in the local museum. The genealogy research detail frequently faced almost unsolvable problems, since the trail of ancestors often disappeared as a consequence of numerous illegitimate ancestors in the wide fields of the Slavic east.

Photo Department. Established for the identification of prisoners, this department served primarily for the production and reproduction of amateur photographs, as well as the design of splendid photo albums for SS members, their relatives, friends, and acquaintances. This particularly well supported work detail, established by Commandant Koch, was not without dangers for prisoners, as the camp administration feared that pictures of their atrocities might reach the outside world. When this actually happened in 1939, the kapo at that time, the political prisoner Alfred Opitz, was thrown into the cellblock and, after painful torture, was garroted by Sommer.

Bookbindery. Lithography and the book printing press were attached to the bindery. Primarily luxury bindings were produced here, along with all types of greeting cards, presentation volumes, the illustrated newspaper *Der Pelikan* for comradeship evenings, plaques with maxims, and calligraphy.

Agricultural Enterprises. These included the pigsty; the horse stable, including riding horses; the sheep pen; a poultry farm; a hutch of angora rabbits; the gardening detail; and extensive fields in the immediate vicinity of the camp.

The pigsty eventually had 800 old and young animals, most of which the SS took during the evacuation of the camp. It was a place that remained engraved in the memories of the prisoners because of an event that cost about 250 comrades their lives. On November 16, 1935, a pig was stolen, the remains of which Koch supposed were buried somewhere in camp. At first he made the entire camp stand for ten hours in miserable weather in roll call square and had a number of men whipped. Then he ordered that no food be given out to the prisoners until the pig was found. The search lasted a full three days, until it was revealed that the pig had been stolen and slaughtered by SS men. (On the preceding five days, all Jews in camp had received no food because of an alleged bomb attempt on Hitler at the Bürgerbräukeller in Munich. They had been locked into the darkened blocks, where they passed the time in agonizing uncertainty.)

The angora rabbit station and the poultry farm provided a steady supply of good food and a source of income for the SS administration. The gardening detail

---

18. Schobert was tried at the Buchenwald camp guards trial and was sentenced to hanging. NA, RG 338, case 000-50-9, box 426, "Review," 83–84, 94–95.

was the most feared detail, second only to the stone quarry. It stood under the direction of SS First Lieutenant Dumböck, a native of Salzburg, who with his own hands killed at least forty political prisoners, doggedly persecuting the Austrians in particular. Greenhouses, specially built at great expense for the Buchenwald gardens, were strong competition for Weimar businesses. Flowers and occasionally vegetables were sold to prisoners at fantastic prices.

Whole sections of the general enterprises and work areas of the camp were temporarily diverted for the private interests of the SS administration, especially in the weeks before Christmas and special SS celebrations. Up to half the working time of the prisoners in these enterprises, including those in the purely military factories like the German Armament Works (DAW), was spent in so-called boondoggling [*Pfusch*], that is, illegal activity for the private purposes mentioned above. Special woods, copper, bronze, gold, silver, all sorts of wrought iron, and an abundance of other raw materials vital to the war effort were constantly diverted in large quantities for the private benefit of SS officers. The prisoners not only went along with this practice because they were compelled but even encouraged it because it further corrupted the SS and presented an opportunity to sabotage the war effort. A multitude of luxury articles, some of great artistic worth, was produced—interior decoration for entire rooms, inlaid wood furniture, valuable individual pieces, paintings, objects made from metal, busts and sculptures—for which nothing was paid, except occasionally a few cigarettes to the deliverer.

These items circulated not only in the area of the Buchenwald guard battalion but went far beyond, to every friend and acquaintance of the SS leadership clique in Thuringia, throughout Germany, and even to other lands of Europe. Especially talented artists among the prisoners were at times "loaned out" for weeks to Berlin or other cities and camps so that they could satisfy the SS officers' desire for luxury. For Christmas 1939, Heinrich Himmler received a desk set of green marble finished by the prisoners' sculpture studio of Buchenwald and valued at approximately 15,000 to 20,000 marks.

In 1938 the construction of a personal falconry for Hermann Göring was begun near the headquarters, the completion of which took until summer 1940. The cost of materials alone was reckoned at approximately 135,000 marks. The falconry encompassed an area that included the actual aviary, in old Germanic style, with artistically carved massive oak timbers; the hunting hall, with hand-carved oak furniture, large fireplaces, and hunting trophies; a circular gazebo; and the house of the falconer. In this house the French prime minister Léon Blum and other prominent personalities were later interned. A special deer pen and cages with wildcats were attached to it. The entire facility had to be designed and maintained by landscape gardeners. His excellency, the Reich hunt master [Göring], never entered the falconry given to him and never even saw it. However, the SS publicized it in advertising brochures for Weimar and the vicinity and charged visitors entrance fees of 1 mark.

At the special request of Frau [Ilse] Koch [the commandant's wife], a private riding hall was constructed in the first year of the war.[19] A huge, costly wooden building was erected, rectangular in form, approximately 120 by 300 feet and a good 60 feet high; it was decorated inside with wall mirrors, as in a riding school. Construction had to be accelerated to such an extent that up to thirty prisoners were fatally injured or driven to their deaths as they worked on it. Building costs ran around a quarter of a million marks. After its completion Frau Koch held her morning ride there for a quarter to a half an hour a few times a week, during which the SS band had to provide the musical accompaniment. After Frau Koch was delivered to the police prison in Weimar in 1943, as a result of the Koch trial, the riding hall served as a lumber storage room and warehouse.

On the climatically milder south side of the Ettersberg, the camp inmates had to build an asphalt-paved road (Eicke Street). From the beginning the officers' houses were built along it. Eventually ten luxury villas stood there, each equipped with every modern convenience. They were stylish wooden villas with massive basements, private garages, and spacious terraces that offered a view over the Thuringian countryside. The large stone slabs used for fences around them had to be dragged from the stone quarries by long columns of prisoners. In the officers' houses lived the camp commandant, the deputy commandants, the commander of the guard battalion, and other higher SS officers, their families, and servants. In addition, prisoner domestic servants, mainly male and female Jehovah's Witnesses, were assigned to them. The private central heating and hot water systems installed in each house were also serviced by prisoners. Into these officers' houses, year in and year out, in quantities difficult to describe, flowed the fruits of an economy built on corruption. To give just an indication of the extent of the corruption, it should be mentioned that once in 1942 the commandant sold to some of the prisoners 200 preserved ducks that were about to spoil.

SS mess halls originally consisted of three categories: the men's mess, the headquarters staff mess, and the officers' mess. The highest-ranking officers always reserved for themselves the right to eat privately as well. The various grades were sharply distinguished, both quantitatively and qualitatively. When in 1941 SS Major [Otto] Barnewald replaced the previous administrative officer, SS Captain

---

19. Ilse Koch, known in the popular press as "the bitch of Buchenwald," was tried at the Buchenwald camp guards trial. Her collection of human skin and tattoos received extensive publicity. She was sentenced to life, but the sentence was reduced to four years. A public furor resulted, including an investigation in 1948 by a U.S. Senate committee headed by Homer Ferguson of Michigan. Koch was released in 1949, rearrested by German authorities, retried, and sentenced to life imprisonment. She committed suicide at Aichach prison in Bavaria in 1967. NA, RG 338, case 000-50-9, box 426, "Review," 62–65, 94–95; Frank M. Buscher, *The U.S. War Crimes Trial Program in Germany, 1946–1955,* (New York: Greenwood, 1989), 54–55; Louis L. Snyder, *Encyclopedia of the Third Reich* (New York: McGraw-Hill, 1976), 198.

Weichseldörfer, the differences were formally abolished.[20] As a result, the private "organizing" of the officer corps came into full bloom. The extent it reached can be seen in the example of a master sergeant named Henschel, for years the work detail officer of the prisoners' tailor shop, who had 1,000 jars of tomatoes, peas, and green beans canned for his own use in a single winter. As payment, the work detail officers from the gardens, the prisoner kitchen, and the German Armament Works received dozens of the best-tailored civilian suits and uniforms made from stolen material. For years, eggs by the thousands ordered for sick prisoners were consumed by SS officers.

A nest of corruption without equal in this regard was the camp canteen led by SS Technical Sergeant Hans Schmidt, a corpulent black marketeer. Schmidt was an almost pathological case. He liked to urinate in champagne glasses and in February 1945 had his penis washed by his prisoner servant in the presence of his wife and daughter, who were visiting him. Using whatever telephone he pleased, this man could summon Deputy Commandant SS Major Schobert with the often overheard words, "Maxie, come immediately and pick me up in your car!" upon which the deputy commandant would always promptly obey the staff sergeant's instructions. [Through the black market] Schmidt disposed of all PX wares intended for the troops.

Although strict rations on tobacco and wine were imposed for the SS rank and file, for example one bottle of wine for six men, champagne literally flowed in rivers for the SS officers. Frau Koch took baths in Madeira that was poured into the bathtub. Cigarettes by the hundreds of thousands were put at the disposal of SS officers for their own use and for profiteering. In their insatiable greed they did not even shrink from exploiting the Croatian, Hungarian, and Transylvanian ethnic German [*volksdeutsche*] guard troops. In return for bacon, lard, and sausages out of packages sent from their farm homes, they received special leaves and lighter duties. SS man Ortner from Romania, a member of the Second Company, served no duty for two full years because he made himself useful to his superiors in this manner.

A special chapter in this connection was the so-called comradeship evening. They began in 1938 with a pompous open-air festival at the Bismarck Tower (an observation tower on the south slope of the Ettersberg that could be seen from a great distance) and were held approximately once a month for the headquarters staff. These were binges of eating and drinking that almost always ended in wild orgies. The funds for these occasions were raised by "punishing" the entire prison camp at regular intervals with twenty-four-hour fasts, which brought in a sum of 6,000 to 10,000 marks for the headquarters staff each time. The Weimar profiteers from these feasts were primarily the firms of Daniel (fine meat and sausage wares) and Fischkettel (a delicatessen).

---

20. Barnewald, tried at the Buchenwald camp guards trial, was sentenced to hanging. The sentence was commuted to life, he was paroled in 1954, and the sentence was remitted in 1957. NA, RG 338, case 000-50-9, box 426, "Review," 38–40, 94–95; appeals, box 452.

It is not possible in this framework to present even a roughly complete picture of the depth, extent, and complexity of the network of corruption in the drone existence of the SS officer corps. Hundreds and hundreds of prisoners were constantly employed as slaves for these pinnacles of achievement of the National Socialist folk community; thousands had to starve for them.

VI The Living and Working Conditions of the Prisoners

The life of the camp inmates stood in sharp contrast to the life of the SS. Crowded quarters, cold, hunger, slave labor, and constant fear governed their existence.

On arrival at the camp, the prisoners had a foretaste of what awaited them. After a railroad journey that was often days long, crowded together in railcars, constantly harassed by the guards (and in many cases by the police), they arrived in Weimar only to face another challenge. They were either marched up the 5-mile-long road at double time, with arms raised in the air while receiving blows from a cane, or, threatened with rifles and pistols, they were squeezed together in trucks to be transported to the camp. A total of 233,868 people traveled this path, not counting the tens of thousands who were brought back to the base camp a second time from subsidiary camps as wrecks, after their bodily and spiritual strength was worn out.

Arrival was followed by a "reception ceremony." In most cases a ring of SS sergeants who were hanging around lusting for new booty immediately lunged at them. There was a hail of kicks and blows; the "new ones" had stones thrown at them and cold water poured on them. They had to stand for hours in front of the political department in the so-called Saxon salute: arms crossed behind the head, frequently with bent knees, too, so that temporary paralysis set in.[21] In this manner their morale was broken. Then with further kicks and blows to the head from the sergeants, they were led into the political department for the initial recording of personal information.

The following example illustrates the manner of questioning. To fill in the space for "parents," a prisoner was asked, "Which whore shat you into the world?" It came out that the prisoner being questioned was one of six children whose mother had received the Mother's Cross in gold from Adolf Hitler.

Questioning was followed by entrance into the camp itself through the famous gate with the inscription in the stucco, "My country, right or wrong" ["Recht oder Unrecht mein Vaterland"] and in iron letters on the bars of the gate, "To each his

---

21. The "Saxon salute," in which the arms are crossed behind the head and the hands placed on the back of the neck, apparently came from Sachsenburg concentration camp. *KL Bu* (Weimar: Thüringer Volksverlag, 1946), 108. It became a regular Nazi practice in World War II and can be seen in many war photos.

due!" ["Jedem das Seine!"][22] For hours at a time, the new arrivals had to stand with their faces toward the cellblock wall, again in the Saxon salute, alternating with deep knee bends.

Block officers who happened to be passing by considered the new entrants fair game. If it amused them, they chased people, sometimes those who still had their suitcases with them, until the victims fell in complete exhaustion in roll call square, or they would force them to roll in the dirt in their civilian clothes. Next came the "lecture" by the deputy commandant or the roll call officer that was supposed to represent the first introduction into camp life. But it was limited to the threat of the death penalty, repeated twenty to thirty times, for a series of so-called offenses. As long as the gallows still stood in roll call square, the "lecture" was held there.

Next the prisoners marched at double time to the bathhouse. They undressed (at which time part of their possessions disappeared) and then were brought to the barbers, who used hair clippers of less than the highest quality to shear the prisoners from head to toe. Next came either a hot or an ice-cold shower, according to the whim of the SS, after which the prisoners were led to the clothing room to get dressed. Often this side trip took place in winter. Prisoners were led in the nude over camp streets and roll call square, which cost hundreds of victims their lives either immediately or from the pneumonia that followed. From 1941 on, disinfection preceded the bath. The brutally shorn prisoner had to jump into a vat with a disinfectant that was gradually becoming horribly dirty. It burned the injured parts of the skin terribly. For "inspection" each of the disinfected prisoners had to bend over with his back to the sergeants and his legs spread, which gave special pleasure to the perverted, especially when the prisoner was a prominent personality.

Each new admittee was issued striped prison duds [*Klamotten*], without consideration of size, build, or physical peculiarities. It consisted of a pair of underpants, a shirt, pants, a jacket, a cap, and a pair of shoes. These civilized terms, however, give no indication of the actual condition of the articles of clothing. Some were lucky if a new supply had suddenly arrived. The majority received absolutely worn-out goods that they could improve slightly over the course of time only through patient "organizing."[23] In fall 1942 several hundred thousand pieces of clothing from those murdered at Auschwitz arrived. It ranged from infants' diapers to women's underwear and men's shirts; almost half of it had to be thrown

---

22. The American Steven Decatur is credited with "My country, right or wrong!" The second motto, "*Jedem das Seine*," is a Germanization of the Latin phrase *suum cuique*, which can be found in several citations from Tacitus, Cicero, and Justinian. It appears, for example, in the first sentence of the Roman emperor Justinian's *Institutes* as part of the definition of justice. The German motto appeared on medals of the Prussian Order of the Black Eagle (1701–1918). Georg Büchmann, *Geflügelte Worte* (Berlin: Haude und Spenersche Buchhandlung, 1910), 466.

23. This was a widely used term in concentration camp jargon. Des Pres writes, "The word *organize* [was] used to cover all forms of illegal, life-sustaining activity"; *Survivor*, 105.

out, since it was full of bullet holes and large bloodstains. The remainder were mainly nightshirts, as well as numerous choir robes from priests. Men ran around the camp in this clothing. Especially catastrophic was footwear; many comrades, in particular those who were given wooden shoes, could hardly walk anymore after just a few days. Those who received the "Dutch wooden shoes" were in the worst shape. If one were not used to them, one could hardly walk much less run in them because of their sharp edges, especially if one went without socks or foot coverings. The number of foot injuries and inflammations [*Phlegmone*] they caused eventually forced the SS, when the work capacity was vital to the war effort, to permit prisoners to have shoes sent from home.

The next station on this path of suffering was the personal property room. There the few remaining personal possessions prisoners had brought along were sorted, cataloged, and put into a sack to be held for the duration of time in the camp. All money had to be turned over, along with any other valuables, such as wedding rings, watches, and the like.

Opportunities for common theft at each of these stations were shamefully exploited not only by the SS but also, unfortunately, by many a fellow prisoner. Yet other comrades did all they could to help new arrivals improve their situation and lighten their burden during this first passage. For example, they often hurriedly whispered valuable words of advice.

Through this advice the new arrival was promptly and immediately removed from the claws of the SS. There were not many individuals who could survive without inner damage the process of breaking the will and dehumanization. Many could protect their inner worth only by simultaneously entering a state of split consciousness, whereby the body was wholly turned over to the arbitrary outside power while the true self absented itself from the body, observing it psychologically and objectively.

The new arrival was normally received in the prisoner records office, entered into the card catalog, and assigned to a block on the same day. A medical examination and the filling out of a lengthy questionnaire for the medical records followed a few days later.

At the residential block an abundance of confusing impressions and experiences flooded in upon each new arrival. Every wooden block had two wings; each stone block had two stories and four wings. Each wing consisted of a dayroom and a sleeping room, occupied by 100 to 200 prisoners. The beds in the sleeping room were stacked above one another in three or four levels. They contained straw mattresses, which were covered with checkered bed covers until the end of 1941. Each prisoner had one or two thin blankets at his disposal. A particular form of persecution on the part of the SS consisted of so-called bed construction [*Bettenbau*]: Lumpy or sagging straw mattresses had to be made flat as a board each day; the checkered bedspread had to be arranged in straight lines before inspection by the kapos; the misshapen pillow had to be placed in the right corner; and all the other nonsense that belonged to Prussian barracks drills as sharpened by SS practices had to be carried out. A single crease in one bed could lead to the most depraved harassment of an entire block. Room attendants responsible for bed making therefore often developed a hardness and ruthlessness that made understandable other acts of roughness or injustice, especially considering the lack of experience, indifference, or lack of discipline of many prisoners.

The dayrooms contained a row of tables with benches and a locker with cubbyholes to hold each person's basic utensils: a metal bowl, a metal pot, and a spoon. It was a constant struggle to keep at least a few things there that one was able to acquire over the course of time; often enough they were simply thrown out or seized during inspections. On such occasions Block Officer Uhlemann took special pleasure in simply tipping over the entire locker. The prisoner had no other place to store his miserable possessions.

Except during working hours, the life of the camp inmate was spent in these rooms. Between the two wings of sleeping rooms there was a washroom and a toilet facility with an open cubicle. Men would secretly smoke there whenever they could, since it was strictly forbidden in the blocks. Washrooms and toilet facilities were first made available in mid-1939.

The daily routine went as follows: At dawn the camp was awakened by a whistle. One had thirty minutes to wash, dress, eat breakfast, and "construct" the bed, often an impossible feat. In late winter 1942, Deputy Commandant SS Second Lieutenant Plaul introduced "morning calisthenics" that began half an hour before the normal waking time of the block; it later had to be canceled because of numerous deaths and cases of pneumonia. Plaul was one of the worst oppressors of the prisoners. In fall 1943 he was sent to external work detail Laura near Saalfeld (which had a very high death rate) and later to Hasag-Leipzig.

Breakfast for the prisoners consisted of a piece of bread from the daily ration that each received and either a pint of thin soup or a pint of "coffee" without milk and sugar. Then everyone went to roll call, which as a rule lasted an hour, until it became light enough to work. If the roll call tallied—and in the morning it was speeded up because of work—the army of bald-shaven heads heard the command "Caps off!" and then "Caps on!" If the orders were not carried out smartly enough, they had to be repeated as often as necessary. Next came the feared announcement, "The following prisoners to the gate!" This announcement affected all those who on the previous evening had received a note from the records office to report to one of the six signposts that were fastened to the left wing of the gatehouse building. Those summoned had to wait there for the anonymous terrors that had been decided for them. Whenever the prisoners had eventually determined which signpost indicated the political department, which were for punishments or more or less harmless things (inquiries, signatures, notarizing of documents, and the like), then the sequence was suddenly changed again.

Immediately afterward came the command: "Report to work details!" Now everyone rushed in a wild helter-skelter, running as quickly as possible to the assigned gathering spot for the work details. To the cheerful accompaniment of the camp band, which in winter had to play their instruments with stiff fingers, prisoners marched out in military ranks of five abreast. While passing through the gate, prisoners had to snap their caps off their heads again and align their hands on the seams of their trousers. Then they marched to the work sites at double time, singing songs.

Work either continued till late afternoon, with a half hour midday break in the open air (it was long forbidden to bring bread for this break), or work details returned to camp about noon for thirty to forty-five minutes to gulp down the midday meal. This was the only warm meal of the day, as a rule consisting of about a quart of more or less watery and insubstantial stew. The worst food was in the first year of the war, 1939–1940, when rutabagas, jokingly called "German pineapples," were almost always the daily fare. After 1938 midday roll call was no longer held; however, time taken for marching in and out was calculated as part of the midday break.

Evening roll call seldom took less than an hour and a half in any sort of weather. It was particularly bad if a prisoner was unaccounted for. The entire camp had to stand in roll call square until the person was found. The search effort was conducted by the senior block inmate and the room attendants. In 1939 the entire camp once had to stand a full nineteen hours, that is, through the entire night and into the next morning at eleven. Two professional criminals had hidden themselves in the pigsty.

In the latter years of daylong, uninterrupted work, food was given out only in the evening; it was, of course, cold after a lengthy roll call. In the block each prisoner found his daily portion, which the room attendant had in the meantime distributed: bread, margarine, and either a small piece of sausage or a spoonful of yogurt [*Quark*]. Most went right to bed after eating. After the evening whistle, which depending on the season was between eight and nine o'clock, everyone had to be in his block and a half an hour later in bed. Only a shirt was allowed for sleeping, even in the most extreme cold and often in ice-cold sleeping rooms. Block officers would frequently order inmates to stand in their shirts by their beds, or even outside in front of the blocks, to catch those who had on another piece of clothing. Anyone who was found wearing long johns or socks had to reckon with the most severe punishments.

As far as work was concerned, it is essential to distinguish between work details employed inside camp and those employed outside camp. In general, inside work details were the easier ones. Of these, however, there were a few major exceptions: the gardening detail, stone breaking on the camp streets, and the so-called 4711 squad (named after the famous Cologne perfume brand, this was a Jewish work detail that had to empty the latrine trenches). Other internal details, such as the prisoner hospital, always carried heavy responsibilities. Many prisoners met their deaths in the stone-breaking detail, which was exposed to all sorts of weather. At one time the Austrian minister of justice, [Dr. Robert] von Winterstein, and the Austrian state youth officer, Baron Duval, among others, belonged to this detail. The most important internal work details were the kitchen, warehouse, laundry, bathhouse, personal property room, clothing and supply room, shoemaking, tailoring, sock darning, cabinetry, locksmith, and a series of other workshops. There were also the lumberyard, pigsty, gardening detail, prisoner hospital (with its pathology section), prisoner records office, labor records office, prisoner post office, library, and the camp maintenance detail. After 1943 a clinical station for the Department for Typhus and Virus Research (Block 46) and a typhus vaccination production facility (Block 50) were created.

In 1942 a camp fire department was created, in 1943 a camp police; the latter had the task of maintaining order in the camp, something that was not always easy. This institution existed only in Buchenwald. The camp police became a well-disciplined executive organ in the hands of the inmate leadership. It was a concession wrangled out of the SS administration, and for a long time it was reserved for German prisoners because the SS could communicate only in German and believed that Germans could more easily become tools. In the course of time, especially after the bombardment of Buchenwald on August 24, 1944, the German prisoners opened the institution more and more to all groups of foreigners. They made out of it a basic cadre for self-defense, which achieved an extraordinary significance in the final months during the prisoners' preparations for the end of the camp. Thousands of prisoners who lacked deeper insight did not understand the functions and methods of the camp police, even less so when there were occasional excesses both in tone and action in its use of authority.

Many internal work details such as sock darning and the lumberyard were turned over primarily to comrades who were invalids. Along with service in the blocks and work in the German Armament Works, approximately 40 percent of the working prisoners were employed in internal work details.

Conditions were much harder in external camp work details. Work began with a struggle over tools, which were available only in limited numbers and variable quality. Anyone who did not manage to get a tool was under the constant, immediate danger of "standing out," that is, of being reported for not working hard enough. There was strict supervision under the work detail officers and the sergeants hanging around them, who for their part constantly "worked" their nightsticks. The main principle of prisoners therefore was always to "work with the eyes." They set up their own warning system, activated immediately by the code word "Eighteen!" [*Achtzehn*] (which meant "Watch out!" [*Achtung*]) that was passed along as soon as one of the slave drivers appeared.

Unlike at the Moor camps, the type of work at Buchenwald did not generally allow for production quotas, so as little as possible was accomplished. The system was the purest form of education for aversion to work [*Arbeitsscheu*]. One of the worst injuries the SS inflicted on the prisoners was instilling in them poor work habits, so that they were unable to do any real work for years, if not for life. It probably would have been possible to accomplish two or three times as much work with one-fifth the work force through a more reasonable and humane work system that included incentives. But for the SS it was not so much a question of work output as one of senseless torment. External work details were in many cases also used as convenient opportunities for "liquidations."

Even the selection of the work force was usually carried out by a life-threatening means. Skilled workers were ordered to step out. Then the remaining prisoners were beaten and ordered into the heaviest work details, like stone quarrying or tunnel building, without any consideration for physical strength, suitability, or previous experience. To be a skilled worker was in any case to have a life insurance policy. Anyone who had the courage and presence of mind to present himself as some sort of skilled worker, and was able to withstand with boldness and inventiveness any difficulties that developed later, had at least a chance. In contrast, members of the intellectual professions, especially those who wore glasses, were from the beginning on the road to ruin. It was a fearful and grotesque version of survival of the fittest.

The most important external work details were as follows. The stone quarry was the truest of the "suicide" work details where several thousand comrades met their deaths through blows from stones, caning, "accidents," deliberate pushes over the precipice, shooting, and every other type of torment. A favorite practice of the sergeants was to have candidates for death, especially Jews, push an empty or even a loaded cart up a steep slope—an impossible task for one man or two prisoners together. They would be killed by the weight of the cart as it rolled back on them or by the beatings that accompanied the task. Primarily the punishment company worked in the stone quarry, along with those who were specifically condemned to it. These were the hunting grounds of the infamous Staff Sergeants Hinkelmann and Blank (a Bavarian forestry apprentice and poacher who in 1944 hanged himself in the cellblock during the Hoven affair [Chapter Eleven, §152]).

The tunnel work detail was almost as infamous. Under the kapo Heusgen of Tunnel Detail I, the foreman Tennenbaum drowned a family man in 1939 by holding him down in a pool of water. Another foreman beat a prisoner so severely with a new hoe that the tool broke. And those were not isolated examples. Kapo Heusgen, who wore the red triangle, died an unnatural death in camp in 1942 because of his misdeeds, but the foreman Tennenbaum, likewise a political, had earlier escaped his well-deserved fate by an unexpected "release."

Similarly bad conditions existed for excavation workers in the construction details (garrison garage, SS housing), whereas the situation was more bearable for skilled workers. Terrible conditions always existed in the stone-carrying detail. It was composed largely of Jews; they were driven into the sentry line by the dozens. The other horrible torments they had to undergo (having their faces rolled in thorns, etc.) were like those in Dante's *Inferno*. It was almost a relief for them when they were merely forced to build stone walls that would be carried away the next day in order to be built up again elsewhere, and so on.[24]

The prisoners who worked in the headquarters area had it better than those in all other work details. They had numerous advantages, in particular that of being able to relieve the SS of highly pleasurable things. Many of them used the items only for their own advantage; others smuggled whatever they could into the camp. The greatest risks were attached to theft: Many went to the whipping block for it and were relieved of their duties. In all work details prisoners were interested in two basic things: being under a roof and getting near a source of heat. For the

---

24. Dante's description of the figures condemned to carry heavy stones is from *Purgatorio,* Canto X.

bad weather season, which in Buchenwald lasts from September to the end of May, there was enormous competition to get into work details that offered those advantages. To kapos and foremen who could be bribed, high prices were paid for workplaces close to a source of heat, even in the open air.

Just as work began with the struggle over tools, it ended with the struggle over the stones that every member of external work details had to haul into camp at the close of the workday. Under considerable danger, in the last few minutes before work ended, one had to glance around for a stone to carry. It had to look large and heavy but not be too sharp-edged and had to be reasonably clean so that it would not dirty one's clothing. So laden, the columns of work slaves marched in the gathering darkness "from the day's toils and burdens" back into camp, carrying with them dead and collapsed prisoners and still facing hours of evening roll call.

Free time was scarce and filled with the necessary cleaning of clothes, shoes, and lockers, and the SS cut into it at every opportunity.

In 1938 and 1939 the entire camp regularly had to report for work after the evening meal until late at night. Floodlights glared over the camp to create the brightness necessary for work and supervision. After 1939 this night work was a "privilege" of the Jews, until in 1942 the inmate camp leadership successfully insisted that other categories of prisoners also be assigned to this shift so the Jews had to do night work only two or three times a week. Night work often lasted until one in the morning, but sometimes even through the entire night. Of course, little was actually accomplished, but the torment was great. For years work was performed on Sundays until noon or early afternoon, with relatively short breaks. The special activities for the entire camp on these days were stone carrying and hauling tree trunks. Block officers assigned to Sunday duty avenged themselves for the loss of their free time with particular cruelties.

Considering these living and working conditions, the daily rations for the prisoners were completely inadequate. Up to March 1938 the permitted expenditure was 55 pfennigs per head per day; from April 1938 to the outbreak of war it was 5 pfennigs more.[25] During the war food was rationed for prisoners as well as for the entire population, although after August 1940 there was a slight improvement. By bribing SS officers involved in food rationing and every other possible maneuver, a number of work details managed to get additional food rations for heavy labor or long hours of work. In the final weeks before the end of the camp, the food situation became so catastrophic that many comrades died of hunger. The nature of the food—deficient in fats, proteins, and vitamins—along with the general living conditions through the years, was responsible for horrible epidemics and diseases. The most serious was a severe epidemic of tuberculosis.

The need to supplement the subnormal daily food rations offered the SS an opportunity to conduct a profitable business. They allowed prisoners to make can-

---

25. The allocation for the daily ration amounted to about 22 cents at the 1938 exchange rate (1 reichsmark = 40 cents).

teen purchases. The prisoners' canteen at Buchenwald was, like those of other camps, centrally supplied from Dachau until late 1942. Prices were rather arbitrarily determined. Up to the outbreak of war there was a relatively broad selection of things to buy in the canteen, at least for those prisoners who had money. On the average they made up at most one-third of the camp population, which would explain part of the terrible corruption.

In principle each prisoner was allowed to receive 30 marks a month from home. The funds were deposited for him in an account at the prisoners' bank. Money was paid out at irregular intervals two to four times a week. Prisoners had to wait for money for hours, putting up with all sorts of harassment, especially before major holidays like Christmas, when a withdrawal often took two or three days of waiting in the cold. Waiting prisoners were thrown down into the dirt or forced to lie on their stomachs for half an hour at a time; then there were the reversals, in which the first few rows, who had already waited four or five hours, were suddenly made last. It goes without saying that in the haste with which the teller threw sums of money at the prisoner, many a banknote or 5-mark piece was missing by the time the prisoner had the funds in his own hands. SS First Lieutenant Driemel, who for a long time directed the bank, was not above holding back even small sums, not to mention larger ones. It was a favorite "joke" of his, after the close of disbursements, to inform the senior block inmates of the Jewish blocks that "a Jew had swindled him out of 10 marks." After that each Jewish block immediately had to reimburse him 10 marks.

Prisoners had only two possible uses for the money: canteen purchases and bribery. By using the most improbable tricks, the well-to-do managed to have extra money sent from home. They kept it off the books of the prisoners' bank—Driemel was not seldom in on the profits—in order to help out dozens of comrades. Those who brought a lot of money into the camp at the beginning became targets for robbery, especially by the green kapos. Many of them possessed not just hundreds but thousands of marks. They used the money to support a fitting lifestyle. The differences that existed in this regard caused trouble until, finally, besides tobacco, the canteen had nothing more to offer other than "Viking salad," a multicolored, undefinable product of the German chemical industry.

"Coupled sales," strictly forbidden in German retail trade, were developed into a specialty by the SS in selling to prisoners. Because smoking materials were usually extraordinarily scarce, a small quantity of tobacco, cigarettes, or cigarette paper was coupled with a pair of suspenders, a kilo of mussels that were no longer fresh, spoiled herrings, red beets, or the ubiquitous Viking salad. The greatest specialist in this area was SS Master Sergeant [Gotthard] Michael, nephew of Commandant Koch. From him came the slogan, "To each his own and to me the most!" He once advertised among prisoners for a purchasing expedition to Holland. Taking along 15,000 marks, he traveled in a first-class sleeping car and spent fourteen days living there luxuriously. When no one in camp believed in his return any more, he came back. For 6 to 10 marks he offered a few paper cigars, some cigarettes of the worst sort, a bar of chocolate, and a can of condensed milk for every three men. He was tripped up over the following affair: Although alcohol was strictly forbidden in camp, he brought into the canteen 3,000 quarts of apple wine that was "improved" there to 9,000 quarts. He had purchased it at a price of 35 pfennigs per liter and sold it at a price of 1.20 marks. Envious SS buddies turned him in because of it.

Canteen purchases for prisoners were made through agents, block purchasers. No more needs to be said about the double-sided nature of this function. In 1942 a special canteen building was opened in camp. Very few prisoners saw the lavish salesroom from the inside. The administration of the prisoners' canteen performed a service by "organizing" large quantities of food through the most wide-ranging channels. This they supplied to individual work details in the form of nourishing soups and similar things. These special food distributions in the individual work details even benefited prisoners without money. After 1944 the kapo of the canteen was able to find ways of offering light beer for sale with some regularity.

Prisoners were forbidden to receive packages from home. A single exception was made in winter 1939, so that prisoners could acquire their own warm clothing; many items naturally disappeared. The second deputy commandant at the time, SS Captain [Hermann] Florstedt, for example, seized sacks full of items from the Jewish blocks and distributed them among the SS.[26] After fall 1941 the ban on the receipt of packages was lifted. Formally, from then on a prisoner could receive as much food as he could eat in one day. The rest was seized by SS men in the package distribution office.

What sort of life these package robbers were able to lead can be imagined. Relatives of prisoners understandably sent whatever they could, often food touchingly saved out of their own rations. Food packages also arrived in considerable number from agricultural areas or from solidarity actions, especially from Bohemia and Moravia in Czechoslovakia. For this reason rigorous control could no longer be maintained, and a portion of the camp received the means to hold out to the end. Severe antagonisms, animosities, and nationalistic hate psychoses were also a consequence of this development, since general distribution [of package contents] was not possible. Only assistance on an individual level came into question—though of considerable extent.

In the winter of 1941–1942, Adolf Hitler called on the German people to collect wool. The appeal was also graciously extended to the concentration camp inmates, who had been excluded from the folk community. Requests for donations in the blocks were passed on by senior block inmates in the following manner: "We must voluntarily contribute to the wool collection. Everyone who gives something will get a positive mark in the records. Anyone who gives nothing goes to the whipping block. Do whatever you want!" Many a comrade then gave a halfway sparable piece to a needier prisoner in camp with the words, "That is my wool donation. The others can kiss my ass!"

---

26. Florstedt was later commandant of Maidanek and was found guilty of corruption by an SS court. He was executed by the SS in April 1945. Feig, *Death Camps*, 455.

Nevertheless the 12,000 Buchenwald prisoners gathered together a nice pile, which was praised in the *Thüringer Gauzeitung* as the "contribution of the SS headquarters staff Buchenwald." The blocks of Dutch prisoners and Jehovah's Witnesses openly and unanimously refused any contribution. Although the SS did not dare take action against the Dutch for this, the Jehovah's Witnesses were punished: They had to stand in the cold in roll call square all day on New Year's Day, perform punishment exercises, and work until late at night. They were removed from all preferred work details—an order that of course had to be revoked a few days later because they were needed.

Every two weeks a prisoner could write a letter and a postcard of a prescribed number of lines to immediate relatives. Jews were often not allowed to write for months at a time; members of the punishment company could write only every three months. From time to time, for one pretext or another a general ban on letters was levied on the camp. Frequently a prisoner would receive only an empty envelope in the incoming mail. The ministry secretary, Dr. Franz von Nagy from Vienna, was called to the gate on Christmas 1939 to receive a telegram. After two days of waiting in the icy cold, he was handed a telegram informing him of the death of his father. Roll Call Officer Hackmann once notified a prisoner of the death of his brother. When the prisoner asked which of his several brothers had died, he received the answer, "You can pick one out yourself!" Once Block Officer Kubitz brought all the mail for Block 36, showed the stack around, read the individual names, and stuck the entire packet into the stove with the words, "So, you swine, now you know that you have received some mail!"

Censorship depended on the mood of the SS men responsible for it, who were in part [functional] illiterates. Every card or letter that was in the least objectionable was not sent back but was simply torn up. Thus the prisoner, who had carefully formulated an appropriate text with the most urgent information, never knew whether or not he had made contact with his family. Weeks of anxious waiting would pass, filled with tormenting doubts about the fate of relatives, the fidelity of wives (the Gestapo often used the most shameless lies to pressure women to seek a divorce), and the development of children, of whom one no longer had any vivid memories. This terrible war of nerves represented one of the most depressing burdens of life in camp. No wonder many attempted again and again, under great danger to their lives, illegally to smuggle mail out of the camp. An SS man who in this regard accomplished extraordinary feats for a great number of comrades was SS Sergeant August Feld from Lummerscheid, near Saarbrücken. In addition to being above all reproach, he was also exceedingly willing to help. Feld did not belong to the camp itself but was assigned as a courier to Block 50.

As a rule visits to camp inmates were not permitted at all. Only rare exceptions were allowed when it was a question of foreign intervention that could not be avoided or because special permission was granted by Gestapo headquarters in Berlin. In the last years of the war, especially distinguished soldiers from the front who had relatives in the concentration camp were allowed to visit.

Still rarer than visits were leaves from the concentration camp. During the entire existence of Buchenwald concentration camp, perhaps two dozen comrades received the opportunity to visit their relatives temporarily. Occasions for this were severe illnesses, deaths, and the liquidation of businesses. This list of reasons as such gives a false impression, as permission for leave in fact depended on luck in having good connections with either a Gestapo official or the camp administration. Business transactions that promised one of the granting authorities some advantage ranked far higher than the death of a mother or father.

Most prisoners came into the camp under an illusion encouraged by the Gestapo or police. They believed that they were to remain here for a limited period of time, maybe three or six months, "depending on conduct." Nothing was farther from the truth. Release from the concentration camp, if it ever came into question at all, was a purely arbitrary matter, even a question of chance. (In 1936 Himmler had declared publicly that he would keep thousands of politicals behind barbed wire for life.) The Gestapo headquarters formally required the camp administration to file conduct reports on individual camp inmates at intervals of three to six months. These reports were one of the craziest chapters of camp life. In thousands of cases the camp administration gave information without knowing anything about the prisoner or his case, stating that the prisoner concerned was especially recalcitrant, incorrigible, and absolutely not suited for release.

The results were often written entreaties, complaints, and reproaches from relatives, especially from mothers, as well as numerous divorces. The prisoner never had the least opportunity to answer directly with even a single word, which aggravated the situation immeasurably. The role chance played was shown in that negative "conduct reports" could be issued and yet the inmate would be released a few weeks later anyway. If a prisoner was actually called in for "questioning" by one of the camp officers, a practice that went on at Buchenwald according to whim up to 1942, the results were nevertheless not authoritative. Information was given out by the camp administration as it suited them. Apart from that, "questionings" were linked to beatings, insults, and often transfers out of one of the better work details. It should be obvious with what feelings a prisoner was overcome when he received a slip in the evening ordering him to report to the "questioning post" the next morning. From what has been said, it should be clear how little weight the Gestapo placed on the intervention of the prisoner's relatives.

The greatest release action that ever took place in Buchenwald concentration camp followed Adolf Hitler's fiftieth birthday in [April] 1939, when approximately 2,300 prisoners, primarily antisocials, were sent back to their homes. Between February and August 1939, some 2,000 Jews who already had emigration papers were eventually released—a measure the SS later bitterly regretted.[27]

---

27. A Gestapo directive signed by Reinhard Heydrich and dated January 31, 1939, provided for the release of Jewish prisoners from concentration camps if they had emigration papers. They were to receive verbal threats of lifelong imprisonment if they should return to Germany. John Mendelsohn, ed., *The Holocaust*, vol. 6: *Jewish Emigration, 1938–40* (New York: Garland, 1982), 202–203.

Every prisoner who left the camp had to sign a declaration in the political department to stipulate his later behavior on nine points. Three points should be emphasized: total silence about all conditions in camp, no contact with former fellow prisoners, and an obligation to inform against others. Ex-prisoners were threatened with appropriate(!) retaliation for violating any one of the nine points. Most ex-prisoners were also required to report to the police on a regular basis. It is only too clear that almost every released prisoner, burdened by the impressions of his experiences and under constant threat, lived on only as a broken man.

VII Punishments

There is one path to freedom. Its milestones are called obedience, industry, honesty, order, discipline, cleanliness, sobriety, willingness to sacrifice, and love of the fatherland.

At Himmler's order large placards with this inscription were placed everywhere in the camp, which could only have had a laughable effect on concentration camp prisoners. The actual path was the path to the crematorium. Its milestones were the whipping block, the cellblock, hanging, shooting, freezing, starving, fatal beatings, and torture of every type.

The SS had made use of these and other opportunities to achieve the true goal of the concentration camp: "to finish off" the rejected ones both physically and spiritually. The primary method of achieving this was through punishment.

The SS used a variety of excuses to inflict punishment—having one's hands in one's pockets during cold weather, having one's collar turned up in wind and rain, or having the most trivial defects in one's clothing, such as stains, missing buttons and small tears, shoes that were not thoroughly cleaned when there was foot-deep mud, and shoes that were polished too brightly. (A much-feared special clothing inspection took place for this purpose over many years during free time on Sundays.) Violations of saluting rules and a so-called bad attitude were further reasons for punishment, as was entering the block during work hours, even when it was only a question of using the toilet. Another infraction was taking too long to use the toilet on work detail; for a time it was strictly forbidden to use the latrines before 10:00 A.M. (after the thin morning coffee!). Other violations were standing up straight even once during work that required bending over, eating during working time, and smoking outside of free time or in the block. "Butt sticking" (picking up cigarette ends) cost many antisocials their lives. Another offense was so-called camp cooking [*Abkochen*], which was understood as any attempt to obtain food outside the distributed portions, as well as other forms of begging food and every type of "organizing."

The SS, a dissatisfied kapo or foreman, or frequently even a civilian employee in the armaments factories would gladly file a report on a prisoner for so-called laziness on the job, which was interpreted as broadly as possible. Mix-ups in prisoner numbers were not unusual, so that the doubly innocent were punished. Defense of any sort was completely out of the question because it would immediately be claimed that the prisoner was accusing an SS man of lying. One time a new prisoner received the number of a released prisoner against whom a report had been lodged; in his place he then received twenty-five lashes with the cane. There were of course terrible punishments for whatever could be interpreted as sabotage. Cement, for example, was delivered in large paper sacks that lay around the building sites; using this paper to protect clothing while carrying stones or wearing it under a thin prisoner's coat to protect from the rain led to an immediate report or to being struck down on the spot. Genuine sabotage, which will be discussed later [Chapter Nine, §137–139], was never discovered by the numskulls in the SS Death's-Head units.

The maintenance of order in the blocks was an almost inexhaustible source of punishment, as is clear from everything that has been said. Bed making in the blocks gave SS officers hundreds of excuses to inflict punishment on individuals or groups. Because many block officers even checked the insides of stoves for remnants of paper or trash, room attendants ended up wiring stove doors shut. At times officers would climb on the tables to check with their fingers if there was dust on the beams. Every roll call was a true nightmare for the prisoners because of the possibilities for punishment. If the numbering off for the first few rows of blocks did not go quickly enough or if language problems developed, there was a hail of slaps, kicks, and commands to stand up and lie down. (For this very reason German prisoners often had to take over the dreaded front row to protect the foreigners.) Ridiculous mistakes in aligning rows or in lining up prisoners according to height, the slightest movements, sneezing, coughing, and so on provoked the SS to wild excesses.

If actually punishable cases of theft did not occur, they were invented by the SS. Most of the real cases of theft were caused by hunger. Theft from comrades was taken care of by the prisoners themselves, who took thorough and ruthless revenge. A bread thief, for example, was done for as soon as he was caught; he simply could not be tolerated in camp, even when he had acted out of hunger, as otherwise the remaining comrades, who also had only the barest necessities, would suffer further hardships. Moreover, many stole not out of hunger but to trade bread for chewing tobacco or cigarettes.

From its own standpoint, the SS of course considered some offenses as ones that had to be rigorously punished, for example, creating political propaganda, listening to foreign broadcasts, establishing illegal contact with the outside world, subversion of the SS, and acts of sabotage. Other offenses were the organization of antifascist gatherings, any type of political work in the camp, the smuggling of letters, and attempted escape. Escape by prisoners had terrible consequences for the entire camp, especially in the early years. The political prisoners therefore rejected escape as a purely individual action that was pointless and enormously disadvantageous to the whole. Only at the end, when the approach of the front changed the situation, was it seen as a necessary step for certain persons who were acting on behalf of the illegal camp leadership. Prisoners who abused their comrades or even beat them to death were typically never punished by the SS and so had to be hunted down under the prisoners' own form of justice. That was often quite difficult and took considerable time, as these figures stood under the eye and enjoyed the special protection of the SS. Many comrades who lacked a deeper insight into camp affairs simply could not understand that such murderers could be allowed to "continue to do as they pleased."

Even old, experienced concentration camp veterans must have wondered how it was possible to pass alive through the jungle of punishments in the concentration camp. This feat was no doubt possible above all thanks to the solidarity of the prisoners and the stupidity of the SS, who attended only to minor details and external things because they completely lacked any deeper insight.

Many types of punishment were imposed: withholding food, standing in roll call square, punishment work, punishment exercises, transfer to the punishment company, or transfer to a less desirable detail. There were also lashes with a whip or cane; hanging from a post or a tree, the arms drawn high behind the back; detention in the cellblock; fatal beatings; hanging; shooting; and an abundance of other cleverly devised torments.

For punishment by whipping there existed a uniform regulation from the SS Main Economic and Administrative Office, under which all concentration camps stood. Whipping was to be performed upon the so-called whipping block, a specially created wooden table upon which the delinquent was strapped down. He had to lie on his stomach with his head down, his legs bent under, and his bottom stretched up high. Anywhere from five to twenty-five lashes with the cane or the whip were delivered at intervals of every fourteen days, repeatable up to four times.

On April 4, 1942, a circular letter arrived at the camp commandant's office from the chief of the central office of Section D, Concentration Camps, SS Lieutenant Colonel [Arthur] Liebehenschel.[28] It had the following text:

> The Reich SS leader and chief of German police [Himmler] has decreed that in his orders for punishment by whipping (for male and female prisoners alike in protective or preventive custody), if the word *severe* is included, the execution of the punishment is to be upon the naked bottom. In all other cases, execution of punishment is to follow the previous orders of the Reich leader.

In principle the camp administration had to seek confirmation for punishment by whipping from Berlin. Nevertheless, up to the takeover of command of Buchenwald by Camp Commandant SS Colonel [Hermann] Pister in 1942,[29] the practice was such that the prisoner first "went on the whipping block" and re-

---

28. Liebehenschel later served short terms as commandant at Auschwitz and Maidanek. He was executed after a trial in Poland in January 1948. Feig, *Death Camps*, 318, 457–458.

29. Hermann Pister assumed command of Buchenwald on January 21, 1942, and remained in command until the end. He was tried at the Buchenwald camp guards trial and was sentenced to be hanged. He died of a heart attack in Landsberg prison on September 28, 1948. NA, RG 338, case 000-050-9, box 426, "Review," 74–76, 94–95; box 450, "Status of Individuals Listed in Report of 24 April 1945."

ceived the desired number of blows. Afterwards the procedure was performed once again—this time officially—upon receipt of confirmation from Berlin. If they did not enthusiastically volunteer for the job, sergeants were commanded to carry out the punishment by whipping. If one of them showed signs of sympathy or insufficient force, then the specialist Sommer intervened, lending his experienced hand to blows aimed especially at the kidneys.

The camp doctor attended the procedure. Only four or five cases are known where camp doctors stopped the delivery of further blows in the interests of the prisoner—in one case by SS Captain Dr. Blies, when Sommer, claiming the victim (who had to count aloud the lashes with the cane) had cheated, wanted to start all over again on a nearly finished whipping. For a time prisoners themselves were forced to carry out the punishment of whipping on their comrades. Some lacked the courage to face the consequences of refusal; others were not unhappy to volunteer. The politicals refused or else dealt the blows in a manner that did not suit the SS; for the most part they were then condemned to receive the same punishment themselves.

If SS officers turned the beating into a private pleasure—laying prisoners over tables and chairs in their "workrooms" and thrashing them with whips—it was naturally impossible to prepare any self-defense. Otherwise, something could still be hastily devised. For example, one could put on thick underwear or a layer between the underpants and shirt. If, however, a prisoner was caught doing this, he received the blows on his naked bottom. The comrades in the prisoners' hospital always did everything possible to get the frightfully mauled victims back on their feet and nurse them to health.

Hanging from a tree was feared even more than the whipping block. As long as there were still woods left in camp, condemned inmates were hung from trees for anywhere from half an hour up to three hours and longer. They had their arms pulled up high behind their backs so their toes no longer touched the ground. Horrible cries echoed through the camp when Hackmann and Sommer went around with dog whips and lashed the unfortunate victims over their entire bodies. If the comrades did not die, they almost always came away with severe injuries for life.

The punishment exercises imposed upon entire work details and whole blocks at a time were also such that many, understandably, could not endure them. Exercises often lasted for hours at a time on the uneven ground of roll call square, with its scattered potholes and network of drainage channels. The exercises represented an evil combination of the normally sadistic Prussian barracks drill with the usual concentration camp practices. The punishment of standing at attention was spiced by the SS with its favorite "variations."

The maximum penalty that could be levied for an actual or an alleged offense was, with the exception of the already described regulation on caning, in no way fixed. Rather, even when the entire camp had been sentenced—or especially in such cases—the punishment was entirely up to the mood and the whim of the SS.

VIII Health Conditions

To fall sick in the concentration camp was a catastrophe from the outset. And when they were torn from their normal living situations and suddenly plunged into this vale of misery, with all its horrible concomitant circumstances, thousands fell ill. It was not just the difficult physical conditions that played a considerable role for those who became sick; it was also the psychological factor, the feeling of having become from that point on completely superfluous and worthless. From other camps, as well as from practices carried out before one's eyes in Buchenwald, one knew the fate that awaited (or was chosen for) a sick prisoner. At any moment sickness could result in a death sentence, coming from the person who for the rest of the world brought healing to the sickbed: the doctor!

If the prisoner lacked a thorough knowledge of the organization of the infirmary [*Revier*] and good personal connections there, as most did, he was already hindered by the general fear of coming into contact with it. In the hospital there was outpatient treatment, inpatient treatment, the dental clinic, and so-called convalescent treatment [*Schonung*]. For years simply getting to the outpatient clinic was an ordeal. Since 1938 the infirmary had been located in the remaining camp woods. The sick man had to drag himself to the infirmary barracks on a path through knee-deep mud, over tree trunks and roots—assuming that he was even able to get away from his work detail, after he had taken part in the mandatory roll call with a very high fever. The single gravel-covered path that led to the infirmary was reserved for doctors and SS personnel; any prisoner who used it was driven off with blows from a cane.

Once the sick person finally reached the infirmary, he had to stand in a long line, waiting in the open air in all sorts of weather. Because it was simply not possible to treat everyone who was sick and because there were always prisoners who simply wanted to get out of work, a robust prisoner gatekeeper made the first radical selection of the sick. If by chance the SS camp doctor appeared in the morning to take care of the despised "dirty" business of treating prisoners, then the gatekeeper made a second selection, during which he delivered kicks and slaps right and left. Anyone who in the meantime had not voluntarily fled or been chased away had to be allowed in as sick without any doubt. Before entering the infirmary barracks, prisoners had to take off their shoes (which often enough were stolen, an unimaginable catastrophe).

Some of the sick were taken care of by the prisoner orderlies; the remaining special cases were brought to the SS doctor for examination. Prisoners had to undress in a drafty corridor, which was, of course, unheated, and had to wait there naked until they were admitted. They had to be fairly hardened already to withstand this method of treating patients. It certainly wasn't difficult to acquire an infection or develop an inflammation of the lungs here, too. The actual outpatient care was performed by prisoners, doing whatever they could with what was available. That often meant just following the familiar saying, "Above the navel aspirin, below the navel castor oil." An outstanding exception was the treatment of flesh wounds, to which the prisoners devoted the greatest possible care.

Dental care for prisoners took place in a well-equipped special room separate from the infirmary in Barracks 7. The dental clinic was directed by SS oral surgeons and dentists and the work performed by trained prisoner specialists. The treatment there was on the whole good. Exceptions on the part of the SS proved the rule. Indeed it was an SS dentist who decided which tooth had to be pulled and which filled. (It sometimes happened that healthy teeth or those with gold fillings were extracted, the patient never allowed to protest.) However, the work was always done professionally and usually even almost painlessly. It was fortunate that the SS dentists and oral surgeons active in Buchenwald were open to influence by some of the more capable prisoners, so that here some of the conditions reported in other camps were avoided.

According to orders from the Reich SS leader [Himmler] of September 23, 1940, and December 23, 1942, SS dentists had to take out the gold teeth of dead prisoners and remove from the living those gold fillings that were no longer "repairable." According to the available monthly reports of the camp doctor, between 6 and 16 ounces of gold per month were taken as booty in this manner. Out of this gold, Commandant Koch had a student-style watch fob [*Bierzipfel*] made for his watch chain on which, significantly, he engraved the birthdates of his children. The living prisoners who were robbed in this way had a laughable amount of money credited to their accounts. With the exception of tooth extraction, dental care had to be paid for. Thus for most prisoners, there was only the choice between extraction or the illegal treatment provided by the comrades of the dental station at their own considerable risk yet organized in a remarkable fashion.

Inhospital care in the infirmary was always a difficult matter. Because of the constant bed shortage, only the most severe cases could be admitted. The principal criterion was the degree of fever. The right to admit someone for hospital treatment was granted solely to the camp doctors; because they were rarely in attendance and had no real overview of the situation, the right eventually fell into the hands of the kapo of the infirmary. That was not only of extraordinary significance for the sick, it also offered comrades who were in danger of being liquidated the possibility of "submerging."[30] They were saved by exchanging their names and numbers with those of a dead person or through some other tactic.

Work in the infirmary was very difficult and involved a great deal of responsibility. In the beginning equipment was worse than primitive, and for years it was inadequate. In particular, sufficient medication was lacking. The possibility of performing operations existed only after 1939, when the camp doctor at the time, Dr. Ding (who later carried the name Schuler), created an aseptic operating room. In winter 1939–1940 a separate, illegal operating room was built with the help of a series of work details and the tacit approval of the camp doctor, Dr. Blies. In retrospect, the project seems hardly conceivable, yet it was extremely character-

---

30. *Submerge* (*untertauchen*) was a common word in prisoner slang to describe hiding by the exchange of names and identities. See Des Pres, *Survivor*, 120.

istic of camp conditions. The workers who built it were compensated with food from the infirmary kitchen. Most prisoners who knew about the improvement in their comrades' meals but were unaware of the reason whispered about further "corruption." In truth, deaths were being reported months after they happened, so the extra meals had been ordered for dead inmates.

The SS medical administration was organized in the following manner. The garrison doctor of the Waffen SS Weimar was in charge; subordinate to him was the camp doctor. The two positions were united in 1942. The garrison doctor was independent of the camp administration. (Under certain conditions this allowed for interventions and influences of great significance, as, for example, collaboration between prisoners of the SS hospital and of the prisoner infirmary.) The doctor stood under the control of the SS Main Economic Office, Office Group D (Health Affairs of the Waffen SS, Section 3 II), directed by SS Colonel Dr. [Enno] Lolling, chief doctor of all concentration camps. Subordinate to the camp doctor were, when it was deemed necessary, a second and third camp doctor, in addition to several medical corpsmen [SDG]. The best-known member of the medical corps was the almost sixty-year-old master sergeant [Friedrich] Wilhelm.[31] His duties included giving prisoners lethal injections for Dr. Hoven and later for the camp doctor, Dr. Schiedlausky, who did not want to concern himself with such things at Buchenwald.

Among the camp doctors, the following names held special significance for the prisoners: SS Lieutenant Colonel Dr. [Werner] Kirchert, SS Major Dr. [Erwin] Ding (Schuler), SS Captain Dr. Blies, SS Second Lieutenant Dr. Wagner, SS First Lieutenant Dr. [Hans] Eisele, SS Captain Dr. [Waldemar] Hoven, SS Captain Dr. [Heinrich] Plaza, and, finally, SS Captain Dr. [Gerhard] Schiedlausky.[32] The professional quality and character of these camp doctors varied greatly. Among them were a few who could not bear the conditions and transferred out of the camp as quickly as possible. One in particular was the very decent SS Captain Dr. Hofer, for whom even the function of acting camp doctor was enough to persuade him to volunteer immediately for the front. Of the camp doctors named above, the worst were Kirchert and Eisele. Under Dr. Schuler the health conditions in the camp improved for the first time; Dr. Blies (SS Reserves) understood the needs of

---

31. Wilhelm was tried in the Buchenwald camp guards trial and sentenced to be hanged. NA, RG 338, case 000-50-9, box 426, "Review," 89–90, 94.

32. Only a few of the camp doctors were tried. Dr. Ding-Schuler was captured by the U.S. Army, made a statement about his activities, but committed suicide before his trial. Dr. Waldemar Hoven was tried as one of the doctors in what was called the SS medical case (*United States v. Karl Brandt et al.*), where he was found guilty, given the death sentence, and hanged at Landsberg in June 1948. Dr. Hans Eisele was tried in the Buchenwald camp guards trial at Dachau, found guilty, and sentenced to be hanged. Eisele's sentence was later reduced to ten years, then remitted on February 19, 1952. *Trials of War Criminals Before the Nuernberg Military Tribunal Under Law No. 10* green series, vol. 2, (Washington, D.C.: U.S. Government Printing Office, 1949–1953), 300; NA, RG 338, case 000-50-9, box 426, "Review," 94; Eisele appeals, box 453.

the prisoners. Dr. Hoven had many positive and at least as many negative sides. Dr. Schiedlausky brought with him a miserable reputation from the women's concentration camp at Ravensbrück. At Buchenwald he played an outwardly proper but in secret remarkably dark role.

In the early years prisoner health personnel consisted of completely unskilled workers, but they gradually acquired great experience. The first kapo of the infirmary was actually a book printer by profession; his successor, Walter Krämer, was an ironworker. Krämer was a strong, bold personality, tremendously industrious and very gifted in organization; he developed excellent skills in treating wounds and assisting during operations. In November 1941 he was shot by SS Master Sergeant Blank in the Quedlinburg work detail, where he had been taken in chains along with his closest collaborator, Peix. Soon afterward the prisoner hospital was taken over by the former Communist Reichstag deputy Ernst Busse, who confined himself to the purely organizational and personnel side of the steadily growing infirmary operations. Together with his assistant, Otto Kipp from Dresden, he contributed considerably to the further consolidation of conditions in the infirmary.

The shortage of SS health personnel, on the whole seen by the prisoners as a blessing, led to the employment of prisoner doctors in the infirmary in 1941–1942. Jewish doctors had been used earlier as a result of the special actions directed against the Jews in 1938. Out of a total health care staff of 280 at the end, there were around seventy prisoner doctors of all nationalities in 1945. From the end of 1944, doctors were appointed to each of the individual blocks through the skillful organization of the internal camp leadership.

The infirmary was not just the place where the sick were supposed to be cared for and made well again, but it was also a place of experimentation for SS doctors. In this connection the camp doctor Eisele (from late fall 1940 to late summer 1941) probably exceeded every possible baseness. For his own personal "professional" training, he conducted vivisections on human beings. The sole surviving witness among the Dutch Jews is Meyer Nebig. The camp doctor, Dr. Neumann, equaled Eisele, qualitatively if not quantitatively, by conducting experimental sectionings of the liver to "study" the effects of such operations on healthy humans. Dr. Wagner wrote a doctoral dissertation on tattooing, had the entire camp searched for people with tattoos, and had them photographed. The prisoners were later called to the gate by Commandant Koch, selected according to the splendor of their tattooed skin, and sent into the infirmary. Soon thereafter the best examples of skin appeared in the pathology department, where they were prepared and were shown to SS visitors as special treasures for years. Koch had an "artistic" table lamp made for himself out of human bones stretched over with human skin. Hundreds of prepared human skins were sent to Berlin on orders of the chief doctor for the concentration camps, SS Colonel Dr. Lolling.

Hospital statistics are incomplete up to December 1939. Approximately 2,065 deaths are recorded until then. From then on the statistics include the number of inhospital patients and from April 1941 the outpatient cases. Under the changing conditions the numbers naturally rose and fell. Monthly averages of death rates varied between 0.5 percent and 8 percent of the population, the monthly average of outpatients between 2.5 percent and 14 percent, the inpatient cases between 1.5 percent and 8 percent. From the beginning to the end of Buchenwald, a total of 32,887 prisoners died, not including those who were executed, those sent on death transports, as well as those in the worst condition who were transferred to other camps. An estimated death toll of 55,000 in seven and one-half years—an average of 7,300 per year—would not be too high [Chapter One, §2]. That means that year by year almost the entire camp at the time died off, since only after 1943 did the population exceed 10,000. Without the continual delivery of new prisoners by the SS, after six to eight months, statistically speaking, the camp would have been only a pile of corpses.

From fall 1943, as the population grew rapidly to a peak of 86,000 prisoners, including the external work details, the horrible death tolls of course no longer kept pace with the number of new admissions. The absolute number of deaths became higher; the percentages dropped. If one viewed the Buchenwald concentration camp in isolation, it would be unjust to blame the high death toll solely on the health facilities and the individual SS camp doctors. Transports brought in prisoners who were already so weakened by the hardships they had just endured that they died like flies day after day, immediately after their arrival. The SS command was accustomed to telling the other camp administrations in such cases, "You have sent us all your scrap [*Schrott*]!" Conditions in other concentration camps were the same or similar, so all the camp administrations and the higher SS administration shared in the guilt, from which any single camp doctor, even if he himself was of better intentions, could not escape.

If a prisoner had recovered from an illness but was not yet able to work, was still in outpatient care, or, as the case may be, was not so sick that he required treatment in the hospital, he could receive a so-called convalescent slip. This was an arrangement by which a prisoner could remain in the block or in a special room of the hospital for a few days. "Recovery" consisted in the early years of allowing convalescents to carry wood in the open air in all sorts of weather. In January 1942 out of 7,964 inmates, eighty-two were in convalescence. In March 1945, when out of the total of around 82,400 prisoners in the concentration camp, approximately 30,000 were in the base camp, 1,542 were convalescent. Camp doctors, the camp administration, and the work detail officers tried again and again to exercise strict control over convalescence. But the prisoners gradually made that impossible, so that many comrades could be helped in this way, too.

Additional health facilities in the camp included the bathhouse and the disinfection facility. The bath, a well-designed shower facility constructed in fall 1938, was an amenity the camp was lucky to have. But because Buchenwald suffered from chronic water shortages, it was often not usable for months at a time. These shortages considerably worsened the general hygienic conditions. The camp's sewage system was designed for 20,000 persons. Because of the sudden increase in usage at certain times of day, it was usually overburdened, so that very serious problems resulted when there was also a shortage of water.

Transports full of dirty and lice-infested prisoners arrived from other disease-ridden camps. Thorough disinfection was therefore an iron necessity. It was gradually set up not by the SS but at the initiative of the prisoners themselves, who went through the difficult process of acquiring disinfectant chemicals so that a still greater disaster could be prevented. The strict lice inspections carried out twice a week in the blocks by the inmates' own hygiene wardens also contributed to keeping Buchenwald relatively free of epidemics. After 1939 all inmates of the camp were immunized against typhoid fever and dysentery. After 1943 the French of certain age groups were immunized against scarlet fever, to which they were particularly susceptible. After 1944 the entire so-called functionary personnel were immunized with typhus vaccines produced in Block 50. A few camp doctors supported these measures to some extent. Indeed the SS feared that any outbreak of infection could easily spread to their own ranks.

On the orders of the Reich SS Leader, every prisoner who died had to be burned. Often the numbers of dead were so large that difficulties arose in storing them. Until a special morgue was constructed, the bodies of the dead lay in piles in various rooms of the camp, some in the toilets. At first there were often those among them who were not yet completely dead. They were carried off by the corpse-carrying detail, which early on consisted of Jews, later of Poles. Of course any sort of pious handling of the dead never came into question. At any hour of the day, one could hear the call over the loudspeakers, "Corpse carriers to the gate!"

Corpses of prisoners were burned in the crematoriums in Weimar and Jena until 1940. In theory the corpse was to lie in a coffin, wearing a shroud with his name and number. Often they were simply thrown naked into primitive crates—in pairs if they were thin enough. On the way to the crematorium, a hearse from Buchenwald concentration camp once lost a coffin in front of a coffee house in the middle of Weimar; the coffin sprang open and two emaciated corpses fell out. In winter 1940–1941 the camp acquired a motorized crematorium that could be loaned out wherever needed. The number of corpses was so great and the crematorium's capacity so small that bodies were literally stuffed into it. At times body parts failed to burn and fell out into roll call square, a gruesome affair. Buchenwald's own permanent crematorium was being built during this time and was finished in 1941. The facility consisted of a large morgue, an autopsy room, two ovens with an enormous chimney, and some rooms for the service personnel. The whole thing was in a spacious courtyard and was surrounded by a high wall.

An autopsy had to be performed on every corpse and an official report made of the findings. The prisoners assigned to this task in the early years were a former baker and a pimp, then a former carpenter. They were, of course, hardly suited to these enormous tasks, even if they had had the desire and the sense of responsibility. The autopsy reports were simply fabricated. When it was necessary, the SS, too, was often kept in the dark. A real autopsy was only made on special request or if the pathology section or a Berlin authority demanded tissue samples.

The pathology department was created in 1940. The autopsy room in the crematorium was under its control. It prepared all sorts of pathological specimens, which were sent either to Berlin or to the SS Medical Academy in Prague for teaching purposes or were displayed in the department's own exhibit case. The Buchenwald collection gradually became very wide ranging. The department had gained scientific significance insofar as the specialists employed there presented training courses in medicine, physiology, and biology for a circle of interested comrades. The medical students among the Norwegians brought here in 1944 were able systematically to continue their training there.

The last year, up to fall 1944, the autopsy room was directed by a Czech Premonstratensian monk. He had been spared from transfer to Dachau again and again because of his extraordinarily humane qualities and his radiant, good-natured personality.[33] Using a wooden platform set up over the stairs to the crematorium basement, he had repeatedly celebrated mass, especially on Catholic high holy days, for a few of the faithful, an activity that carried with it the danger of a death sentence for all participants.

It seems not inappropriate to say a few words here about the complete lack of pastoral care in the concentration camp. The SS, of course, allowed nothing of the sort. On grounds of long-expressed views that were based in very old, deep-rooted beliefs, even the otherwise most distinguished comrades of the Left viewed pastoral care as laughable and reactionary. A few of them, nevertheless, in the last years revealed greater understanding. They used their decisive positions to assist in keeping a few priests in the camp, that is, by protecting them from transports. Their influence was, however, kept secret and was therefore limited.

There is no doubt that even only limited pastoral care, especially for the Poles, would have prevented much despair, much sadness, much baseness. It would have given thousands hope, would have strengthened hundreds in their last minutes, and would have given countless of the sick and infirm the new inner strength needed for bodily recovery. Instead, these blessings were confined to a tiny, insignificant circle of especially brave and therefore strong people, as well as a few orthodox Jews. Only within the French ranks in the last months was an "underground church" [*ecclesia abscondita*] possible, so that a ray of light fell upon the dying on their path to the crematorium.

The ovens were always operated by professional criminals. When the burnings did not take place daily but, as per regulations, only twice a week, enormous mountains of corpses sometimes formed. The crematorium was heated with coke. Often the "unholy" flames rose day and night over Buchenwald, up to a yard high out of the chimney. The prisoners faced this drama with both horror and apathy. All sorts of jokes about the crematorium were made in roll call square. Depending on the curve of the smoke plume, for example, inmates joked about which category of prisoners was being burned. "You will go on the grill" or "up the chimney" were constant expressions in the camp. The roll call officer would often call over the loudspeaker to the professional criminals who were working in the oven

---

33. Kogon identifies him as Father Josef Thyl. *SSS*, 179.

room and were not taking part in the roll call. "Let's have the birds in the crematorium take a peek outside!" Then these fellows would grab corpses and hold them up to the windows. The mood in which the final act of mourning for thousands took place is well characterized in this example.

Relatives' requests for prisoners' ashes were handled with the same lack of reverence. One of the professional criminals grabbed a handful of ashes from the great pile, threw them in a box, and sent them to the post office. The political department was informed, the infirmary (camp doctor) issued a certificate of authenticity for the remains, and the Registrar's Office issued a death certificate. If the person in question was not a Russian, a Pole, or a non-German Jew, some SS member in the political department wrote a "sympathy letter" that always read the same:

> Dear Frau (name)! Your husband (name) died in the hospital here. I express to you my deepest sympathy at this loss. (Name) was delivered to the hospital on (date) with signs of severe exhaustion and complained about difficulties in breathing and chest pains. Despite the best medications and dedicated treatment, it was unfortunately not possible to save the patient's life. The deceased did not express any last wishes. The Camp Commandant.

In the final months there was a great shortage of coal. When the number of corpses became too large and the rats that ate them threatened to spread disease in the camp, the SS, with Himmler's permission, switched to emergency burials in mass graves located at the Bismarck Tower. To a very limited extent cremation continued, mostly for Germans, because you could not expect them to lie together with Jews in a common grave, as the sergeant in charge of the crematorium thoughtfully expressed it.

In the last years the crematorium also served as a place of execution. Again and again people were brought from outside the camp or prisoners were called to the gate, taken directly to the crematorium, and there, always in the presence of the camp doctor and a representative of the camp administration, they were strangled with a rope while hanging from a hook mounted on the wall.

IX "Special Facilities"[34]

Buchenwald concentration camp had a range of facilities that require detailed explanation.

1. The members of one work detail, the punishment company, received the harsher concentration camp treatment in every regard. They were isolated in their

---

34. The word *special* became virtually synonymous with torture and murder in Nazi jargon, even though the term is not always used precisely in that way in this section. *Special treatment* (*Sonderbehandlung*) became a code term for murder, particularly for Jews. On this and related words, see Joseph Wulf, *Aus dem Lexikon der Mörder: "Sonderbehandlung" und verwandte Worte in nationalsozialistischen Dokumenten* (Gütersloh: Sigbert Mohn, 1963).

own separate block so that even in their limited free time they had no chance to go anywhere [Chapter Seven, §81]. The punishment company worked primarily in the stone quarry, usually for longer hours than other work details. It regularly worked on Sundays, with shortened midday breaks, so that the prisoners could scarcely even eat any more. They frequently had rations withdrawn, at the beginning always on Sundays. What is more, they were called upon for any unpleasant and difficult work, were not allowed to receive money, could write letters only every three months or were not allowed to write at all, and frequently had to perform punishment exercises.

Life in the punishment company was pure hell. The men in the punishment company were helped by their comrades whenever possible; otherwise no one would have survived the treatment there. The company's composition further contributed to the almost unbearable conditions. New admittees of all colors, Jehovah's Witnesses, homosexuals, and those singled out for special punishment formed its membership. Men were also assigned to the company on the grounds of certain remarks in their records—whether by the Gestapo or the camp administration. Some stayed in it permanently, others only temporarily. Even that was mostly an arbitrary matter. The politicals by no means played the most important role in the punishment company, making its disunity all the more apparent. At the beginning of 1944, it was dissolved on the basis of an order from Berlin.

2. The Special Section directed against the political leadership existed for three months, from March to May 1942. It was created as a consequence of the battle raging in camp at the time between reds and greens. The professional criminals had started a comprehensive wave of denunciations against the politicals and put themselves behind the infamous Plaul, then deputy commandant. The Special Section, to which were assigned about 100 people from the German Left, primarily Communists, lived in conditions equivalent to those in the punishment company but stood directly under the spotlight of the SS administration. Undoubtedly, the intention was to liquidate these leading political figures of the camp at the first favorable opportunity. In the meantime, however, the professional criminals had overextended themselves. Certain SS officers, for example, camp doctor Hoven, who possessed considerable influence, at the time leaned more to the politicals. One by one, the leading greens ended up in the punishment company themselves, where they were helped along in their rapid decline. With the gradual strengthening and final triumph of the influence of the reds, the Special Section was dissolved.

3. The black cellblock was one of the most horrible inventions of Senior Camp Inmate Richter mentioned above, who later had a chance to experience it for himself [Chapter Five, §61]. The facility lasted from the beginning of 1939 until April 20, 1939. A wing of Block 3 that bordered on roll call square was shut off, completely darkened, and left unheated. It was also favored with numerous visits by the supervisor of the cellblock, Sommer. Frequent punishment by whipping was particularly severe there because it was always levied collectively for the slightest infraction. Food rations were set at the lowest possible level. The last survivors came out of the black cellblock looking like corpse-colored skeletons.

4. The camp jail was located in a wing of the gate house. It was composed of a series of small cement cells with stone sleeping benches and window holes near the ceiling. Although central heating was available, it was not used for the cells. The already hard conditions took on terrifying and almost unbearable proportions because of the rages of SS Master Sergeant Sommer and the cellblock servant, Fischermann (who was later taken away from the camp by the SS) [Chapter Five, §55]. When anyone was delivered into the cellblock, his comrades in camp immediately wrote him off. Many were not able to withstand the torture and made use of the rope that Sommer liked to bring to the cell after a period of time. After SS Colonel Pister took command, things changed; people were still tortured in the cellblock but no longer killed.

5. After the beginning of the war with Soviet Russia, the horse stable near the riding hall, outside the barbed wire around the camp, was used as a liquidation site for the first Russian prisoners of war who arrived at Buchenwald [Chapter Seven, §86]: political commissars, officers, Komsomol leaders, and Russian Communist party personalities who had been recognized or denounced in various stalags. A detailed plan of this place of execution is included as an appendix with this report.[35] Except for a few prisoners, camp inmates were kept away from the horse stables. The camp had no possible means of rescuing these victims. Immediately upon delivery at the political department, they were led into "special treatment," without being allowed to come into contact with the camp at all. The shootings took place by day and by night. The total number amounted to at least 7,000, probably more. (Well-grounded estimates run up to 9,500.) After every liquidation, trucks full of bodies drove from the horse stables to the crematorium in camp, from which the approximate numbers estimated here were derived. In the last two years, numerous German and foreign (non-Russian) civilians, men and women, were shot in the same manner. It was accomplished by a refined technique of shooting through the base of the skull [*Genickschuss*], which is described in a special account in the appendix [Chapter Seven, §86].

6. In a wooded part of the headquarters area between the actual camp and the officers' houses stood the confinement barracks. It consisted of two parts: the so-called Spruce Grove Camp and the I Barracks [Chapter Seven, §82]. In the Spruce Grove Camp, between 150 and 200 Romanians of the Iron Guard were interned. Originally housed in an isolation block in the camp, they were employed in precision mechanical work. After the bombardment on Buchenwald that killed a number of them, Himmler ordered them sent to a convalescent home in Hohenlychen. The so-called I Barracks located next to Spruce Grove was surrounded by a high wall that prisoners could neither see over nor climb. High-ranking personalities, prominent figures from Germany as well as abroad, were interned there. Their names, insofar as they are known, are listed in a special report [Chapter Seven, §100]. The servant in the I Barracks was a woman Jehovah's Witness. Contact

---

35. "Genickschuß-Anlage," *SSS*, endpaper 2; "Murder Plant," *TPH*, frontpaper 2.

with the occupants occurred only occasionally, through skilled workers among the prisoners who were sent there to carry out repairs.

7. One of the most feared special facilities of the camp was Isolation Block 46, which was surrounded by double barbed wire. It was opened in late fall 1941 as the clinical station of the Department of Typhus and Virus Research of the Hygiene Institute of the Berlin Waffen SS. Its foundation was the result of the consultation with and approval of the health inspector of the German army; the general staff chief doctor, Lieutenant General Dr. [Siegfried] Handloser; and State Secretary of the Reich Health Leader and SS Lieutenant General Dr. [Leonardo] Conti. Also involved were the president of the Reich Health Office, Professor Reiter; president of the Robert Koch Institute Berlin (Reich Office for the Prevention of Infectious Diseases), Professor Gildemeister; and SS Brigadier General Professor Dr. Med., Dr. Rer. Nat. Joachim Mrugowsky, director of the Hygiene Institute of the Berlin Waffen SS and chief hygiene officer of the SS.[36] A diary entry on the founding of the clinic states concisely under the date December 29, 1941, "Since animal experiments do not permit sufficient evaluation (of typhus immunizations), experiments must be carried out on humans." SS Major Dr. Ding-Schuler was assigned the task of carrying out the experiments.

Up to the end of 1944, experiments were carried out in twenty-four series of tests involving a varying number of persons, ranging from four to at most forty to sixty, though one group included 145. The tests involved the evaluation of typhus immunization substances of varied origin. They included acridine and methylene blue from I.G. Farben, yellow fever immunizations, and immunizations against smallpox, typhus, paratyphoid A and B, cholera, and diphtheria. They also included tests of substances for chemical warfare and various other poisons and of substances to treat burns from phosphorus canisters from the Berlin Military Medical Academy, and the production of a typhus convalescence serum for the SS. The chemical pharmaceutical and serobacteriological departments of the I.G. Farben Industries in Frankfurt am Main–Höchst, the Behring Works in Dessau, and a series of German scientists, as well as various firms who had something to test, collaborated with the director of the Hygiene Institute of the Berlin Waffen SS and the department. They even made proposals and offered contracts. Officially, it was announced in individual cases that those being experimented upon were certain dangerous criminals chosen by the Reich SS leader [Himmler] himself.

For a year and a half, the camp administration's practice was to send the test victims to Block 46 according to "proven" principles. They were primarily profes-

---

36. Handloser and Mrugowsky were tried at Nuremberg in the medical case. Mrugowsky was sentenced to death and was hanged on June 2, 1948. Handloser was sentenced to life imprisonment, the sentence was later commuted to twenty years, and he was apparently released along with other Nazi war criminals in the early 1950s. *NT,* vol. 2, 296f.; Alexander Mitscherlich and Fred Mielke, *Doctors of Infamy,* trans. Heinz Norden (New York: H. Schuman, 1949), 146f.; Thomas A. Schwartz, "Die Begnadigung deutscher Kriegsverbrecher," *Vierteljahrshefte für Zeitgeschichte* 38 (1990), 406.

sional criminals, homosexuals, and in part politicals. The prisoners made use of the practice to get rid of those who worked with the SS against the camp and to save endangered political personalities (the most famous case: three officers of the English secret service in fall 1944). After 1944 the camp SS administration no longer wanted to carry the full responsibility for Block 46. Designation of the test victims was left to the Reich Criminal Office in Berlin and the infamous SS Lieutenant General [Arthur] Nebe. He also wanted to send Gypsies, who were rejected as unsuitable by Dr. Ding-Schuler, at the urging of the prisoners.

As will be explained in a detailed special report, these experiments had almost no real scientific value.[37] A total of 1,000 prisoners were taken to the experimental station. A few of them had the good fortune to be used only for blood donation examinations or for experiments that had to be given up for external reasons before infection. The remainder included approximately 450 persons, of whom 158 died, not counting those who were delivered to the station month after month in groups of five for so-called passage purposes—that is, having been infected with highly contagious blood from typhus patients, they served as hosts to keep the typhus germs alive. Almost all the prisoners used for "passage" died. The remainder came away with severe, lifelong damage to their health, as every expert on typhus can confirm: permanent weakness of the heart, loss of memory, paralysis, etc.

Also quarantined in Block 46 (which was a model of cleanliness and was well equipped) were all prisoners who had been naturally infected with typhus in camp or were already infected when they were delivered into the camp. Insofar as they survived the dreaded disease, they were well cared for there. The director of the block on the prisoners' side was Arthur Dietzsch, who gained his first medical knowledge through this practice. Dietzsch had already spent twenty years in prison and was a very hardened man.[38]

8. In August 1943 a previously independent department for the production of a typhus vaccine (Block 50) was attached to the clinical station (Block 46). The best available experts from the camp, among them physicians, bacteriologists, serologists, and chemists, were selected for this task. Clever politics on the part of the prisoners made it possible to bring into this work detail endangered comrades from all stations. Because they feared infection with typhus, the SS showed the same respect for this block as for Block 46. This taboo-anxiety of the SS was fostered for different motives by SS Major Dr. Ding-Schuler, under whom both blocks stood, as well as by the prisoners. Candidates for death found refuge there with the knowledge and approval of Dr. Ding-Schuler. Among them were Dutch

---

37. This was the view of the French scientist Alfred Balachowsky, a former Buchenwald prisoner who testified on the experiments in Block 46 and Block 50 at the Nuremberg trials. *Trial of the Major War Criminals Before the International Military Tribunal, Nuremberg, 14 November 1945–1 October 1946* (*IMT*), blue series, vol. 6 (New York: AMS, 1971; reprint of 1947 ed.), 302–321.

38. Arthur Dietzsch was tried in the Buchenwald camp guards trial and received a fifteen-year sentence. NA, RG 338, case 000-050-9, box 426, "Review," 43–45; 94–95.

physics professor Van Lingen; the legal adviser of the Netherlands Sports Society, Jan Robert; architect Harry Pieck and other Dutchmen; Austrian journalist Dr. Eugen Kogon; the department head of the Pasteur Institute in Paris, Dr. [Alfred] Balachowsky; and seven Jewish comrades. A statement by Schuler (which Kogon proposed, drew up, and presented to Schuler for his signature) provided protection from the Reich Central Security Headquarters against participation in any immediate actions, death transports, and so on. *Ultimum refugium judaeorum,* "last refuge of the Jews," Dr. Schuler once jokingly called Block 50, not without justice.

Vaccine was produced from the lungs of mice and rabbits following a procedure created by Professor Giroud of the Pasteur Institute in Paris. The valuable instruments, apparatuses, microscopes, and the like were mostly from France and were either "war booty" or were "purchased" from French firms without payment. Typhus microbes (*Rickettsia prowazeki*) were cultivated by injecting 2 cc of blood from typhus patients in Block 46 into guinea pigs. Two official types of vaccine were produced: a normal one for the fighting troops of the Waffen SS and one that had a somewhat cloudy appearance, known as the red-dot vaccine, for the prisoners. In truth—without the knowledge of Dr. Schuler—another vaccine of the highest quality was produced in relatively small quantities. It was used only for endangered comrades among the prisoners in exposed positions. A vaccine of the second quality, which to be sure did no harm but was also not very effective, was produced in considerable quantities for the SS.

9. Between Block 46 and the infirmary stood the "special building" [Chapter Seven, §84]. Under this charming name the camp brothel was chastely concealed. It was created in summer 1943 on orders of Himmler. Construction had to be accelerated, thus delaying the much more urgent project of the expansion of the infirmary. Eighteen girls were brought to Buchenwald from the women's concentration camp at Ravensbrück, under the leadership of two female SS sergeants who conducted themselves like Amazons. The girls had supposedly volunteered for this purpose. Their medical records nevertheless showed that they had had diseases of the sort that did not exactly imply proper moral conduct before they were brought into the concentration camp. Other than a single exception, who died of illness soon afterwards, they seemed to adapt themselves to their fates without any inhibitions. Right from the time of their arrival, they acted in a completely unambiguous and provocative manner.

For the SS, the purpose of this exercise was to corrupt the politicals who had gained predominance, to gain information about them, and to distract them from politics. Among themselves prisoners had spread the word not to use the facility, not only for the reasons given above but also for ethical reasons. It was, for example, an unparalleled disgrace when the money wives and mothers of prisoners had worked so hard to save and had sent to sons and husbands in the camp was used to pay the 2-mark entrance fee for the brothel. But right from the beginning, the camp administration forced the senior camp inmate at the time to use the special building. If the senior camp inmate had not yielded to the pressure, he would at the very least have been removed, which would have brought upon the camp serious consequences. He complied after two days of refusal but never went there again.

On the whole the politicals held the line, so that the intentions of the SS were thwarted. But the special building did bring corruption of all sorts into the camp, including the theft of packages and the like. The visiting time allowed for men without connections was twenty minutes, after prior examination in the prisoner hospital and the subsequent cleansing.

The "sexual needs" of men imprisoned for a long time (which has been fully discussed in numerous publications) were by no means satisfied in the special building, for the reasons given above and because the worthiest men of course did not use it. Dissolute men, many of them politicals, too, developed some disgusting relationships through pederasty. A considerable number of young Poles and Russians who came into the camp as twelve- to fifteen-year-olds were brought to total ruin by enticement (good food!) and also by force. The so-called doll boys [*Puppenjungen*] played a disgusting role, especially in 1943 under Senior Camp Inmate Wolff. He was a former riding champion and German Nationalist who seriously exploited his position. He was brought down by the camp when he began to work more and more with the SS and against his comrades. All the more praiseworthy, therefore, was the example of those comrades who selflessly helped the children and youths in camp. That sexual repression was nevertheless widespread in camp and that it was even aggravated by the example of the SS, with its inclination toward sadistic brutality, almost goes without saying.

SS officers also used the special building for true orgies. Two of its occupants were reserved for the use of the Ukrainian guard troops.

10. An entertainment facility of another and better sort was the cinema. It was created in May 1941 at the suggestion of the kapo of the photo department. Once or twice a week, or sometimes at longer intervals, entertainment and cultural films were shown for an entrance fee of first 40 pfennigs, then 20 pfennigs. Considering the generally terrible conditions in camp, many a comrade couldn't bring himself to go to the cinema. Others, for equally justifiable reasons, were able to rise above this psychological qualm and given new strength by the few hours of illusion. Nevertheless, it was repugnant to sit in front of the flickering screen in the evening, knowing that just a few hours before, comrades had been beaten terribly or killed on the very same spot. For in the cinema stood the whipping block that was carried to roll call square like an exalted throne for special "show" beatings. In it were also stored the gallows and the poles that were mounted in special holes to hang prisoners.

X "Special Actions"

Buchenwald concentration camp not only had "special" facilities that threatened to go beyond the boundaries of an already abnormal existence, but its history was unfortunately also rich in "special actions" of terrifying dimensions.

Mention should first be made of special actions undertaken by the SS against the Jews. In November 1938 more than 10,000 German Jews were delivered to Buchenwald concentration camp after the assassination of the German embassy secretary [Ernst vom] Rath in Paris[39] [Chapter Seven, §95]. What took place in camp at that time cannot be described in just a few words. It can only be mentioned that sixty-eight of the Jewish prisoners went completely insane and were beaten to death like mad dogs. In Blocks 1a to 5a, which later became infamous and were eventually torn down, lived about 2,000 Jews each. The normal capacity of these primitive emergency barracks was calculated at only 400 to at most 500 people. The sanitary conditions were unimaginable. Hundred-mark notes were used as toilet paper. (The Jews had brought along a great deal of money, in some cases tens of thousands of marks.) SS sergeants pushed people's heads into overflowing toilet bowls until they drowned. In a few weeks hundreds of these "action Jews" had died. Then, for obscure reasons that lay with the Reich authorities, most of them were released—after the SS and a portion of the prisoners had vied with one another to rob them of all their money and jewelry, using both the clumsiest and most cunning methods.[40]

The next large action against the Jews followed in November 1939, after the assassination attempt against Hitler in the Bürgerbräukeller [November 8]. Jews were seized at random (three men from each of the seven Jewish blocks) and immediately shot. All the others were locked into darkened blocks for three days without any food—in constant, demoralizing uncertainty about what might happen to them. On the fourth day they were given half rations. The action then came to an end, amid measures already described that were taken against the entire camp because of the alleged theft of a pig.

In October 1942, Jews began to be transported out of Buchenwald to death camps. That lasted until summer 1943 and created a state of intense anxiety that even the most hardened men found almost unbearable. Incoming reports and earlier experiences left no doubt about the character of these transports. In fact only a very small percentage lived, their survival frequently depending on extraordinary shrewdness, presence of mind, capability, and decisiveness. It was often a question of whether one or another prisoner could suddenly grab a lifeline with which he could then find his way to the rescuing solidarity of some of his fellow prisoners. Up to 200 Jews who passed themselves off as skilled construction workers (among them lawyers, authors, doctors, and artists!) were held back by the camp administration. All the rest were sent away at that time.

The number of Jews in camp rose again for the first time toward the middle of 1944, primarily because of a large number of new prisoners from Hungary. Life

---

39. In recent historiography this event has become known as *Kristallnacht,* the attack on synagogues throughout Germany and the subsequent arrest of thousands of Jews. See Anthony Read and David Fisher, *Kristallnacht* (New York: Peter Bedrick Books, 1989), 111f.

40. Bruno Bettelheim was a prisoner at Buchenwald and Dachau during this period. He published one of the first scholarly articles on the concentration camps, "Individual and Mass Behavior in Extreme Situations" (1943), reprinted in Bruno Bettelheim, *Surviving and Other Essays* (New York: Vintage Books, 1980), 48–83. See also his later work, *The Informed Heart* (New York: Free Press, 1960).

became halfway bearable for the few remaining Jews in camp, although they came into the spotlight one more time in 1943. At that time it pleased the third deputy commandant, [Erich] Gust, together with the labor service officer, to summon two or three Jewish brick masons at a time to the infirmary for lethal injections [*zum "Abspritzen"*]. Normal work situations turned into childish occasions for punishment with fatal consequences.

The sort of atmosphere in which such things sometimes played themselves out may be seen from the following example: Five young Jews—splendid men, among them a medical student—were taken into the infirmary. (It was later revealed that as a consequence of the intervention of the camp doctor, Dr. Hoven, this was the last of these pleasure actions of Herr Gust and his colleague.) On the way, a former fellow student encountered them. "Where are *you* going?" "We're going to be knocked off!" answered the student gaily, and they went on their way, holding their heads high. For several days SS Staff Sergeant Wilhelm hesitated over them, because by then he was tired of the constant killing with the injection needle. He wanted to wait until the return of the camp doctor, who was absent at the time. Precisely one day before Hoven's return, he killed them, as he could no longer resist the pressure from his superiors.

Many, especially foreign Jews, had survived in camp unrecognized, that is, not recognized as Jews by the SS. Even if they were not directly in the line of fire, they did not have an easy existence. They were constantly exposed to the danger of either being discovered or denounced by their fellow prisoners. The SS had originally gone far beyond the Nuremberg laws in marking as Jews all those who had even one Jewish grandparent and were not able to hide this because of existing notes in their records. In many actions the nose alone was sufficient for the SS men; anyone whose looks displeased them was therefore a Jew. Later the "quarter Jews" and "half Jews" were in part "Aryanized" and thereafter no longer wore the yellow triangle. For most, this change came too late.

Of the approximately 600 Dutch Jews who were brought to Buchenwald in February 1941, the survivors were sent in the summer of that year to Mauthausen, where they went to their deaths within a few days in a tragedy without equal [Chapter Seven, §97]. One of them, on whom the camp doctor Eisele had undertaken an experimental stomach section, remained behind. He was saved by the TB station, despite repeated demands from the political department.

The permitted number of TB patients appears to have been limited by one of the Berlin authorities. This was the case in Auschwitz, where the total number of patients in the infirmary could not exceed 10 percent of the camp population. The remainder were all automatically sent to the gas chamber. In any case, Eisele suddenly decided in summer 1941 that Buchenwald had "enough" TB patients. He switched to the system of killing whole groups of them by intravenous injections of evipan sodium[41] or by injecting the same substance directly into the heart.

---

41. Evipan sodium is a hexobarbital used as a general anesthetic. The lethal dose in rats is 50 percent. *The Merck Index,* 9th ed. (Rahway, N.J.: Merck, 1976), sec. 4577, 616.

Panic seized everyone who was ill, especially when all prisoners in camp who had tuberculosis were simply gathered up and sent to their destruction.

It is difficult to make comprehensible the sort of rescue actions and delay tactics that went on at that time. People who innocently reported to the infirmary for treatment were often forcibly turned away by the hospital orderlies in order to save their lives. (In this strange village, with its hidden paths, its relatively closed off castes and work details, and its loners, there were always some prisoners who despite everything were completely uninformed.) Since the reasons could not be stated openly, this seeming "barbarity" led to the most terrible misunderstandings on the part of fellow prisoners. Eisele's action killed at least 300 people. These victims and indeed whole rooms of patients usually received a sleeping medication before the lethal injection. Sometimes a patient with an especially strong heart survived two injections and died only after the third shot.

Summer 1941 was terrible for the camp in every aspect. The first transports for gassing were assembled. The order came from Berlin and affected professional criminals, sex offenders, and the politicals who were most offensive to the SS. The transports went to an unknown destination; by the next day the prisoners' possessions, including the contents of their pockets, their dentures, etc., were returned to camp. Through a sergeant of the accompanying guards, it was learned that they had been sent to Pirna and Hohenstein and were killed there as part of a test of a new gas. The substance had already been tried out on cows. The gassing was conducted underground, but all vegetation on the surface was killed within a circumference of 60 to 80 yards. Those regarded as dangerous persons—by both the camp administration and the prisoner leadership—were thrown into these transports. Among the first to be gassed in this manner was the Austrian security director from Salzburg, Dr. [Ludwig] Bechinie. In putting together the third transport in spring 1942, the camp administration committed the error of placing on the list politicals who were well liked and occupied important positions. The prisoners mobilized the camp doctor, Dr. Hoven, to the point that this transport was finally canceled, after months of intrigues and tugs of war.

In the meantime Jews were selected in the winter of 1941–1942 on the basis of their ability to work. Instead of going on the transport mentioned above, invalid Jews were sent on the same path in four groups of ninety men each. They went to Bernburg via Köthen, where at the local "health and nursing facility"(!) a doctor by the name of [Imfried] Eberl served as a willing tool of the SS[42] [Chapter Seven, §92]. The first two transports for gassing each comprised something over 100 men.

Gassings never took place in Buchenwald itself. Probably near the end of 1943, an order from the Central Building Office of the Waffen SS in Weimar arrived to build a gassing facility at Buchenwald. Influential and daring comrades delayed

---

42. Eberl later became the first commandant of Treblinka, where he presided over the newly installed gassing facilities. Feig, *Death Camps*, 296, 299, 454–455.

the start of planning by destroying the telegram and other maneuvers, so the first actual attempt to carry out the building plans collapsed with the increasingly negative developments for the SS in the second half of 1944. If it had come to the construction of the facility, not a single inmate of Buchenwald would have remained alive in March and April 1945.

The action against the Russian prisoners of war has already been described. It began in late summer 1941 and eventually concluded toward the end of 1943 and beginning of 1944, clearly as a result of international complications. Nevertheless, shootings of individual Russians or of small groups continued thereafter. As became known from the reports of prisoners from transports, the action was not limited to Buchenwald concentration camp. At least in Dachau and Sachsenhausen, shootings of this sort were also carried out to a considerable extent.

Special actions were also ordered against Poles. Like the Russians, they were treated as an inferior race. Aside from the large action after the end of the Polish campaign, which will be described later, there were two other principal measures against the Poles. In 1938–1939, Jews, primarily those in Vienna, had been forced to give up their houses and property by signing them over to party members and their beneficiaries. The prices ranged from 10 marks upward. With the Poles it became simpler: They were paid absolutely nothing. People were simply called and informed that their families had to leave house and home. To refuse to sign the papers transferring ownership was tantamount to committing suicide.

In dozens of letters from relatives who had been forced out, Poles learned that the German conquerors and their followers had not even allowed a full hour to pack. The Poles could take only a suitcase full of possessions and 30 marks per person! As the tens of thousands of Polish slave workers wearing defamatory signs were dragged into the interior of Germany, it naturally happened in cities and on farms, that Polish men and German girls entered into sexual relationships. On Himmler's orders, such Poles were hanged. The German girls were sent to the women's concentration camp at Ravensbrück; they received twenty-five lashes with the cane on the naked bottom three times in succession. Prior to that, they had been "spontaneously" pilloried by the public under the direction of efficient party members: Their heads were shorn and they were led through the streets of the town.

In 1941 an effort was suddenly begun to search Buchenwald for Poles who might have had such liaisons; denunciations from inside and outside the camp played a large role. Young Poles were pressed into becoming hangmen of their own countrymen. These "Pole hangmen" were then sent out of Buchenwald concentration camp and used for these purposes over wide areas of Thuringia. They traveled under SS guard to the cities and villages of the land with a two-armed gallows, on each side of which three persons could be hanged, performing public executions to scare the workers from the East. If there was any sort of violent action by a Polish worker in the vicinity of the camp, then thirty Poles were immediately sent from the concentration camp to the site of the offense and hanged there as a "deterrent." The young Poles who had been forced to be hangmen stood under the strictest oath of silence and in any case were unfamiliar with the areas outside the concentration camp, so it was unfortunately not possible to get accurate information on the names of towns where these executions were performed.

After 1944 individual actions of a special type began against pregnant women on the basis of general decrees that had existed earlier. Whenever it became known that a female prisoner in an external work detail of Buchenwald concentration camp was pregnant, the Jewish women were sent to Auschwitz, the non-Jews to Ravensbrück. They were informed that only at those locations were maternity facilities and kindergartens available. What sort of kindergartens these were can be seen from the following example.

A Jewish doctor from the Netherlands had a wife who was not Jewish, and the couple had a five-year-old girl. He was to be transferred from Vught concentration camp, near 's Hertogenbosch, to Auschwitz. Without any idea of what that meant, he asked whether his wife and child could accompany him. The SS approved with pleasure, highly praising the kindergartens there. The wife declared herself ready to go immediately; she went on the very first transport, even before her husband. When the Jewish doctor arrived in Auschwitz, his first concern was to inquire about the women's home and the kindergartens. With guffaws, the SS pointed to the gas chamber. His wife and child were already dead; the man himself died a few days later.

When the gassings were stopped at Auschwitz because of the planned evacuation of the camp, pregnant Jewish women and later all others were sent to the "residence camp Bergen-Belsen." There they were left to starve. Since such horrors could not be kept completely secret, pregnancies were often concealed by any means possible. If it came to a birth, then the mother and child ended up on the same path.

In fall 1944 the Danish SS Major Dr. Vaernet, who had his headquarters in Prague, arrived in Buchenwald. He started a series of experiments to cure homosexuality, with the approval of Himmler and the Reich medical chief of the SS and the police, SS Lieutenant General Dr. [Ernst-Robert] Grawitz, and SS Brigadier General [Helmut] Poppendick, Berlin (via Experimental Department V, Leipzig, of the Reichsführer SS).[43] Implanting a synthetically produced hormone in the right side of the groin was supposed to effect a change in sexual drive. The SS doctors made terrible jokes about it; the prisoners spoke of "flintstones" that were supposed to help those implanted with them along the proper path. Vaernet also experimented with castration. It was tried on a total of about fifteen men, of whom two died. Doubtless that was a result of the operation, since one of them developed a major infection and the other died a few weeks later as a result of general weakness. Otherwise the human guinea pigs of this special series of experiments were not treated badly. But no positive findings were ever obtained.

One ruthless and very dangerous man was SS Major Dr. Ellenbeck from the Department for Blood Preservation of the Berlin SS hospital. He was a conceited,

---

43. Poppendick was tried at the Nuremberg medical case trial He was sentenced to ten years but was released in February 1951. (*NT,* vol. 2, 298f.; Schwartz, "Begnadigung," 407.)

vain nincompoop who had a guest laboratory in Block 50 that had nothing to do with the production of typhus vaccines. For a year and a half, Ellenbeck came to Buchenwald for a few days every three weeks to practice "nutritional physiology." "Fetch me some of your chaps so I can tap some blood from them!" was one of his favorite expressions. Men even came willingly to some extent, in the hope of receiving some additional nourishment or at the very least of being freed from work. Ellenbeck, who flattered himself enormously about his scientific knowledge, made them do strenuous exercises—knee bends, etc.—so that the blood that was to be examined would have a different oxygen content at the time it was collected. Incidents of fainting or the danger of collapse among the undernourished prisoners held no interest for Ellenbeck. With the approval of the camp doctor, Dr. Schiedlausky, he also had two medical corpsmen sent from Berlin every three weeks to take blood for the SS hospital from hundreds of prisoners in the invalids' block of the Little Camp. A slice of bread and a piece of sausage were offered for 200 cc of blood, but sometimes up to 400 cc of blood at a time was "tapped." A few days before the end of the camp, the gentlemen came back once more for such an exercise but found no one willing to put himself at their disposal. By this time the SS no longer had the power to assemble the men.

One of the most upsetting special actions of the SS was the execution of thirty-eight members of the Allied secret services in fall 1944 [Chapter Seven, §89]. They were English and French, almost all of them officers who had been brought from France to Buchenwald concentration camp by the Gestapo in August 1944. A total of forty-three men were housed in Admissions Block 17. In the first half of September, sixteen of them were suddenly called to the gate without any advance warning and were immediately hanged in the crematorium. After that efforts were made by various quarters in camp to save as many as possible of the remaining men. The prisoner hospital could not take on the matter because the camp doctor, Dr. Schiedlausky, in contrast to his predecessor, Dr. Hoven, would not collaborate with the prisoners in any way. This group of endangered men also still stood very much in the spotlight of the SS. Some of them, among them the English lieutenant colonel Southgate, were nevertheless taken in as sick, although that offered no real security.

Rescue was only possible if the threatened person formally "died" and then exchanged his name and number with one of the actually deceased. A few brave comrades of Block 50 declared themselves prepared to undertake the daring transaction through Block 46. Naturally only a limited number could come under consideration. It was a tragic moment when the leader of the group, Lieutenant Colonel Dodkin, who was still alive, undertook the selection in a certain sequence. Because of his importance, his comrades urged him to move his own name to the very top of the list [although by doing so they might condemn themselves to death]. These Englishmen and Frenchmen demonstrated amazing spirit. Only three of them could be saved (aside from Dodkin, whose real name was [Wing Commander Forest Frederick] Yeo-Thomas): Captain [Harry] Poole, the man known to the Gestapo only under the French name Peuleve, and Lieutenant Stephane Hessel from the secret service of General de Gaulle.

The course of the rescue, which was full of dramatic high points, is described in a special report [Chapter Seven, §89, list only]. On October 5, 1944, an additional twenty-one men, among them Peuleve, were summoned and twenty of them shot, while Peuleve made a hair-raising escape. A telegram reporting his successful execution was sent to Berlin in the name of the camp commandant, who had not the slightest hint of what had actually happened. Peuleve was struck off the list. The supposed deaths of Dodkin and Hessel were also reported to the political department. Fourteen days later an additional member of this group, a Frenchman, the father of four children, was taken to be executed. For him, as for the others, the extreme circumstances meant there was simply no hope of rescue, especially without endangering those who had already exchanged numbers. The remaining three men waited week after week for the arrival of an order of execution from Berlin. As a rule the order came on Wednesday and was carried out on Thursday; luckily, however, it never arrived.

Southgate was thus able to stay alive; the two Frenchmen among the survivors went to external work details. One of them by the name of Guillot escaped at the beginning of April 1945, was caught again, and was brought to the cellblock. He was later liberated there. On April 5, 1945, an order of execution suddenly arrived for Dodkin (the report of his death of October 1944 had not reached the proper authority!). The order was also directed against another Englishman in the camp named [Martin] Perkins, a very popular young English officer who had already been in Buchenwald for a year and a half.[44] As a result of fateful complications, the order to execute Perkins was carried out six days before the American troops' liberation of the camp. The four remaining English officers, at their head Southgate and Captain Burney, were protected from the danger of liquidation at the last moment. With the help of a few who were in on the secret, they disappeared into an underground hiding place until the liberation of the camp.[45] In the confusion of the last days of the camp, no further isolated actions were taken against the Englishmen.

XI The Permanent Underground Struggle Between the SS and the Antifascist Forces in Camp

In this hell created by the SS, Buchenwald concentration camp would never have experienced so much that was positive without the tough, death-defying work of

---

44. This account apparently contains a few errors. A young Englishman listed as Martin Perkins was hanged on March 29, 1945 ("Liste der Exekutionen"). His real name, however, was Maurice Pertschuk. Christopher Burney described him as his best friend and dedicated his book *The Dungeon Democracy* "to the memory of Maurice Pertschuk, hanged in Buchenwald Crematorium on the 29th of March, 1945, who fought more gallantly than any of us and died more sadly." *Dungeon Democracy*, (New York: Duell, Sloan, and Pearce, 1946), 122.

45. Ibid., 127f.

the leading political men among the inmates. Nor would so many have been saved in the end if these men had not successfully held their own over the course of the years.

The main point of this earnest, unrelenting work was to build an impenetrable wall against the SS that was invisible but went up wherever an SS man appeared. The handful of men in the camp administration, with their approximately 120 executive organs, were in no position to control the tens of thousands of the enslaved, other than externally and sporadically. What actually happened behind the barbed wire remained hidden from them. The SS foresaw this, suspected it, feared it in the dark hours during the gradual decline of the last years. But they could not seize anyone, could not strike at the anonymous. They attempted, therefore, to obtain through informers knowledge of internal events in the camp, especially about opposition sentiments and organization. Leclaire and Driemel at times went around the camp in prisoner's clothing—a childish method of finding something out, as they did not know a lot of the typical details of prisoner life and were immediately recognized and shadowed.

The result was only sharpened watchfulness and increased distrust. Even the planting of Nazi prisoner informers did not work for the Gestapo and the SS. Even before a new admittee entered the actual camp (that is, the area surrounded by barbed wire), if he belonged to any sort of Nazi or related circles, a signal went out to the internal camp leadership and the leading men on the prisoner side. Reliable eyes and ears were directed at the "new ones" from the very first moment; for hours, even for days, they were put through a series of tests so that the prisoners could judge their very hearts and souls. Nazi sympathizers remained cut off in camp until they could either be rendered harmless or proved themselves without any doubt as innocuous (which luck only a very few had).

The SS had success only with informers from the camp itself: professional criminals, antisocials, and even politicals. Collaboration with the SS developed gradually as a result of the positions the "rats" occupied, which kept them in constant contact with the SS. Or it grew out of motives of personal revenge or a need for power or prestige. A few were also forced into serving as informers by the Gestapo or the camp administration.

The best-known and most infamous case of voluntary denunciation in Buchenwald concentration camp occurred in 1940–1941. A White Russian emigrant, Grigori Kushni-Kushnarev, allegedly a former general, had spent months systematically working himself into the confidence of wide circles. After that he began to deliver comrades of every sort, but especially Russian prisoners of war, into the clutches of the SS [Chapter Seven, §86; Chapter Eight, §113]. This miserable Gestapo agent brought several hundred comrades to their deaths. He did not even shrink from brazenly denouncing anyone with whom he once had even the most trivial personal conflict. One of the chief tasks the SS assigned him was sorting out the Russian prisoners of war who had been brought into camp. He did this according to secret guidelines that had been set up with the Reich Security Main Office with the approval of the Supreme Command of the army. He claimed he was usually able to tell whether people were dangerous or not simply by looking them in the face.

To relate the history of the Kushni-Kushnarev case would make a suspenseful criminal novel in itself. It was finally possible to bring the rascal down with a lethal injection in December 1941. The official cause of his death was given as an acute infectious disease.

The danger of unforeseeable consequences that spies and informers posed for the whole camp was so great that even the possibility of betrayal had to be prevented. Many who unknowingly came into contact with such persons were themselves drawn into a life-threatening circle. Only in rare cases could one know in advance what sort of connection it was and where it might lead, even against the will of the individual concerned. Here, too, mistakes were made that, though never excusable, were understandable given the overall danger of the situation. It took at times laborious and burdensome interventions in order to free a truly innocent person from the fatal web. A few were first turned into "rats" by unjust persecution in camp. Out of despair and lack of experience, they could see no other way out than collaboration with the SS, which sooner or later would also bring them down.

The invisible wall of separation from the SS could only be kept up if the camp was strictly organized and had unified leadership on the prisoners' side. Those elements who stood outside the organization, who either knew nothing about it or were too undisciplined, could on the one hand be kept in check and on the other even appreciated. The German Communists brought with them the best prerequisites for this task. In contrast to the liberals and democrats they were already long accustomed to strict party obedience. Therefore they alone were up to the means and methods of their opponents. Furthermore, they possessed the longest camp experience. That in the process, especially in the early years, valuable antifascist personalities of other [political] directions were often shut out was regrettable. In some cases it was even disadvantageous, but practically nothing could be done about it.

The antifascist forces' struggle for self-preservation had one prerequisite: Under all circumstances the power in camp had to lie in the hands of the political prisoners. The SS principle of mixing categories, encouraging natural distinctions and creating artificial ones, had to be overcome and rendered harmless through constant struggle. No other group ever made an attempt to take into its hands the internal camp leadership; it remained in the ranks of the politicals and professional criminals. The reds' motives were clear; on the greens' side the grounds were anything but political: They wanted a free hand for their accustomed practices—corruption, extortion, and material gains. Any form of control, but especially one that came from within the camp, was unbearable to them. In their opinion, within the framework of what was possible, they could fare just as well with the SS as with the politicals. For the reds, political differences created an insuperable barrier between themselves and the enemy and oppressor. That did not exist for many of the greens.

When therefore the camp administration lay in the hands of an SS officer who showed a preference for the professional criminals, there existed the immediate danger of a change of internal regime. At the beginning Buchenwald concentration camp, as has already been emphasized, was primarily under the rule of the greens. When the majority of them were transported to the newly founded Flossenbürg concentration camp, things gradually became better. With the outbreak of the war came thousands of new professional criminals as a consequence of a massive roundup by German police. In 1942 they once again gained the upper hand under Senior Camp Inmate Ohles. The consequences revealed themselves drastically enough in the Special Section already described. The means that the greens used (establishment of a thoroughly organized system of informers, secret installation of illegal radio devices to compromise the politicals, etc.) is described in a separate report [Chapter Eight, §101].

Active conflict against the SS in camp was completely impossible. As a result, attention had to be directed toward undermining them, primarily through corruption, which benefited the prisoners not only materially but also politically (although the risk-taking was one-sided on the part of the prisoners). Corruption also provided the preconditions for making the brighter SS men uncertain of their own ideals, insofar as they had any. It could even bring them to total ruin [by transfer to the front], with the increasingly deteriorating situation at the front. The basic goal was to put them under so much pressure that they were forced to keep silent or to tolerate certain actions of the prisoners, especially the saving of lives.

The political camp inmates cleverly fostered and exploited the basic tendency of the SS toward corruption. More and more of the actual power in the camp—that is, its inner structure and driving forces—thus came into the prisoners' hands. Under the cover of a dense network of intertwined interests, their work was also advanced by other circumstances, such as the war and the problem of foreigners. In the last year Buchenwald had such a thoroughly developed self-administration that the SS no longer had any real insight into the most important affairs. They had become tired; they were now accustomed to having things "run by themselves." On the whole they allowed the politicals to have their way. The fruits of long years of struggle and effort had ripened; preparations could be made for the expected end with some degree of certainty.

Neither the SS nor the Gestapo ever again succeeded in carrying through measures that would have cut through all the lines of communication of the politicals. The Gestapo tried it once more, much to the displeasure of the SS camp administration, which felt itself accused, interfered with, and hindered. In summer 1944 up to thirty political prisoners, among them important people of the Left, were arrested as a result of denunciations by two new prisoners. After staying a week in the cellblock, they were let out. The investigation of the Gestapo led to no useful outcome. Except for a few, about whose fate nothing further is known, the comrades were gradually released again. In any case, during those months an air of general depression hung over the camp, and in the early weeks any sort of political activity was almost impossible. Slowly the leading forces retreated, organizing themselves along new lines.

The entire political organization and the training of antifascist forces were based on the precondition of maintaining internal power in the camp.

The widespread view in Germany that the inmates of the concentration camps received National Socialist political instruction and would then be released into the community as "better men" was pure nonsense. The SS never even introduced any type of political "reeducation" or anything similar, much less carried it out. The only things that might remotely be interpreted in this sense were transmissions from the German Radio network. In every block and in many work details, loudspeakers that broadcast the German station were turned on at the pleasure of the SS. At first all prisoners had to stand at attention in roll call square as they listened to Adolf Hitler's speeches. They were as endless as the rain that poured on their shaved heads, and their effect was the same: The prisoners simply shook them off. When it later became possible to remain in the blocks during the so-called Führer speeches, Hitler was already so crowned with defeat that he spoke only briefly and less often. That brought some disappointment to the camp, since most amused themselves or took refreshing naps during the speeches.

With much enthusiasm and devotion, the prisoners planned and executed their own projects and measures to keep up their strength for moral and political resistance. Party organization on the Left, by Communists as well as by Social Democrats, was thoroughly developed. Training courses took place rather regularly, if only in the smallest cells. After the eradication of the informer system and the unambiguous clarification of power relationships in the camp itself, everything became tremendously politicized. After 1944 it was actually quite open and unrestricted. Daily newspapers were available; one could read the *Thüringer Gauzeitung* and the *Völkischer Beobachter,* or even subscribe to a hometown newspaper.

In camp a sort of propaganda ministry formed that collected and passed on small items of significant information that at times Goebbels allowed to be published only in border newspapers. Sharp political minds analyzed the situation and provided clarity and an overview for interested comrades. This was especially critical during the times when it appeared as if Hitler's trees would actually grow into the heavens,[46] and as a result many comrades were very depressed. Ironically, there was probably no other place in all Germany where politics could be discussed so clearly—even if illegally—as in the concentration camps. Foreign news was provided by a listening service in the electricians' work detail, whose reports were passed along twice a day to trusted contact men. Work at this location was in any case linked with the constant threat of death. In Sachsenhausen concentration camp in fall 1944, over 100 comrades were arrested for listening to foreign broadcasts; more than two dozen of them were hanged.

---

46. This is a reference to a German proverb: "It has been provided for that trees do not grow into the heavens."

Lasting contacts with the outside world were carefully maintained. They were established in part by released protective custody prisoners, in part by the external work details and civilian workers. In this manner the picture of conditions in the country that came from reports by new arrivals could be constantly corrected or amplified. Important political news from the camp could also be launched to the outside.

Antifascist celebrations took place repeatedly in Buchenwald concentration camp, though the necessary security precautions were always taken. Naturally only longtime camp inmates of absolutely irreproachable character were invited. The celebrations consisted as a rule of a serious and a humorous part, the latter part featuring sharp political satire at its best. Even antifascist literary readings took place. Out of books in the camp library, everything usable was carefully sought out, especially from the works of the German classicists. Each time the success was enduring. What an effect the reading of scenes from Georg Büchner's *Danton's Death* had. Again and again, during so-called recycling, valuable books from confiscated libraries were found. (Among others, Justinian's *Pandects* and other famous legal works were found, along with many Bibles in old and new editions, which had been designated for use as toilet paper.) Through them the programs could be extraordinarily enriched. Heine's satirical and revolutionary poems came into the prisoners' possession in this way.

Whenever there was enough free time, the prisoners provided for entertainment. In the early years, according to the whim of the SS, prisoners could be severely punished for holding musical evenings or cabarets in the blocks. Later they were allowed to organize concerts or variety shows in the cinema, which were well attended. In part they offered outstanding programs, for among the prisoners were performers of renown and reputation and more than a few with serviceable talent. Even sports were played, though within a relatively modest framework, which managed to divert comrades for an hour or two from the horror and the drudgery of everyday life.

To carry out and maintain everything that was illegal, a truly effective prisoner self-defense force had to be created. The prisoners decided to present this idea to the SS itself, suggesting a police force that could act as an extended arm of the SS in the camp, though in fact it would serve the well-understood goals of the prisoners. The danger that the SS could effectively misuse the organization against the prisoners was no longer very great at the point when the camp police was created. This speculation proved to be correct.

The camp administration regarded the camp police as a deputized representation of SS power in camp, which lightened its task of control and domination of the camp. As has already been mentioned, the camp police was formed as the core unit of the prisoners against the SS. It was of course a difficult and moreover, as seen from the outside, a thankless task. For example, the camp police had to take over new admissions, transports, organization of roll call, search actions, and similar activities that took a firm hand.

The Buchenwald camp police seldom administered beatings. New prisoners who came from other camps were at first frightened when they were received by the men of the Buchenwald camp police, then soon saw it as a relief. Naturally, now and then there would be a member of the camp police who seemed to take the tone of a frustrated SS man. But that was hardly conclusive: If the camp police had not maintained an irreproachable camouflage of order toward the SS, how would it have gone for the camp as a whole and for thousands of individuals during deliveries, during transports, in punishment actions? "Last but not least" [phrase in English in the original], how would it have gone in the final days of Buchenwald before the liberation? This enormous service far overshadows any mistakes that were made.

Furthermore, entry into camp lost much of its hardness and roughness when it became possible to internationalize the camp police. It was precisely the German comrades who talked the SS into this. All the other prerequisites were already in place in order to unify and provide a common direction for the camp in the final months. New auxiliary groups of the camp police were created for all possible reasons and pretexts, as well as new institutions that could stand side by side with them in an emergency. In addition to the fire department that already existed, there were the fire wardens, the medical corps, and the rescue squad. More than 1,000 men who were well disciplined and obedient to the orders of the prisoner camp leadership stood ready.

The SS never succeeded in seeing through this gradually forming power structure. One can imagine the degree of courage, of selfless sense of responsibility toward one's own camp forces, the cleverness and detailed work that were needed to create this effective protective force as part of the permanent underground struggle of the antifascist forces. Its influence and example were so great that political comrades from other camps who had been terrorized by the greens sent for information and for help. Elements of camp police from Buchenwald were sent along with outgoing transports; they could not immediately change conditions at the place of their destination, of course, but they could nevertheless improve them.

XII The Camp Since the Outbreak of the War

Up to this point the account of Buchenwald concentration camp has primarily described conditions typical of German concentration camps in general. Without a knowledge of these incidents and institutions, it would be impossible to understand the changes that the war brought about in camp.

In general it must be said that the war, contrary to the expectations of most, did not worsen conditions in camp but actually improved them somewhat. That seems contradictory but is in fact so. A series of circumstances, especially the growing difficulties [posed by the war] in all areas, meant that SS actions were no longer marked with the same degree of aggressiveness and brutality as in the early years. The pressure that constantly weighed upon the prisoners, pressure that in part had made them compliant, thus lessened. The war also increased the inmates' chances of eliminating harmful elements in their own ranks and of abolishing or tempering unbearable conditions.

A considerable number of the atrocities described here were gradually stopped after about 1940–1941. Beatings seldom occurred thereafter—aside from "official" whippings. New prisoners were delivered in a more or less bearable manner; the bathhouse, the disinfection station, and the supply rooms functioned more or less "normally." They remained stations of dehumanization, but [without?] the special torments and shameless excesses that long characterized them. In the blocks a deputy senior block inmate from each nation was named. The block officers now cared little about such things; the old work detail officers either left or became relatively tame. The last two circumstances in particular rid the camp of any number of terrors.

Objectivity demands that these changes be pointed out. One should not, however, believe that through them the camp turned into a recreational facility. Anything but! It was only that the overwhelming terror, which in the early years was hardly bearable, disappeared more and more. What remained was the "normal" hard existence for the 12,000 to 35,000 people living in about 1 square mile in conditions that were still inhuman, even if they could no longer be made worse through demonic minds. Perhaps what has been said is only understandable from the standpoint of an old concentration camp veteran; for someone who had adapted to the lowest possible level during years of horror, this felt like a relief. Foreigners and other new arrivals were horrified even by the improved conditions because they were unaware of their origins and development.

In addition the transformation occurred only very gradually, unequally in the various areas, and was often accompanied by severe setbacks. There were fewer atrocities against individuals, yet certain mass actions increased, as already described.

After the Polish campaign and up to spring 1940, it almost seemed as if the circumstances of the war would bring about the destruction of the camp. As early as August 21, 1939, Buchenwald had reached its absolute lowest point with 5,376 prisoners. After August 23, 1939, with the signing of the German-Russian friendship treaty [the Nazi-Soviet pact], numerous so-called action prisoners were delivered into camp. The National Socialists did not want to leave them at large because they believed they might torpedo the policy toward Soviet Russia. It was also feared that they might cause difficulties in the army if the long-prepared-for war were to begin. They were therefore declared "militarily unworthy." The Dachau concentration camp was completely evacuated: 2,000 comrades from there came to Buchenwald. Clothing and food were miserable; the winter was immeasurably severe.

On one cold day in 25-degree weather, after the work details had dragged dozens of badly beaten and frozen prisoners to roll call, the camp doctor ordered that at least on days when the temperature dropped below 15 degrees, work details would no longer have to move out of the camp. But this "improvement" could no longer halt the outbreak of epidemics, since the nutritional condition of the prisoners was already catastrophic. Buchenwald had survived the typhus epidemic in winter and spring 1939; now dysentery broke out to such an extent that the camp had to be quarantined.

Into this milieu of horror—made up of hunger, cold, epidemics, and misery of all sorts—181 people from the Polish minority in Germany were delivered after the end of the Polish campaign. On October 15, 1939, 1,000 Poles were delivered; on October 16 an additional 1,098; from the Jewish nursing home in Vienna 200 old people; and, finally, about 2,000 Jews who had emigrated from Poland to Germany and Austria in earlier times. They were housed next to roll call square in large, open tents, without heat or blankets and with half rations of food and only one loaf of bread for ten men.

Every day the SS pulled out of the Little Camp (which was surrounded by extra barbed wire) people they considered to be so-called snipers [*Heckenschützen*], thus Polish partisans. They were brought to a "house" on the edge of the Little Camp that was called the "rose garden." Barbed wire was all it consisted of. There, in temperatures of 22 degrees below zero at night and 5 degrees above zero in the day, the victims died of starvation—in sight of their comrades, who never knew when their turn would come. One time all the Poles in camp were mustered in front of the window of the roll call officer, man by man. A German woman had come in order to find the "murderer of her husband." It was never determined if someone whose facial features she believed she recognized was among the candidates for death who had been thrown into the "rose garden" that day. A total of 123 men died of hunger there, not counting victims in the Little Camp.

With the conquest of one European land after another, more and more transports of foreigners arrived in Buchenwald. There were Dutch, French and Belgians, Spanish republicans, Ukrainians and Russians, Yugoslavs, Norwegians and Danes, and finally Hungarians and Italians and citizens of two dozen additional states. The condition in which the people sometimes arrived is impossible to describe. In summer 1943 hundreds of French, some completely naked, some in the shabbiest underwear, were unloaded at the Weimar train station. They arrived along with their numerous dead in the freight cars into which they had been crammed together for a transport from Compiègne.[47] They were forced to walk the 5 miles to Buchenwald; among them were high government officials, professors, officers (especially from the French police), and engineers. The first Russians had behind them hunger marches of 600 miles or more. When they staggered through the camp gate, they were like human wrecks; out of the baths came walking skeletons. The comrades immediately took up a bread collection to benefit the unfortunates. The SS responded with harsh sanctions against the politicals who had organized the charitable work. The entire camp was punished by the withholding of food. "If one of the Reich Germans [helps] these dirty dogs from the east one more time … ," threatened the first deputy camp commandant over the microphone. It continued to go on, of course, but only in secret.

Children were delivered into the camp in growing numbers, too. The youngest "partisan" was three and a half years old. They were housed in a wooden block,

---

47. Frenchman Jean Michel gave a similar account of his own trip to Buchenwald in September 1943. Jean Michel and Louis Noucera, *Dora* (New York: Holt, Rinehart, and Winston, 1980), 32.

where they were entrusted to more or less reasonable prisoners. In the course of time, they were given a little employment during the day; they eventually entered all sorts of work details, where the comrades treated them well. Of course the rough conditions had some long-lasting effects on them. In the end there were 877 boys between three and a half and twelve years old whom the National Socialists had preserved as special examples of the "protective custody" methods they undertook for the good of the German people. It went right to the hearts of hard-boiled men when the SS sorted out and herded together all the Jewish children and Gypsy boys for transport to Auschwitz for gassing. The SS used carbines and pistols to drive away the screaming, crying children, who desperately wanted to return to their fathers who were staying behind or to their prisoner guardians in the individual details.

In 1945 the camp included prisoners from a total of thirty nations. A few words about the conduct of the most numerous foreign nationals in the camp: The Poles adapted to the situation relatively well. It was not easy on them, as even in camp they received little sympathy. What is more, they were very divided politically. During the course of the war, some of them were brought into significant positions of leadership on the prisoners' side. They were strongly represented among the room attendants and in some preferred work details because they pursued systematic personnel policy. In 1942 they suffered a setback under Senior Camp Inmate Wolff. Poles who came from Auschwitz brought with them bad reputations and immediately sought to obtain power in Buchenwald. After the defeat of this extremely dangerous attempt to force the internal development of the camp onto a different path, it was a long time before the Poles were able to reconsolidate their position.

The Czechs had come into the camp as so-called protectorate prisoners [i.e., from Bohemia and Moravia] with special privileges. They lived in their own blocks, wore their hair long, and did not need to work for months at a time. That caused much envy and ill will toward them. But their helpfulness, especially their willingness to distribute surplus food and smoking materials, dispelled much of the hostility. When more and more of them gradually reported for work in the camp before their privileges were taken from them, they had the opportunity to seek out the very best work details. Hardly any of the Czechs were in a difficult work situation for any length of time. After overcoming their own party political differences, they lived with the other nationals on either friendly or merely civil terms.

The Soviets fell into two rather sharply divided groups: the prisoners of war along with Russian civilian workers, and the Ukrainians. The latter group represented the overwhelming majority. The prisoners of war, at the end about 800 men, formed a splendid, well-disciplined team. They were properly and skillfully conscious of their own collective interests but also kept the interests of the entire camp firmly in mind. The mass of Ukrainians, in contrast, were a rather unqualified people. They were at first favored by their German party comrades in such a way that it was almost impossible to put forward even the smallest complaint against a "Russian." The impudence, laziness, and uncomradely behavior of many of them nevertheless brought a quick and thorough change so that they were no longer able to gain positions of leadership. In the last year the Russian prisoners of war, together with some of the outstanding Komsomols from the Ukrainian ranks, had begun to educate and integrate into the rest of the camp at least the usable portion of this hodgepodge society that knew no inhibitions. This difficult task was to some extent successful.

Because of their temperament and their generally weak constitutions, the French suffered more than others under the unfavorable conditions. Their pronounced individualism, their predominantly intellectual character, and the fact that among them were a number of disguised criminals and other doubtful elements brought them into many difficulties that could have been avoided. From other quarters they often received little sympathy. A number of French personalities achieved the very best relations in camp, but on the whole they were poor at it and were not very popular. It proved impossible to unite their ranks in order to make them capable of more resistance and more valuable to the "community of the oppressed" because they were politically so incredibly splintered. Only the French Communist minority had close connections to the internal camp leadership. The result was not only protection for themselves and those they recommended but also considerable injustice for the others, the overwhelming majority who were helpless and lived in a state of constant fear from every quarter. Much of what occurred, even after the liberation of the camp, can be explained thereby.

The Dutch conducted themselves very bravely. At the beginning there were sharp internal differences, but these were essentially moderated and bridged over, especially at the end. They were freedom-loving men who hated every form of compulsion, no matter where it came from. But their efficiency always helped them overcome the difficulties that arose. Between them and the other nationalities in the camp prevailed not only proper but in many cases warm relationships. Precisely the same can be said of the approximately 600 Yugoslavs in the camp, who were very popular.

The almost 2,000 Danes, mostly police officers, came to Buchenwald in 1944. They formed a unified block who kept to themselves and lived under more favorable conditions. There were never any conflicts with them. Again and again they were able to help the camp to a certain extent by their own means, which stood at their disposal in relative abundance. That was even more true of the approximately 350 Norwegian students, splendid men who brought with them their sporting nature and were good comrades. It would be wrong not to mention in this place the 167 Allied pilots who found themselves in Buchenwald concentration camp for several months in 1944, before they were shipped elsewhere. Organized along strict military lines, they stood in close contact to the leading non-Communists in camp. They showed complete loyalty to the German Communist leadership and maintained highly useful contact with the Russian prisoners of war. At the end of the camp, many first-rate plans of action that were regarded—and rightly so—as extremely critical were built upon their cooperation.

In addition to orders directed against Russian prisoners of war, orders from SS headquarters were also directed against the Dutch, French, and Belgians. These involved the so-called NN transports. The SS had the uncanny ability to give romantic names to the death to which they condemned others. Action Ocean Foam and Action Spring Wind were names for the SS manhunts in France, whose victims were deported to German concentration camps. Starting in summer 1943 the code word *NN transport* began to appear in the political department. One might believe at first that it was a special measure directed at the Netherlands. Soon, however, the real meaning became clear. The "Night and Fog" [*Nacht und Nebel*] transports comprised several hundred Dutch, French, and Belgians who, after "investigations of biological race" were taken to other concentration camps, especially the infamous Natzweiler, for special medical experiments. Through skillful intervention, about two dozen comrades were nevertheless saved from the fate determined for them, seven of them by way of Block 50.

Housing the thousands of foreigners in Buchenwald was problematic from the beginning. In 1942 the SS therefore arranged for the building of the so-called Little Camp, which eventually comprised seventeen barracks, adjacent to the last row of stone barracks. Until the final completion of the primitive wooden barracks, new admissions were housed in tents. It scarcely needs to be said what that meant for many, even for the majority. But even in the Little Camp conditions were such that anyone who was able made every effort to escape and to be transferred into the large camp. In bunks densely stacked on top of one another to the right and left of a central corridor, six to ten men apiece were housed without proper light or sufficient ventilation, each with a single blanket—if he was lucky. A latrine was located outside. Each block housed 1,500, or 2,000 people instead of the intended capacity of 500.

Tragedies of unimaginable dimension occurred here; the longer the war lasted, the greater. It got worse starting in fall 1944. The daily death toll in the Little Camp alone grew tremendously, sometimes up to 150 to 200 men. At times corpses lay in the open because there had been no time to carry them away, the living having simply thrown them out of the barracks in the middle of the night in order to make room. "Renovations" by the SS consisted solely in having Block 61 erected. Every day up to 200 people from the Little Camp were brought there to be given lethal injections, thus freeing up more space in the other barracks. Because of the extent of this miserable situation, in which among others the Allied pilots and the Danes had to live, the SS opened a separate infirmary in the Little Camp. To be sure, it had less to do than Block 61.

The organizing forces inside the camp as a whole were almost powerless in the face of this mass death. The appointed senior block inmates had an almost unmanageable task, since hunger and deprivation in many cases reduced the prisoners to animals. There were wild fights to the death over the meager daily rations, so the room attendants were hardly able to maintain control.

To relieve conditions somewhat, the new arrivals were sent away again on transports to subsidiary camps as quickly as possible. Years earlier the base camp at Buchenwald had already established subsidiary camps. Their number and distance grew with the duration of the war. Construction brigades from Buchenwald went as far as the Channel Islands; thousands of comrades went to excavation trenches and factories along the Rhine. In the north the external work details stretched to Magdeburg; in the east, beyond Leipzig. The greatest number of prisoners were required in the so-called closed area [known as Dora], a terrain of several thousand acres around Nordhausen, about 42 miles north of Buchenwald. There alone approximately 150,000 men worked in underground tunnels of the Dessau Junkers Works in inhumane conditions, alongside foreign workers and German civilian employees. Slave workers were also sent from Buchenwald to other closed industrial areas that stood under the SS.

In total the base camp possessed seventy subsidiary camps (fifty for men, twenty for women), not counting the Dora camp near Niedersachsenwerfen in the county of Nordhausen. Dora became an independent camp in October 1944, and to it were assigned the camps of the so-called B Project. Under Commandant Förschner, a man who had no special preference for the greens, Dora eventually fell under the control of the professional criminals. Förschner ordered prisoners themselves to hang comrades who were condemned to execution. The politicals firmly refused, after which he removed them from their leading positions and replaced them with the greens.

In fall 1944 Förschner, clearly on orders from the Security Service (SD) [*Sicherheitsdienst*], had more than 100 politicals arrested. Among them were prisoners of all nationalities, including doctors, a number of whom were hanged for sabotage. The conditions in these subsidiary camps were of course known in Buchenwald, although no one was ever allowed to return from the closed area. Through the prisoner hospital attendants and occasionally through SS men, it was nevertheless possible to get around the regulations and find out about at least the most important events that took place there.

Under these circumstances, to be sent on transport obviously meant something terrible. The subsidiary camps all had to be built from scratch. Sanitary conditions were horrible; the workday long, mostly spent underground; the food miserable. Men frequently could not change clothes for four to six weeks at a time; clean underwear was not available. Epidemics reaped a rich harvest among the slave workers. Convalescent duty was granted in only the rarest cases. Precisely this threat of being transported held an advantage that the base camp Buchenwald utilized, for anyone who was not "indispensable" or did not have the best connections could suddenly be sent on such a transport. Under the best conditions, they would disappear in a single stroke.

The war production effort was put in place with a great expenditure of organizational effort, like almost everything the SS undertook. Factories were built everywhere; machines were procured from all over Europe; directors and SS officers ran about everywhere. Commands were given, deadlines set, the army of slaves was pushed harder—and out of it came relatively little or nothing. The main reason for this was that everywhere the prisoners applied the work methods of the camps, reinforced by deliberate sabotage, at times on a significant scale. Thus, for example, in the Gustloff Works, instead of 55,000 barrels for carbines per month, only 33,000 were produced in six months. Another striking example was the building of the railroad link between Weimar and Buchenwald. It was to be a traffic artery to the Gustloff Works, which had a branch factory with thirteen large buildings on the edge of the concentration camp. Himmler himself had ordered its completion by June 1943. The deadline was in fact met, but it was a Potemkin railroad: It ran for precisely one day, namely, the opening day, on which the foundations gave way after the first locomotive passed. The actual completion took an additional six months.

The camp was so strongly drawn into war production not only because of centralized orders but also because of efforts by the SS to expand their own power base as far as possible so as to protect their own members from being sent to the front. After 1943 the concentration camp served as a base for the slackers among Himmler's elite troops. When they could no longer avoid pressure from above, they finally offered prisoners as material for the front, though only to a modest extent.

A certain [Oskar] Dirlewanger had placed himself at the disposal of the SS in Dachau to reeducate camp inmates as volunteers for the front. This man was later decorated with the Iron Cross and made an SS brigadier general. Although he was able to obtain only a few prisoners with red triangles for his undertaking, he had more success with greens and blacks. In 1945 the last effort of the Dirlewanger action was directed at the homosexuals, but it was too late for them to take part in the honor intended for them.

Insofar as the professional criminals volunteered to show their solidarity with the Waffen SS (in Buchenwald no fewer than 500 joined), they contributed not a little to augmenting the reputation of the SS as butchers. They were used in the battle against the partisans in the east. If they were not killed in action, they were occasionally brought back into the camp after a period of such "testing at the front." This could be a source of amusement for the prisoners and the cause of some chagrin for the SS. It was especially the case when a professional criminal who had received a whipping from a work detail officer or had been sent to the whipping block now suddenly sent a field postcard to the same SS man. It would be signed with the words, "With comradely greetings, yours, _____." The politicals remarked in derision that the Dirlewanger men should wear a green triangle on their SS uniforms as a mark of differentiation from their comrades.

In fall 1944 all German political protective custody prisoners in Buchenwald received a gracious letter from Himmler urging them to volunteer for service, too. Only 100 appeared for mustering, almost all of them unsuspecting new arrivals. Commandant Pister gave little publicity to Himmler's friendly encouragement to volunteer, which offered prisoners the opportunity to fight for Himmler and for National Socialism after they had spent five to ten years in a concentration camp. Pister saw the impossibility of the situation and, for reasons already mentioned, was not very interested in losing German prisoners. They were the ones with whose help the SS believed that they could master the almost unmanageable problem of the growing foreign population.

Starting in 1942, Russian volunteers, who had placed themselves at the disposal of the SS in prisoner of war camps for the fight against the partisans, were also trained in Buchenwald concentration camp.

The bombardment by the Allied air forces on August 24, 1944, completely destroyed the "industrial development work" of the SS in Buchenwald in one single, well-aimed blow. The factory was just coming into full production.[48] In the camp itself there were only two large fires caused by incendiary bombs. But because at the time prisoners were not allowed to retreat to the camp in the event of an air raid alarm, there were no less than 384 dead and 600 seriously wounded among the prisoners. These casualties resulted mainly from a direct hit to the quarry by a bomb intended for the SS barracks. On the SS side only eighty men were killed.[49]

The bombardment made an extraordinarily deep impression on the SS. From then on they were rather intimidated, fleeing to the shrapnel trenches at the slightest air raid alarm. They viewed the camp as a place of refuge and protection for themselves. Every visit by Allied planes encouraged a mood of confidence among the prisoners, in addition to bringing welcome leisure time for the period of the alarm. Besides that, the water supply in the camp suddenly functioned better than before because consumption by the armaments factories ceased. German airplanes were viewed with great mistrust when they flew over the camp, as it was feared that one day Himmler might give the order to liquidate the camp and its inmates in a manner that could be represented to the public as an act of the Allies. Ernst Thälmann, the leader of the German Communist party [KPD] arrested in 1933, had been smuggled into the camp by Goebbels around the time of the bombardment of Buchenwald and had been shot about the same time.[50]

Buchenwald prisoners suffered serious losses on February 9, 1945, during an air attack on Weimar. Out of about 2,000 comrades employed in the Gustloff Works,

---

48. Postwar reports identify this an RAF raid. The liberated prisoners praised the precision of the raid and the relatively few casualties it caused. NA, RG 338, box 444, "Buchenwald Camp: The Report of a Parliamentary Delegation," 5; United Nations War Crimes Commission, "Visit of a Delegation to Buchenwald Concentration Camp," NA, RG 338, box 444, 5.

49. Among the casualties were the wife and daughter of Commandant Pister. NA, RG 338, box 444, "Parliamentary Report," 5. Damage to the camp itself was slight. The wind blew a couple of firebombs into the camp, destroying the camp laundry, disinfection, tailor shop, and shoe repair, without causing prisoner casualties; *KL Bu,* 53. Goethe's Oak, near the laundry, was also destroyed; Pierre d'Harcourt, *The Real Enemy* (New York: Scribner's, 1967), 157.

50. Postwar accounts revealed that Hitler ordered Ernst Thälmann's execution on August 14; he was transferred from Bautzen to Buchenwald and killed at the crematorium there on August 18, 1944. The Allied air raid on August 24 provided the Nazis with a convenient cover. The official party newspaper, the *Völkischer Beobachter,* announced on September 16 that he had been a victim of the bombing raid on Buchenwald along with Social Democrat Rudolf Breitscheid. For a modern account, see Emil Carlebach, *Buchenwald: Ein Konzentrationslager* (Frankfurt: Röderberg-Verlag, 1984), 81–83.

more than 300 were killed and hundreds were wounded, the prisoners having been forced to sleep in the factory building or nearby. The German Red Cross in Weimar refused to receive wounded Buchenwald prisoners at city hospitals, in particular at the Sophie Hospital. They had to be transported back, during which time some of them died; others were not even given first aid.

During clean-up work in Weimar and the digging of mass graves, duties assigned to prisoners, the National Socialist Public Welfare (NSV) nurses[51] brusquely refused to give prisoners water and small slices of bread. In some cases private citizens of Weimar were willing to make food and drink available to the prisoners.

At this stage of the camp's development [early 1945], the food supply became steadily worse. The greatest assistance to the camp came from the International Red Cross of Geneva, whose rather substantial shipments began at that time, primarily for the French protective custody prisoners. At first, with their wonderful contents, the Red Cross packages understandably caused strong dissension in the camp. When the French comrades expressed their willingness to turn over a considerable portion of the shipments to the entire camp, by blocks, their act of solidarity was gratefully received. In practice, however, the distribution was rather a scandal for weeks. For example, the Little Camp received only one package for every ten Frenchmen, while their compatriots who were entrusted with the distribution reserved whole piles for themselves. Of course the SS administration also brazenly made off with a share of these shipments. It was amusing to see how hastily the camp officers cleared their rooms of empty Red Cross boxes as the front approached, so the Americans would not come to the obvious conclusions when they saw them.

XIII   The Dramatic End of the Camp

The influential men among the prisoners were long prepared for the various possible outcomes at the closing of the camp. The average prisoner looked forward to the expected event with considerable anxiety. It was generally assumed that Himmler would give an order from headquarters for the liquidation of all inmates of the camp at the appropriate time, either by poisoning, transports to gas chambers, mass shootings, or bombing by the German air force. If one analyzed these possibilities, it became clear that these types of measures, if they were to be completely successful, would not be so simple to carry out. The camp could without a doubt have prevented a general poisoning, yet it was not in a position to guarantee its own continued food supply. An attempt at mass shooting, such as by machine-gun fire from the towers or through flamethrowers, would have led to

---

51. The Nationalsozialistische Volkswohlfahrt was a social welfare organization that worked with pregnant mothers and juveniles.

an uprising. The electric barbed wire fence would be knocked down immediately; hundreds, perhaps thousands would fall, but more would escape. Admittedly, their individual fates in the surrounding countryside would then have been very doubtful.

The least protection would be possible against a German aerial bómbardment. But general factors—such as a consideration of the mood of the population, the command structure in the German air force, and the like—moderated these fears, although they could not be completely put aside. The camp was most defenseless against an evacuation for the purpose of gassing. Group or individual flight while under way and resistance immediately at the gas chambers remained the only means of defense, and they would be relatively ineffective.

The argument that eventually proved to be the most correct, advanced by only a few at the time, was the least persuasive. It was that any sort of centralized order would simply be out of the question because by that stage of general dissolution, concentration camps would have moved to the periphery of attention for Himmler and his staff, and the SS command structure would no longer be fully functioning.

One could see that the local SS, as a consequence of its manifold disintegration, was no longer an effective executive organ against the masses. But this factor was too uncertain to rely upon. Clear and definite preparations had to be made for a negative outcome. The setting up of a self-defense force has already been mentioned. At the time of the bombing on August 24, 1944, immediate efforts were made to secure weapons. The general confusion was used to conceal whatever machine guns, pistols, carbines, and hand grenades could be taken from the SS division's armory. The weapons supply was carefully secured in the camp, partly buried, partly hidden in walls, with the knowledge of only a few trustworthy contact men.

To the extent feasible, the arms were supplemented. Even this part of the preparations could not have been carried out without two preconditions: The internal organization had to have functioned perfectly, and the camp had to have already been systematically cleansed of all doubtful or treasonous elements after lengthy struggles.

The possession of weapons created a feeling of security for the first time. At least one did not have to die without a fight, to simply allow oneself to be slaughtered. With their strengthened self-confidence, the comrades could be more easily calmed with logical arguments. The enormous difficulty of the situation cannot be underestimated. The struggle had to be directed not only against the SS but almost equally, at the decisive moment, against weakness, cowardliness, and unavoidable panic [among the prisoners].

When the first large return transports to Buchenwald from evacuated camps began, a curious situation resulted: The SS, seeing the end coming from the outside, feared the anonymous mass of tens of thousands of prisoners. The mass of prisoners feared the SS. In these days the people in the area, especially in Weimar, were as afraid of the camp as of the devil himself. All three groups, each working from a different set of perceptions and assumptions of facts, had good reason for grave concern.

For the SS and the prisoners, considering their relationship, the reasons for these fears were clearly apparent. The people, in contrast, could have remained calm, but they, too, operated under impressions created by continuous propaganda. They believed that the prisoners of Buchenwald were all criminals, and they saw the tattered, zebra-striped clothing and the familiar markings as outward confirmation of the correctness of this discrimination. But there were also people who had come into contact with prisoners on external work details and had learned to recognize prisoners as individual human beings with their own fates. Word of this had spread. And a residual consciousness of humanity still played a certain role, even though it had been repressed to some extent. Together with a hidden, all too willingly suppressed sense of guilt, it caused people to fear the end of the concentration camp in the event of a German defeat.

Undoubtedly the anxiety was greatest among the civilians employed in the SS factories. (They had certainly behaved despicably often enough.) They always feared that they would simply be slaughtered if it ever "came to that." The desire for revenge among the political prisoners was great, especially toward the city of Weimar—which through hundreds of channels had received money and all types of benefits from the "death factory" yet had never shown any feelings of compassion or understanding, much less offered any active assistance. But despite their vindictive urges, the forces of order in the camp had an interest in their political reputation; they didn't want chaos coming out of Buchenwald—for the sake of the country as well as the future. Therefore everything possible was done to master the approaching circumstances.

As the situation became ever more acute, months before the actual end, a question began to be discussed: Armed uprising or continued waiting? Only through great effort could we unite on a basic policy. We would not provoke a fight; we would not create pretexts; we would resist only when matters became serious. We set about preparations even more intensively, amidst continued difficulties with the SS and many of our fellow prisoners. In every block there were contact men for each nationality. The self-defense troops were expanded further. Everything finally revolved around the question of what Himmler would order. It had already become clear that the SS camp administration would no longer undertake anything of its own accord.

Independently of each other, two groups had prepared clear plans for taking over the camp after the defeat of the SS and the arrival of the Allies. They were the Communist party and a non-Communist group under the leadership of Captain Burney. The plans differed little from one another, as became evident after the liberation, since both were based on the same camp experience. The difference consisted principally in that the KPD proceeded from a position of real power in the camp. It acted out of old habits and an understandable feeling of cohesion, providing for the use of its own people almost exclusively in the takeover. The other group proceeded only on the principle of personal ability without any consideration of party affiliation. A good third of the proposed functionaries of this group were also Communists. Both groups worked on an international basis.

Already by mid-March 1945, it was obvious that the Western Allies would come to central Germany. The camp directed its hope primarily toward help from the air when it came to the final showdown. In case of a landing on the plain north of Buchenwald, it was decided to intervene directly from the camp, no matter how difficult things might become. Everyone expected, though, that the SS would still move toward evacuation before then. At the beginning of April, preparations were made for that: The SS division supplies were removed. The camp was in a constant state of internal alert, although the situation never came to a clear resolution. It was known that the commandant, SS Colonel Pister, was by nature a bureaucrat, that he would never undertake anything on his own initiative, and that he liked to postpone decisions.

Through the prisoner secretary of SS Major Dr. Schuler, it was known that at Ohrdruf (S III) on April 2, a telephone conversation was held between the Weimar police president, SS Colonel Schmidt, and Himmler, at the urging of the Ohrdruf camp commandant, SS Captain Oldeburhuis. (Ohrdruf was an infamous subsidiary camp about 30 miles southwest of Weimar, where one of the proposed Führer headquarters was located.) On the basis of that telephone call, it was left to the Ohrdruf commandant's discretion to get rid of the professional criminals and "those politicals thought to be dangerous," but nothing should be allowed to happen to the Jews—a paradox that could be explained only out of the curious international expectations of the Reich SS leadership. The rest of the camp, however, would be sent off on transports. The death transport of 12,000 men from Ohrdruf to Buchenwald did then take place, thousands meeting their deaths through shooting. On the road from Weimar to Buchenwald alone, the last short stretch, seventy-four prisoners lay in pools of blood on April 5. Earlier, hundreds had been shot down by fanatical Hitler Youths and even by women.

The number of deaths in S III itself amounted to more than 1,500. There were now 47,700 people crowded together behind the barbed wire of Buchenwald. The food supply was in doubt, the misery immense. American tanks were waiting west of Erfurt, from which the thunder of shooting could be heard, until they could resume their advance. These were days of extreme nervous tension.

On the afternoon of April 4, 1945, the Jews of the camp were suddenly summoned. No one appeared in roll call square. Such a thing had never before happened in a concentration camp. It was inconceivable that the SS would no longer dare to use extreme violence to enforce their orders. A precious night passed, during which hundreds of Jewish comrades of the camp's "old guard" had the opportunity to "submerge." Names, numbers, markings, and work details were switched; blocks were changed. The next morning the SS ordered the inmates of the camp to appear by block. "Jews step forward!" came the order. Some obeyed the order; the rest the SS had to try to find "by face," since after the bombardment they no longer possessed adequate records.

It came to strange scenes; the sergeants of Buchenwald concentration camp performed the task casually. Some were butchers from Auschwitz. They walked around the Little Camp with nightsticks, smoking cigarettes and pulling out those who suited them. But the camp police of the prisoners, without which they could no longer work, did nothing that would have assisted them in their exercise. Indeed, it even allowed men, insofar as they were vigorous enough to take action themselves, to disappear without hindrance back into the ranks that had already been sorted through. At the end, out of 6,000 Jews in camp, 1,500 were assembled. Their numbers were increased on the next day by the Hungarian Jews who had just arrived from Ohrdruf.

On April 5 a tip came from the SS side that the liquidation of the Englishmen in camp—along with two Americans, twenty altogether—was being planned. A few of the faithful quickly helped four officers among them, at their head Southgate and Burney, to "submerge" by hiding them in a 2-foot-deep crawl space underneath Block 56. As they climbed down into the crawl space, they found a Jew who by chance the day before had found a hole under a bed leading to it. Now the Russian prisoners of war who guarded the hiding place would not let him out because they feared that the spot would be revealed. The poor man remained four more days in this horrible situation—without light, in damp dirt, motionless, with the sound of the tramping of 1,500 wooden shoes constantly above him—and he was fed along with the other concealed men.

In order to relieve the extremely tense situation, as early as April 3 four leading personalities among the foreigners in camp—the Belgian minister [Paul] Soudan, the French under secretary of state [André] Marie, the English captain Burney, and the Dutch naval officer [Pieter] Cool—wrote a carefully worded letter to the commandant. They acknowledged the commandant's loyal and proper behavior and expressed the hope that when the undersigned returned to their homelands, they would find the opportunity to bring this to public attention in their lands. The commandant's barber delivered the letter. And it worked: Pister regarded it as a document that would provide security for himself and his family. "In an emergency a period of time can elapse between an order and its execution," he said.

Naturally neither side could openly call things by their real names. Pister hesitated; that was the main thing. One could hear the thunder of cannons; American planes swooped over the land—gaining time was everything. Had anyone known that the liberation would take another eight days, the delay tactics could never have been kept up. Furthermore, the commandant never took an unambiguous position in favor of the prisoners but on the contrary leaned toward the side of the SS leadership, indeed increasingly so.

The decisive showdown came on April 5. Days earlier SS officers had destroyed the most important papers. SS Major Dr. Schuler returned once more to camp and informed his prisoner secretary [Eugen Kogon] that an order had gone out from the Gestapo in Weimar—he knew this from Dr. Schiedlausky—to kill forty-six political prisoners immediately, before the camp was evacuated. Parallel orders to Ohrdruf! Schuler knew only four names: the kapo of the infirmary and his deputy, the kapo of Block 46, and the above-mentioned secretary of Schuler in Block 50. The warning was of incalculable value because it provided almost eight hours of lead time.

In no time the entire apparatus of the internal camp leadership was put on alarm. A resolution was adopted to take the challenge seriously, to refuse the handing over of the forty-six men, even if it should lead to open conflict. But who were the forty-six outside of those already mentioned? In the evening the list came from the roll call officer to the camp records office. The prisoners were to report "to the gate" the next morning [Chapter Ten, §147]. The composition of the list was rather uneven; it did not correspond in every case with the people's actual importance. Important names were missing; others were of no account. It was a true Gestapo measure, clearly based on one of the denunciations known within camp.

Months earlier a certain Duda, who had gone over to Dirlewanger, had "ratted." Now it was obvious that he had given out all the names that *he* thought were important, some rightly, others wrongly. The camp doctor, Dr. Schiedlausky, had probably expanded the list. Two days earlier he had been seen handing over a handwritten letter to the head of the Weimar Gestapo just as the latter was leaving camp. For the rest, it went back to information from Schuler. That hardly a single functionary of the actual illegal camp leadership stood on the list showed what good conspiratorial work had been accomplished.

That same night all those threatened except for the French manufacturer [Pierre] Bloch (no one knew how he had come to be on the list) managed to "submerge" in secure hiding places.[52] Except for Bloch, no one appeared at the gate the next morning following roll call. Bloch was sent away again after a while, apparently out of tactical considerations, in order to allay the fears of his fellow victims. After this second refusal of the camp to follow SS orders, the commandant called the senior camp inmate and demanded that he locate the missing men using the camp police. The senior camp inmate thereupon "searched" for eight hours, naturally without finding a single one of the submerged men.

Now the danger of a general roll call existed. The internal leadership decided not to appear for that either if it were ordered. A concentration camp without roll call! With that the SS would lose its most important instrument of control. From then on, no one went to the gate when any sort of group or a "prominent" individual of the camp was called and was presumed to be in danger. It was an open declaration of war. When night fell, the SS dared enter the camp only heavily armed. They saw that the politicals were determined to fight.

The responsible leaders in camp were absolutely clear about the prospects of success in an armed confrontation between the SS and the prisoners. The battle would surely end, after at most a few hours, to the disadvantage of the camp. But we counted on the arrival of the liberating troops, who were expected almost

---

52. D'Harcourt described Pierre Bloch as a French aircraft manufacturer; *The Real Enemy,* 173.

hourly. To avoid the danger of a last-minute evacuation, it was decided to smuggle a representative out of the camp who would reach the Allied lines and at the same time send a letter to the commandant of Buchenwald concentration camp.[53] Forty paratroopers in civilian dress had been dropped on both sides of the autobahn the previous night, the police radio had reported, without having been caught. (The well-functioning information service of the camp had passed the report on.)

A letter purporting to come from one of these paratroopers was composed:[54]

TO THE COMMANDANT!

Transports are leaving Buchenwald. They are death transports—like those from Ohrdruf!

The horrible tragedy of Ohrdruf must not be repeated. We have seen for ourselves the victims of the guard troops and the frenzied population.

Woe to those responsible, woe to Thuringia if it is repeated! We understand that you—like the entire land—are in a dilemma that you believe you can overcome by sending thousands away. It must cease! Stop immediately!

Our tank commanders are on their way to settle your account. You still have a chance!

> **James McLeod,** *Major*
> *War Office, London*

On April 6 more than 3,000 Jews had left Buchenwald on foot. The camp representative could escape by only one route at this point. It had to be through Block 50 and Dr. Schuler because, except on transports, no one else left the camp. His secretary [Kogon] emerged from his hiding place, although SS patrols searched the camp. He presented himself to Dr. Schuler, who through Sergeant Feld, the courier previously mentioned in this report, agreed to the daring enterprise. (The agreement alone represented unprecedented boldness.) On the next day, April 8, a truck from the Weimar police was to be sent to pick up valuable instruments and vaccines for the battle group of SS Colonel Schmidt. The representative was to hide in one of these crates and be brought into Schuler's house in Weimar.

On April 7 the commandant had ordered 14,000 men to be transported out of Buchenwald. After constant delays and difficulties, 1,500 were turned over to the SS. When 200 heavily armed SS men entered the camp with machine guns, a further 4,500 men were put at their disposal in order to make the impending struggle in the camp easier. One of the greatest problems was the food supply; another was the large number of people in the camp—professional criminals, blacks [antisocials], and others—who might attack the combatants from behind or otherwise

---

53. It was Kogon himself who was smuggled out of camp, although in this report he seems too modest to claim credit for it. See *SSS,* 360; *TPH,* 285. Burney also described the event using the fictionalized name of Emil Kalman, his pseudonym for Kogon throughout the book; *Dungeon Democracy,* 132–133. See also d' Harcourt, *The Real Enemy,* 178.

54. Letter reprinted in *SSS,* 359; *TPH,* 284.

hinder them. There was no other way. The two transports left, destination unknown.

On the morning of April 8, after a lengthy air raid alarm, the entire camp was summoned for the move out at 12:00 noon. The truck from Weimar had not yet arrived. It finally came in about 12:45 with four unsuspecting SS men. Under Feld's supervision the loading of the crates went smoothly. Four hours later the [McLeod] letter was delivered to the commandant in Weimar. It, too, worked.[55] Pister wavered still more.

On April 9 an additional 4,880 comrades and on the morning of April 10 9,280, mostly from the Little Camp, had either voluntarily reported for transport or were brutally assembled and taken away. After April 10 the commandant could no longer avoid forceful, drastic measures. SS General and General of the Waffen SS Prince Waldeck-Pyrmont came to Buchenwald in order, as he expressed it, "to make Pister toe the line."

Up to then the commandant had played a double game. He had pursued it in accordance with his position, acting ruthlessly only in partial actions, without issuing any general commands to the camp to carry out SS orders. Now when Waldeck himself finally intervened, it was already too late, for by April 11 the final decision was made.

The action against the remainder of the Jews and the forty-six political prisoners had in the meantime foundered in the general confusion. Only during the evacuees' march out could the remaining forty-five men have been found at the gate and shot—if they had appeared at all. But they were determined to remain along with the sick and the functionaries, in any case not to leave the camp. They would protect themselves in secure underground hiding places if at the end the camp was destroyed. (Waldeck had actually expressed the intention of blowing up the remainder of the camp, including the sick and the prisoner doctors, as had been done in Auschwitz.[56])

At midday on Wednesday, April 11, there were still 21,000 prisoners in camp. Provisions for effective armed action were made. But the SS took no action. Around 10:30 the first deputy commandant declared to the senior camp inmate that the camp would surrender. This declaration possessed at least some value, yet it was already known that the SS had ordered dive bombers from the nearby air-

---

55. Apparently the letter did have some effect. A copy was found among the papers of Himmler's adjutant, SS Colonel Rudolf Brandt. The text reproduced there varies slightly from this one. It refers to the crimes of Koch and says that much has improved under Pister. NA, RG 331, SHAEF, G-1, 000.5-12, "War Crimes," Letter to A.C. of S., G-2 SHAEF from HQ, 21 Army Group, June 1945.

56. It cannot be determined if an order to destroy the camp was given. An Allied intelligence report, conveyed via the Swiss government, stated that a Swiss professor visiting Buchenwald had heard "that just before the arrival of the Allied troops a German called Schmidt had telephoned to the camp from Weimar ordering that all remaining prisoners be finished off," telegram from Berne to the Foreign Office in London, dated 28 April 1945; NA, RG 331, SHAEF, G-1, 254 PW Camps. See also §146 of Chapter Ten for the report of a phone call after the departure of the SS.

field Nohra to destroy the camp. Accordingly, all forces in camp remained in a state of full alarm. When about an hour and a half later it was announced that all members of the SS were to report immediately to their stations outside the camp, expectations of a crisis rose to their highest level. Shortly afterward, however, the SS began to withdraw.

The die had been cast. The sentries at the guard towers had stayed behind, but as the sound of battle grew ever closer, they retreated into the adjoining woods shortly before 3:00 P.M. Then the comrades of the camp police, who had taken cover with their arms, immediately cut through the barbed wire, occupied the towers themselves, took the gate and the camp entrance, and raised the white flag over the first tower. Thus the first American tanks that rolled in from the northwest found a liberated Buchenwald. A relief action out of Weimar was no longer likely; Weimar was taken by the Americans that same evening.

The jubilation of the 21,000 rescued men was tremendous. The organizational system the Communist party had prepared for the takeover of the camp was immediately put into effect. It consisted of an international camp committee and separate committees for each of the individual nations. These groups cooperated with the arriving American military authorities in order to restore their freedom at last. On April 12, 1945, they appeared at roll call for the first time no longer as slaves of the SS but voluntarily and finally as human beings! Buchenwald concentration camp had ceased to exist after eight years of the bloody enslavement of hundreds of thousands. It was temporarily converted into the Displaced Persons Center in which all those remained who—unlike many Frenchmen and members of other Western nations—were unable to return to their homes immediately.

Today the flags of the United Nations fly over the former concentration camp. They are the symbols of victory over the crushed Nazi dictatorship and its barbaric places of terror—the camps, of which Buchenwald was only one among numerous examples.

XIV   Afterword

This report was composed on the grounds of information provided by experienced camp inmates of all the nationalities represented in Buchenwald. The national committees submitted their own reports.

The arrangement and text of the report are not based on the individual reports, which are included in the appendices [Part Two]. Those arose independently from the main report; they serve the purpose of supporting it with facts and experiences, as well as making it more concrete. The individual reports of the appendices have been left as they were given in order to preserve their originality. Because their authors at times saw things from their own perspective, were unaware of some of the complicated relationships, or were unable to see the whole picture, it was unavoidable that here and there some contradictions arose between the main report and the appendices. In such cases the official report is the sole definitive source, as it has been checked in every detail and is reliable.

Some of those who gave information appeared especially qualified on the basis of their positions and significance in the camp; the following should be named:[57]

DR. EUGEN KOGON	Vienna, author, first medical secretary in Block 50
DR. WERNER HILPERT	Leipzig, leader of the former Saxon Center party, member of the International Committee
FERDINAND RÖMHILD	Frankfurt a. M., author, first medical secretary of the prisoner hospital

The three named above stood in constant friendly contact with leading men of the foreign groups: Wing Commander [Forest] Yeo-Thomas, London; Captain Southgate, London; Captain [Christopher] Burney, Edinburgh; Under Secretary of State [André] Marie, Rouen; M. Julien Cain, director of the Bibliothèque Nationale, Paris; Professor A[lfred] Balachowsky, Pasteur Institute, Paris; M. Maurice Suard, member of the medical faculty, University of Angers; Lieutenant Stephane Hessel, War Ministry, Paris; Jan Robert, Amsterdam, legal adviser of the Netherlands Sports Society; Professor Dr. Marius B. Telders, University of Leyden, leader of the Dutch Liberal party; Lieutenant Pieter Cool, War Ministry, The Hague; Dr. Miroslav Klinger, Prague, former leader of the Czech Sokol Society; the attorney Dr. Polansky, Prague; Dr. Marian Ciepielowski, Kraków, physician; and many others.

HEINZ BAUMEISTER	Dortmund, longtime executive member of the camp records office, Buchenwald, second secretary of Block 50
FRANZ HACKEL	Prague, author
WALTER BARTEL	Berlin, chairman of the International Camp Committee
HANS EIDEN	senior camp inmate
ERNST BUSSE	Solingen, former Reichstag deputy, kapo of the prisoner hospital
OTTO KIPP	Dresden, deputy kapo of the prisoner hospital
BAPTIST FEILEN	Aachen, kapo of the laundry, member of the illegal internal camp administration
WALTER WOLF	director of the camp information bureau
ERNST THAPE	leader of the German Committee
OTTO HORN	Vienna, leader of the Austrian Committee
STEFAN HEYMANN	editor, Mannheim, member of the camp information bureau

---

57. The German manuscript includes handwritten notes on party affiliation—Kogon: "Nonpartisan"; Römhild and Hackel: "Nonpartisan Socialist"; Baumeister and Thape, "Social Democrat"; Bartel, Busse, Feilen, Heymann, Horn, Kipp, Wolff: "Communist."

HERBERT FROEBESS	Fulda and Brazil, Franciscan monk, preparer of secret plans for the commandant's office at Buchenwald
[NIKOLAI] KALTSHIN	Russian prisoner of war, officer, member of the Russian Committee
BORIS DANILENKO	Ukrainian Komsomol leader, member of the Russian Committee

Weimar-Buchenwald, May 10, 1945
Det. "B" 4th MRB Co.   (signed)
PWD SHAEF   **ALBERT G. ROSENBERG**
                                                         2nd Lt. Inf.
                                                         C.O. Det. "B" 4th MRB Co.
                                                         PWD SHAEF

Individual Reports

Chapter One
Statistics and General Information

1. Total Number of All Admissions.   The following table shows the total number of all prisoners who came to Buchenwald as new admissions. Death tolls contain only those registered in the hospital as deaths; not included are the numbers of murdered Russian prisoners of war, executed prisoners, and those prisoners sent on death transports. Also missing is the number of victims who died or were beaten to death on the way to and from Weimar during transports.

	Admissions	*Deaths*
1937	2,912	48
1938	20,122	771
1939	9,553	1,235
1940	2,525	1,772
1941	5,890	1,522
1942	14,111	2,898
1943	42,177	3,516
1944	97,867	8,644
1945 (3 months)	43,823	13,056
TOTAL	238,980	33,462

Buchenwald had its highest number of prisoners on October 6, 1944, with a total of 89,134.

2. Nations Represented in the Camp.

Germans	Austrians	French
Spanish	Italians	Swiss
Czechs	Yugoslavs	Croats
Albanians	Greeks	Bulgarians
Romanians	Poles	Russians
Belgians	Dutch	Luxemburgers
Latvians	Lithuanians	Estonians
Danes	Norwegians	English

Americans	Mexicans	Brazilians
Chinese	Egyptians	Canadians
Members of various African nations		

3. War Events and Transports.   It is extraordinarily interesting to link the transports that arrived during wartime to the events of the war. The type and nation of origin of the transports give a clear picture of the constantly changing difficulties Nazi Germany had to struggle with during the war. At the same time the transports reflect the progress of the war. The first expressly identified war transports arrived in Buchenwald shortly after the declaration of war. They were Reich Germans, primarily members of the former parties of the Left who were designated as "militarily unworthy." The Nazis feared antiwar propaganda from their own people and tried to lock up those they suspected might present such a threat.

The same was true for the Protectorate of Bohemia and Moravia, where antiwar propaganda of course started up from day one. Czech hostages and Czech Jews were thus sent to Buchenwald immediately after the war began. Among the hostages were many government officials whom the Nazis apparently did not trust to comply with war measures.

Finally, all Jews who had emigrated from Poland to Germany were arrested and brought to Buchenwald and other camps. The war against Poland offered a useful pretext for a new action against the Jews.

After the occupation of Poland, the first Polish prisoners were brought here. A total of 4,800 Poles were dragged into the camp, among them the so-called snipers, a group of 123 residents of Bromberg [Bydgoszcz]. Because the year 1940 was marked by great military successes for the Nazis, they did not concern themselves much with actions against possible opponents of the war. That summer only a transport of Dutch hostages was brought to the camp; it was made up in part of high state officials who were released again relatively soon, that is, transferred to a Dutch camp.

In 1941 there were only two large actions linked to the war. In February 1941 a general strike against the Nazis took place in Rotterdam. In connection with that, 750 Dutch Jewish workers were brought to Buchenwald. After the outbreak of war against the Soviet Union, the first Russian prisoners of war were interned in the concentration camp, in violation of all international agreements.

After the occupation of large parts of the Soviet Union, the Nazis began to deport many civilian workers to Germany. In 1942 the first such transport of civilian workers arrived in Buchenwald. It contained mostly those foreigners who had either practiced industrial sabotage (totally harmless, of course) or had attempted to escape. Many Poles who had had [sexual] relationships with German women were also brought into the camp.

In addition a special action was carried out in 1942. As is well known, from the first day of their attack on the Soviet Union, the Nazis attempted to undermine that state from the inside. To that end they recruited men from the prisoner of war camps who were anti-Soviet and whom they hoped to use as their own tools.

It was mainly a question of members of the former ruling classes, officers, owners of large estates, intellectuals—notably absent were ethnic Russians, but there were Georgians, Tartars, Ukrainians, etc. These Russian White Guards were prepared for their tasks and trained militarily at Buchenwald. They remained in the camp about nine months.

With the fall of Stalingrad in 1943, the problem of foreign workers became increasingly urgent. Under the direction of [Gauleiter Fritz] Sauckel, millions of foreign workers were forcibly sent to Germany. Of course these people used every opportunity to commit sabotage or escape to their homelands. Therefore, from this point on an unceasing stream of foreign workers arrived in camp. During the retreat from Stalingrad, the Germans took with them as many Russians capable of working as possible. But because they were mostly "unreliable" elements, they were put directly into the camp as prisoners, assigned to war production. In that year 5,394 Russians came directly to Buchenwald from Russian cities.

At the same time the great actions began in France, where after the fall of Stalingrad, the Maquis movement took on ever larger dimensions. Under the poetic names "Ocean Foam" and "Spring Wind," thousands of French workers were forcibly deported here. In this year, and in the early months of 1944, a total of 21,851 prisoners were brought to Buchenwald from France.

In addition several thousand Belgians and Dutch were deported to Buchenwald for the same reasons. Their exact number is difficult to determine because they did not come here in closed transports but mostly in so-called daily admissions. (There were two exceptions, the "Night and Fog" transports.)

In 1944 Nazi rule fell apart everywhere. It was all the more criminal to continue to deport these victims of Nazi barbarism from all parts of Europe. But the German arms industry needed cheap workers and could find them best through the SS. Therefore strong men were transported to Buchenwald from every direction, soon to end up as starved wrecks in the crematorium. The first transports were Jewish transports. Because there was no longer any arms industry to be supplied in eastern camps and because the Nazis preferred to squeeze every last drop of blood from Jewish workers through work rather than gassing them, Polish and Hungarian Jews no longer went to Auschwitz but to Buchenwald. They amounted to a total of 5,745 Polish Jews and 6,115 Hungarian Jews. After the Warsaw uprising 4,560 Poles were brought to Buchenwald.

After July 20, 1944 [the plot against Hitler], began the "Iron Bars" [*Gitter*] action, in which former functionaries of anti-Nazi parties were arrested and brought into the camp. There were a total of about 750, the majority of whom were released again after a short time mainly because of complaints from the arms industry.

The anti-Nazi student movement in Oslo led to the deportation of 349 Norwegian students to Buchenwald. In mid-March 1945 they were sent to Neuengamme camp near Hamburg. And when unrest developed in Denmark, as is well known, the entire Danish police force was replaced by the SS; 1,953 Danish policemen were brought to Buchenwald as a result of this action. The last of them were released just a few days before the liberation of the camp.

In all these actions it was a question of arrests in firmly held territories that were to be cleansed of Nazi opponents. At the beginning of 1945, the first transports of a new character began—evacuation transports from camps that were soon to be freed by Allied troops (in this case Russian troops). Tens of thousands came in open freight cars or on foot, staggering into camp half-starved, half-frozen, and almost naked. In three months more people were brought to Buchenwald from the evacuated camps than in all of 1943. That was the end! Anyone who saw these figures knew for certain that the bloody rule of the SS could only last a short time longer.

STEFAN HEYMANN, Mannheim

2. THE DEAD OF BUCHENWALD

1. Dead.　In this number are included all those who died in camp, were beaten to death, or were shot from October 1, 1937, to April 10, 1945, in addition to the external work details (with the exception of women)......................................34,566

Those who died in January 1945:	2,039
February 1945:	5,661
March 1945:	5,588
April 1–10, 1945:	913

2. Liquidations.　Number of Russian prisoners of war murdered in the horse stable by a shot through the base of the skull estimated at 7,200

Estimated number of executions based on the clothing of murder victims received in the Personal Property Room..1,100

Precise figures are available only from the end of March 1944; before that there was no opportunity to gather information.

3. Liquidation Transports.

Gas transport to Sonneberg, July 1940... 100
Gas transport of Jews to Bernburg, [February] 1942 500
Gas transport of Jews to Bernburg, [March] 1942........................... 200
Transport of Dutch Jews to Mauthausen, 1941..............................341
Various transports to Auschwitz in the year 1943 1,180
Transport of children to Auschwitz, 1943.......................................200
Transport of Jews to Auschwitz, 1944.. 2,101
Deaths in Dora, disguised as liquidation transport to Auschwitz 3,000
Transports to Bergen-Belsen, 1944 3,438

11,060

[TOTAL DEATH TOLL]　　53,926

This number must be regarded as the minimum number of deaths brought about by Nazi barbarism in Buchenwald. Not included in these numbers are the many hundreds who froze or starved to death on transports to and from Buchenwald. Not included in these numbers are the numbers of dead from transports to liquidation camps that did not leave Buchenwald solely as liquidation transports. That, too, would amount to several hundred victims. It is therefore certainly still too conservative to set the number of those who died or were murdered under the immediate influence of Buchenwald at 55,000 victims.[1]

3. STATISTICAL OVERVIEW OF THE DEVELOPMENT OF BUCHENWALD

| | | Departures | | | | Camp Pop. |
	Admissions	Rel.	Transf.	Deaths	Total	at Month's End
July 1937	930				1	929
August	1,414			8	48	2,295
September	180			7	55	2,420
October	109			2	60	2,469
November	133			9	75	2,527
December	146			22	112	2,561
TOTAL 1937	2,912			48	351	
January 1938	139				67	2,633
February	140				45	2,728
March	138				60	2,806
April	236				42	3,000
May	1,785				54	4,731
June	3,103				111	7,723
July	463				258	7,928
August	348				485	7,791
September	3,059				379	10,471
October	428				711	10,188
November	10,098				2,181	18,105
December	185				7,262	11,028
TOTAL 1938	20,122			771	11,655	
January 1939	184				1,727	9,485
February	113				949	8,649
March	45				30	8,664
April	13				2,314	6,363

---

1. Leni Yahil estimates the actual number of deaths in Buchenwald at 70,000, or 30 percent of the total of all prisoners admitted there. She includes in this number the figures given here, plus the number of prisoners evacuated in the week before liberation in April 1945. Leni Yahil, *The Holocaust: The Fate of European Jewry, 1932–1945* (New York: Oxford University Press, 1990), 536.

	Admissions	Rel.	Transf.	Deaths	Total	Camp Pop. at Month's End
May	20				713	5,670
June	103				250	5,523
July	166				297	5,392
August	155				165	5,382
September	3,334				62	8,634
October	5,373				1,232	12,755
November	50				448	12,377
December	17				587	11,807
TOTAL 1939	9,553			1,235	8,774	
January 1940	24				875	10,936
February	21				654	10,323
March	14				1,518	8,819
April	67				900	7,986
May	19				372	7,633
June	26				321	7,338
July	250				318	7,270
August	1,168				239	8,199
September	52				144	8,107
October	196				502	7,801
November	96				286	7,611
December	592				763	7,440
TOTAL 1940	2,525			1,772	6,892	
January 1941	50				128	7,362
February	452				217	7,597
March	236				513	7,320
April	505				336	7,489
May	288				992	6,785
June	231				209	6,807
July	2,695				920	8,582
August	396				496	8,482
September	251				363	8,370
October	251				468	8,153
November	277				520	7,910
December	258				257	7,911
TOTAL 1941	5,890			1,522	5,419	
January 1942	554				479	7,986
February	480				349	8,117
March	2,843				2,154	8,806
April	521				673	8,654
May	452				1,505	7,601
June	1,019				620	8,000
July	1,996				1,147	8,849
August	1,715				678	9,886
September	1,709				1,520	10,075
October	984				2,228	8,831
November	794				533	9,092
December	1,044				619	9,517
TOTAL 1942	14,111			2,898	12,505	
January 1943	2,500			111	742	11,275

| | | Departures | | | Camp Pop. |
	Admissions	Rel.	Transf.	Deaths	Total	at Month's End
February	1,291	94	377	175	646	11,920
March	2,474	40	1,582	311	1,933	12,461
April	2,773	1,102	299	507	1,908	13,326
May	2,339	38	807	379	1,224	14,441
June	1,858	122	348	211	681	15,618
July	1,727	39	1,317	191	1,547	15,796
August	4,537	57	517	118	692	19,641
September	5,444	41	233	123	397	24,688
October	9,048	41	209	109	359	33,377
November	4,454	27	2,378	314	2,719	35,112
December	3,734	35	525	967	1,527	37,319
TOTAL 1943	42,177	1,636	8,592	3,516	14,375	
January 1944	8,017	49	1,454	1,000	2,503	42,833
February	1,979	44	2,648	880	3,572	41,240
March	5,065	96	1,527	1,311	2,934	43,371
April	4,788	120	1,649	560	2,329	45,830
May	9,655	133	675	390	1,198	54,287
June	9,986	464	2,193	460	3,117	61,156
July	7,398	311	1,287	347	1,945	66,609
August	17,170	217	429	742	1,388	82,391
September	4,221	1,139	471	497	2,107	84,505
October	6,728	981	34,047	732	35,760	55,473
November	10,305	698	5,207	612	6,517	59,261
December	12,555	2,076	5,579	1,113	8,768	63,048
TOTAL 1944	97,867	6,328	59,166	8,644	72,138	
January 1945	24,197	190	4,756	2,002	6,948	80,297
February	13,066	257	1,351	5,523	7,131	86,232
March	6,560	488	6,337	5,531	12,356	80,436
TOTAL 1945	43,823	935	12,444	13,056	26,435	
GRAND TOTAL, 1937 to March 31, 1945	238,980			33,462	158,544	

4. SIZE AND LAYOUT OF BUCHENWALD: ITS WATER SUPPLY AND SEWAGE FACILITIES

THE ETTERSBERG is one of the most unfavorable places possible for human settlement. It belongs to the middle German border mountains and has the typical climatic disadvantages: relatively large amounts of rainfall. The highest point of the camp is 1,568 feet above sea level, the lowest 1,230 feet above sea level. This altitude means frequently occurring and abrupt temperature fluctuations.

Originally, barracks were planned for the Death's-Head units, in addition to housing for approximately 5,000 prisoners. At the time of liberation, the entire camp (including headquarters) covered 371 acres. There were 99 acres surrounded by the electrically charged barbed wire fence; the territory of the German Armaments Works encompassed 11 acres, roll call square was 3.7 acres; the Gustloff Works covered an equal area. The entire area inside the sentry line comprised 0.75 square miles; the electrified barbed wire fence was 2.2 miles long.

From the beginning, water supply and sewage removal posed special difficulties. The SS managed to improvise for a year before it actually began to set about solving the problems. Because no usable water was available in the immediate vicinity of the mountain, the water had to be brought from the variegated sandstone area southeast of Bad Berka, the so-called Tannroda saddle.[2] The pipeline was about 12 miles long, but not wide enough (10 inches in diameter). Near Tonndorf two well-pumping works (to a depth of 656 feet) were constructed. The well water was piped over the pipeline, through a pumping relay station erected near Daasdorf to raise the water pressure, and up to a water tower in the Buchenwald headquarters. This facility was not ready for operation until the end of 1942. But because of the construction of the Gustloff Works and the expansion of the camp, the supply had in the meantime become inadequate. Two additional pumping works with the necessary pumping relay stations were to have been added to the network. But the expansion has not yet been completed to this day.

A conservative estimate of the total capital invested in the water supply would be 3.5 million marks. Without counting the backup generators, approximately 400 horsepower is needed to power the facility in its present dimensions. After the expansion an estimated 800 horsepower would be needed. The amount supplied by continuous operation of the facility is 4,444 to 6,535 cubic yards per day. The total length [of pipe] amounts to about 31 miles.

Removal of sewage proved to be equally difficult. The principal deficiency was above all the lack of an efficient main drainage canal. The first makeshift solution, which lasted about a year, took the form of latrine trenches. In the meantime a 2.8-mile-long sewage pipeline with a diameter of 7.8 inches was built to the Vippach, a tributary of the Unstrut. Sewage was routed to a reservoir with a capacity of 1,308 cubic yards, which was spread over 25 acres of swampy land near the village of Berlstedt [a few miles north of Buchenwald]. The beneficiaries were united in a soil cooperative. After epidemics arose in camp, it became necessary to build a full-scale sewage treatment plant. It was begun in 1939 but was not ready for operation until June 1941. It was designed for a daily capacity of 3,924 cubic yards, corresponding to a total population of 20,000 in the camp and military base. In the final months, however, the actual head count was 50,000. An expansion was urgently needed but was no longer even considered.

Sewage and rainwater were carried off in separate pipelines. The total length of the pipelines in the drainage network comprised about 37 miles; the building costs ran to an estimated 5 million marks.

---

2. An area about 10 miles southwest of Weimar.

Planning and construction of these facilities was in general contracted out to private firms. The blueprints these firms supplied, however, were usually so sketchy and incomplete that the prisoners themselves almost always had to make entirely new ones. Although we had only a few skilled personnel, we had to undertake this because the life and health of thousands depended on this work. Technical shortcomings were therefore unavoidable; frequent interruptions in service can be traced back to them. Nevertheless, these building projects were the result of mutual effort accomplished under inhumane conditions.

CONSTRUCTION OFFICE, Buchenwald Concentration Camp

5. The Political Department

THE POLITICAL DEPARTMENT was concerned with the precise registration and documentation of all prisoners living in camp, those who died in camp, those who were transferred out of camp, those who were released, and those who were sent on transports. Of primary importance was the correct registration of the prisoner at the time of his delivery into camp. For every prisoner a so-called personnel form was filled out. In addition to personal data and information on military service, the form included a personal description, the referring government agency, any previous punishments, and the prisoner's category. The prisoner had to sign the form himself to verify the accuracy of the information—or else reckon with severe punishment. Until June 1942 registration was carried out only by SS members in the political department. After the German occupation of various European lands, the SS used the appropriate interpreters to communicate with the non-German prisoners being admitted.

When after June 1942 deliveries began to climb and the sergeants were no longer able to complete the work promptly, prisoners were allowed to work at registration. Identification cards that were issued along with the personnel forms were provided with a photo of the prisoner. Only after the aerial bombardment on Buchenwald on August 24, 1944, was the photographing of prisoners dispensed with, as there was a great shortage of materials and the number of new arrivals had increased tremendously. To the personnel forms were later added the so-called documents (for example, order of arrest, protective custody order containing the reasons for such custody, the signed interrogation by the Gestapo, and other documents). Together these formed what were called the prisoner files.

In addition, birth and marriage certificates were requested from either registrars' offices or parish offices to confirm the information the prisoners gave at the time of registration. The camp administration thus had a clear picture of each prisoner's past. Completed prisoner files were presented to the camp commandant; at other times they were kept in steel cases in the office of the political department, arranged alphabetically and always at his disposal. From the prisoner personnel cards the so-called card catalog was created, which, likewise alphabet-ized, made it possible to determine the name of a prisoner and his personal data in an instant. For archival purposes the personal documentation of the prisoners who died or were released was kept separately in the so-called documents room.

The old wooden barracks of the political department had the following arrangement: four interrogation rooms, one large office room, an office for the director of the political department, and a documents room. After prisoners be-came auxiliary workers in the political department, two of the interrogation rooms were placed at their disposal.

In the last half year of the camp's existence, the death division of the political department was heavily burdened with work, since the number of dead prisoners grew day by day. Death certificates were issued only for Reich Germans and citi-zens of the Protectorate of Bohemia and Moravia.

Those who were released made up only a tiny percentage of prisoners. Release followed after a telegraphed order was received from Berlin. The camp comman-dant could, however, postpone the release for days if he was not satisfied with the conduct or work effort of the prisoner concerned. After he had changed into civil-ian clothes, the released prisoner came to the political department to receive the so-called release certificate, on which appeared his personal data. He was also no-tified of the Gestapo office to which he had to report. If he had no funds, he re-ceived a coupon, redeemable in Weimar, for a ticket to his destination. Before his release he had to sign a statement that sharply warned him not to pass on any in-formation that he had obtained during his stay at Buchenwald concentration camp.

After the second half of 1943 there was an increase in escape attempts by pris-oners—not from the camp itself but from the various external work details, whose number had constantly risen with the development of the German war in-dustry and war needs. It did not take much effort to escape from an external work detail, but the prospects of remaining in freedom were very slight for an escaped prisoner.

A recaptured prisoner was locked into the cellblock immediately after being re-turned to the camp and was later interrogated by the political department. Many escaped prisoners were hanged in the basement of the crematorium as a result of the interrogation. In later times those who remained were assigned to the garden-ing detail and were supposed to perform the heaviest work. In the last half year, countless escaped prisoners were brought into the camp and interrogated. Among them were mostly Russians and Poles; very rarely did Czechs and Ger-mans escape. The political department was by this time scarcely able to perform all its duties, since escaped prisoners often changed their names and thus made the work all the more difficult.

The last director of the political department was the detective inspector SS Ser-geant Major Walter Serno, who loved to strike prisoners on the buttocks with a metal ruler now and then during interrogation. This treatment was almost exclu-sively reserved for Russians and Poles; Germans, Czechs, Dutch, and French were very seldom abused.

The SS men in the political department in the last months were:

Detective Inspector and SS Sergeant Major Walter Serno (director of the political department)
Detective Constable and SS Master Sergeant Noske (deputy director and head of interrogation)
SS Sergeant Franz Hennemann (office director of the political department and correspondence)
SS Technical Sergeant (former Wehrmacht member) Hebenseder (private matters)
SS Corporal Franz Heiling (releases)
SS Sergeant Kuss (correspondence)
SS Corporal Gebauer (mail)
SS Corporal Rottig (director of the death department)
SS Corporal Hans Wiech (death department)
SS Technical Sergeant Lemke (death department)
SS Technical Sergeant (former Wehrmacht member) Hepp (inquiries)
SS Technical Sergeant (former Wehrmacht member) Utz (escapees)
SS Private First Class Ewert (interrogation of escapees)
SS Sergeant Harwart
SS Sergeant Franz Hoffmann (registration)

In addition the following SS members were employed by the political department:

SS Second Lieutenant Danel (director)
SS Master Sergeant Pfaff (releases)
SS Master Sergeant Höhring (death department)
SS First Lieutenant Stolberg (office director)

Prisoners began to share in the work of the political department starting in June 1942. They were entrusted with clerical services (registration, taking of statements, typing, interpreting, pulling cards, labeling file folders, handling requests for birth and marriage certificates, and other things). They were supposed to lighten the workload of the SS members. At the beginning, the work detail was composed of a kapo and six prisoners. In the course of time, as thousands and thousands more prisoners arrived in camp, the number of prisoners employed in the political department increased, so by the end eighty-five worked there. After the aerial bombardment on August 24, 1944, when almost all records of the department burned, the entire card catalog had to be copied.

The work detail was divided into two day and night shifts that worked in the political department and the Personal Property Room. These prisoners always considered it their duty to make things easier for the other prisoners during their stay in the political department and to be as helpful as possible to them.

Up to 1944, visits to camp by members of the prisoners' families were rare. An SS man would accompany the visitor to the political department, where he had to show permission to visit from the Reich Security Main Office. Then the prisoner concerned was summoned and could speak with his visitor—only in the German language—for approximately an hour, usually under the supervision of the director of the political department. It was laughably apparent how politely the SS members treated civilians. Officials of the Gestapo seldom came to the political department. They almost always had their own interpreters with them, so little is known about the interrogations. During their interrogations blows and cries could often be heard.

Family members of various prisoners took steps at home to get their loved ones out of the camp. When the Gestapo office involved wanted to show interest, it demanded a so-called conduct report from the camp administration. The camp commandant had to say whether he was satisfied with the prisoner. In most cases the conduct report was unfavorable, that is, negative. Even with a favorable conduct report, the chances of release were small, for again and again the other agency showed a lack of goodwill.

Often attempts were made to recruit a prisoner as an informer for the Third Reich. Some of these attempts were successful, the prisoners becoming so-called confidential agents. After their release, they were supposed to put themselves at the disposal of the German secret service and inform on their incautious countrymen.

It is a fact that in camp countless persons disappeared without a trace. Their files were confiscated by the headquarters staff. There remained only their personnel cards, without any cause of death filled in, only the remarks "died on _____," "see _____ file," or "see headquarters." The files themselves could certainly tell us more. They unfortunately no longer exist because the SS consigned them to flames just before their flight. Only the card catalog was left behind. This can at least offer an overview of all the prisoners delivered into the camp.

JAN SOBOTTKA, Prague
Kapo of the political department

Chapter Two
Luxurious Living and Corruption of the SS

6. LIST OF SS MEMBERS

[A list of 355 names mentioned in the report is included in the original manuscript at this point. The list has been omitted from this edition.]

7. BARBER TO THE COMMANDANT

I WAS the regular barber to the commandant since almost the beginning of the camp, first with Koch, then with Pister. In this post I was always able to see and hear more than was possible for other prisoners. I always put my experience and knowledge at the disposal of the prisoners who participated in the antifascist struggle against the SS and thus helped prevent many a planned crime. I describe here some of my experiences during this long period of terror. I want to emphasize, however, that this represents only a small excerpt out of all that happened during my time in Buchenwald.

How Koch Was Bribed

Because Commandant Koch never seemed to be able to make ends meet, despite his high salary, he never rejected enormous bribes. Koch's main supplier was the criminal Meiners, who administered the prisoners' canteen and created shameful price markups—once, for example, prisoners were sold vegetable salad for 2.60 marks per pound though it had cost 80 pfennigs to purchase. Thus, he brought in 50,000 to 60,000 marks a month on the side, all of which ended up in Koch's pockets. The other gifts that Meiners distributed likewise amounted to many thousands of marks. So, for example, Frau Koch received from him a diamond ring that cost 8,000 marks. For deputy commandant Hackmann he bought a new car; he even donated the money for a villa on the Edersee near Bad Wildungen, though it was never built because of the objections of SS General Prince von Waldeck-Pyrmont. He also bought Koch a motorboat on the above-named lake

121

from the money he swindled out of prisoners. Meiners is unfortunately still free and today drives around Jena in an elegant automobile that he likewise bought with money stolen from the prisoners.

As can be seen from what has already been said, Koch was not popular, and everyone tried to find a way to trip him up. Once a truck full of lemons for SS members came to Buchenwald. Koch seized the entire shipment, kept most of it for himself, and gave only a few lemons to some of the higher-ranking officers. At that time the rumor spread that I had rubbed down Frau Koch's naked back with lemons, but this was not the case. Still, this example shows how "popular" the commandant was with his own men.

50,000 Bottles of Cognac for Göring

During the campaign in France, Göring had 50,000 bottles of the finest cognac—Hennessy—stolen. This gigantic booty he had stored in Weimar with Gauleiter Sauckel. About ten days before the advance of the American troops, this loot was picked up by military vehicles and driven off to an unknown location.

Bribery to Save Comrades

All SS men from the top to the bottom were corrupt through and through. In some cases we were able to make good use of that corruption to help our comrades in camp. When, for example, a comrade was to receive a caning, the commandant would tell us about it the day before. Then we would go to the deputy commandant at the time, Florstedt, bringing him a can of caviar or some other delicacy, after which the punishment was always canceled. Later Florstedt stood under our influence to the extent that the waiter of the officers' quarters could say to him, "You will receive no breakfast today until this or that punishment is canceled!" And he did so every time. It was the same with Staff Sergeant Jacobs of the Gustloff Works. This sadist beat the prisoners terribly but was not afraid to sponge a pack of cigarettes at least once a week from the prisoners' canteen. Since he did not stop the beatings, the comrade in the canteen simply refused to give him any more cigarettes. Jacobs promised to improve if he could receive cigarettes again, and he actually did so.

Conflict Among the SS Officers

There was constant conflict among the SS officers. In particular, Prince von Waldeck could not stand Commandant Koch, feelings that were reciprocated. Waldeck frequently came to Buchenwald, where he always became totally drunk. In a drunken state, he once took with him 30,000 cigarettes designated for the SS officers. When Koch found out about it, he raised a giant uproar and issued an order forbidding anything to be given out to an SS officer who came from outside the camp, regardless of who it was.

The Proper Pister

Under Koch a regime of true arbitrariness prevailed, whereas Pister attempted to organize the Nazi terror more correctly and bureaucratically. He was of course brutal and ruthless, but always within the framework of his orders—to which he adhered in a painstakingly exact manner. Toward the end of the Nazi regime at Buchenwald, Pister became basically cowardly, as at heart all Nazis were, and wavered in his measures. He tried to find a way to cover his rear in the hope that he could go over to the Americans together with the prisoners. A letter he received from prisoners who had been prominent personalities in freedom (a Belgian labor minister, a former French justice minister, a Dutch officer, and an English officer) confused Pister so much that he no longer offered any serious resistance to the delay tactics of the prisoner leadership.

Seventeen English Officers Hanged

In 1944 thirty-seven English and French officers were brought to Buchenwald to be killed here. When seventeen of them were ordered to the gate one day, it was clear that this was a death sentence. I spoke to the English comrades and showed them how they could attack their murderers at the gate and at least put up a fight for their lives. They answered me more or less as follows: "We have already given up our lives. If we attempt a mutiny now, there is the danger that the entire camp will suffer because of it, which is something we don't want. So we will not fight." When the comrades were led to the crematorium, they requested that they at least be shot like honorable soldiers. Despite that the Nazi beasts hanged them.

Starved to Death in a Crate

In spring 1938 a Gypsy made an escape attempt but was soon caught. As exemplary punishment, the sadist Koch thought up the following gruesome treatment: The Gypsy was placed in a wooden crate that had wire netting in the place of wood on one side. The poor victim had to sit in this crate in a bent-over position. In addition the crate was held together by long nails driven from the outside to the inside, so that with his slightest movement the nails dug deep into his flesh. In this cage the Gypsy was placed on display in roll call square for two days and three nights. His horrible cries no longer sounded human. Finally, on the morning of the third day, he was put out of his misery with a lethal injection.

Koch's Syphilis

During 1940 Koch was in Norway for a short time—but long enough to infect himself with syphilis there. Because he rightly did not trust the healing powers of the SS doctors, he had himself treated with Salvarsan by the prisoner orderly Walter Krämer. In order not to be known as a Salvarsan user, he had the medication ordered from the SS health supply depot in Berlin under the name of the prisoner

Rudi Hach. When Koch was healthy again and a blood test repeated several times showed his complete recovery, he gave a special gift of thanks to his savior Krämer. Afraid that Krämer might say something about this cure, Koch had Krämer and his comrade Peix, whom Koch feared as an accomplice, arrested and shot after a few days by the mass murderer Blank. As an excuse Koch cited political discussions the two had allegedly carried on in the infirmary.

Mass Murderers as Educators

One of the chief murderers of the Buchenwald SS was Sergeant Major [Wolfgang] Otto, by profession a teacher.[1] Otto was a participant in almost all executions; in particular he played a leading role in the murder of Russian prisoners of war. Precisely this mass murderer, who almost every day slaughtered several people, was hired by Koch as a teacher for the children of SS officers.

There is another experience I will never forget. The adjutant, SS Captain Schmidt, came home from an execution in which he himself had hanged nine prisoners in the crematorium.[2] In front of the door to his home stood his wife and children. Schmidt took his youngest child in his arms and played with him, even though the same hands that stroked the child had previously strangled nine men! And when the ropes in the crematorium were not quick enough on the job, the victims of the Nazi bandits were hanged on hooks and beaten to death.

Gypsy Woman Shot

At the end of December 1944, a young Gypsy woman was to be hanged. On the way to the place of execution, she threw herself on the ground and howled and wailed. The SS men could not bring her to her feet. Then deputy commandant Gust, who happened to be passing by, shot the young woman in the head with a bullet from his revolver.

"All Jews to Koch!"

Every morning when I came into the commandant's house, I immediately rushed into the office, because there were always some decrees or orders lying there that were important for us prisoners. I could stay there undisturbed for at most four

---

1. Otto was tried at the Buchenwald camp guards trial and sentenced to twenty years, but he was released in the amnesty program of the early 1950s. In 1986, however, a West German court in Düsseldorf again tried him on charges of participating in the execution of Ernst Thälmann at the Buchenwald crematorium. He was acquitted. NA, RG 338, case 000-50-9, box 426, "Review and Recommendations," 73–74, 94–95; *Der Spiegel* 20 (May 12, 1986) and 36 (September 5, 1986).

2. Schmidt was tried in the Buchenwald camp guards trial and sentenced to hanging. He was given a stay of execution in 1949 and after a series of appeals was apparently released. NA, RG 338, case 000-50-9, box 426, "Reviews and Recommendations," 81–83, 94–95.

to five minutes before I had to report to the commandant, who around this time sat in the bathroom. I followed this practice under both commandants. It would take too long here to list every important document. But I would like to mention one. One morning, shortly after commandant Koch was transferred to Lublin [Maidanek], instructions addressed to all camp commandants lay upon the desk of the new commandant, Pister, with the following text: "All Jews of Europe to Koch—Lublin. Himmler."

FRANZ EICHHORN, Weimar

8. MASSEUR TO THE SS

IN APRIL 1942 I was placed in the prisoner hospital at Buchenwald as a masseur. Although I was supposed to work only for the prisoners, the camp doctor, Dr. Hoven, brought me into the houses of SS officers, so that from then on I massaged almost only SS men. Hoven did this to ingratiate himself. I massaged almost all the higher-ranking SS officers.

I had my worst experiences with the adjutant, Captain Schmidt. For two long years I had to treat him every morning. Because he was drunk almost every day and the drinking bouts took place in his room, the work was highly unpleasant. In addition Schmidt pressured me to get eggs, butter, and milk for him, in Hoven's name, out of the hospital kitchen every day. One day the commandant saw this, and of course I told him truthfully what I was doing—or was forced to do. The adjutant received a stiff reprimand, and the camp doctor ordered me not to leave the hospital anymore. It was obvious that Schmidt had instructed the camp doctor to kill me. For when the adjutant came to the hospital after about six weeks, he was clearly astonished that I was still alive. But he immediately ordered me to massage him again.

Now he tried to draw me into all sorts of black market activities. I was to supply him with soap, jewelry, even food from Red Cross packages; of course I always declined. As the defeat of Nazi Germany became ever clearer, he tried to create a safety net for himself and asked whether he might be allowed to visit me in Holland after the war. But one day in February 1944, he said in a drunken state, "You should not imagine that any prisoner will come out of here alive if we are defeated. We have prepared everything so that the camp can be destroyed in a few hours."

I had another experience with SS Captain Dr. Morgen, who had come to Buchenwald as the investigating judge in the case of the previous commandant, Koch. Although he was not sick, he took a steam bath and got a massage every morning. The electrical heating box was broken, and one morning, despite my warnings, he played around with the hinges on the box and burned himself horribly. The box snapped shut and the ten heat lamps burned his skin. He accused me of intentionally abusing an SS officer. That would have meant an unconditional death sentence. Since Morgen was very unpopular with all the SS officers, who were afraid of him, nothing happened to me.

Despite this work, I was able to help my comrades quite a bit. Above all after abuse or punishment by beating, massage was often of great value. Especially in the difficult early years, many of the German orderlies collaborated with me.

JAN ROBERT, Amsterdam

9. CONVERSATIONS OF SS OFFICERS

AS A BARBER for SS officers, I had the opportunity to hear many an interesting conversation. When in December 1944 the German counteroffensive [Battle of the Bulge] began in the west, Deputy Commandant Schobert believed it would be possible to drive the English and Americans back into the sea. First Lieutenant Kampen shared that opinion; he worried only about the Russians. Deputy Commandant Gust reassured him with the words, "For them, the German fire department is enough."

When in December the topic of discussion in officers' circles was that there were no more shoes for the prisoners, Gust offered his opinion: "Wait until spring; then we will have won and will be able to supply ourselves with boots from abroad."

An "ass full," that is, twenty-five lashes with a cane, was a punishment prisoners usually received from the roll call officers. Once the roll call officer Werle asked his sidekick, Hofschulte, whether he wanted to give three prisoners twenty-five lashes each. Hofschulte answered, "But of course! I always like to do that!" Hofschulte alternated between a cane and a whip for the beatings.

Once fifteen prisoners were ordered to receive punishment. I was supposed to shave a roll call officer, and when I arrived, the punishment had already been performed on thirteen unfortunates. Hofschulte and another SS technical sergeant were clothed only in shirt and trousers, despite the cold, and were sweating heavily. "These dogs make hot work for us," Hofschulte said.

One day in November 1944, 400 Yugoslavian prisoners of war were brought into the camp. Since I am a Yugoslavian, the commandant asked me whether I knew if these men were strong. The camp needed strong men. Three days later these comrades were sent to the infamous camp at Ohrdruf.

In December 1944 I met two young German manufacturers at the adjutant's. One of them disappeared with the adjutant into his office while I shaved the other one. When the first manufacturer came out of the adjutant's office, he said to his companion, "I've made a good deal; now I'll get some prisoners for work."

ALOIS SARATCHEVIC, Jesenice

10. Luxurious Living at the Expense of Prisoners

I ARRIVED at Buchenwald concentration camp on August 25, 1938. After a temporary assignment in road construction, my next work detail was in the prisoners' kitchen. There I was under the command of Technical Sergeant Schmidt, Leipzig, who sold the prisoners' food supply wholesale on the black market. Then in November 1938 I became a waiter in the SS officers' quarters [*Führerheim*]. The officers' casino was under the command of SS First Lieutenant Jacobs, who diverted to SS Colonel Koch an estimated quarter of a million marks that he had obtained by overpricing goods in the prisoners' canteen.

In the SS officers' quarters, "comradeship" evenings were held at intervals of every two to four weeks. At every place setting there were six to eight wine glasses.

After the outbreak of war, cars went to France and Holland at regular intervals and picked up mainly alcoholic beverages. The trips were carried out by the director of the motor pool at the time, SS Master Sergeant Rieger. The best items went to Koch's house, and then the headquarters staff took its share. What was left over went to the canteens or the officers' casino. The specialist for this entire activity was SS Master Sergeant Michael. On the basis of his kinship with Koch, he decided on the life and death of prisoners in a whole variety of work details.

Koch established a restaurant in the officers' quarters that served the officers at Buchenwald. Dinner there cost these bandits 0.75 marks; obviously, the salad alone was often worth more than the cost of the entire meal. At Christmas large packages were given to the headquarters staff, the cost of which amounted to several hundred marks. During visits by high-ranking SS officers (generals), up to six "breakfasts" a day were regularly consumed. They often lasted until late at night. All these things were paid for by SS Captain Florstedt with money from prisoners. The prisoners of the officers' kitchen were harassed and threatened with pistols if they ever dared speak about things they had heard or seen in the officers' quarters.

Later I went to the prisoners' canteen. The head of the canteen was SS Technical Sergeant Schmidt. So the SS officers could pay less for goods purchased in the SS canteen, the prisoners' canteen had to be burdened all the more. Thus there were price markups of 100 to 300 percent. Through these and other manipulations, Technical Sergeant Schmidt had accumulated 60,000 to 70,000 marks. In the final weeks before the liberation of the concentration camp by the Americans, the SS canteen was the site of daily orgies. Participating in them were above all SS Major Schobert, Administrative Officer Barnewald, Sergeant Krone, Private First Class Besier, a millionaire from Wiesbaden, and Sergeant Berger.

Barnewald maintained a personal friendship with canteen administrator Schmidt and covered up every form of corruption. For his silver wedding anniversary in August 1944, Barnewald received eighteen tortes and an enormous quantity of tea biscuits. The ingredients for these delicious treats had been stolen out of the supplies in the prisoners' food warehouse. The intermediary in these black market activities was the administrator of the warehouse, SS Master Sergeant Pack of Leipzig. As a witness to all these things, I was placed on the list of forty-six prisoners who were supposed to be liquidated a few days before liberation.

CARL GÄRTIG, Kretzschen über Zeitz

11. Corruption in the SS

THE DEPUTY COMMANDANT, SS First Lieutenant Hackmann, once had to pay 186 marks for auto repairs. He summoned Wolff, the senior block inmate of the Jewish block at the time, and demanded this sum of money from him within an hour or else he would report him for violations of camp discipline. Of course Hackmann received the money. The incident occurred in summer 1939.

In winter 1939 a stove in Block 42 burned through. Deputy Commandant Rödl ordered each block to pay 50 marks toward the repair of this stove. At the same time, however, he informed the senior camp inmate that blocks that paid "only" the 50 marks would have to do punishment exercises the following Sunday. Of course most blocks paid sums up to 100 marks. The money disappeared into Rödl's bottomless pockets.

In summer 1942 SS Master Sergeant Pfaff bought 50 gallons of gas for his private car from the Hille company of Weimar. The Staupendahl company delivered it to Pfaff's private dwelling in Klein-Obringen. When the bill for the gas was presented at headquarters, of course no one knew anything about the delivery. To get headquarters to pay for the gas nevertheless, Pfaff persuaded SS Technical Sergeant Halter to write a false receipt for it. Halter did this and received as a "reward" three days of special leave.

In a bombing raid on Düsseldorf at the end of 1943, all the windows in the residence of SS General Weitzel were broken. For the repair of the window frames, the DAW of Buchenwald received especially valuable lumber. Instead of being turned into the window frames that had been ordered, the wood was used to make a gift for Koch: a luxurious smoking room. Since Koch already had a smoking room, he gave the new room to the police president of Weimar at the time, Hennicke. But since Hennicke, too, already had a smoking room, he passed the gift on to the man responsible for the food supplies for Weimar, the president of the Raiffeisen Society of Thuringia.

JOSEF SCHAPPE, Düsseldorf

12. Excuses for Collecting Money

To take money away from the Jews and rich Aryans the SS robbers invented the most grotesque pretexts. In winter 1939 a wolf in the large zoo of the megalomaniac commandant SS Colonel Koch had rubbed open a wound from a chain around its neck and had to be killed. The blame for this, of course, was laid upon the Jews. During a snowball fight among the Jews, a snowball had allegedly struck the wolf, after which the animal tried to tear itself loose from its chain. A collection was ordered for the purchase of a new wolf, raising a total of 5,000 marks. A bear once broke out of the bear pit that had been built entirely out of concrete. This created a threat to the entire population of the vicinity, and the bear had to be hunted down and shot. The "hunter," Deputy Commandant Rödl, had himself photographed proudly standing next to his victim. Of course the Jews had to pay for a "replacement bear"; over 8,000 marks were collected.

Other pretexts were used to collect larger or smaller amounts almost exclusively from Jews: a broken cart axle in the transportation detail, repainting the staircase in the Personal Property Room, replacements for flowers allegedly stolen from the gardening detail, replacement of an allegedly broken lamp shade in the SS lodgings, replacement of a freshly cemented slab on which footprints were found. These were some of the "reasons" the SS used to extort money.

The collections were at their greatest during the time that Jews could still emigrate. Some of them had all their available cash sent to the camp in order not to be totally without funds at their eventual release. One example out of this period stands for many: In March 1939 Rödl claimed that the Jews had torn towels and broken bowls. Each of the eight Jewish blocks had to raise 500 marks—a very nice extra income for these SS robbers!

GUSTAV HERZOG, Vienna

13. Nazi War Profiteers

The bloody beasts of the SS, who had the words "love of the fatherland" on their lips at every opportunity, meant this only for others. They themselves betrayed and swindled their fatherland in the most shameless manner.

This happened above all in the "normal" camp enterprises. The value of vital war raw materials the SS bandits used for their private consumption ran into the millions, not counting the tens of thousands of skilled workers who were deliberately withdrawn from the war industry. What the SS did to maintain its private life of luxury was sabotage on a grand scale. Not only were vital raw materials (iron, copper, brass, hardwoods, etc.) used for the elegant dwellings of SS murderers; there was also senseless waste and the hoarding of food supplies by SS men. Long punishments, in many cases even the death penalty, were levied against the rest of the population for every pound of hoarded butter, whereas the cellars and pantries of these criminals with swastikas were full of lard, sausage, hams, eggs, preserves, etc.—not to mention countless bottles of schnapps!

But in other ways, too, the SS bandits were war profiteers on a grand scale. Under SS control the so-called German Armament Works (DAW) was founded. Through good connections with the Armaments Office, this factory was able to receive enormous contracts that generated fantastic profits. This was because the prices were calculated normally, yet the factory's work force cost almost nothing. Moreover, some of the SS officers were personally involved in these large profits. Camp Commandant Pister, for example, was also a director of the DAW in Buchenwald, with the large salary and expense allowances that entailed.

And, finally, the slave trade of the SS was a profitable business for both sides— for the SS and the industrialists of the arms industry. The factory directors naturally knew very well that the work of the prisoners was unsatisfactory, that only poor-quality arms and munitions came from the hands of the prisoners. But these patriots were not concerned about that. The state paid them their high prices, and the SS delivered cheap slave labor to them. The extra profits were by no means to be dismissed. SS earnings from the slave trade are reflected in the camp administration's income from prisoners' "wages": between 1.5 and 2 million marks per month during 1944.

Special branches of production, for example, the manufacture of rocket weapons, were directly reserved for the SS. This was because it seemed that absolute secrecy could be guaranteed nowhere better than among prisoners who were not allowed to come out from behind barbed wire.

That is the true face of the SS, which called its "highest commandment loyalty." But in reality it was committed to dirty profits at the expense of its own country.

WILLI SEIFERT, Plauen

14. THE FALCONRY

FOR ENTERTAINMENT and diversion of the Nazi criminals, a falconry was built at the order of Reich SS leader Himmler. It was a group of turreted houses that held eagles, falcons, hawks, and other birds of prey, some of which were also used for hunting.

After the completion of the falconry, a standing work detail six to ten prisoners strong was employed to feed the birds and clean their cages. The wages for this strenuous work were injuries from the raptors' biting and clawing, which almost always led to blood poisoning; nor did the SS spare the prisoners any beatings on the job.

To the falconry belonged a series of other wild animal cages in which stags, does, wild pigs, a mouflon,[3] foxes, pheasants, peacocks, hens, rabbits, squirrels, and other animals were kept. Outside the falconry, in the so-called zoological gardens, were cages in which five monkeys and four bears were housed. Earlier there was even a rhinoceros there.

As late as 1944, when great hunger prevailed in the camp, the birds, bears, and apes received meat every day. Of course this came from the prisoners' kitchen and so was subtracted from prisoners' rations. The bears also received honey and marmalade, the monkeys mashed potatoes with milk, oatmeal, zwieback, white bread, etc. Such food had not appeared on the prisoners' tables for years. Even in times of the greatest shortages in camp, the falconry was maintained to its fullest extent, while the prisoners received only one-sixth of a loaf of bread a day and cooked rutabagas for lunch. The entire falconry was a completely unproductive enterprise, and its management could only be covered up by robbery and murder.

LEOPOLD REITTER, Brünn (Brno)

15. The Photography Department and Cinema

THE PHOTOGRAPHY DEPARTMENT was conceived and operated mainly for the private use of the SS; in addition, it had the official function of providing identification. Out of the smallest, most primitive beginnings, it was expanded into a modern department. Its work detail had up to thirteen men, who were thus removed from war production. During the bombardment of August 1944, the entire photography department went up in flames, unfortunately destroying many valuable pictures, for example, photos of suicides, accidents, executions of Poles in the villages, SS celebrations, etc.

Also under this work detail stood the establishment and operation of the camp cinema, the first cinema in a German concentration camp. Against the will of Administrative Officer Weichselsdörfer and with great difficulty, it was constructed as a separate building. The comrades of the camp electricians' detail and camp carpentry played outstanding roles in this effort, and the name of comrade Helmut Wagner must not be forgotten in the history of the Buchenwald cinema. Official tolerance of the camp cinema's operation was achieved only by making the matter as palatable as possible. With an admission of 30 pfennigs per head and

---

3. A mouflon is a big-horned wild sheep from Corsica or Sardinia.

a donation toward expenses of 35 pfennigs, the gross receipts were so high that it was profitable to permit the prisoners this pleasure. Even in the first six months, it was able to contribute 23,000 marks to the headquarters treasury—to be used for celebrations and drinking bouts. Even the later reduction of admission to 20 pfennigs still made the business profitable, since attendance rose with the growth of the camp population. The procurement of films from the UFA Corporation in Berlin was not always so easy. SS men had to be bribed and all sorts of diplomatic tricks had to be used to be able to send a courier to Berlin over and over again.

On April 26, 1945, the first American film was shown in the camp cinema.

EBERHARD LEITNER, Neckarwestheim

16. Prince von Waldeck-Pyrmont

W HEN THE POLICE ADMINISTRATION in Kassel was bombed out, we were assigned to build barracks to house the higher-ranking police and SS officers. These barracks, which were of course equipped with every sort of luxury, contained living and working rooms for the SD [Security Service], the SS staff, and high-ranking police officers, who were naturally SS men one and all. In addition, a whole harem of beautiful women was housed there, allegedly as typists but in reality only to satisfy the officers' sexual desires, since there was actually only enough "work" to employ these painted and powdered young women for two to three hours a day. This office bore the formal title "Office for the Germanization of Eastern Peoples." It stood under the direction of the chief of Military District Nine. This military district chief was none other than SS Lieutenant General Prince von Waldeck-Pyrmont. Under this respectable firm name, he had gathered together his SS drinking and murdering buddies.

There were problems right from the beginning of construction. In particular, the site the prince had chosen stood under "cultural preservation protection" and could not be altered or built upon without permission of the Reich government. The building commissioner of the city of Kassel forcefully insisted on this principle, which indeed he was obligated to do. But if there is one thing an SS officer is good at, it is getting his way. Two days later the building commissioner was ordered to report for military service—specifically, to the Waffen SS! That certainly shut him up. Thus the German cultural landscape was covered with barracks for orgies of drinking and lovemaking.

Since at the time of the building (summer 1944) there was already a great shortage of materials, the prince ordered that all the plumbing materials be stolen from bombed out houses. Columns of prisoners under the leadership of SS bandits had to break into townspeople's bombed-out homes to dismantle and steal the water pipes. Of course this was all done under the authority of a pass bearing the prince's name.

Extended drinking bouts took place almost daily. Of course we saw only the remains: broken glasses and plates; dirty tablecloths and carpets; broken chairs, mirrors, and other furniture—in short, it always looked as if another bombing raid had hit. The prince constantly trembled with fear; he was cowardly and nervous and could hold himself upright only when drunk. In that state he played the brave one, only to collapse a minute later if a tire exploded nearby.

This degenerate criminal executed his masterpiece during and after the large bombing raid on Kassel on October 22, 1943. Because of insufficient warnings and protective measures, a large number of children were killed during this attack, leading to an investigation on the part of the superior offices. The two persons responsible for Kassel, the Gauleiter Weinrich and the commanding SS officer, Prince von Waldeck-Pyrmont, had not even been in Kassel that night. Weinrich was on one of his drinking tours at Bad Wildungen, where he spent the entire night with four women, drinking and womanizing. Indeed, this pig was not ashamed to visit the wounded citizens the next morning, while he was still completely drunk. And the prince had climbed into his car at the approach of the British planes and roared away at 60 miles per hour. To cover up this cowardly and criminal behavior, the prince made SS Major General Harnes responsible for the mistakes of this fateful night. Harnes was immediately locked up, held for many months in the I Barracks at Buchenwald, and was finally shot by the SS. But his murderer lives on!

Toward the prisoners the prince showed a double countenance. When a prisoner was employed for his personal comfort, whether as a manservant [*Kalfaktor*],[4] waiter, or craftsman to decorate or maintain his home, the SS lieutenant general was extraordinarily friendly. When it was a matter of the prisoners in general, from whom this cowardly bandit derived no personal advantage, then he was for total extermination. Thus on the day before the arrival of the American troops—in the drunken condition that was his normal state—he tried to incite the commandant of Buchenwald, Pister, to take sharper measures against the prisoners. This crime ran aground on the determined and skillful tactics of the prisoners' leadership.

JOSEF MILDENBERGER, Saarbrücken

---

4. *Kalfaktor* has no exact equivalent in English. It refers to a personal servant or valet for SS officers. See Chapter Eleven, §152.

17.° SS Sergeant Bayer, Administrator of the Supply Room

THE SS ADMINISTRATORS of the rooms [for supplies and personal property] were all thoroughly corrupt bandits, soft and personally cowardly. A model of this was the administrator of the supply room at Buchenwald, SS Master Sergeant Bayer, who knew how to avoid front duty to the end, although he was completely fit for it. But of course this coward did not shrink from killing defenseless humans. He had taken part in the shooting of the Russian prisoners of war in the horse stables, for which he received the Military Service Cross. When after the shootings the victims' belongings were brought to be disinfected, he would always rummage through the things to see whether he could find any "objects of value." This murderous swine was also corrupt to the bone, as the following examples will show.

During the Rath action 12,500 Jews were housed in temporary barracks. Bayer allowed metal bowls and metal spoons to be sold there for 5 marks each. Under the pretext that he could not make change, he frequently pocketed a 20- or 50-mark note. Furthermore, he was so clever that he shared a portion of the swindled money with the commandant at the time, Koch, to protect himself from grumbling from SS circles.

During the exchange of dirty hand towels in the supply room, a favorite sport of Bayer's was to discard some of the towels as "unusable" and make the blocks pay for them, especially the Jewish blocks. Once he collected 750 marks from the Jewish blocks for the "repainting of the stairwell in the Personal Property Room." To the commandant, however, he reported a collection of only 600 marks. This of course the two robbers "honestly" divided up.

He had the Jewish blocks pay 500 marks for disinfection of the blocks, even though the administration provided the materials for this. Disinfection became a source of torment under Bayer's orders: Buildings were sprayed with more than the prescribed amount of Super-Tox, and Jewish prisoners were required to remain in their beds during the procedure.

The other small sums that flowed into Bayer's pockets over the course of years probably amounted to a considerable sum. The entire ledger of income and expenses had to be rewritten at least three times. Each time Bayer deleted a large number of entries and stuck the money into his own pocket.

WALTER WOLF, Gotha
Last kapo of the supply room

18. High-Ranking Visitors to Camp

WITHIN SS CIRCLES Buchenwald concentration camp was considered to be a model camp to be showed with pride to visitors from outside. Of course visitors never got to see how the prisoners were abused and beaten. On the contrary, all objects and facilities that hinted at this torture were hidden. For example, the infamous whipping block, which always stood in roll call square so that it was immediately at hand, was kept inside one of the blocks until a visit was over. Once, however, it was forgotten. When a visitor asked what kind of instrument it was, the deputy commandant (I no longer remember whether it was Florstedt or Schobert) replied that it was a table from the model building shop for the production of special molds. Gallows and posts for hangings were always hidden, too. Visitors were led around the "model enterprises": infirmary, pigsty, cinema, the [supply and personal property] rooms, laundry, kitchen, and library. If visitors were actually taken into one of the blocks, then it was only into the block of the so-called service detail [*Kommandierten*], where the SS barbers and manservants as well as especially privileged prisoners were housed. This block was not heavily occupied and was always clean. In the gardening detail, and at times in the sculpture studio as well, the visitors received "souvenirs" of Buchenwald.

There were group and individual visits. Individual visitors were especially frequent during vacation time, when the SS officers showed their friends and relatives the camp. Most of the visitors were SS or SA officers; occasionally there were Wehrmacht and police officers. Group visits were of a totally different sort. Classes of police or gendarmes from the nearby police school frequently came, as did classes of SS cadets. After the beginning of the war, visits by Wehrmacht officers were very numerous, especially from the general staff in Weimar or pilot officers from the airbase at Nohra. Occasionally, civilians came to visit; from their guilty looks it was easy to tell that they were Gestapo or criminal police officials. A special highlight was the visit of youth groups from fascist lands who had gathered together for a "cultural congress"(!) in Weimar and came to Buchenwald to observe new Germanic culture. Gauleiter Sauckel, the president of the Weimar police, Hennicke, Prince von Waldeck, Count Ciano, and sometimes even Himmler were guests of the camp administration. All were allowed to see only what the prisoners had accomplished in exemplary fashion. Behind the walls of this Potemkin village were only misery and hunger.

Of course, despite the very best management, not every sign of the bloody face of SS terror could be hidden. Starving and, in winter, half frozen figures often staggered past the visitors. We never found out what sorts of lies the distinguished visitors were then told. But the camp administration sought to get rid of the bad impression that such miserable figures no doubt made, pretending that the prisoners led a happy life. So, for example, they usually sought to keep the visitors away during the evening roll call by taking them to the top of the main watchtower near roll call square. From there they had an overview of the entire camp. After roll call the prisoners had to sing in order to heighten the good impression. The marching out had to follow with special precision. If a block attracted attention during the march, then the block or in some cases the entire camp inevitably received punishment exercises the following day. Each of us therefore pulled himself together, even though we knew that it was all merely show.

They were especially fond of having the so-called Jewish song performed for visitors. It was a barrage of defamation and vilification of the worst sort that the Jews themselves had to sing [see Chapter Three, §37]. With grinning faces the officers on the tower listened to how the Jews had to ridicule themselves.

It was carefully seen to that no visitor ever talked with a prisoner. When some Swiss journalists visited the camp in 1938, they were presented to a few individual prisoners who had been precisely coached in advance. Through this route, of course, none of them found out the truth about Buchenwald. Two Reichswehr officers once visited the camp without SS accompaniment. When the deputy commandant found out, he flew into a terrible rage and immediately dismissed the SS block officer who had gate duty at the time, jailing him for allowing the officers into the camp without accompaniment and without the commandant's permission. But even though the SS bandits did everything possible to prevent the truth about Buchenwald from reaching the people, visitors must have recognized what sort of system of hunger and barbarism prevailed here.

STEFAN HEYMANN, Mannheim

Chapter Three
Daily Life in Camp

19. ROLL CALL

THE ROLL CALLS THAT took place daily were feared by all prisoners, especially in the early years. Often one had to stand for hours in the icy cold or in stormy weather, after a hard day's work. But the SS wanted to count their slave workers precisely every day, as many of them of course harbored thoughts of escape and often enough even attempted to flee—which always meant retaliation against the entire camp.

Of course the statistics for roll call had to be prepared by prisoners because no SS man could ever have carried out these painfully exact mathematical calculations. We constantly strove to avoid mistakes in setting up the lists because searching them out during roll call would have unnecessarily prolonged the process and robbed exhausted comrades of their free time. This meant special care in counting the numerous service detail prisoners, who because of their work were not required to appear at roll call.

It is clear that with a camp population of 5,000 to 7,000, a missing person is rather quickly noticed. It is different with 35,000; because of the overcrowding of the blocks, a precise check was almost impossible. In addition, many foreign prisoners thought of roll call as a Prussian drill that one should simply avoid. They unfortunately gave no thought to the fact that by doing so they endangered the free time of tens of thousands. For if a single person was missing, often 800 numbers and names had to be called, usually with the help of interpreters. One can imagine how long that took, especially when furious SS men struck prisoners and shouted at them during the process. Thus in the final years roll call was never completed in less than an hour and a half.

Roll call square saw many horrible tragedies. How often, when a prisoner had escaped, did the entire camp have to remain standing! Twice, in 1938 and 1939, the camp had to stand for eighteen or nineteen hours straight, costing many people their lives. We were often frisked in roll call square; that is, we had to empty our pockets, and the SS inspected the contents, during which a great deal of money and tobacco disappeared. One time we had to undress completely and stand naked for two hours while we were frisked. All executions until the end of 1942 took place in roll call square. The whipping block in particular was put to use at almost every roll call.

137

At the same time roll call accomplished its function in the Nazi annihilation plan against antifascists. Many met their deaths after hard hours of standing in the square. In the famine of winter 1939, when the horrible grub led to a dysentery and typhus epidemic, hundreds literally fell: The square was covered with the dead and dying at every roll call. Anyone who had died in the block or work detail during the day had to be dragged to the square. In many blocks sixty to seventy lay dead and dying. Gypsies in particular died like flies during this winter. Only a few out of several hundred were still living by summer. Yet even in "normal" times the dead and murdered comrades lay alongside their blocks for a final roll call, for the SS insisted on "order" down to a prisoner's last breath. Only after roll call were the dying allowed into the hospital; the murdered were taken to the morgue.

When the great evacuation transports came out of the east, an orderly roll call was no longer possible. SS sentries only hastily counted the half-starved figures who staggered through the gate, so an exact determination of the number of prisoners in the camp was no longer possible. Moreover, of course, there were no transport lists—which would have been inaccurate anyway, as on every transport many comrades escaped and still more died and were thrown out of the train. The confusion during roll call was so great that, on one evening, for example, the books would show three prisoners missing, but by the following evening there would be seventeen too many, even though no new transport had arrived. Roll call had by then lost all meaning even for the SS.

After April 3, 1945, therefore, no more roll calls were held under SS command. At that time there were 80,900 in the Buchenwald camp system, of which 45,000 were in external details and about 36,000 in the base camp. Through continuous arrivals from subsidiary camps, the number in Buchenwald itself rose very rapidly to 48,000. Then began the evacuation of the camp, which went on until 21,400 comrades remained. These comrades then took part in the first "freedom roll call" on April 12, 1945.

MAX MAYR

20. Senior Camp Inmates and Camp Leadership

BUCHENWALD CONCENTRATION CAMP, like all such camps, was directed according to the principle of self-administration. The SS had disciplinary power but left the internal, technical administration to the prisoners. In time, under the methodical leadership of the antifascists, the prisoners were able to expand their positions until the SS had practically nothing more to say in camp affairs.

From the beginning the SS administration believed such a development was possible and sought to protect itself by appointing as senior camp inmates those prisoners who could be expected to support their criminal activities. The first senior camp inmates were therefore professional criminals. The very first was Hubert Richter, previously a member of the infamous Berlin SA murder unit, Storm Unit Thirty-three. He was active in camp as an executioner and murderer for the SS but was later himself killed by his bosses as an inconvenient witness.

His successor was another criminal, Paul Henning, who did not differ essentially from Richter. After his dismissal he went to Mauthausen. Nothing is known about his later fate.

The first political prisoner who became senior camp inmate in Buchenwald was Paul Mohr of Wiesbaden. He in fact tried to alter the course of the professional criminals but was himself too closely involved with the criminals to be able to act energetically enough. In the course of a corruption scandal, he was beaten to death by the SS.

After him the senior camp inmate was Fritz Männchen of Dresden, who once more took an energetic antifascist course. He was dismissed when he failed to inform against a drunken prisoner.

His successor, Arthur Wischka of Beuthen, led the camp in a model manner. He understood perfectly well how to deflect the constantly reawakening mistrust of the SS and to continue on a clear antifascist course.

After Wischka's release and after the short term of the antifascist Karl Bartel of Dresden, Ernst Frommhold of Erfurt became senior camp inmate. He was certainly the most active and energetic senior camp inmate the camp had up to the final months, organizing the antifascists in camp in the struggle against the criminals. He was released on April 20, 1939.

After another short term in office by Karl Bartel and immediately afterward by Hans Becher, Ernst Busse of Cologne became senior camp inmate. He remained in office until the deputy commandant at the time, Plaul, helped the criminals in another attempt to take over camp positions. His proper conduct in office won him such trust that he was immediately named kapo of the prisoner hospital. He remained there until the liberation by the American army.

Then followed the short but tragic intermezzo of dominance by the criminals again under Senior Camp Inmate Ohles. He was beaten to death in the punishment company after his dismissal.

After him followed the former [Reichswehr] first lieutenant Wolff of Ratibor. Since Wolff, with the help of Polish fascists, attempted to battle the antifascists in camp, he was brought down. Because of his homosexual tendencies, this was not difficult. He was sent to a subsidiary camp, where he died soon afterward.

His successor was the longtime deputy senior camp inmate, Erich Reschke of Hamburg. Through an informer, he was denounced for his antifascist activity. He was jailed by the Gestapo in Weimar on October 30, 1944, and was hauled off to an unknown location before the arrival of the Americans.

The last senior camp inmate, who had also long been deputy senior camp inmate, was Hans Eiden of Trier. At a time when SS mistrust [of inmate leaders] had grown tremendously, he had the difficult and demanding task of overcoming this mistrust while at the same time safeguarding and concealing antifascist preparations for the liberation of the camp. Hans Eiden played an important and often decisive role in sabotaging the evacuation ordered by the SS. Through his courageous and skilled actions, he overcame many difficulties for the camp and greatly facilitated our antifascist tasks. He himself could fulfill his duty only because he had at his side two reliable antifascist comrades: Deputy Senior Camp Inmate Karl Pankow (LA 2) of Berlin and Second Deputy Senior Camp Inmate (LA 3) Paul Schreck of Mannheim.

WALTER BARTEL, Berlin

21. THE BUCHENWALD SONG

When the day awakes,
before the sun smiles,
the columns march
to the day's toils
into the breaking dawn.
And the forest is black and the heavens red,
and we carry in our bags a piece of bread
and in our hearts, in our hearts the sorrows.

O Buchenwald, I can never forget you
because you are my fate.
Whoever leaves you, he alone can measure
how wonderful freedom is!
O Buchenwald we do not lament and wail,
whatever our fate might be.
But we want to say yes to life,
for someday the time will come when we are free!

And the night is hot and my sweetheart far away,
and the wind sings softly, and I love her so,
if she stays true, yes if only she stays true!
And the stones are hard, but our stride is firm,
and we carry our pickaxes and shovels along
and in our hearts, in our hearts, love.

O Buchenwald, I can never forget you, etc.

And the day is short and the night so long,
yet a song rings out that was sung at home:
We will never be robbed of our courage!

Keep in step, comrade, and don't lose heart,
for we carry in our blood the will to live
and in our hearts, in our hearts, our faith.

O Buchenwald, I can never, etc.

This Buchenwald song is heard today in all the world, just like the songs from other concentration camps.[1] But few know how it arose, and fewer still memorized this song in camp. Therefore it is documented here.

At the end of 1938, the deputy commandant at the time, Rödl, declared, "All the other camps have a song; we have to come up with a song for Buchenwald. Whoever writes one will receive 10 marks."[2]

"Poets," composers, and others submitted many proposals, but none was judged suitable or met with the approval of the SS administration. Only the song above was accepted and was declared the official "Buchenwald hymn." This was because the kapo of the post office at the time, a professional criminal and by vocation a master of ceremonies, made use of the necessary connections with the SS. This kapo identified himself as the composer of the words and melody. In truth the song was composed by two Austrian Jews. The lyrics were by [Fritz] Löhner-Beda, a librettist for [Franz] Lehar; the music was by [Hermann] Leopoldi, a Viennese cabaret singer. Löhner-Beda unfortunately died in a subsidiary camp of Auschwitz; Leopoldi was able to emigrate to the United States in time.[3] Of course the camp administration never found out who the actual composers of the song were.

The words and melody of the song had to be practiced in the blocks during free time, until one evening at roll call came the command, "Sing the Buchenwald song." It was the end of December 1938, bitterly cold, with everything covered by deep snow.

Of course it didn't come off the first time (7,000 men stood in roll call square). An enraged Rödl, who was stinking drunk at the time, gave the order to stop. He ordered each block in the square to practice by itself as long as necessary until the song was learned. One can scarcely imagine the infernal concert that broke out in

---

1. Both the German lyrics and a translation of the song can be found in Walter Poller, *Medical Block Buchenwald*, (New York: Lyle Stuart, 1961), 162–163; in German in *SSS*, 107–108 (but not in *TPH*); Erich Fein and Karl Flanner, *Rot-weiß-rot in Buchenwald* (Vienna: Europaverlag, 1987), 68–69. Fein saw the song as a positive affirmation of the prisoners' will to live, their saying "yes to life," and he noted that the second stanza—which ends in "free!"—was sung in a loud, enthusiastic chorus.

2. Tom Segev described Arthur Rödl as "probably a sadist" in his short biographical description in *Soldiers of Evil* (New York: Berkley, 1991), 135–139.

3. Fritz Löhner-Beda died at Auschwitz-Monowitz on December 4, 1942, after a terrible beating by a camp guard. Hermann Leopoldi, born Ferdinand Kohn, emigrated to the United States before the outbreak of war, returned to Austria after the war, and died in Vienna in 1959. Fein and Flanner, *Rot-weiß-rot*, 70–73.

the square. When Rödl realized that this would not work either, he had it sung in unison verse by verse and repeated again and again. Only after the entire camp had stood in this manner for four hours in the bitter cold did he give the order to march out. But while usually each block simply turned and went back to the camp, this time it was different. Lined up in rows of ten, each block had to march stiffly past Rödl and the other drunken SS officers at the gate while singing the Buchenwald song. Woe to the block that did not march by in perfect order or whose singing did not quite live up to Rödl's expectations. Finally, around 10:00 at night, we came back to our blocks starving and frozen stiff.

Starving and freezing men standing and singing in deep, bright white snow in roll call square in the dead of winter, under the glare of searchlights: This scene has burned itself permanently into the memory of every participant.

STEFAN HEYMANN, Mannheim

22. BLOCK INSPECTIONS

AMONG THE DUTIES of the block officers was the inspection of prisoner lodgings for cleanliness and order. In reality the inspections existed solely to put the prisoners through new ordeals and forms of persecution. The daily inspections were so feared that as an SS inspection neared, only the most necessary personnel remained in the block; the others fled. The anteroom, the washroom, the toilet, the dayroom and the sleeping rooms were searched to the furthest corner for the slightest trace of dust or dirt. Woe if a speck of dust was to be found on a wooden ledge—which of course a block officer simply had to claim to see. Likewise if the stove did not look as if it had been licked clean. If a prisoner's locker contained a crumb of bread or if a spot was on a prisoner's bowl or knife, the [whole] locker was tipped over. Room attendants had to fetch buckets of water and pour it over everything. Of course there were blows and kicks during the inspection.

A special chapter was bed "construction" [*Bettenbau*]. The straw mattress had to have square corners like a cigar box; the checks on the bed and pillow covers had to run at right angles. It was not just that the block officers tore up beds that were made differently and thus "badly." At times they overturned the beds, throwing the straw mattresses, pillows, and blankets in a heap and even tipping over the bed frames. In the evening after rations were distributed, the occupants had to restore the sleeping room to order or else the entire block could be reported, leading to collective discipline such as punishment exercises or standing at attention for hours and the withdrawal of rations. There are countless examples of abuse of room attendants and senior block inmates as a result of block inspections. These inspections also tended to turn the prisoner functionaries against the occupants, forcing them to take sharper measures against their own comrades.

Even during the night there were frequent inspections. In the middle of the night SS men would storm into the sleeping rooms, armed with truncheons and whips, and wake up the occupants. They would search to see whether someone had committed the crime of sleeping in the unheated sleeping room in long johns or even in socks. Then the entire block, barefoot and in nightshirts even in the deepest winter, was chased around the outside of the block for half an hour or even a whole hour.

GUSTAV HERZOG, Vienna

23. THE EARLY YEARS OF THE CAMP

BUCHENWALD CONCENTRATION CAMP was built solely by the Reich German prisoners. With few exceptions all camp functionaries until the end of 1938 were professional criminals or their friends among the reds (pimps, Foreign Legionnaires, former Nazi party members, etc.). These bandits stole whatever they could from their comrades. Food rations were only partially distributed, most ending up in the pockets of the room attendants. Mortality as a result of undernourishment was extraordinarily high at this time. The professional criminals and their friends were closely entangled with the SS in a web of corruption. Only when close connections between the SS and prisoners reached the point where the most corrupt SS men no longer dared act against the prisoners did the SS administration draw the right conclusions and change the prisoner leadership by replacing professional criminals with politicals. That severed the corrupt ties between the SS and prisoner functionaries, at least in part, and at the same time the internal camp leadership became cleaner and more honest.

The workday lasted from 6:00 A.M. (in summer from 5:00 A.M.) until 8:00 or 9:00 P.M. During construction of the water pipeline, prisoners regularly worked under floodlights until 10:00 or 11:00 P.M., in many cases until 2:00 or 3:00 A.M. The camp leader was the infamous professional criminal Noack, who beat many comrades to death.

As "punishment" there was no meal almost every Sunday in addition, there were days of fasting to pay for the comradeship evenings. Standing in roll call square was a constant torment for the prisoners. One Sunday in February 1938 the prisoners had to stand naked in the square for three hours while SS men searched their clothes. During this time the wife of the mass murderer Koch and four other SS officers' wives stood at the barbed wire fence and stared lewdly at the naked prisoners.

In addition to the regular places of punishment, the so-called black cellblock was constructed at the suggestion of the senior camp inmate at the time, the professional criminal Richter. The sleeping room in A Wing of Block 3 was completely vacated; the windows were nailed shut and darkened. Prisoners who were locked in there had to stand day and night, clad only in twill, without blankets and heat, although at that time (January 1939) it was often only 10 to 12 degrees. Every day the locked-up prisoners received twenty-five lashes with the cane. Day and night the block officers came into the room and tormented the prisoners. Of the thirty or so comrades in the black cellblock, six died there. The others came out only as skeletons and perished soon thereafter.

FRITZ MÄNNCHEN, Dresden

24. Sidelights from the Early Days

In the following I will give some of my own observations, which stretch over the time from September 1938 to the middle of 1939. They will serve to give an approximate impression of conditions in the early days of the camp.

Reception in the Political Department

Amid blows from sticks and rifle butts, we were forced out of the trucks that had brought us from Weimar to Buchenwald. We were herded along and brought to the political department. There the SS men standing in the corridor received us with kicks and punches. It was a favorite pastime of the SS men to ask new arrivals the reasons for their delivery and then abuse them accordingly. I remember a sex offender from my group who immediately got fifty lashes with the cane. The next day he died of the consequences of this abuse.

The Prisoners' Bank

Kapo Edmund Röttgen and the three other prisoners (criminals) employed in the bank worked closely with the directors, SS Lieutenant Driemel and SS Sergeant Döring. Every week a maximum of 10 marks [per prisoner] was paid out, for which two or three evening pay periods were announced. Driemel paid out the money and regularly forgot a few marks when it came to the Jews. If he decided the throng of waiting prisoners was too large, he grabbed the revolver lying near him and shot out the window.

Jewish prisoners were especially dependent on purchases from the canteen because of the constant withdrawal of food rations. Röttgen turned his sympathy for the Jews into a good source of income: For a 50 percent share, he arranged a higher payout for the rich prisoners.

One day the SS needed a new typewriter. Six Jews were summoned, informed that they must each donate 100 marks for a machine, and had to sign for the withdrawals. The machine SS Sergeant Döring purchased had a value of 350 marks.

SS Master Sergeant Michael, brother-in-law of Commandant Koch, sold sweaters and underwear to prisoners for a good profit. The remaining goods that could not be sold were donated to the professional criminal prisoners. To protect himself from losses, Michael let all Jews order with funds from the prisoners' bank and allowed them to withdraw on the spot a third of their account. An additional source of income for the criminal prisoners in the prisoners' bank was represented by transfers to needy prisoners. With the agreement of the sergeant, the sum of 5 marks was regularly deducted from the accounts of the Jews.

With the release of the 10,000 Jews as a result of the Rath action, horrendous sums were deducted from the refunded accounts by the prisoner Katz. These monies were allegedly destined for the less wealthy Jews, but most flowed into the pockets of Deputy Commandant Hackmann. He was present at the payouts and therefore encouraged Katz to make hefty deductions.

The Roll Call of the Seventy-five Dead

At the evening roll call of December 14, 1938, two professional criminals were missing. Despite a temperature of only 15 degrees and the prisoners' insufficient clothing, we had to stand for five hours in roll call square. I still have in front of me the image of an already weak old man who had lost consciousness. A few of the younger comrades had grasped him under the arms and pulled him behind our block, rubbing his body to keep him from freezing. That same evening twenty-five prisoners froze; by the following morning the number increased to seventy-five.

Christmas 1938

Christmas Eve 1938 the SS had prepared a special surprise for us. On the snow-covered roll call square, a gallows had been erected. After roll call the commandant informed us over the loudspeaker that on the orders of the Reich SS leader, Himmler, the political prisoner Forster was to be hanged. Forster had escaped to Czechoslovakia in May 1938 with another prisoner after knocking down an SS man, but he had been extradited. And before our eyes Forster was led to the gallows and hanged.

Hangman Osterloh

Up to the beginning of 1939, with the exception of the political block, all the senior block inmate and room attendant posts were occupied by professional criminal prisoners. All of them had the liberty to give free rein to their criminal activities. So one morning a prisoner was found hanged in one of the blocks. Through an oversight of the administration, the state attorney in Weimar found out about it. The investigation revealed that the "hanged man" had several broken ribs from brutal punches and kicks. He had been killed and then hanged by the room attendant under the direction of Senior Block Inmate Osterloh to disguise it as a suicide. The murdered man had protested the room attendant's black marketing of bread. Through the intervention of the camp administration, the matter was hushed up and the murderer restored to his post.

FRITZ MÄNNCHEN, Dresden

25. THE FOOD SUPPLY

Until the beginning of the war, a lump sum was budgeted for the prisoners' food supply. From July 15, 1937, up to February 28, 1938, only 55 pfennigs per day per prisoner could be spent. Since this amount of money proved to be too low even for the SS administration, it was increased to 65 pfennigs a day from April 1, 1938, until the sixteenth of the same month. Then as of April 17 [1938] the sum stood at 60 pfennigs per day. The administration held to this amount until the outbreak of the war.

With the outbreak of war in 1939, the most important foodstuffs were rationed. The food supply became worse. Only after August 1, 1940, were rations for camp inmates fixed according to the following guidelines:
Weekly Ration:[4]
(a) Meat or meat products, 400 g
(b) Total fats, 200 g
 Margarine, edible fats, or oils, 150 g
 Lard, bacon, or suet, 50 g
(c) Yogurt [*Quark*], 100 g
 or lowfat cheese, 50 g
(d) Bread, 2,740 g
(e) Sugar, 80 g
(f) Marmalade, 100 g
(g) Processed foodstuffs, 150 g
(h) Flour or flour mixtures, 225 g
(i) Coffee substitutes or coffee additives, 84 g
(j) On the average, potatoes, up to 3,500 g
(k) Fresh vegetables (rutabagas, etc.), 2,800 g
Heavy Labor Supplements
 For a limited number of prisoners who were designated as heavy laborers, the following additional amounts per head per week could be issued:
(a) Meat or meat products, up to 400 g

---

4. Weekly food rations per person are calculated in grams. For approximate conversions: 1 ounce equals 28 grams; 1 pound equals 448 grams.

(b) Total fats, 100 g
   Margarine, edible fats, or oils, 75 g
   Lard, bacon, or suet, 25 g
(c) Bread, up to 1,400 g

As of October 1, 1941, the rations were reduced. The amount available per week per prisoner was:
(a) Meat products or meat, 320 g
(b) Coffee substitute, 63 g
Heavy Labor Supplements
(a) Meat or meat products, 320 g

All other food rations remained unchanged. As of January 1, 1942, the meat ration was reduced to 280 g for normal prisoners as well as for heavy laborers. As of May 15, 1942, new reductions went into effect. The food rations looked as follows:
(a) Meat or meat products (from the food bank or horse meat), 280 g
(b) Total fats, 170 g
   Margarine, 130 g
   Fat from pork scraps, 40 g
(c) Yogurt, 100 g
   or lowfat cheese, 50 g
(d) Bread, 2,450 g
(e) Sugar, 80 g
(f) Marmalade, 100 g
(g) Processed foodstuffs, 150 g
   (cereal products, 50 g; other foodstuffs, 100 g)
(h) Rye flour, 75 g
(i) Bread flour, 50 g
(j) Coffee substitute or coffee additives, 63 g
   (If "German tea" was issued instead of a coffee substitute, the daily quota
   was 4 g, a saving of 9 g of coffee substitute.)
(k) Potatoes, 5,000 g
(l) Fresh vegetables, 2,600–3,000 g
Heavy Labor Supplements (permitted for only a limited number)
(a) Meat or meat products (if possible, food bank or horse meat), 280 g
(b) Total fats, 100 g
   Margarine, 75 g
   Lard, 25 g
(c) Bread, up to 1,400 g

As of May 31, 1943, the meat portion of the normal rations was reduced from 280 g to 200 g a week. As compensation there was [an additional] 75 g of bread and 12.5 g of fats each week.

Prisoners who were sent on transports received a daily ration of 500 g of bread, 50 g of sausage, and 60 g of margarine. (These portions made a complete daily ration.)

On April 28, 1944, when the Buchenwald concentration camp went to Level I (work camp), the following weekly portions were defined as the camp food ration:
(a) Meat and meat products (if possible from food bank or horse meat up to base portion), 200 g
(b) Margarine, 182.5 g
(c) Yogurt (or 50 g of cottage cheese), 100 g
(d) Rye bread, 2,600 g
(e) Rye flour, 125 g
(f) Sugar, 80 g
(g) Marmalade, 100 g
(h) Processed foodstuffs, 150 g
(i) Coffee substitute and additives, 62.5 g
(j) Skim milk, 0.25 l
(k) Potatoes, 2,800 g
(l) Fresh vegetables, 2,000 g
    Rutabagas, 2,000 g
(m) Processed foodstuffs, 105 g
(n) Rice or legumes, 175 g
With this the camp food rations were about equal to the basic rations for the civilian population. In general the food rations for camp inmates remained constant up to February 1945.

With the flood of soldiers returning from the east and the evacuation of the eastern camps and the German civilian population, food rations for camp inmates were radically reduced.

As of March 1, 1945, all prisoners received the following allotments:
Weekly
(a) 250 g food bank or horse meat
(b) 83.33 g fats
(c) 1,366.67 g rye flour (or bread in ratio of 3:4)
(d) 250 g marmalade or 125 sugar
(e) 41.66 g yogurt
(f) 20.83 g cottage cheese
(g) 33.33 g coffee substitute
(h) 125 g fresh vegetables
(i) 250 g rutabagas
(j) 0.25 g dried milk powder
(k) 3,500 g potatoes
The prisoners who were not actively employed (about two-thirds of the inmates) were allowed only 80 percent of the above-listed rations.

For heavy laborers (an extremely limited number), there were the following supplements:
(a) 350 g meat
(b) 56.66 g margarine
(c) 1,100 g bread

ERICH LOCH, Essen

26. ANIMALS LIVED BETTER THAN HUMANS

IN THE PREPARATION of meals for prisoners, even meat was used in small quantities. Two to three times a week, 26 to 33 pounds of meat were put into a pot that held 260 gallons. (After liberation of the camp, it was 220 pounds.) The prisoners' kitchen received meat only from sick animals, so-called food bank meat that spoiled very quickly and had to be consumed in two to three days at the latest. But in Buchenwald meat was often distributed to the kitchen after a week, so that it was already in such a state of decomposition that it could no longer even have been given to animals.

In camp were two dog kennels that the SS used for the breeding and care of about 120 to 150 guard dogs. The dogs were trained exclusively to "attack prisoners." These well-trained beasts, who mauled many a prisoner, were excellently housed. Each had its own stall with a "dayroom," "sleeping room," and "running space." The dogs were cared for by SS men; prisoners were strictly denied admission. Only later, after the kennels were taken over by members of the Wehrmacht, were prisoners used to do gardening, cut wood, etc. The dogs' food consisted of oats, potatoes, and meat; sick animals received a special milk diet. No wonder that starving prisoners were delighted to use every opportunity to steal food from the kennel kitchen. But no prisoner ever got hold of any of the fresh eggs and red wine that was set aside for the dogs of SS officers. At liberation a carload of dog biscuits stood in the kennel. Mobs of hungry prisoners descended upon it to eat their fill.

In the pigsty about 700 to 800 pigs were kept to breed and to sell. Scraps from the prisoners' kitchen were sent there. But especially while Koch was commandant, the food of an entire block, all Jewish blocks, or even the entire camp was often seized and turned over to the pigs. Because the raising of the pigs was not carried out professionally, chronic swine fever prevailed. The animals ready for slaughter were of course consumed exclusively by the SS.

DR. JAN POSPISIL, veterinarian, Boudnice

27. SS Men as Postal Thieves

I WAS ACTIVE IN THE post office from January 1943 until fall 1944. At my arrival letters and packages alike were still handled in the office of the block officers. Only later, on the orders of the commandant, were packages distributed separately; out of Block 12 and later Block 2. The letters prisoners received were treated rather casually. Depending on mood and whim, letters and cards were not passed on or were torn up or cut to pieces. SS men frequently wrote dumb comments about the contents of letters; seriousness and professionalism were completely lacking.

In the parcel post office, packages for prisoners were considered free booty for the SS robbers. Packages were systematically plundered. SS men simply took whatever they may have needed out of the packages. The SS bandits sent most of the booty home. Food from the parcels they ate themselves, or they used the stolen goods for barter.

In these postal robberies the following bandits especially stood out:

SS Master Sergeant Dottermusch of Saxony
SS Technical Sergeant Ebeling of Berlin
SS Corporal Bielek of Vienna
SS Sergeant Rabe of Halle, who was also a member of the infamous shot-in-the-
    neck Column Ninety-nine.

The direction of this band of robbers was in the hands of SS Sergeant Klett, who himself stole indiscriminately. SS Technical Sergeant Marx played the gentleman yet liked to let lie packages that should have been passed on. "Let them rot," was his favorite expression.

The so-called inspection and security office stood under SS Sergeant Bretschneider of the Sudetenland, also a member of Column 99. Here the SS rummaged through packages from abroad that of course contained foodstuffs no longer available in Germany, especially in later years. Plundering went on in grand style here.

ALFONS MARINCOVICH, Innsbruck

28. Divorce Among Prisoners

According to the new National Socialist divorce law, a marriage could be ended if it was determined that marital cohabitation had been disrupted. Proof that a marriage was disrupted—among other criteria—was that the spouses had lived separately longer than three years.

In 1940 and 1942 individual Gestapo offices showed a strong tendency toward pressuring the spouses of political concentration camp prisoners. They were urged to divorce their husbands, who had been jailed for treason. In the strict sense of the law, the separation caused by imprisonment did not constitute sufficient grounds for divorce, but under pressure of the SS—often continuation of welfare support depended on it—wives of political prisoners complied and filed petitions for divorce. The prisoner had no opportunity to have himself legally represented.

Against the orders of the SS, the undersigned has offered legal counsel to numerous comrades and has discovered that in clear violation of the law, lower courts in particular have pronounced a divorce and even declared the husband as the guilty party. Only in two cases of the twenty or so on which the undersigned worked was it possible to reverse the verdict on appeal.

DR. WERNER HILPERT, Leipzig

29. Human Remains in the Sewers

I arrived at Buchenwald concentration camp on September 26, 1939, and was employed in the work detail for prisoner housing in the gardening section, assigned to earth leveling. On September 16, 1941, several captured Russian officers were brought into camp as prisoners of war after the evening roll call. Around that time a few covered trucks drove in the direction of the crematorium. On September 18, thus two days later, a pipeline from the sewage system was clogged beneath the ground on which we were working. Although I had nothing to do with the sewage system, SS Sergeant Döring reproached me because the system was not working. With a Dutch comrade, I set about to clear the blockage. We found that a heap of human bones, some still covered with pieces of unburned flesh, were the cause of the damage.

SS Sergeant Döring commanded us to scatter the ashes and remnants of flesh on the ground and bury them in the course of our leveling work. I said to my comrades, "We will dig a hole and bury everything properly." Against the orders of Sergeant Döring, we carried out this plan and buried the bones as properly as possible. The exact spot is still clear in my memory.

From another source I know that experts from the Bremen sewage works likewise found that the cause of the stoppage was half-burned human body parts and bones.

ANTON JANACEK

30 Nazi Beasts of Buchenwald

In April 1938 I was brought to the Gestapo in Berlin. I was held there and put through many interrogations until I was finally sent to Buchenwald concentration camp in mid-September.

When I was delivered to Buchenwald, I found the camp still under construction. Along with about fifty men, I was delivered to the political department. We were received with beatings and insults and had to remain in the Saxon salute until we were summoned to have our personal information recorded. As personal information was taken, we were again beaten and kicked then sent into camp at double time. At the gate we had to stand in the Saxon salute for about three hours before we were brought to the Personal Property Room to change our clothes. Here, too, the sergeants abused the majority of those who arrived.

The next day I was made a mason—urgently needed at the time—and assigned to the "garrison garage" work detail. Already on the first day I witnessed the sights and sounds of SS bestiality that I will never forget. I was working on one of the first massive blocks; from the scaffolding I could look over everything. A colleague called my attention to a troop of prisoners being led into the woods by SS Sergeants Sommer and [Anton] Bergmeier.[5] I could see how the prisoners had their hands tied behind their backs and how one after another they were hanged from trees with their hands thus bound. They were hanged so high that their feet were 18 inches above the ground. These people remained hanging from the trees between half an hour and three hours. The cries, howls, pleas, and entreaties were unceasing until the victims were finally taken down.

SS Sergeant Abraham was a vulgar beast. He tortured, beat to death, and drowned many people in Buchenwald. He targeted the Jews in particular. Out of his multitude of crimes, I give just a few examples.

In November 1938 deep mud lay everywhere. When prisoners had to use the toilet, there was no choice but to wade through the deepest mud and dirt. Because

---

5. Bergmeier was tried at the Buchenwald camp guards trial and was sentenced to death by hanging, but he was covered by a stay of execution in 1949. Although an appeal for clemency was rejected in 1950, he was most likely released along with other prisoners in the early 1950s. NA, RG 338, case 000-50-9, box 426, "Review and Recommendations," 41–43, 94–95; appeals, box 452.

there were only a few latrines in camp, they were always occupied. The SS sergeants made a sport of chasing prisoners away from the latrines before they were able to use them. The worst were Abraham and Zöllner. I once saw how both armed themselves with truncheons and stormed a latrine that was occupied by twenty prisoners. They beat the prisoners over the heads so that most of them fell into the latrine. The latrines were full of excrement. If one of the prisoners tried to climb out, Abraham and Zöllner would beat him with their truncheons again. A large number of the prisoners thus drowned in the latrine.

On another occasion in 1939, I saw how Abraham drove four Jewish prisoners into a deep water hole and repeatedly struck them to keep them from getting back out. In this instance one prisoner lost his life. The other three were able to save their lives because the author of these lines and several other prisoners rushed to answer their calls for help, and Abraham preferred to simply walk away. A complaint against Abraham lodged with Roll Call Officer Strippel not only had no success but led to my being reprimanded and threatened with punishment.

On yet another occasion Abraham struck down a prisoner with a truncheon. When the prisoner failed to respond to his order to stand up, Abraham shoved his truncheon against the prisoner's throat and trampled on him with both feet until he was dead.

Another beast was SS Sergeant Schmidt (Thuringia). During the building of the Gustloff Works at Buchenwald in 1942–1943, Schmidt abused numerous prisoners so severely that they died. Already in the early morning he would strike prisoners like a madman, using truncheons, spades, and hoes. He conducted himself with special brutality against Russian, Polish, and Jewish prisoners. Repeated attempts were made to put an end to Schmidt's activities. But all complaints failed.

The prisoner Schreiber, who belonged to my work detail as an apprentice, was one of Schmidt's favorite victims. Almost every day Schmidt abused him. He had to undress himself completely, climb a tree and shout, "I am a filthy Jewish pig!" Schreiber was often too slow in climbing; Schmidt beat him until he was up in the tree. When I told Commandant Pister this, he doubted it was true but promised to forbid SS Technical Sergeant Schmidt from carrying out such abuse. But Schmidt continued his handiwork.

Another dirty dog was SS Technical Sergeant Greul. This beast simply could not survive unless he began his day by beating a number of prisoners. One day I myself witnessed how Greul used a truncheon to beat about fifty prisoners—Jews and Russians—until they collapsed. After many attempts to put an end to Greul's activities, it was finally possible—because of his thefts—to have him transferred from his post as construction supervisor.

Another blossom in this wreath of dirty dogs was SS Sergeant Klinger (who lived in the vicinity of Wurzen). He, too, targeted Jews and Russians in particular. With two other SS bandits, he would catch a victim and lead him into a closed room in order to abuse him viciously. One day my apprentices called me to witness the following scene: Klinger and his two helpers had two Russians in front of them. They beat them with truncheons and kicked them until blood ran from their mouths and noses. Then they had to press their fingertips together and hold out their hands. The three bandits then beat the prisoners' fingertips until they bled. The victims bellowed with pain and called for help. I tore open the door and at the top of my voice shouted, "What's going on in here?" The bandits stopped the beating right away. When I addressed Klinger, he said the Russians had threatened him and tried to attack him. He said he could have them shot immediately. Through an interpreter I was able to determine that Klinger's assertions were false. In this case, too, I went to the commandant to protest against this sort of abuse, but everything remained as usual.

ROBERT SIEWERT, Berlin

31. SS Sadists

May 1938. Work details report to roll call square. We stand for an hour. During this time I went to the block to use the toilet because I was sick. SS Master Sergeant Bräuning reported me. I was punished with half an hour of "hanging from a tree." Hanging proceeded as follows: The hands were tied tightly together behind the back with a cord. Then the body was lifted up, and the fetters were hung over a large nail that had been driven in at a height of 6.5 feet, so that the feet dangled freely. Thus the entire body weight hung from the arms, which were bent backward. The result was the dislocation of the shoulder blades, causing horrible pain. Thirty to forty comrades were hung along with me, but I was there for only half an hour. Many were there up to three hours, some even four to five hours, until they became unconscious or indeed even died. Howls, cries, shouts of pain filled the forest. SS Staff Sergeant Sommer used a stick to beat the helpless victims on the feet, the face, and the genitals. Victims tortured to the point of madness cried out for water, for their wives and children, to be shot in order to end their torture. The cries went beyond the fence of the camp and into the community. The German people never reacted to these cries. The world, however, heard them and has finally put an end to the activities of this fascist plague.

October 1937. There were still no toilet facilities in camp and no washrooms. Great latrine trenches were dug, about 25 feet long, 12 feet wide, and 12 feet deep. Once two boards were nailed across them, the toilets were finished. On each of these boards sat ten to fifteen men. From behind came SS Sergeants Abraham and Zöllner, both with large truncheons. They beat the prisoners with the truncheons until they fell into the trenches. Ten prisoners drowned in excrement. Woe to him who dared to aid those calling for help. He ran the danger of being beaten to death himself.

Winter 1943.   Kommando Laura, Deputy Commandant Plaul. A prisoner was talking to a woman whom SS Sergeant Heinrich had chosen as his sweetheart. Heinrich was irritated and forced the prisoner to take off his clothing and climb into the water when the temperature was only 50 degrees. Then the prisoner had to warm himself again by running laps. After a few laps Heinrich ordered him to halt and demanded that the prisoner masturbate. The prisoner refused, was again beaten by Heinrich, and then was forced to do laps again. Heinrich repeated this until the prisoner, half out of his mind, tried to masturbate. A number of SS men witnessed this incident without making even the slightest attempt to restrain Heinrich as he carried out the abuse.

WILLY APEL, No. 582

32. A HANDFUL OF HORSE FODDER

AFTER THE OCCUPATION of Poland by the German Wehrmacht, when I was sixty-three, I was arrested by the Gestapo and taken to Buchenwald along with many of my countrymen. Out of the long years of horror, I would like to emphasize only one experience.

On May 2, 1943, I was sent to the external work detail in Goslar. The work was hard, the food completely insufficient and of poor quality. Of course we suffered from hunger; our strength was completely exhausted. One day—it was in July 1943—I was working in a horse stable at the camp there. One of the SS men, moved by pity, allowed me to take a handful of horse fodder. The fodder consisted of slices of sugar beets, oats, barley, and peas. Joyfully I crept into a corner to grind the grain with stones and then eat it. The work detail officer, Master Sergeant Höber caught me at it. He attacked me with incredible anger. Punches and kicks rained down upon me. When I fell to the ground, he worked me over with kicks so severe that for weeks afterward I had pains in my back and hips. In the days after the incident the SS master sergeant supervised me himself. Despite great pain I had to perform the heaviest labor under his supervision.

When I returned to Buchenwald from the Goslar work detail in November 1943, I found I had been reported for "theft" of state property. I received ten days in the cellblock, a sentence I served there.

KARL PETEREK, No. 374

33. BEATINGS WERE PART OF THE DAILY ROUTINE

I BELONGED TO the so-called Action for the Polish Ethnic Group in Germany, a group called the Polish minority in camp. We were part of a group of 181 prisoners delivered to Buchenwald on the evening of October 15, 1939. For this reason we were not brought directly into camp but into the cellblock at the camp gate. In groups of ten to twelve men, we were crammed into cells that were only about 4 feet wide by 6 feet long. With kicks and blows from a truncheon, Sergeant Sommer finally managed to get the doors closed. The windows were shut tight and covered with shades. The heat was turned up full blast and could not be turned off from within the cells. After only an hour or two in these terribly overheated cells, in which there was a severe shortage of oxygen, we were more or less unconscious. Finally, after the morning roll call, the doors were torn open and the terribly battered mass of men was allowed to begin the march into the Little Camp.

We were commanded to carry stones in the stone quarry. Each day we had to make up to seventeen trips. SS Technical Sergeant Emde had us run at double time not only on the way to the stone quarry but also going uphill with a full load. On the way from the quarry to the watchtowers and back, we had to run the gauntlet of infamous SS men, among them Sergeants Jänisch, Kostial, Chemnitz, Kubitz, Waletzko, Hentschel, Hättig, Blank, and Hinkelmann. By the second day sixteen men could no longer stand up because of exhaustion. By the third day it had reached thirty. By the fourth day half the remaining men on duty were carried into camp on stretchers by their fellow prisoners.

This unimaginable existence lasted for ten days, then we were assigned to Block 34 in the large camp. I was sent to carry tree trunks. We waded into the deepest mud. From the forest to the sawmill on the grounds of the German Armaments Works, the trunks had to be dragged through the mire exclusively by human power. The tempo was kept up by blows from SS men's truncheons.

When the day was over and the evening roll call was behind us, the other side of camp life began. A sergeant would enter the block and while still standing at the door would bellow at us, "You're still not under the table yet?" Benches were flung onto the table, bowls rattled, and there were always a few who could find no place under the table, no matter how hard they tried. These unlucky ones then became the whipping boys to an even greater extent. These games varied. Block Officer Roscher would have us vacate the barracks and order us to stand on our heads in the snow. The headstand in the snow was of course also expected of elderly men, as if those who were barely able to put one foot in front of the other could run laps as well as those far younger.

Once a man who had passed out lay in front of the office of the roll call officer. Second Lieutenant Driemel came up to him and stepped on his hands. The unconscious man did not stir. Then Driemel stepped on his head. After Driemel kicked him in the sides with his boots, he finally groaned and began to stir. To make him still more lively, a bucket of water was fetched and the water poured over his body. (Only the highlights can be described here.) The SS men Stoll and Grundel threw a Jew into a ditch full of water. He tried to climb out. Both of them sprang at him, threw him into the ditch again, and managed to hold him down to drown him.

SS man [Hubert] Krautwurst was angry that a large number of prisoners were lying in the sunshine in the woods one Sunday afternoon.[6] Although this was by no means forbidden, seventy comrades were reported and for several consecutive Sundays had to haul excrement under the constant torments of SS Sergeant Döhring II. Beatings were part of normal daily routine.

On April 8, 1945, the sergeants appeared at Block 33 to clear the block of prisoners. The way they did this, prisoners flew out into the streets along with entire window frames. I was an eyewitness when Master Sergeant Rackers beat the pile of prisoners with a squared piece of timber that was completely covered in blood.

THEODOR GADCZINSKI

34. Cold-Blooded Double Murder

On a cold November day in 1937, we came back from work in the camp, dead tired and hungry, as always, and reported for the evening roll call. During roll call it was discovered that two prisoners—"green" criminals—were missing. As punishment, Commandant Koch ordered the entire camp to stand in roll call square until the two missing men were found, dead or alive. We stood at attention the entire night; anyone who moved received twenty-five lashes with the cane.

In the morning around 9:00—we were still standing in the same spot—political prisoners Oskar Fischer and Brehm were called to the gate. The commanding officer, Deputy Commandant Rödl, and some SS men disappeared with them into the forest. A few minutes later two shots rang out there, and when we went out to work the next morning, we saw two large pools of blood at the spot. Around noon the two escapees were caught and shot. The corpses were placed in a wooden crate and were carried around from block to block as a deterrent. Only

---

6. Krautwurst was tried at the Buchenwald camp guards trial and sentenced to death by hanging. The sentence was sustained but apparently never carried out. He was probably released in the 1950s. NA, RG 338, case 000-50-9, box 426, "Review and Recommendations," 67–69, 94–95.

around 2:00 P.M., after we had stood for eighteen hours, did Koch let us move out. Dead tired, we immediately fell into a leaden sleep—but no one could wake up the two comrades any more. Approximately six months later the manservant of Deputy Commandant Weissenborn showed me a skull on his writing desk. It was that of our comrade Fischer, which I recognized immediately from the rather large protruding front teeth. It was the victory trophy of a headhunter!

MAX GIRNDT, Oppeln, Upper Silesia

35. TORTURE METHODS AND ATROCITIES OF THE SS

IN SUMMER 1939 the deputy commandant at the time, Rödl, sent a prisoner to his dwelling without a pass: When the prisoner reminded him that it was forbidden to go there without a pass, Rödl forced him to go nevertheless. Because the prisoner did not walk quickly enough in Rödl's opinion, this murderer drew his revolver and shot after the prisoner. The sentries stationed along the camp street took that as a signal to shoot, so the comrade was murdered in front of what was then the post office.

One day in summer 1940, during the building of the pipelines to the water towers in the camp, Master Sergeants Becker and Weihrauch and Technical Sergeants Müller and Halter were sitting around the materials-receiving depot of this detail. They were drunk and were target shooting. When this became too boring for them, they arbitrarily picked a prisoner out of the detail, brought him to the booth, and gave him twenty-five lashes on the rear with the cane. Then they ordered him to run to the sentry line. When the prisoner replied that he was not crazy yet, he received twenty-five more lashes with the cane. Since he was still not ready to obey the death command, he was beaten by all four SS bandits at the same time. Then they ordered the prisoner to run around a tree for ten minutes until he became quite dizzy. Afterward they forced him toward the sentry line. Just as the comrade was about to run across the line, another prisoner came and pulled him back. After that the four sadists brought both prisoners back to the booth and beat them steadily, saying that the work detail could only return to camp after one of them had run across the sentry line. The comrade who had come later decided to sacrifice himself. He lit a cigarette and walked very slowly across the sentry line. As he stepped across it, he told the sentry he should at least shoot him in the head so that he would die immediately. The sadistic sentry, however, shot the brave comrade in the stomach. He lay on the ground for ten minutes in terrible pain, screaming horribly. Then the work detail officer came and gave the comrade a "mercy shot" in the head with his revolver.

Riedl, the owner of a transport firm from Weimar, was a witness to this murder and declared, "If I were a sentry, I would shoot down twenty a day!" The camp doctor at the time, Hoven, wrote on the death certificate that the prisoner was shot from a distance of 20 yards, although the comrade was in fact only 3 yards from his murderer.

In summer 1940 six to eight Jewish comrades in the Jewish stone-carrying detail were regularly driven across the sentry line and shot. The chief murderer was the SS sentry Zepp, who received three days of special leave for each prisoner he shot. Zepp had made a regular "contract" with some of the more criminal kapos, who had to drive the unfortunate victims to him.

The kapos who drove the prisoners to the line were Vogel (political), Herzog (Foreign Legion), Strenzel (Foreign Legion), and Gross (a Jewish professional criminal). Of these only Strenzel is still alive today. Vogel and Gross were executed in camp by their fellow prisoners. After his release from camp, Herzog was killed by another prisoner who recognized him. These four kapos received a package of tobacco for each victim they drove to the murderer Zepp.

In 1940–1941 the most infamous sadists among the block officers were the Sergeants Roscher and Kubitz. Roscher, who was soon promoted and became roll call officer, had prisoners buried alive. Then he murdered them with blows from a shovel when they pushed their heads through the dirt. As he made his rounds through the camp, he also used to seize a victim at random, take the unfortunate prisoner to the nearest washroom, and then hold his head under water until he drowned. Roscher killed about thirty-five to forty comrades in this manner.

Kubitz had the habit of ordering any prisoner he encountered on the street to bow. Kubitz would then strike the prisoner on the base of the skull until his neck was broken. Thus he murdered twenty to twenty-five comrades.

A German political prisoner was taken before Deputy Commandant Rödl in summer 1940 because of a complaint about a letter. Asked whom the letter was from, the comrade answered, "From my mother." Rödl then said cynically, "The old sow doesn't need to write." When the prisoner naturally became upset about this remark, Rödl pulled his revolver. He forced the comrade into the corner of the room and had him shot there by the roll call officer, on account of the prisoner's alleged "resistance."

In summer 1941 two priests from [the Benedictine monastery at] Maria Laach in the Eifel were brought to Buchenwald because they had refused to give the Hitler salute. Their "punishment" was as follows: In front of the cellblock on roll call square, a chair was placed and on it an SS cap. From early morning until night, the two priests had to walk back and forth in front of the chair, giving the Hitler salute each time they passed. This was a special source of amusement for the block officers.

In March 1942 an antisocial prisoner from Berlin was transferred to the gardening detail as punishment because he was caught smoking during working hours. There he had to carry dirt and manure at double time. After five to six days, he collapsed, primarily because he wore wooden shoes and as a result had badly wounded feet. SS Sergeant Krautwurst, who was stationed in the gardening detail, threw the collapsed man into a sewage ditch full of excrement.

The prisoner was pulled out again and sprayed off with cold water from a garden hose. After that he had to work again at double time until he finally collapsed around 4:00 in the afternoon. The corporal put his foot on the throat of the collapsed man until the poor man suffocated.

The homosexual sadist SS Technical Sergeant Zöllner was widely known by the nickname "Aunt Anna." Young, good-looking prisoners were the victims of his perversities. In summer 1942 he locked himself into the washroom of Block 13 with a young antisocial. A few days later, in a conversation with a comrade, this prisoner said that Zöllner could do nothing more to him, that the prisoner need only lock himself into the nearest washroom with him. This conversation was overheard by SS Technical Sergeant Beyerlein. The young antisocial was transferred to the Daasdorf work detail the very next day. That evening he came back as a corpse: "shot while attempting escape."

Just as great a homosexual sadist was the work detail officer Greuel. Greuel would bring a prisoner to his room in the morning, right after the work detail moved out, and give him twenty-five lashes on the rear with a cane. Then he would say, "Now I'll enjoy my coffee more." On August 22, 1942, he beat a prisoner from his detail with his own hands until he crossed the sentry line. The sentry Nief shot this comrade while he was still 3 yards in front of the line.

In February 1943 a transport of women came into camp. Among them was a young Ukrainian woman who was seven months pregnant. Her buttocks were completely torn open and covered with blood. According to her testimony, she had been abused on the transport.

A special annihilation action against the Jews was carried out in the months of May and June 1943. Fifteen Jewish prisoners, most of them very young, were given lethal injections as "punishment" by the medical corpsman SS Master Sergeant Wilhelm, because their work detail officer had reported them for alleged laziness at work. The above-mentioned Greuel was involved in most of the cases.

In summer 1943, during the unloading of gravel from a truck from the transport firm Klawitter of Weimar, a prisoner smashed his finger. When the driver gave the prisoner a bandage for the wound, SS Technical Sergeant Halter of Füssen in Allgäu and Sergeant Thamke of Grünberg in Silesia reproached the driver, Klawitter, saying it would be better to kick the prisoner in the stomach than to help. But Klawitter answered the SS men, "That's what you're here for; I'm no SS man." For this Klawitter received an eight-day ban on entering the head-quarters area again. Only because no other transport operator was available was he given permission to enter the headquarters area again.

In mid-February 1945 five Polish comrades from Block 37, of which I was the senior block inmate, were summoned to the political department. They never came back into camp but were hanged, as I later found out. On the next day another Polish comrade was again summoned; he ended up the same way.

When the next day a Russian comrade was ordered to the gate for the same purpose, he went to the infirmary. There he was admitted under the name of a Russian prisoner who had just died, while the name of the prisoner ordered to report to the signpost was reported as dead. When I made this report to Roll Call Officer Hofschulte, he merely said, "Well, once again we have saved ourselves a little work!"

JOSEF SCHAPPE, Düsseldorf

36. History of the Jews in Buchenwald

THE FIRST JEWS came to Buchenwald in spring 1938. At that time the camp was still essentially in the hands of the criminal prisoners, who allowed themselves to become total creatures of the SS and their methods. The arrested Jews were of such varied ages and social origins that they could never act as a homogeneous unit. They had to camp out in a cattle barn without any furniture, getting 4 ounces of bread and less than 3 pints of watery soup a day to live on—and they were largely swindled out of the soup by their criminal overseers. They worked fourteen to fifteen hours a day. Sleep was possible only about five hours a day because of the living conditions and the harassment. Through systematic harassment and beatings, especially in the stone quarry, three to four of them were forced to run into the sentry line every day. There they were shot "while attempting escape." Apart from a very small number who were released, all the others were murdered down to a remnant of about twenty, who are still alive in Buchenwald today.

On September 23 and 24, 1938, an additional 1,000 Jews per day came from Dachau concentration camp to Buchenwald. The overwhelming majority of the Jews in these two transports had been arrested in "actions" after the German march into Vienna. In addition, there were among them a considerable number of long-time prisoners who had been imprisoned earlier for their antifascist convictions. In the following weeks and months, the systematic struggle of the imprisoned German antifascists reached its first crisis. It concluded with the removal of the criminal element from positions of leadership at the start of the new year. The

Jews now found themselves in an essentially more favorable position. By January 30, 1939, at the urging of the German antifascists, the commandant ordered Jews to take their prisoner foremen out of their own ranks in the future. Even among these, a number proved to be negative and dangerous elements, but they could be more easily eliminated than the so-called Aryans.

On November 9, 1938, through the Rath action, 12,000 Jews were delivered into the camp. During their march into camp along the road from Weimar, they had to go through a gauntlet of SS men armed with sticks and whips, so that only a few arrived in camp completely uninjured. These thousands were housed in five emergency barracks, without latrines, without sanitary facilities, without straw mattresses or blankets. They had to lie on top of one another, four to a bunk. Under those circumstances, and with the added abuse of SS men who chased people around with whips and pistols, such a chaos arose in the first night that it could only be described as a riot. Of the many who had been shackled together by their hands in a circle and had dogs turned upon them, seventy went mad that night. They were temporarily placed in a wooden cage, from which they were taken in groups to the camp jail, where they were personally beaten to death by SS Technical Sergeant Sommer.

Among these 12,000 were a relatively large number of well-to-do businessmen. Thus the SS took advantage of this action not only to satisfy their lust for murder but also for their own personal enrichment, down to the lowest-ranking SS man, in an almost unimaginable manner. Through the loudspeaker it was announced that those who placed their automobiles and houses at the disposal of the camp administration would receive preference for release. Gold jewelry and bank notes circulated constantly in the circles of the SS and their criminal assistants. Every day collections amounting to thousands of marks were taken under various pretexts: for damages, compensations, and release expenses.

When after a few weeks the action—which had cost hundreds of lives—ended with mass releases, property worth millions had passed through the camp. The demoralization of the SS through this corruption and the resulting close business ties with the criminal prisoners contributed more than a little to the decision of Commandant Koch. He swallowed the bitter pill and placed political prisoners in leadership positions in order to regain control of his headquarters staff.

At the beginning of the war (September 1939), an order from the commandant banning Jews from treatment in the prisoner hospital in the future was quietly ignored by the comrades in the infirmary.

The next large mass action was the delivery of approximately 2,500 mostly stateless Jews from Vienna and the occupied territories in the east. They were housed in five large tents behind barbed wire in roll call square [in the Little Camp]. The methods employed in their treatment and care, the taking over of this special camp by the infamous SS sergeants Blank and Hinkelmann, and frequent declarations of SS members all indicated that they were to be liquidated to the very last man. There were among them residents of entire homes for the elderly and students from boarding schools. Deputy Commandant Hüttig, shaking his head, said of them in my presence, "It is unbelievable that they have let such people run around free until now."

At first the SS attempted the liquidations by the usual method, shooting prisoners while they "attempted escape." Then they switched to keeping those in the special camp behind the barbed wire and giving them only half rations of food. They had to stand in roll call square in winter weather without underclothes or coats until the daily quota of sixty dead was reached. In addition, Sergeants Blank, Hinkelmann, and Sommer busied themselves with special pleasures, such as giving out kettles of poisoned food on a number of occasions.

From the very beginning we carried on a struggle to put a stop to these things, a struggle that because of the balance of power could of course be carried on only indirectly against the SS. Its immediate target was their prisoner collaborators. The foreman of the column that carried the food to the special camp was brought down and the comrade Curt Posener put in his place. He was at least able to smuggle additional food into the special camp at the risk of his own life. Indeed the two worst collaborators (Wolff and Rosenbaum) remained in their positions, but we were able to place the Polish comrade Vulkan as clerk. Through his dedication he was able to save the lives of many people.

In spring 1940 the German antifascist Walter Krämer (murdered in November 1940), kapo of the prisoner hospital, was able to achieve the dissolution of this death hole by constantly working on the garrison doctor. He used the reasoning that epidemics were being spread from there into the camp, to the SS, and to nearby villages. Five hundred skeletons, barely alive, were brought into the large camp through this rescue action.

Prior to that, soon after the start of the war, the following incident happened there. On November 9, 1939, the day after the assassination attempt [on Hitler] in the Bürgerbräukeller, all Jews were locked into darkened barracks. A group of SS members, among them the sergeants Blank and Jänisch, selected twenty-one strong young men. They took them to the stone quarry, where they were shot "while attempting escape." The others remained five long days without food, locked inside the blocks, uncertain about their eventual fate. Since after this the entire camp received no food for three days—because a pig had allegedly been stolen—these measures had especially serious consequences.

The inmates of the Little Camp mentioned above were all sent to the stone-quarrying or stone-carrying work details (again, the work detail officers were Blank and Hinkelmann). There, with the usual beatings and shootings, the bloody work was brought to an end, in general successfully. The ongoing struggle to eliminate a series of SS collaborators among the functionaries of the Little Camp and the stone quarry led to the dismissal of the Jewish antifascist [Rudi] Arndt of Berlin. He had been the senior block inmate of Block 22 and was murdered in the stone quarry on May 3, 1940, as the result of a denunciation. Along with the released senior camp inmate, the Thuringian comrade Ernst Frommhold, he had been the principal organizer of the struggle against SS measures. Fourteen days later the above-mentioned comrade Max Vulkan was murdered in the same manner. I myself was a witness when Wolff threatened him: "If you ever mention anything about the occurrences in the Little Camp, I will see that you do not leave the camp alive."

In summer 1940 Commandant Koch, Deputy Commandants Schobert and Florstedt, the camp doctor, and some other members of the headquarters staff visited the sock-darning detail, an invalids' work detail. They chased all Jewish invalids into the stone quarry. Among those shot on the first day of work was our Austrian comrade Hans Kunke.

It must be noted that in addition to these special actions against Jewish individuals or groups, mass death—through poor treatment, hunger, and attempted poisoning by the camp doctors—of course struck the Jews especially hard. This was because the Jews, under pressure from the SS, were always placed in the worst work details in the camp, despite the resistance of the antifascist groups.

In February 1941, 400 young Dutch Jews were brought to Buchenwald. Because the improved camp conditions fought for here did not allow their liquidation to the extent the SS desired, they were transferred after a short time. They went to camp Gusen near Mauthausen and within three weeks were murdered to the last man.

That same year the first case of open resistance to an SS murder took place. SS Technical Sergeant Abraham drowned the Jewish prisoner Hamber in a pool of water. His brother—questioned as a witness on the cause of death—told the truth. Thereupon the entire work detail was called to the gate, but understandably none of the others dared to say that they had seen anything. All names were recorded. Immediately afterward they were all sent to their blocks.

The brother of the murdered man told me, "I know that I must die for my testimony, but maybe these criminals will restrain themselves a little in the future if they have to fear an accusation. Then I will not have died in vain." About 9:00 P.M. he was again called to the gate and much to our surprise returned to us after about half an hour. Commandant Koch, the adjutant, the deputy commandant, the camp doctor, and the roll call officer had interrogated him. The commandant told him the following: "We want to know the whole truth. I give you my word of honor that nothing will happen to you." Hamber repeated his previous statements one more time. About 11:30 P.M. he was called out of the block again, was placed in the camp jail, and was dead after four days. (It should be noted that at least up to the year 1942, no Jew ever left the cellblock alive, no matter what the grounds were for his having entered it.)

One by one the twenty-nine other Jews of this work detail who were on the list were brought to the camp jail, where each died after a few days. Only one, a forty-year-old shoemaker, Löwitus, was released before his name came up; as a citizen of one of the Baltic states, he could emigrate to the Soviet Union.

The following examples describe the events in the camp jail. The Jewish antifascist Jochen Pickard from the Rhineland, who was sent from Dachau to prison for political offenses, was transferred to Buchenwald concentration camp after completion of his sentence. The SS had not forgotten that for years in the concentration camp he had denied all the charges against him. A few days after his arrival in Buchenwald, he was sent to the camp jail, which he did not leave alive. The Social Democratic president of the Prussian Landtag, Ernst Heilmann, was brought into the cellblock in 1940 without any formal charges and was dead after a short time. Kurt Eisner, the son of the famous Bavarian prime minister of the same name, successfully survived several murder attempts because of his extraordinary coolness. Then he was interrogated as a witness in a minor, nonpolitical matter involving another prisoner. He declared to the deputy commandant: "I have been a prisoner for ten years. You should not expect me to denounce another comrade." He died in the cellblock.

In winter 1941 the infamous experiments at the Typhus Station began. Ten Jews were selected as the first victims. Among those in the next groups were fifty Jews. Then the racial doctrines of the Nazis prevented the further use of Jews, since Aryans were not allowed to be vaccinated with blood serum from Jews.[7]

In spring 1942 approximately 400 Jewish prisoners who had been declared incapable of work were sent by the camp doctor, Dr. Hoven, on a so-called invalid transport to a secret destination. It was an experimental poison gas institute [Bernburg] [Chapter Seven, §92]. Over a year later the prisoner records office was instructed to list the members of this transport as dead. Hoven declared to the comrade Weingärtner (Karlsruhe), at that time kapo of the prisoner hospital, "If things turn around sometime, we will both be hanged for this." He did not know that his apparent accomplice had in fact saved a number of comrades by falsifying the lists.

In general, insofar as we could not prevent this sort of thing, we saw it as our principal task at least to protect the comrades who had good characters and clean reputations and were capable of offering resistance. This goal was justified through success on April 11, 1945.

The transport mentioned above was conducted as follows: For four consecutive days three trucks drove up to the roll call each morning, and the thirty Jews whose names were read were loaded in. On the last day a truck drove to the hospital, where the selected sick prisoners, in nightshirts and without blankets, were thrown in and driven away.

On October 17, 1942, Jewish prisoners from all the camps, prisons, and penitentiaries were transferred to the liquidation camp at Auschwitz. From Buchenwald 450 Jews were sent away. We were left with 200 comrades who had been exempted as skilled workers in the defense industry.

Our situation in camp was now, temporarily at least, essentially improved. For one, the systematic struggle of the illegally organized antifascists had led to almost complete elimination of anti-Semitism, the majority of the camp having been immunized against this plague. For another, the SS believed that they needed us as skilled workers and therefore moderated their persecution.

---

7. This is one of several references to Nazi racial theory, which had developed into an elaborate pseudoscience. For some valuable insights into Nazi views of biology, genetics, and euthanasia, see Benno Müller-Hill, *Murderous Science: Elimination by Scientific Selection of Jews, Gypsies and Others, Germany, 1933–1945* (New York: Oxford University Press, 1988).

In summer 1943 we faced a new crisis. Sergeants Schmidt and Greuel, Labor Service Officer Simons, and Roll Call Officer Hofschulte, in cooperation with Deputy Commandant Gust, the camp doctor Hoven and the medical corpsman Wilhelm, began a new liquidation action. The two first named indiscriminately reported a number of Jewish comrades for alleged laziness at work. Simons and Hofschulte ordered whipping and carried it out themselves. Gust placed the victims in the camp jail and the next day transferred them to the hospital. Lethal injections from the responsible authorities there took care of the rest. The self-sacrificing work of our comrades in the hospital succeeded in saving a few victims and finally putting an end to the action. Bribery of the SS bandits in charge played a role in this instance as it did so often. But fifteen comrades, among them the Czech antifascist Max Galandauer, met their deaths.

Because of the tension that this crisis created, for the first time we confronted the question of resisting with force. In discussions with the comrades responsible for the camp, it was made clear to us that an attempt at a general uprising would have been hopeless. It would therefore have served only as a provocation. But as those responsible for the Jewish group, we had decided that if the usual attempts to stop this series of murders in camp failed, we would rather fall in a hopeless struggle than let ourselves be slaughtered like sheep one by one. Then the effects of our work up to that point became apparent for the first time. The majority of Buchenwald Jews would have taken this road with us, in contrast to all those millions who let themselves be slaughtered without resistance. Up to now the Warsaw ghetto uprising unfortunately represents the sole exception.

In the same period food rations for the Jewish block were regularly withheld, allegedly as punishment. Food that was saved in this manner was distributed as a supplement to a series of work details. Once again the solidarity of the camp became obvious: A number of work details decided to give this food back to us, although they would have to reckon with punishment if it became known. The [supply] rooms, the camp police, and the fire department in particular should be mentioned here. Because of the danger of betrayal, other work details whose membership had not been selected so carefully for their antifascist sentiments could support us only through the individual actions of decent comrades. To the work details named above should be added the prisoner records office, the labor records office, the senior block inmate, and the inspectors [*Kontrolleure*]. As is clear from the above, all these incidents had to be kept strictly secret, so the majority of the inmates of Buchenwald concentration camp never knew about them.

In 1944 the situation changed because of the arrival of mass transports of Jews from the east. First, with the complete enslavement of Hungary, came the male Jewish Hungarians who had been selected at Auschwitz as fit for work. They arrived in transports of 1,000 to 1,500 men. In addition, with the advance of the Red Army, more and more evacuation transports from Polish camps arrived here. The possibilities of providing for them were as slight as for the thousands and thousands of non-Jews who were deported in the same manner. The deputy commandant took the standpoint, "As long as the gate is not shut, the camp is not overfilled." The untiring, self-sacrificing work of the prisoner leadership, above all comrade Hans Eiden, succeeded in providing emergency housing, at first in tents and later in emergency barracks. This was done through the more or less open theft of SS property.

The arriving mass transports were designated entirely for reshipment to external work details. There they would all have been condemned to a more or less gradual wasting away if they had not had leaders who could have prevented the worst. Thanks to the comrades of the labor records office, we were able to pull out not only the most actively useful elements but also hundreds of children and youths who would otherwise have been sent to a certain death. To the Hungarian and Polish comrades in particular, along with our longtime prisoners who volunteered to be room attendants, we owe the possibility of sorting out prisoners in the short time at our disposal—often the transports of 1,000 to 1,500 people were in camp for only three or four days. Through this sorting we rid ourselves of the most dangerous Nazi informers; at the same time we tried to give the transported prisoners their own leadership.

A pleasant exception that filled us with pride was the evacuation transport from Auschwitz-Monowitz. It had a clean, well-organized antifascist prisoner leadership: They were our Buchenwald comrades who had been taken away two and a half years earlier. One of our best, however, the Austrian antifascist Erich Eisler, had been murdered in the jail at Auschwitz.

By fall 1944 the external work details had made cripples out of many of the men from the transports who were once fit for work. So-called invalid transports began to stream back here before reshipment to liquidation camps. The external work details Magdeburg and Zeiss alone sent back 1,500 candidates for death. The efforts of our comrades in the infirmary succeeded in taking 500 of them off the list. A number of them whom the SS had put on the transport lists were even held back here. This was done through rather open sabotage by the labor records office and the prisoner records office. But over 900 had to ride to their deaths in Auschwitz, just before the Red Army put an end to SS activity there. Immediately afterward the labor assignment officer demanded a list of children in order to send them to the infamous Bergen-Belsen camp. Once again the labor records office succeeded in limiting the victims to twenty-one, although there were several hundred children here. The prisoner hospital, which in general accounted for most of what was accomplished in Buchenwald, cooperated in this instance as well.

With the constantly increasing overpopulation of the camp, SS control was no longer as intense as it once had been. The segregation of Jews and non-Jews was therefore imposed less rigorously over the course of the years. During 1944 the Jewish comrades more or less joined their respective national groups.

The constant defeats of the Nazis and the advance of the Allied armies of liberation led to the belief that a special SS action against Jewish prisoners was no longer possible. Then all of a sudden, on the evening of April 4, 1945, came the command, "All Jews report immediately to roll call square." None of us had any doubts about the meaning of this measure. A short, spontaneous discussion produced the following picture: In consideration of the military situation, an open mutiny of the entire camp would represent a pointless suicide. But obeying the order, which a few weeks earlier we would not have been able to avoid, would represent an act of cowardice, considering precisely this situation. Therefore we turned to open sabotage. At the urging of activist elements, no one would report. Hundreds, if not thousands, fled to their non-Jewish comrades in other barracks. The card files in the blocks were burned; the prisoner records office declared itself incapable of preparing a precise list of Jews in camp in such a short time. The camp police maintained that it was not able to find the Jews, quite apart from the fact that with only 100 men it could not forcibly assemble 8,000 men! The SS hesitated and postponed the roll call to the next afternoon.

Through the open mutiny of activist elements among the Jews and deliberate passive resistance of the non-Jewish comrades, the Nazis' objectives ended in a complete fiasco. Approximately half the Jews, around 3,000—those who were the most active and decisive in their resistance, of course—had again fled and hidden themselves among the others. Following our motto, "No surrender without resistance," our comrade Kurt Baum of Herne attacked with a spade the sergeant who stumbled on his hiding place. Baum, an antifascist jailed since 1935, fell as the first victim. But the block officers were startled. The search action was not continued. There were 3,000 Jewish prisoners illegally in the camp; the SS had lost all control over the situation. Already by the next day, the favorable effects of this development were visible. Hiding the forty-six comrades who were to be liquidated became much easier. (The camp administration had added me to the list because of the sabotage of the Jewish transport.) The developments of the following week do not belong here; they affected the entire camp. With the afternoon of April 11, 1945, this chapter closes.

The above report can of course give merely a rough framework for the development of the history of Jews in Buchenwald. Details can be given only insofar as they are especially representative. Yet the complete significance of things is understandable only in connection with the whole history of Buchenwald. In all the facts discussed here, I was either a participant myself or found out about it directly from the participants.

The course of our work and our struggle has taught us something. It would not have been possible to use as guidelines for action the familiar and accepted viewpoints of Jewish life as it had been in freedom. We could not conduct our struggle for our survival against the SS as either conservatives or liberals, Zionists or socialists. There was only one possibility: solidarity of all those capable of resistance on the grounds of antifascism.

EMIL CARLEBACH, Frankfurt am Main

37. Memories of a Young Jew

Sachsenhausen. I came into this camp at the age of seventeen. But January 7, 1940, a cold winter day, will always remain in my memory. We had to stand at attention in rank and file in the blocks since there was not enough work for all the prisoners. All of a sudden five block officers stormed in. They bellowed, "What kind of pigs are standing at ease here?" Then stools flew over our heads one after the other. Full jugs of water followed. Since the doors were blocked by SS men, everyone jumped out of the windows, full of fear. Outside stood additional troops of block officers armed with sticks with which they struck at everyone. Many dead men lay on the floor; we stumbled over the bodies and were beaten again, but in the end we all got outside the block. Then we were chased at double time around the barracks. SS men would stick their legs out to trip us, then strike us with rubber truncheons and iron bars.

After two hours, the command was suddenly given to halt. Despite the bitter cold, we were bathed in sweat. Then we had to do knee bends for an hour and stay in the "Saxon salute." Woe to him who fainted! Our block had thirty-seven dead that day. These actions continued every day the entire winter; the Easter holidays in particular were occasions for the most brutal abuses.

Dachau. Because of extreme bodily weakness, I was transferred there in the year 1941. I worked in the plantation, turning over fallow land. Our foreman went up and down the rows, striking everyone on the back with the blade of a shovel. Many ran into the sentry line because they could no longer stand the torture. In the evenings we had to use wheelbarrows to bring back into camp the dead, the wounded, and those beaten to the ground.

Buchenwald. After a relatively short stay in Dachau, I was sent here. I want to present only one memory—our torment over the "Jewish song." It went as follows.[8]

For centuries we have deceived the people,
no swindle was too large or too bad for us.
We have lied, cheated, and swindled
whether it was with the mark or the crown.
Now the paradise has come to a sudden end;
gone is the filth and all the swindling.

---

8. The text of the Jewish song can also be found in Feig, *Death Camps,* 95–96; *SSS,* 308–309; *TPH,* 81.

Now must our crooked dealer's hands
be used for the first time in honest work.
We are the Cohens, the Isaacs, and the Wolfensteins,
known everywhere for our ugly mugs.
If there's a race that is still more base,
then it is surely related to us.
Now the Germans have finally seen through us
and put us securely behind barbed wire.
We deceivers of the people have long feared
what has suddenly come true overnight.
Now our crooked Jewish noses mourn;
in vain is hate and discord sown.
Now there is no more stealing, no feasting and
no debauchery.
It is too late; it is forever too late.

This song was "composed" by a German antisocial. Even for Rödl, the deputy commandant at the time, it was too stupid. He had it sung two times and then banned it. But Deputy Commandants Florstedt and Plaul brought the song out of obscurity. Then there was a regular command at the end of the evening roll call: "Jews remain!" When the rest of the camp had moved out, we had to stand in roll call square and sing the Jewish song continuously for hours at a time—often until late at night. If by chance an outside visitor was present during evening roll call, Florstedt had "his" Jews sing the song for the visitor. He was especially proud that Buchenwald concentration camp had its own Jewish song. It goes without saying that many a Sunday afternoon, which was usually free of work, had to be spent singing this product of German culture. All this, which happened mainly in 1941–1942, ceased in 1943 when workers, not singers, were needed.

MANFRED LANGER, Gelsenkirchen

38. THE MURDER OF ERNST HEILMANN

ON SEPTEMBER 25, 1938, Ernst Heilmann, chairman of the Prussian Landtag faction of the Social Democratic party (SPD), was transferred from Dachau to Buchenwald.[9] At first he was in a transport work detail. Later, at the suggestion of the camp administration, he was employed as a room attendant.

From the prisoners' side objections were raised against Heilmann for having initiated concentration camps in Germany through his motion in the Reichstag.

---

9. For more on Heilmann, see Poller, *Medical Block*, 152–161.

Heilmann explained this by saying that in the Landtag he had only discussed the possibility of isolating inveterate professional criminals for an indeterminate amount of time. Since he otherwise conducted himself in an uncomradely manner in the block, he was not very popular among the prisoners. Despite that, a general outrage spread through the ranks when he was called to the gate on March 31, 1940. For everyone knew that this meant a death sentence.

He immediately went into the cellblock. The SS then allowed the rumor to spread that Heilmann had it good, that he received all possible advantages in the cellblock. But on April 4 he was brought to the crematorium; Sommer had poisoned him with chloral hydrate.

Heilmann was the only Jew at Buchenwald whom the SS put to lie in state and whose relatives received permission to see the corpse once more before cremation. Deputy Commandant Rödl, who was an accomplice in this murder, expressed his sympathy to Frau Heilmann and her daughter. He said that the case was especially tragic because Heilmann was about to be released.

GUSTAV HERZOG, Vienna

39. THE MURDER OF THE HAMBER BROTHERS

IN SPRING 1941 an event occurred that at the time took place almost daily. In the garrison garage work detail (a Jewish work detail), a Jew—namely, the Viennese [Philipp] Hamber—was fatally abused by Technical Sergeant Abraham, one of the worst sadists of Buchenwald. Abraham struck the comrade down and then threw him into a pool of water. There he held him down with a foot on his head until the comrade had drowned miserably. As has been said, this was an everyday occurrence. Not an everyday event, however, was the aftermath.

Hamber's brother lodged a complaint with the deputy commandant over the death of his brother. The surviving Jew, [Eduard] Hamber, was then locked into the cellblock; after three days he, too, was dead. He was beaten to death by Sommer.[10]

After this witness was silenced, the SS band of murderers wanted to be on the safe side. The entire work detail—thirty-five Jews—was called to the gate. There they were interrogated about the murder case by Deputy Commandant Rödl, Roll Call Officer Strippel, and the camp doctor, Eisele. The SS men assured the prisoners that nothing would happen to them. They should just tell the whole truth. But

---

10. The Hamber brothers were prominent Austrian film producers associated with the Vienna studio Ciba. Fein and Flanner, *Rot-weiß-rot*, 74.

the prisoners were familiar with SS practices and unanimously declared that they knew nothing about the murder. Nevertheless, three days later five comrades of the work detail were called to the gate and sent to the cellblock. Within six days not one of the five was alive any more. Two days later the next five victims followed the same path.

I will never forget the blocks of death candidates who waited for the call to the gate and knew precisely that their fate was unavoidable. I myself had a cousin among them, Jakob Pelz of Emden. He, too, was called one day and left the cellblock only as a corpse. Within three weeks the entire work detail of thirty-five inconvenient witnesses was liquidated in this fearsome manner. But we survivors can provide witnesses for these horrible crimes.

HERBERT MINDUS, Hamburg

40. THE SITUATION OF THE HOMOSEXUALS

THE METHOD of diverting internal tensions in critical times by suppressing politically powerless minorities has often been tested in history and in the short run has been successful. It was applied by the National Socialist system in a manner similar to that of criminals who use a modus operandi over and over again once it has proved successful. There is no doubt that this strategy found its most terrible expression in the "solution to the Jewish question." It was used just as deliberately and barbarously against the homosexuals, but on a smaller scale and one that affected the general public less.

In the case of homosexuals, it was even easier to utilize existing and understandable prejudices. Even drawing these men out of the concealment they sought because of hostile social attitudes represented a form of defamation. This stigmatization was made more concrete by their external identification as a clearly designated group in the concentration camps, where they were the favorite objects of exploitation, insults, and abuse.

The extremely varied composition of the men in this category made their situation still more difficult. In it, in addition to worthy men, a large number of unmistakably criminal blackmailers were to be found. Through personal connections of often dubious nature, it was possible for those less inhibited by conscience to secure better treatment for themselves, whereas almost all the worthier ones went to their deaths.

Because of the mentality of the Gestapo, it was of course easy for them to stigmatize as homosexuals those they could not get at in other ways—for example, politicals and Catholic clergy—and make things difficult for them. It often happened in the concentration camp that a single Jewish grandparent was sufficient to categorize as a full Jew a prisoner who by law was classified as mixed race in the second degree [*Mischling*] and so expose him to every sort of danger. Likewise, the mere suspicion of homosexuality sufficed to mark a prisoner in camp as a homosexual and thus submit him to calumny, general mistrust, and the greatest danger to life.

It must be observed that in the cases of homosexual behavior that became known in camp, those designated as homosexual played a relatively small role for obvious reasons. The fact that they had to reckon with the most severe, life-threatening punishments for even the most minor offenses of that sort forced them to refrain. Moreover, because they were openly marked men, they could not be considered for relationships that required concealment in camp far more than they did outside, since at times discovery meant certain death. An additional reason was their isolation in a block surrounded by barbed wire and in a closed work detail. However, precisely this isolation offered to certain creatures without conscience who exercised power over them an opportunity for shameless extortion, abuse, and rape.

Up to fall 1938, the homosexuals were divided up among the political blocks, where they led a relatively inconspicuous existence. In October 1938 they were transferred as a group to the punishment company and had to work in the stone quarry, whereas previously all other work details stood open to them. Other members of the punishment company, except for a few designated in the records, had the prospect of being transferred to a normal block after a certain time and through it into significantly better living and working conditions. This possibility never existed for the homosexuals. Thus in the most difficult years they were the lowest caste of the camp. In transports to designated extermination camps like Mauthausen, Natzweiler, and Gross-Rosen, they represented the highest percentage ratio in relation to their actual numbers. This was because the camp always had the understandable tendency to send away those parts it considered less important and less valuable, or even worthless. No doubt the increased labor needs of the defense industry also brought some relief to homosexual prisoners, since the shortage of workers forced the recruitment of skilled workers from their ranks. But as late as January 1944 most of the homosexuals, with only a few exceptions, were sent to the murder camp Dora, where many of them met their deaths.

Some striking examples of the fates of homosexuals in Buchenwald concentration camp provide a certain insight into the conditions.

L. Adloff, a librarian at the state library in Berlin and a contributor to the left-wing periodical *Die Weltbühne,* was arrested in 1938 as politically suspect. He also stood under suspicion of homosexuality. In summer 1938 he was delivered into Buchenwald concentration camp as a political. When in October 1938 all homosexuals as well as those suspected of homosexuality were sent to the punishment company, he was assigned the emblem of the homosexuals, the pink triangle, and had to work in the stone quarry. In January 1939 he was sent to Mauthausen concentration camp, where horrible conditions prevailed. In the stone quarry there he suffered a leg injury that developed a terrible infection. That same year he was sent as an invalid to Dachau concentration camp. After severe abuse by the hospital kapo at Dachau, the so-called Heiden Sepp, he was sent as an invalid to Buchenwald, went from here back to Dachau, and in fall 1941 finally returned to Buchenwald to die. As a result of this constant shifting, the broken men died off like flies with each transfer into different circumstances. Adloff brought with him from Dachau in 1941 punishment for some minor offense. In Buchenwald, despite having been punished previously in Dachau, he received an additional twenty-five lashes with a cane and several weeks in the cellblock. The cellblock was at that time an absolutely fatal institution. In the block he had already long been written off as dead. His return was a pure miracle. In the meantime the infection in his leg, which had never healed, developed in such a way that it severely damaged his heart. Since he was by nature a strong man and was characterized by enormous willpower, he dragged himself along for months. Finally, pleurisy brought his life to an end in April 1943.

A Berlin author, Dähnke, was brought to the camp in spring 1942 as a homosexual. He was delivered into camp for his political remarks, which had drawn the attention of the Gestapo. After he had worked in the stone quarry for a few months, he was brought into the infirmary one morning by a room attendant. He was presented to the camp doctor as a tuberculosis patient; in fact, he suffered from chest pains. At first the camp doctor wanted to place him in the tuberculosis ward. When Dähnke, out of lack of knowledge of the situation there, said that he was actually here for political reasons, the doctor became suspicious. He realized that he had a homosexual in front of him and admitted him into the ward reserved for death candidates. Two days later he received a lethal injection.

H.D., a white-collar employee in a large firm, was born in 1915 and arrested on April 20, 1938, because of an illegal trip to Prague. He had attempted to make contact with the Russian consulate in order to emigrate from Germany. The Gestapo suspected him of being an illegal Communist courier. At the same time they arrested the friend with whom he had maintained an intimate relationship and forced the latter to confess. The accusation of high treason had to be dropped since they could not prove anything against D. and had obtained nothing from his friend. Thus he only received a sentence of three and a half years' imprisonment for unnatural sexual conduct. In November 1941 he came to Buchenwald after completing his sentence.

The first impressions he had were those of the corpses in the punishment company, which were piled in front of the door like sacks of flour. Besides that, the same evening a young homosexual hanged himself, yet everyone continued eating calmly; no one paid any attention to it. Again that evening a longtime inmate told him that he would have to work in the stone quarry and that the kapo was a terrible person. Above all, he was told, men charged with §176 (sex with minors) were absolutely lost. He should be cautious, but it was no use trying to hide something. After a tormented, sleepless night, D. decided to provide for every contingency. He addressed the kapo, describing what he had been told and saying that he did not want to be hanged from a tree. He asked the kapo for advice on what he should do.

He achieved the exact opposite of what he had wanted out of this action. The kapo, by the name of Herzog, was a former member of the Foreign Legion, an extremely brutal man and apparently a homosexual sadist. He had a terrible tendency toward bloodthirstiness. If Herzog beat a man bloody, he was lost. Herzog desperately wanted to know who had told him these things and threatened him severely. But because D. realized that his companion in suffering would have been lost, he did not reveal the name of the man who had warned him. In the quarry the next day he was assigned to the cart, strenuous and dangerous work. Anyone who was not able to work any more was quickly thrown into the cart and tipped out onto a pile of stones. Herzog either trampled them to death immediately or poured water into their throats until they drowned. If this procedure revived a man, Herzog assumed he was feigning and took that as reason to trample him to death.

Although D. was young and strong, the work was so strenuous for him that only the end of the workday saved him from collapse. The next morning, out of gratitude for his silence, the friend who had warned him took him to another part of the quarry where the work was somewhat lighter and where he moved out of the kapo's sight for the next few weeks. But after about three weeks Herzog remembered him and again demanded he give the name of his informer. He presented him with an ultimatum: At a certain hour he would chase him across the line toward the sentry on patrol. D. knew that Herzog's ultimatum was in earnest and was prepared for anything. His salvation was a pure miracle. An hour before the determined time, Herzog was called to the gate and quite unexpectedly released from camp. (It was later rumored in camp that he was stabbed to death in his own hometown.)

On January 4, 1942, D. was sent to the typhus experimental station, where young homosexuals were preferred as guinea pigs. He withstood the illness well but later suffered from heart trouble as a result. On July 15, 1942, he was transferred out of the station with the stipulation that he do light work in the stone quarry.

In the meantime chaotic conditions had spread through the block. Encouraged by the block's separation from the rest of the camp, the situation was more supported than controlled by the SS. A few bandits terrorized the occupants in the extreme. They stole the packages men had finally been allowed to receive starting in winter 1941. They held genuine orgies of coarseness and the most shameless sadism. Sexual misconduct and the most gruesome manslaughter were the order of the day. In camp the struggle for control still raged between the politicals and the greens, temporarily tying the hands of the reds. Only after months was it possible to clean the Augean stables, a process made easier because the rascals had in part knocked one another off.

An event D. described illustrates the conditions. The punishment company was not allowed to smoke. But the men in the typhus station had the right to make canteen purchases, like all other prisoners. Thus they could also purchase smoking materials. But because the prisoners in the typhus station could not smoke either, each of them of course had accumulated a small supply of tobacco and cigarettes. The first thing the senior block inmate, a former SS man, did was to require men returning from the station to hand over their smoking materials to him. When they hesitated for a moment, he pulled one of them out, stretched him over a table, and counted out twenty-five lashes for him. After that, tobacco and cigarettes quickly ended up in his pockets.

Methods of liquidation had changed somewhat in the meantime. Up to the beginning of 1942, it was possible to sort out the new admissions in the political department. The men, above all homosexuals charged with §176, were ordered to the gate a few days after their arrival and ended up in the cellblock. A few days later came the death report. Since spring 1942, murders in the cellblock had ceased. Therefore Second Deputy Commandant Gust took advantage of the willingness of the kapo in the stone quarry, Müller, generally called "Waldmüller" [forest miller]. Gust visited him almost daily, shook his hand, regaled him with cigarettes, and no doubt gave him instructions. The number of those "shot while attempting escape" rose shockingly during summer 1942. It became necessary to set up trustworthy prisoners as informal sentries to keep men back. D., who stood out from the others because of his human qualities, was selected as a prisoner sentry and witnessed some gruesome scenes on duty.

Müller was a man who had been completely ruined by his position of power and had turned into a shameless sadist because of his undisciplined character. He escaped his fate in the above-mentioned purge of the punishment company; then he went with some of his buddies to an external work detail in the Rhineland, where he was hanged by his own sidekicks. Older and weaker men, men in bandages, and those sent to him for punishment he drove across the sentry line or killed in the most bloodthirsty manner himself. D. unfortunately stood at a spot that Müller preferred to use for his measures. He swore D. to the strictest silence; one word would have meant certain death at the time. The sentries were mostly so-called ethnic Germans [*Volksdeutsche*] (from Croatia and Romania), but there were also many Ukrainians. Between the kapo and the sentries were firm agreements: In return for tobacco and chewing tobacco, Müller delivered the necessary victims. Day after day at least one prisoner, sometimes even two, went over the line. D. counted thirty victims within a short period. The change of guard was at 9:00 A.M., so it was agreed that one prisoner would be delivered before 9:00 and one after 9:00. The sentries decided among themselves who would shoot and thereby obtain the leave and reward.

The methods varied. Either Müller harassed the victim in such a way that he voluntarily went over the line, or he sent the prisoner over it to search for brushwood. Or he would summon an exhausted man and tell him he could lie down to sleep over there. He would ask the sentry to let him pass and thus send the innocent victim over. Once he had taken a few steps, the sentry shot him down. After the shooting an SS commission, consisting of the adjutant or one of his representatives, a camp doctor, and a third man, would arrive. They determined that once again someone had tried to run away at a "pig's gallop," and D. had to serve as witness.

Once it happened that while the commission was there, another prisoner approached and hesitantly remained standing behind a bush. One of the SS men went up to him and asked him what he wanted. When the prisoner answered he wanted to let himself be shot, the SS man replied, "Wait a few minutes!" The commission members then drove off a short distance on their motorcycles while the prisoner was shot. Then the commission drove back to decide on the new escape attempt carefully and objectively.

One cannot deny that in this case the SS showed a certain practical sense. The work detail officer of the stone quarry was SS Sergeant Höber, who of course raised no objections to these practices. D. witnessed a particularly horrible murder on the same spot. A new Jewish prisoner, a well-nourished man who seemed to come from good circles, was turned over to the kapo by Höber. Müller apparently enjoyed having a well-fed victim out of a higher social class. After performing horrible tortures before D.'s eyes, Müller forced the man to hang himself from his own suspenders. When the suspenders broke, he revived the now unconscious man and forced the prisoner to tie the suspenders back together and hang himself again. After death finally set in, Müller opened the pants of the dead man to examine the last erection. He displayed the oddity to the curious sentries who crowded around, while they all made crude comments.

In this case the repulsive details of all these atrocities are intentionally described so completely not to satisfy some desire for sensation but to show the extent to which the National Socialist system had succeeded in educating men to bestiality. It was behavior that can only be described as pathological and in normal circumstances would be unimaginable. For men who came into this hell, three characteristics were basic preconditions to survive the concentration camp more or less intact: complete good health, a clear mind, and a firm character. Many fell victim to the poisoning of body and soul; only a few survived this test of fire completely intact. But even in cases where men sank to a level that can only be described as animalistic, one must say (in order not to libel animals) that they, too, were victims of a system. It was a system that existed for the benefit of a parasitical class that, masking itself with an old culture, represented a school of depravity that has not had its equal in history.

In fall 1942 the shootings in the stone quarry ceased. The increased employment of the prisoners forced the SS to proceed more cautiously with their "human resources." Moreover, the forces of order in the camp had succeeded in knocking the murder weapons out of the hands of the SS. D. succeeded later, when conditions loosened up somewhat, in switching into a special work detail. Through his irreproachable conduct, he was able to maintain himself in camp and to survive the camp, so that he has lived on as one of the few remaining eyewitnesses.

FERDINAND RÖMHILD, Waldacker-Oberroden

41. SUFFERINGS OF THE JEHOVAH'S WITNESSES

SOON AFTER the National Socialists took power, the ban on the International Jehovah's Witnesses Society began.

The largest campaign of arrests began in spring 1936, after the arrest of the leader in Magdeburg in fall 1934. On the basis of a decree from the Interior Ministry dated June 5, 1937, all Jehovah's Witnesses were transferred to the various concentration camps. By fall 1937 the number of Jehovah's Witnesses in Buchenwald had risen to approximately 270, and in fall 1938 it had reached a peak of 450.[11]

Inhuman and degrading treatment became the lot of these people; they were burdened with the harshest labor. In August 1937 the punishment company was established; it was not dissolved until 1944. All Jehovah's Witnesses except for a few special workers were assigned to it.

On September 6, 1938, the Jehovah's Witnesses were offered the opportunity to buy their freedom with their signatures by recognizing the state and abandoning their beliefs. With only a few exceptions, this offer from the deputy commandant met with rejection. Then the abuse and pressure to undermine our morale began in earnest.

From the beginning of March to December 1938, a ban on letter mail and purchases was proclaimed. After the end of this period, it was permitted to send relatives one letter of twenty-five words each month.

On the first day of Easter 1939, the roll call officer made another attempt to persuade us to recognize the state and the Führer. Mocking names like "Heaven's Comedians" and "Bible Worms" were the order of the day. Success was zero. At Pentecost 1939 the entire Jehovah's Witnesses' block was ordered to appear at roll call square. After a speech by SS Second Lieutenant Hackmann, there began a terrible exercise period, divided into two parts. There was rolling, hopping, crawling, and running. This went on for an hour and fifteen minutes, while the block officers urged us on with sticks and the heels of their boots.

After the outbreak of World War II, on September 6, 1939, all Jehovah's Witnesses were called to the main gate. Deputy Commandant Rödl proclaimed, "You know that war has broken out and the German people are in great danger. New laws are taking effect. If you refuse to fight against France or England, then you must die." Two companies of SS guard troops in full battle gear stood at the

---

11. Kogon gives a brief history of the Jehovah's Witnesses in Germany in his book; see *TPH* 32–33. Their refusal to take oaths to the state or provide military service made them early targets of Nazi persecution.

gate. Not one Witness declared himself ready to follow the demand of the deputy commandant to fight for Germany. After a moment of silence came the sudden command, "Hands up! Empty out your pockets!" Then these gifts to the world and representatives of the Reich of Justice and Peace fell upon us and took away our last pennies.

At an inspection of the domestic service detail by the deputy commandant, all Jehovah's Witnesses were gathered together and sent to work in the quarry, even though 90 percent were war casualties. There was during this time no hospital treatment for Witnesses. Only faith in the justice of divine retribution sustained and supported us.

Witnesses were assigned to domestic service [*Kalfaktor*] posts in 1940. Two Witnesses were locked into the cellblock in mid-October 1941. They were accused of having spread stories of atrocities. Though innocent, they sat in the cellblock for eleven weeks. The SS wanted to get rid of the two because they knew something about the "black treasury" out of which the commandant at that time, Koch, took his expenses.

On January 11, 1942, all Witnesses were once again called to the main gate because they had unanimously refused to contribute to the collection of wool for the German troops on the eastern front. The judgment of the roll call officer went as follows: "You traitors! You dogs of heaven! Today you will work under the open skies (it was a cold 20 degrees) until dark. Take off all your underclothes immediately!" The order was instantly obeyed. In the evening when the inmates of the block returned, they had to give up all their leather shoes and exchange them for wooden shoes.

On February 15 the entire block was again called to the main gate, where the roll call officer read out an official indictment. "Twenty Witnesses are charged with insubordination for not observing a camp regulation, for bribery of a block officer, and for turning off the radio during the address of a representative of the Reich government." In 8-inch deep powder snow, winter "sports" began and did not end until all were completely soaked and exhausted.

It was during this time that the Gustloff Works opened. There followed terrible tortures of Witnesses who refused to support the struggle of the Axis powers in any way. Because a few yielded to pressure out of fear of death or beatings and agreed to perform this sort of work, they were soon shut out of our community.

Since at the beginning of 1943 the Jehovah's Witnesses renewed their activity throughout Germany, thousands of them were brought before the people's courts in Essen, Berlin, and Munich. As a result, the Witnesses in the individual camps were broken up out of a closed block in mid-November 1943 and distributed among all the blocks. In mid-April 1944 several Witnesses were locked in the cellblock under charges that they had attempted to form groups in the camp. The plot was successfully thwarted.

In May 1944, representatives of the Gestapo came to Buchenwald. All Jehovah's Witnesses were called to roll call square and were subjected to a thorough bodily search for treasonous literature. Their work stations were also simultaneously ransacked. The inspection was without success.

The long-awaited Last Judgment is now being carried out on the organization behind the Nazi-fascist atrocities.

[no signature]

42. How Jehovah's Witnesses Were Treated

I ARRIVED in Buchenwald on January 12, 1939, without a court hearing. Upon my delivery Sergeant Jung asked me whether I still believed in Jehovah as God. When I answered yes, he beat and kicked me until I could scarcely hold myself upright. Three of my teeth were broken and my left eardrum ruptured. I was immediately placed in the punishment company, where the senior block inmate at the time, Paul Weitz, raged like a madman. I had, however, the good fortune to be spared from his fits of rage. The work was terribly difficult. With loads that often amounted to more than 165 pounds, we had to run at double time and were driven on with truncheons while doing it. We worked from early morning until evening, even on Sundays. When other prisoners' work ended at noon on Sunday, the punishment company had to stand at roll call square until 7:00 or 8:00 P.M. and received nothing to eat.

After three months had passed, I was taken to the paint shop and released from the punishment company. Since that time I personally have suffered nothing more.

KARL SIEBENEICHLER, Leipzig

Chapter Four
The Work Details

THE SUPPLY ROOM [*Gerätekammer*] was responsible for the furnishings in prisoner and SS housing, for the supply of heating materials and cleaning needs, etc. It should be mentioned that all SS officers and noncommissioned officers considered everything that was in the supply room as provided for their own personal enrichment, either directly or through barter, and they used it for such. During the formative phase of the camp administration, in the supply room as in other parts of the camp, the professional criminals exploited their positions to make shady transactions of the worst sort. They were quickly dismissed and replaced by political prisoners. Bayer, the work detail officer in the supply room, also took advantage of the mass deportation of Jews to Buchenwald that followed in 1938 (Rath action). He forced Jews to buy napkins, drinking cups, spoons, etc. at the most expensive prices. Yet this also opened up opportunities for prisoners assigned to the supply room to provide the implements to others free of charge.

In fall 1939 several thousand Poles were deported to Buchenwald, where they experienced gruesome treatment, hunger, and cold and were housed in tents and unheated barracks. They were driven to the point of tearing up a number of blankets to turn them into jackets and vests. This had to be concealed, at least in part. What could not be hidden could be compensated for by paying off the SS. That was not always correctly understood by those affected.

In fall 1941 the first 2,000 Soviet prisoners of war came to Buchenwald. The entire camp did not get anything to eat for a day because we had welcomed them as our friends. Aside from that, a new task arose for us out of their arrival. These prisoners of war were crammed together in only a few barracks constructed out of the worst materials provided in insufficient quantities. It should be clear that we saw it as a natural obligation to equip these barracks like all the rest. It should be just as clear that this could not be done without tricking and deceiving the SS. Equipping the so-called Little Camp, where the "population density" reached well-known figures, was a similar matter. It would take too long to give figures here, but the majority of prisoners had not the slightest inkling of what other prisoners accomplished through write-offs [of surplus materials], juggling figures, etc.

We could tell many a story about the difficulties had by supply room prisoners who were assigned to the SS barracks. They constantly had to serve as the buffer

181

between unreasonable demands of the lower officers, on the one hand, and cautionary instructions of the higher officers of the SS administration, on the other. We will never forget, for example, that at a time each prisoner slept on a straw mattress filled with 15 pounds of wood shavings, a first-class horsehair mattress was produced for Gauleiter Sauckel's dog. The same thing was done for the leader of the administration, SS Major Barnewald. Against these skulduggeries we prisoners were as good as powerless. But we responded in the manner shown above, and the decisive thing is that the majority of prisoners benefited from our actions.

Only thus was it possible that in the final years a considerable number of prisoners got at least two blankets, or in the case of sickness sometimes more, instead of the one the SS allowed. Only thus was it possible, especially in the prisoner infirmaries, to provide them illegally with blankets, towels, furniture, beds, napkins, bar soap, and many other things. Only thus was it possible that in the last year alone 9,000 blankets, 8,000 towels, 5,000 napkins, and 30,000 spoons were taken away from the SS and placed at the disposal of the prisoners, without SS approval. Bar soap—that is a common thread that has run through the entire history of Buchenwald since the beginning of the war. Excess inventory, that is to say inventory that was no longer on the books, was created with the help of the SS. They had in mind only their own personal black market activities. Nevertheless, it went for the most part where it was supposed to—namely, directly to the prisoners, especially to those who needed it for sanitary reasons. The rationing of the supply was so successful that on the day before liberation the last 6,600 pounds of soap were issued to prisoners.

In summary, what could be done was done. The little mistakes that were made only confirm the correctness of the saying that no mistakes are made only where nothing is done.

RICHARD GEORGI, Leipzig

44. The Camp Laundry

ON SEPTEMBER 9, 1938, a work detail of seventeen prisoners was assembled for the first time to put the newly built laundry into operation. Director of the laundry was SS Sergeant Kindervater. The slightest carelessness he observed at work was sufficient for him to have the prisoner concerned stand for hours with his face pressed to the wall or against a pillar, or to make him perform fifty to 100 knee bends. When he was bored, he went to the front of the building and picked out a "loiterer." He brought him into the laundry, laid him over the table, and gave him twenty-five lashes on the buttocks with a cane.

After a short time the work detail grew to about sixty-five prisoners. Work was performed at times determined by the camp administration. Every week each prisoner received one shirt, a pair of pants, a towel, and a washcloth; every two weeks a pair of underpants; and every four weeks clean bed linens. The provision of clean laundry for the prisoners was sufficient and satisfactory.

It became different when the masses of new arrivals came. Then it was no longer possible to supply the prisoners as before.

In 1939–1940 winter clothing was taken back in the spring and summer clothing was issued, something that later could not even be considered. The winter clothing was washed and made ready for issue again the next fall; summer clothing in those years consisted only of the "zebra stripes." Since it would have been impossible for the entire camp to trade in their clothes, the workers in the laundry detail declared themselves ready to sacrifice their free Sunday afternoons so the prisoners could wear clean clothes. They also performed voluntary extra work for the other comrades.

When the SS saw that the prisoner laundry functioned efficiently, the commandant at the time, Koch, ordered that all the laundry of SS members should be washed there as well. Sergeant Kindervater had the task of collecting money for laundry from the SS. After five or six months, Kindervater ended up in the cellblock because he had embezzled the entire amount, spending it on women and drink. After that the laundry of SS members was taken care of without charge.

At that time permission was obtained from the camp administration to wash the prisoners' private laundry.

In 1941 Buchenwald received the clothing and underclothing taken from the prisoners killed at the concentration camps at Auschwitz and Lublin [Maidanek]. The laundry contained over half a million shirts and 280,000 pairs of underpants. Because of the increased amount of work, the work detail had to be expanded. It was eighty-five men strong. In winter 1939–1940, the work detail regularly had to work four times a week until midnight. Expanding the work detail by recruiting new prisoners would have lightened the load for the other comrades. This effort failed because of the ruthless attitude of the SS men. Not until 1943 was it possible to increase the detail to 120 men and, at the end, to 185 men. In the last half year, work went on almost without interruption day and night.

An especially brutal fellow was SS Sergeant Hoppe. Nor did the laundry director for many years, Thierbach, differ from the others in his ruthless attitude. Once he demanded that a comrade braid a cord into a whip so that he could beat Jews with it. When the prisoner refused, both of them threatened to beat him to a pulp.

A special chapter is the one about informers. All the SS sergeants, above all SS Master Sergeant Schäfer, tried repeatedly to find out about any sort of political activity. Targeting prisoners who seemed compliant, they tried to play the prisoners off against each other and to agitate among them. It is telling of the morality of the work detail that they never succeeded in it.

When comrades from all European nations came into Buchenwald concentration camp, an attempt was made to bring foreigners into the work detail. Thus in time it became possible to allow comrades from almost all nations to work next to the German prisoners.

In 1942–1945 a monthly average of over 300,000 pieces of clothing and laundry were washed; in some months, however, up to 650,000 pieces went through the laundry detail.

BAPTIST FEILEN, Oberhausen

45. THE STONE QUARRY

THE TERM *stone quarry* will forever fill us with horror and disgust. The stone quarry—that is one of the bloodiest concepts, one that can never be erased from the total picture of life in the camp. Even the name of the stone quarry detail was enough to fill the strongest men with the greatest fear. It was synonymous with death, murder, and sadistic torture.

Oh, if the hard stones were not dumb, they could tell us about some of the most horrible dramas of Buchenwald concentration camp. They would tell how children and old men were forced to carry stones that in many cases were heavier than the carriers themselves; they suffered forms of abuse that are scarcely conceivable to normal men.

The prisoner Erwin Kohn was forced to carry so heavy a stone that he collapsed under the burden. He was beaten to unconsciousness with truncheons. The kapo at the time, Vogel, poured water over him and continued to abuse him until he died. The death certificate read, "Shot while attempting escape"!

"Shot while attempting escape"—this was the legal formulation for illegal mass murder.

The young Viennese Bergmann was chased over the sentry line in October 1939 while being terribly abused. He, too, was "shot while attempting escape"! In 1940 Koppen, Riebenberger, Keraner, Rappaport, Katz, and many others were driven into the sentry line after the worst torture and abuse. In many cases they were even kicked across the sentry line. If in future times mothers threaten their children, they will speak not of dragons and devils but of the "Satan" of Buchenwald concentration camp.

SS Master Sergeant Blank was one of the greatest mass murderers. On the basis of his orders, and with his active cooperation, a number of people were shot while "attempting escape." When Blank ordered the former Austrian minister of justice [Dr. Robert von] Winterstein to walk to the sentry line, Winterstein lit a cigarette and went toward the sentry line, thus to his death, while smoking. Blank went on a walk with the former Communist Reichstag deputy, Werner Scholem, and carried on a friendly conversation with him for about ten minutes. Then he shot him down from the side with a revolver. On the basis of a special order from Blank, the former Austrian [army] captain [Friedrich] Stahl was likewise chased into the sentry line, where a dumdum bullet shattered his skull. The political prisoner

Rudi Arndt, who had twelve years of prison and concentration camp behind him, was also shot in the stone quarry. This was done on the initiative of Blank, based on a denunciation from a previously sentenced Jewish criminal.

SS Master Sergeant Hinkelmann was another important figure in this bloody drama. He constantly ran around drunk and conducted the worst sort of business and black market deals with the prisoners. To his account must be booked the deaths of many hundreds of people who were forced to carry stones at double time all day long. One of his favorite expressions, addressed to the tormented, bloodily beaten prisoners with a contemptuous smile, was, "Run faster, then you will reach your goal quicker!" Although he was almost always in a drunken state, he was a positive genius at inventing forms of torture.

Hinkelmann forced old men to climb a pine tree, then he would have it shaken until the poor devils, accompanied by Hinkelmann's satanic laughter, fell down. In most cases they broke their necks or were at least delivered into the hospital severely injured, where they died after a time.

Under Hinkelmann's direction columns of stone carriers had to carry stones for three weeks from the quarry to the horse stables at double time. The building of this short, quarter-mile-long road cost twenty-three lives.

Another work detail officer, SS Sergeant Springer, liked to force pairs of prisoners, under threats of death, to beat each other until one was left lying on the ground. Among others he abused the prisoner Weissmann of Hannover so severely that he died of the consequences. He held the head of the prisoner Lindenbaum (who was over sixty years old) under water until he became unconscious.

These were small details, acts committed by SS men who in joining this organized band of murderers had already automatically placed themselves outside civilized society. Unfortunately, there were also prisoners who willingly allowed themselves to be used as tools by these murderous [SS] bandits. In many cases, they even outdid them.

One of these figures was the kapo Vogel, a sadistic homosexual who found sexual satisfaction in abusing people. He was judge and executioner in one. In 1940 the prisoner Bernstein casually commented on the methods of the kapo Vogel. Vogel brought him into the stone quarry and drove him over the sentry line. Thus he was "shot while attempting escape." Once the deputy commandant at the time, Rödl, was inspecting the stone quarry. A man who remained a little behind because he could not keep up with the double time and was no longer able to drag the terribly heavy stone caught the attention of the deputy commandant. Rödl asked Vogel what was wrong with the prisoner and why he was not able to run faster. That was sufficient grounds for Vogel personally to stone the poor devil on the spot. He was the twenty-four-year-old Podvysoka.

A special task of Vogel's was to liquidate those political prisoners the SS perceived as dangerous and had sent into the stone quarry. In the course of a few months, this amounted to fifty men, who had been turned over to him for this purpose by Roll Call Officers Kent, Petrick, and Stribbel. A typical case was that of [Dr. Walter] Gerdes, the brother-in-law of the former Austrian federal president [Wilhelm] Miklas. Vogel denounced him to his boss, SS Master Sergeant Blank, as a political opponent of the Nazis! Then Vogel attempted to extort money from Gerdes—300 marks. When Gerdes did not comply quickly enough, Vogel had him chased by his foreman, Wittvogel, into the sentry line and [he was] "shot while attempting escape." The young Viennese Hans Kunke was also one of his victims.

Karl Müller, No. 4549, who was active as clerk in the stone quarry work detail from January 1940 to March 1941, offered the following information: "In my capacity as work detail clerk, I had to fill out all the death certificates. They all followed a formula: shot while attempting escape! On the average it was eight per day, seven days a week. In fifteen months 3,600 people were struck off the books."

For all eternity the blood-soaked stones of Buchenwald shall remember it!

[no signature]

46. Death Details in Buchenwald

I WAS BROUGHT to Buchenwald on April 24, 1942, and to the infamous stone quarry in May. The work was very heavy, especially the pulling of carts. Every evening the dead, the severely wounded, and the invalids were brought back into the camp on carts. It amounted to about thirty men almost every day. The abuse by the foremen—who were without exception greens, therefore professional criminals—was indescribable. I saw how the kapo made prisoners lie down and trampled on them until they gave no more signs of life. Or he chased the prisoners into the sentry line, where they were shot by the sentries. Prisoners who were caught by their comrades stealing bread and were transferred to the stone quarry for punishment were done away with after a few hours. The kapo once said to a Jew, "Now it is 12 o'clock; by 12:05 you will be with Jehovah." The kapo then summoned his foreman and drove the Jew with punches and kicks into the bullets of the sentries. The family name of the kapo is not known to me, but his first name was Alfred. He later went to Cologne and was reported to have been hanged there.

Later we had to work in a sand quarry at the SS housing area of Klein-Obringen. In the mornings we were greeted there with stones thrown by Hitler Youths. It grew worse day by day, so that some of the prisoners took their own lives.

Another incident has remained in my memory. On May 1 I was caught smoking in the German Armaments Works. As punishment I received five days without bread and five Sundays of punishment labor. At 2:00 P.M. the punishment column had to assemble at roll call square and then march at double time over

Caracho Way[1] to a sand pile. The pile had to be transported by handbarrows over a distance of half a mile, the work performed at double time. Along the stretch, four SS men stood with dog whips and truncheons, which they used to drive the prisoners mercilessly. It was impossible to go even two or three steps at a normal pace. The whip carriers sweated so much that they had to rest after a short time. After half an hour the dead, wounded, and dying lay upon the route. They were pulled to the side and then it started all over again. This torture lasted four hours. By evening the result was seven dead, almost fifty severely injured, and about 100 slightly injured.

GALT VAN RAMSHORST, Driebergen, Holland

47. MAY 1, 1943

SERGEI NIKOLAYEV of Voronezh and Fedya Fedorkim of Stalingrad were friends; they arrived in Buchenwald together and were both assigned to the punishment company. Every Sunday at the end of the normal workday, they were chased into the "gardening" detail or the stone quarry.

May 1, 1943, will always remain fixed in the prisoners' memories. The prisoners reported for punishment labor as usual. For supervision and guard duty, a detachment of drunken SS executioners appeared, accompanied by dogs. A few of these drunks could scarcely stand on their legs. "March!" commanded an SS man. With blows from the cane and the barking of dogs, the march to the infamous sewage facility in the gardening area began. And then a frightening drama unlike any that older prisoners had ever experienced began to unfold. At double time prisoners had to carry away heavy crates of excrement. The SS turned their dogs onto the exhausted men who had collapsed; the animals tore the clothes of the poor men into rags.

Sergei and Fedya were carrying a crate together. They applied every bit of their strength in order not to be noticed, but they did not escape their tragic fate. The completely exhausted Fedya stumbled and fell, tipping out the disgusting contents of the "load." It spattered SS Corporal Fritz Schulz, who was standing nearby. He immediately pointed his weapon at Fedya and shot him while he was lying on the ground. Meanwhile the dogs attacked the disconcerted Sergei and tore him to the ground. Then a furious SS man attacked Sergei from above, kicking him with his boots. Crushed underfoot and his flesh torn by the beasts, Sergei lay in the dirt and bled to death, since no one was allowed to help him.

---

1. Caracho Way was the road into camp, leading to the gatehouse. The word *caracho*, originally derived from Spanish, was prisoner slang for double time. Poller, *Medical Block*, 29.

In the immediate vicinity another bloody scene took place. Vladislav Schezmit, a Pole, had been assigned to the group of stone carriers who had to drag stones out of the gardening area at double time. A sentry ordered Vladislav to carry away an especially heavy stone that weighed over 150 pounds, but this job exceeded the strength of the prisoner. He could not budge the giant stone from its spot. "Lift!" shouted the SS man and threw a brick at Vladislav, who collapsed with blood pouring from his head. "Pick up the stone! You Polish dog, pick up the stone!" screamed the sentry. Vladislav could no longer get up. To start this gruesome game again, they beat him unconscious with sticks, then brought him back to consciousness. Then they leaned him against a tree and shot at him as if he were a target, until he was riddled with bullets. This orgy lasted a full two hours. Six prisoners were beaten to death and three more prisoners died in the barracks that same night as a consequence of the blows and the dog bites.

Similar things occurred in the stone quarry, where likewise a group of punishment laborers was being directed. Here the SS executioners had thought of a special "amusement." They bet each other on who could kill a prisoner in the quarry with a stone thrown from above. (Six cigarettes or two glasses of beer was the stake.) At times a sentry would simply shoot at a prisoner if he had thrown a stone near him. This "joke" cost up to seventeen victims, dead and wounded.

May 1, 1943, is recorded with blood in the history of Buchenwald.

[no signature]

48. The Transportation Detail

ONE OF THE "BLESSED" institutions of Buchenwald concentration camp was the transportation detail, which was an indelible part of the total picture of the camp.[2] This work detail consisted of 130 Jews who were divided into five wagon columns and proved themselves significantly more efficient than horses.[3] One-fifth of a loaf of bread, a quart of watery soup, and a thin slice of sausage or cheese—didn't that fuel matchless labor power?

To give an accurate picture of the life and sufferings of this work detail, a few unretouched reports follow from comrades who had to work for years in this column.

---

2. "Blessed" is of course meant ironically. It is a reference to the fact that this was considered one of the "suicide work details" because of its high mortality rate. In their typical black humor, the prisoners called them "ascension details" (*Himmelfahrtskommandos*).

3. Fifteen to twenty men would be yoked together to pull one of these heavily laden carts. Because they were often required to sing while performing their work, the SS jokingly dubbed them "the singing horses" (*SSS*, 117; *TPH*, 95).

Leo Margulies, No. 4573. In summer 1942 we frequently had to carry stone chips from the quarry. These chips could be loaded by only four men at a time, which we did in alternation. The other men in the crew could rest in the meantime. That was a thorn in the side of SS Sergeant Greuel. While four of us loaded at the quickest pace, he forced the others to carry large stones from the quarry at double time.

Julius Kodicek, No. 6452. In 1940 we in the transportation detail had the following work hours. With the exception of half an hour as a midday break, we worked from 6:00 A.M. until 2:30 P.M. Then there was roll call, after which we continued from 4:00 P.M. until twilight. It often happened that on the way we had to do calisthenics at the command of Sergeant Chemnitz: lying on the ground, then jumping up quickly and running on. There were usually a number of injuries.

Max Feingold, No. 8448. Because only four men at a time could shovel sand and stone chips, it was a specialty of Kapo Ganzer to have us load it with our bare hands. Afterward there were of course bloody, scraped fingers. It was also part of our work to take the disassembled gallows out of the barn in the gardening area and move it to the dog kennels. This was to be done in such a way that the other prisoners would not notice it. At this time—in 1942—hundreds of Poles were hanged for sexual intercourse with German girls.

Moses Einziger, No. 6933. On April 9, 1942, though late in the season, there was a terrible snowstorm, with temperatures of 10 degrees. Although it snowed continuously, we had to shovel snow. It was a completely senseless activity, since new snow was constantly falling. The balance sheet for the day: The young Viennese Fränkel literally froze, and an additional four comrades were delivered to the infirmary with severe frostbite.

Franz Steiner, No. 3949. In April 1942 we had to work three consecutive Sundays in the SS housing area at Klein-Obringen. The adjutant of the camp commandant at the time ordered that we work the entire day at double time. This we did under constant beatings by the SS guards supervising us. The inhabitants usually sided against us; for example, even children threw stones at us.

Hermann Einziger, No. 6932. In April 1942 we had to carry heavy tree trunks into the camp at the quickest pace. We were chased and abused by SS Sergeants Deuringer and Chemnitz. Because all the comrades were already rather nervous and the kapo Jacob Ganzer drove us at an ever quicker pace, the tree trunks were not being carefully stacked. One of them suddenly rolled back and fatally injured the comrade Friedmann of Mannheim; his spine as well as his rib cage was broken. Eight other comrades were delivered to the hospital.

Max Filgur, No. 120559. In March 1940 the kapo Hill gave my uncle Tischler such a terrible kick in the testicles that he had to be taken to the hospital with severe injuries. Thanks to constant chasing by the SS, my work comrade Drucker fell over a tree trunk in winter 1941 and broke his foot. Because of this injury he is still handicapped today.

49. The SS Slave Trade

O N February 1, 1944, I was assigned to maintain the prisoner card index by the labor assignment officer, SS Captain Schwarz. As of September 1, 1944, I was involved in the same task in handling the numerical card index of the roll call officer. The card index of the labor assignment officer was identical to that of the political department but contained only the prisoners in the camp itself or those under the direct control of the camp in external work details. In any case the card index was never in order, as the political department could never keep up with the numerous new admissions in the latter days. At the end more than 20,000 were missing from the card index.

The overall assignment of labor was controlled through the SS Main Economic and Administrative Office in Oranienburg, Office Group D. The orders that came from there were signed *Maurer*. When a factory—whether private or state controlled—wanted to have prisoners as a work force, it had to submit a request to Oranienburg. If the request was approved in principle, then the labor assignment officer in Buchenwald received the assignment to examine the employment possibilities and conditions on the spot. The examinations, the results of which immediately had to be forwarded to Oranienburg, were carried out by SS Captain Schwarz or his deputy, SS Captain Nebel, or by the leader of the SS band, SS Captain Schenk. On the basis of this report, the request was then approved or rejected by Oranienburg. If specially skilled workers were requested, the engineers of the factory itself came to Buchenwald and selected the appropriate prisoners.

Firms had to pay the concentration camp 4 marks per day for every unskilled worker and 6 to 8 marks for every skilled worker. In these sums were included all social benefits, so that the camp was therefore obligated to continue sticking on health insurance stamps. If the firm was not in a position to supply housing for the requested prisoners, a so-called advance work detail was sent. It completed its task only when the required amount of housing was built.

The labor records office selected prisoners on the basis of orders from the labor assignment officer. In certain cases, on the orders of the political department or other camp offices, prisoners were sent to particularly bad work details as punishment. Certain work details were composed only of Jews, others only of antisocials and professional criminals, etc.

The prisoner functionaries for the subsidiary camps (senior camp inmate, senior block inmate, kitchen personnel, records office, etc.) were proposed by the senior camp inmate in Buchenwald. They were approved or rejected by either the deputy commandant or the labor assignment officer. Every work detail officer had to give a daily report on the amount of work done. These reports, which were gathered together by the labor records office, served as the bases for the invoices sent to obtain compensation for the prisoners' slave labor. Private firms had to pay the money into a bank account; state-owned firms paid through transfers into the accounts.

Buchenwald concentration camp had about 100 external work details with around 51,000 prisoners. The sums brought in by exploiting these prisoners amounted to 1.5–2 million marks a month! The SS conducted a profitable slave trade by using its prisoners.

EMIL HOLUB, Brünn (Brno)

50. The Clay Mine at Berlstedt

W HEN A PRISONER at Buchenwald was condemned to especially hard labor, he was usually sent to the external work detail at Berlstedt, about 4 miles away. It was a brick works with the official name German Earth and Stone Works, Enterprise of the Reich Leadership of the SS. All the work the prisoners had to do there was heavy but brought in much money for the SS.

Regulations called for 150 carts of material to be delivered every day from the clay mine. The prisoners were divided into groups of three men each. Each group had to dig out thirty carts of the material every day and break it into fist-sized chunks. This work had to be done in rain and wind, in ice and snow, often while standing knee-deep in water.

Other groups had to pull the carts up a steep incline to the ovens. Woe to the prisoners whose cart slipped off the turntable or derailed. The kapo Johann Küppers beat the poor prisoners mercilessly. In the last years, after his friend the informer Stemann was beaten to death, Küppers became somewhat more cautious.

Most prisoners came to Berlstedt as punishment—that always meant that they were not to return again to the camp at Buchenwald. But only rarely was a prisoner beaten to death at Berlstedt. The work in the clay mine was sufficient to get rid of people in a short time. And a prisoner was usually brought into the hospital at Buchenwald so late that he could no longer be saved there.

Of course there were other enterprises in Berlstedt besides the clay mine. Although these were not quite so murderous as the work in the open air, they, too, meant hard labor. This was especially true for the prisoners at the brick ovens, who in particular had to suffer from the sulfur fumes.

A special pottery department attached to it had its own ovens, in which luxury and consumer goods were produced for the SS bandits.

The commandant of Buchenwald was at the same time director of this factory and received a correspondingly generous salary. This fact was always used by the kapo Küppers as a threat against the prisoners, who for any reason were transferred out of Berlstedt back to Buchenwald concentration camp. Then Küppers always insisted that the prisoner never say anything about Berlstedt in the large camp. Otherwise he would go to the director of the factory—that is, the commandant--and call the prisoner back.

KURT LEESER, Aachen

51. THE HELL OF OHRDRUF

We ARRIVED at Ohrdruf in September 1944 with 1,000 men. The very next morning we went to work at *caracho*. Tunnels were being dug into the mountains. Work was performed in three shifts. The pace of the work was tremendous. Prisoners were often beaten by the supervisory personnel, the SS, Tenos [*Technische Nothilfe*, technical emergency helpers], as well as civilian personnel. These working hours were also maintained in winter, without regard to the insufficient clothing, the long march to work, etc. The wear and tear on work clothing, especially shoes, was enormous and supplies of replacements inadequate. In my five-month stay at Ohrdruf, I was bathed and deloused only a single time, and that was just because typhus had broken out in a neighboring camp.

Later, 500 new admissions came from Flossenbürg. They were in poor physical condition; all but a few died of the heavy work and the inadequate clothing. From our transport no more than 200 had survived; that is, after five months only one-fifth remained.

Gun emplacements and tunnels were later built adjacent to the troop training area, an area that had been set aside as a Führer headquarters [for Hitler]. But the work sites were too far from the camp at Ohrdruf (at first we rode the 8 miles there every day in buses). Because of the shortage of gasoline, two new branch camps were created at Crawinkel and at the so-called tent camp. There the general conditions were still more unfavorable. Food was scarce and the men starved because of the heavy work demanded of them. Many of the sick were transferred to the hospital in Ohrdruf, which was a hell. The hospital lacked doctors, as well as medication, heating fuel, and more. From time to time transports went from this hospital to Belsen on the so-called invalid transports.

Deputy Commandant Stiwitz and SS Sergeant Müller behaved especially brutally, handing out punishments of twenty-five or more lashes with a cane for the slightest reasons.

In Crawinkel there was a special cellblock, Cellblock 2, that the Security Service used for recaptured escapee prisoners. There only a half ration of food was given out every three days. Light and air were nonexistent. I remember an incident where one evening five comrades were hanged because of escape attempts. Among them was a fifteen-year-old Polish comrade who cried in despair, "Mother, Mother, I am still so young, I don't want to die yet!"

On April 4, 1945, the evacuation order came, and we walked the 42 miles to Buchenwald by a circuitous route. The last 1,000 prisoners received no more food. We were under way for three full days and arrived worn out and depressed. The ill and the weak who could no longer keep up on the way were liquidated with a shot in the base of the skull. It is worth mentioning that on the way some members of the SS already took off their insignias in order to pass themselves off as Wehrmacht members.

ROLF BAUMANN, Berlin

52. The Martyrdom of the Women in Altenburg

I CAME to Buchenwald concentration camp with the evacuation transport Auschwitz-Monowitz on January 26, 1945. From there I was sent to the Altenburg subsidiary camp on February 12, 1945. An armaments factory was located there in which 2,500 women prisoners, to a large extent Polish and Hungarian Jewish women, were employed in the heaviest labor.

A factory building was used as the prisoners' camp. The food was meager for the heavy work. Working conditions were very harsh; the sanitary conditions were inadequate, which the women in particular felt. The women were supervised by women SS overseers, the men by the work detail officer. Among the overseers, a Frau Ruprecht (formerly of Block 10 in Auschwitz) stood out. Up to the last days, she struck the women with a whip or a cane on their heads and backs. The women had their heads shaved for the slightest offenses; speaking with men was of course strictly forbidden. SS Technical Sergeant Fretsch (formerly a block officer in Buchenwald) was in charge of the camp; he, too, struck the women often.

On April 12, 1945, the evacuation of the camp was begun. First the women marched out (without food and for the most part in wooden shoes without stockings). Following them came the men; however, ten prisoners remained behind, of which I was one. We were supposedly going to catch up with the others and bring them food. That was only a pretext, for besides some bread for the prisoners, our truck carried mostly luggage and large quantities of hoarded food supplies belonging to the SS. (A large part of the transport seems to have been liberated by the Americans. The press and radio accounts reported that 800 women and 200 men were saved.)

The prisoner Ihr and I, as well as a female former SS overseer, jumped from the truck and tried to escape. We had found out that our journey was to end at the Dresden Gestapo. Shots were fired at us in vain. We made our way to the front line between Chemnitz and Frankenberg and then encountered American officers, who brought us to Buchenwald and the overseer to a prisoner of war camp.

WALTER STRASZ, Brücken/Pfalz

53. THE WEIMAR POLICE WORK DETAIL

IN 1940 I was stationed along with seven other comrades at the Weimar Police work detail. We were employed as skilled workers, shoemakers, and auto mechanics.

My stay there permitted me to obtain many insights into conditions in the police organization. I will report here only on the attitude toward us prisoners.

Because of the war and the occupation duties connected with it, the majority of the active police personnel were withdrawn and replaced with reservists. For some of the prisoners, the long duration of our work assignment meant a relaxation of the guard and, with that, a certain amount of contact with the civilian population. The SS as well as many of the higher police officers presented us as the greatest criminals. It was soon possible, however, for us to convince everyone we came into contact with that the opposite was true. In the beginning we often encountered skepticism when we told of the horrible things that had occurred to us in camp, but some of our sentries were themselves witnesses to these atrocities. They had the greatest loathing for the SS and distanced themselves noticeably from it.

With the increased need for labor in the last years, many prisoners were brought to Weimar and the surrounding territory. Thus the population heard more about things that they had never previously believed. In general they kept themselves at a distance. Whenever we reproached them for having done nothing, they always answered by pointing to the great terror under which they stood. I would like to add that through the years we found support from Police Inspector Heer and First Lieutenant Hebestreit.

AUGUST BERGMANN, Leipzig

54. BURIED ALIVE

IN SPRING 1944 our column—Poles and Jews—was employed in earth moving at the prisoners' canteen. The SS construction officer supervised us personally. Even for strong men the work was very difficult; we lost weight and starved. Men could hardly pick up a pickax or shovel. Every form of digging in the heavy, rocky soil took tremendous exertion. One wanted so badly to rest for a moment, but the constant blows and kicks, the unceasing shouts forced our tired arms to keep shoveling on and on.

Then the gaze of the construction officer fell upon two Jews whose strength had given out. He ordered a Pole named Strzaska to bury the two men, who could hardly stay on their feet. Strzaska froze with horror and refused. The construction officer took the shovel and beat him with it. He ordered him, "Lie down in the trench immediately!" Thereupon he forced the two Jews to cover with dirt the prisoner lying in the trench. These two then did it out of fear for their lives, hoping to escape the same gruesome fate themselves. When only Strzaska's head still peered out, the construction officer called "Halt!" and had him pulled out again.

Now the two Jews had to lie in the trench, and the construction officer again gave Strzaska the order to cover the two with dirt. Slowly the trench filled with dirt; one shovelful after another was dumped in. The face of the Polish comrade was contorted with terror; drops of sweat fell from his forehead. But the construction officer stood next to him with the look of a wild animal that hypnotizes its victims. The trench was now completely covered over. The inhuman SS executioner stamped the dirt smooth himself and laughed while doing it. The rest of us had to keep working without interruption.

About fifteen minutes passed, then the construction officer called two comrades and ordered them immediately to uncover the two buried men. Of course the shovels flew as if it might be possible to save them. The face of one of the men was completely torn open in their haste—but he was already dead. The other man gave only weak signs of life. Then the construction officer ordered that both(!) comrades be taken to the crematorium.

z. MASZUDRO, No. 40991

Chapter Five
Punishments in Camp

ON OCTOBER 15, 1939, I was delivered into Buchenwald concentration camp. Tents had been set up in roll call square to create the so-called Little Camp, in which I had to endure untold agony. On October 27, 1939, I was already sent to the cellblock because I was accused of having shot several German policemen. To force a confession out of me, they tortured me in a manner that a normal human simply cannot imagine. Over a period of four weeks at intervals of ten to fourteen days, I received a total of 175 lashes on the buttocks. About ten times during the same period, I was hanged by the wrists for twenty-five minutes at a time. For four months I was required to sleep on the cement floor next to an open window in the bitter cold, clad only in a shirt and underpants.

I shared the cell with the German Communist Jakob Boulanger of Cologne, who out of sympathy gave me his suit—although this was strictly forbidden and he knew that in doing so he risked his own life. I was often in despair and wanted to hang myself, abandoning such plans only because Boulanger told me not to be a coward. In September 1941 my mother died. The news was brought to me with the words, "Here is your letter. Your sow whore has kicked the bucket!" Since my case fell under an amnesty, I was released from the cellblock in spring 1942.

To my great horror, I was assigned as domestic servant in the cellblock in January 1944; I remained there until November 1944. I was dismissed because I smuggled cigarettes to a few prisoners. I received twenty-five lashes with a horsewhip and was kicked and struck in other body parts, too. Participating in these abuses were Second Deputy Commandant [Erich] Gust, Roll Call Officer Hofschulte, and Block Officer Heinrich. Before I left the cellblock, a stripe was cut through my hair across the middle of my head. The comrades in the hospital gave me treatment illegally and against the will of the SS, but I was nearly at the end of my strength because of the abuse and the constant stress.

Through my always involuntary and long stays in the cellblock, I gained insight into these medieval torture chambers of the twentieth century. The day began with persecutions as early as 5:00 A.M., especially when the infamous mass murderer [Martin] Sommer was on duty. Since men slept in their clothes, at wake up they had to undress with lightning speed. Woe to those who did not immediately run naked to the water pipes after the cell was opened. Woe, too, to those who were not back in their cells again within half a minute. If the prisoner received only three terrible lashes with a riding whip during this half minute, he could count himself lucky.

Fifteen prisoners were once squeezed together in a cell—each cell was about 39 inches wide and 6.5 feet long. They were given only a child's chamber pot, which was not emptied for about ten days. The floor was swimming in excrement. Sommer finally murdered all fifteen unfortunate victims.

Cells 1 to 13 were occupied with camp inmates; the other side of the corridor housed arrested SS men. A special pleasure of Sommer's consisted of driving all the prisoners out into the 4-foot-wide corridor and making them hop and do knee bends until they collapsed with exhaustion. Then with his boot heels he stepped on the heads of those lying on the floor until blood gushed out of their ears and noses. Only then did this beast rest.

Looking out the window of the cell meant certain death. Whenever Sommer caught someone doing this, he beat him to death or gave him a lethal injection. He gave the same punishment to those he saw reading the scraps of newspaper that had been issued as toilet paper. It happened thus to a prisoner named Fischer, who read an old newspaper he found in the toilet.

Lethal injections in the cellblock were given by the SS doctor Hoven; in summer 1941 there were an average of ten a day.

It was forbidden to walk back and forth in the cell; one had to stand stiffly facing the door from 5:00 A.M. until 10:00 P.M. The peephole in the door contained a magnifying glass through which every movement could be observed. Anyone who was caught in violation received twenty-five lashes with a cane. When food was issued, it was usually only a half ration. In winter it was common to pour cold water over a prisoner. His clothing was supposed to "dry" on his body while the prisoner slept on the cement floor.

In one cell lay seven Jews. One day Sommer appeared in the cell with a tin can and struck two prisoners with it. Then he tore a piece of iron from the heating system and struck the others with it. Of the at least 100 Jews who went through the cellblock at that time, not one left alive.

It was also common to give jailed prisoners laxatives in their food, so they suffered from bloody stools. Antidiarrheal medicines were of course nonexistent. There were two toilets in the cellblock: one for the prisoners and one for the SS. When a prisoner received twenty-five lashes with a cane, he had to bend over and stick his head in an SS toilet that was filled with excrement. After the punishment was completed, he was not allowed to wash off the excrement. In the half-minute "morning wash," it was also hardly possible to wash adequately, so the prisoner often had to run around covered with excrement for weeks.

In my time other prisoners also served as domestic servants, in particular Roman Hedelmaier of Vienna. He had been an official in the press ministry and was in the cellblock for four years, working as a domestic servant for two of those years. In general he helped the prisoners as much as he could, yet he often had to strike a prisoner on Sommer's orders. When he had beaten a prisoner, he often secretly brought him bread, placing his own life in great danger. When he refused to strike a prisoner, Sommer said to him, "If you won't beat him, then I'll beat you to death!" Hedelmaier, who knew many things about the cellblock, was released and was sent to the military as a radio operator. The domestic servant Fischermann, a former SA man, was the opposite. He conducted himself in the cellblock exactly as the SS murderers did. He, too, was released.

It was the same with the domestic servant Horesi, whom the SS used as an informant. He saved himself at the expense of other prisoners in the cellblock by betraying jailed comrades to Sommer and delivering many to their deaths. Because he likewise knew too much about the dirty tricks of the SS, he was later shot in the stone quarry.

In the office of Sommer, the infamous overseer of the jail, there was a skull that was constantly lit from the inside. To extort confessions Sommer used the most ingenious tortures. In addition to the methods described above, he often chose starvation. Because he himself issued the food, he could withhold a jailed prisoner's rations until he was dead. In addition to the camp doctors, Sommer himself gave lethal injections to many prisoners. His deputy was SS Technical Sergeant [Anton] Bergmeier, who did dole out terrible beatings but to my knowledge never directly murdered a prisoner.

The reasons for being brought to the cellblock were almost always trivial. One Jew, for example, was brought to the cellblock for smoking during working hours, another for alleged laziness. On a cold winter day, three prisoners carried coke briquettes into the heating cellar. They remained to warm themselves for a few minutes, during which Sommer caught them. He took them into the cellblock and murdered them by injection. If a prisoner stared at the wife of the mass murderer Koch while she was riding by, she wrote his number down, and the unfortunate man usually ended up in the cellblock. And in most cases that meant the crematorium.

Especially in 1940–1941 there were terrible tortures. Seven young Polish prisoners were once suspended by chains from the bunk bed in their cell. They were fed only salt pickles and salt water, and the unbearable agony drove them to madness. All of them died in this brutal manner. The sounds of their cries and shouts of pain for "Father" and "Mother" still ring in my ears.

A Czech Communist in Cell 11 received nothing to eat for seven long days. Then Sommer went into his cell and said to him, "In three days you will meet your savior!" When the comrade was asked how many children he had, he answered "Seven." Sommer replied, "They are all criminals exactly like you!" The comrade was relieved of his suffering after two days.

One morning a crate covered with a white sheet stood in the washroom under the washbasin. When I lifted the sheet, I saw a male corpse whose arms and legs had been separated from the torso.

Once I had to sort out the clothes of the murdered men on the floor of the cellblock (in the room under the roof). There were pieces of clothing from about 800 prisoners, primarily Jews. In summer 1941 Dr. Hoven murdered the Reich

German Bergel by lethal injection. The Pole Wicziak from Mieslowitz was killed in the same manner in January 1941, as was the Polish sergeant Karl Zajac in July 1941, after he had received nothing to eat for seven days. A Polish military chaplain, Galczynski of Kraków, suffered the same fate in May 1941; likewise a prelate from Bromberg [Bydgoszcz], whose name I no longer know. He was accused of having incited the murder of a German, but he told me he had not done it. On the contrary, after their occupation the SS had shot German antifascist workers en masse and put the blame for these murders on the Poles. During my time in the cellblock, at least 300 to 400 prisoners were murdered, but after 1944 the methods changed. The candidates for death were no longer beaten to death in the cellblock but were taken to the crematorium, hanged there, and burned. This way the SS murderers had fewer accessories [*Mitwisser*] and could beter conceal their murderous deeds.

In conclusion, I would like to introduce two special cases. Because of a political memorial service in the Personal Property Room, numerous comrades were jailed. They were terribly abused, above all by the Gestapo in Weimar. They were temporarily placed in the cellblock, where the comrade Willi Bleichert, for example, showed me burns over his entire body caused by lit cigars.

In August 1944, English paratroopers were delivered. One by one they were all brought to the cellblock in the evenings. The next morning they were taken to the crematorium and hanged there. The kapo of the crematorium took part in these crimes and must know the exact number.

RICHARD GRITZ, Antonienhütte

56. INTERROGATION UNTIL CONFESSION

IN THE SO-CALLED *Bunker*, which was officially named the cellblock, the SS personnel were SS Technical Sergeant Sommer and SS Technical Sergeant Bergmeier. The domestic servant was a prisoner from Düsseldorf.

When a prisoner was delivered there, he had to undress himself completely. His clothes were searched with painstaking precision. As his clothes were searched, the prisoner was abused by the SS man and the servant in alternation.

Then the newly delivered prisoner was taken to a darkened cell and shackled to the radiator with handcuffs so he could not move. At night the servant quietly made his rounds in felt slippers. If he found a prisoner sleeping, he struck him with a rubber truncheon. If the prisoner cried out in pain, then Sommer came with a horsewhip and beat the prisoner unconscious. Often in the middle of the night, Detective Inspector Leclaire came and had the prisoner brought before him. To refresh the prisoner's memory, Leclaire first gave him a few lashes over the head with a horsewhip. Then he said the pretty words, "You will never come out of here alive. That should be clear to you, and if you are lying, you'll get lashes until you laugh!" If the prisoner did not say enough or kept silent, then the infamous slip would be sent to the commandant at the time, Koch: "Interrogation until confession."

When this slip arrived, Sommer came with a rope. He tied the prisoner's hands together and pulled the rope through a ring placed in the middle of the corridor. As a result the prisoner swung 12 to 20 inches above the floor. The procedure was cruel and very painful. Sommer and Leclaire also placed a rope around the prisoner's neck and pulled it until he could not breathe; at times they hung onto the legs of the hanging prisoner. After at most twenty minutes, the prisoner became unconscious. Through such torture methods confessions were often extracted that a man would never have given under normal circumstances. But there were also prisoners who said nothing despite this torture. If this "tree hanging" did not succeed, then the prisoner received nothing to eat or drink and was interrogated every day. The interrogated prisoner was hung up as many as three times, and the fast was extended as long as ten days. If the prisoner had said nothing by the tenth day, then came the last trial: "tree hanging" with the head down. I myself was able to hold this out only about fifteen minutes.

If all this had not yet produced a satisfactory result and the political department thought that the prisoner was a difficult case, one evening he would receive a cup of tea that put him to sleep. Then Sommer would give him a lethal injection. The next morning an announcement would come over the radio, "Corpse carriers report immediately to the gate!" The camp doctor wrote on the death certificate: "Death of circulatory failure." If the prisoner did not drink the tea, Sommer or the servant came to the cell window every few minutes to see if the man was asleep. Then the next morning a warm meal that had been poisoned was brought to the cell. If that, too, failed—and if the prisoner had not implicated anyone else—then Sommer would have a remarkable change of heart: He would recommend the release of the jailed inmate, which almost always took place. At the prisoner's release Sommer would usually give him some smoking materials.

KURT LEESER, Aachen

57. THE MARTYRDOM
OF PASTOR SCHNEIDER

IN SEPTEMBER 1937 Pastor [Paul] Schneider of the Evangelical Confessional church was brought to Buchenwald.[1] When he failed to take his cap off at the so-called flag parade, the daily hoisting of the Nazi flag, he received twenty-five lashes on the buttocks and was jailed in the cellblock. Pastor Schneider remained in the cellblock more than eighteen months, until he was finally murdered after painful suffering.

Fritz Männchen shared a cell with Schneider for a while. He reported that every time the infamous cellblock sergeant Sommer opened the cell, he struck Schneider with a horsewhip. Schneider's cell was constantly darkened, water covered the floor 2 inches deep, and the walls were completely wet. Schneider was never allowed to wash during his entire period under arrest. Unlike other arrested prisoners, he was never taken to the bath. His clothes were thus completely infested with lice. He often had fist-sized wounds from beatings over his entire body; they constantly festered, but of course he never received any bandages or the like to treat the wounds. It is inconceivable that a man could hold out under such torture as long as Schneider did. Precisely this particularly agitated the SS murderers, who were trying to torment Schneider to death. Of course he received something to eat only at very irregular intervals so that he had also become a mere skeleton.

Because the SS thought it was taking too long for their unfortunate victim to die, Sommer put a heart-paralyzing drug into his food one day. But since Schneider usually ate very little, the drug had no effect. Sommer therefore had the camp doctor repeatedly apply cold compresses until Schneider had a heart attack and died. On the day before his death, Schneider was called to the gate, where Sommer beat him with a horsewhip.

Schneider's wife and children asked headquarters if they could see their dead husband and father. Koch gave permission for reasons of propaganda. To conceal the corpse's horrible disfigurement by the beating, an SS barber covered the dead

---

1. Schneider belonged to the Confessing Church, a group of German Protestants led by Martin Niemöller who broke away from the official state church and rejected Nazi racial theories as antithetical to Christian doctrine. For a more detailed account of Schneider's days in Buchenwald, see Poller, *Medical Block,* 197–206. For more on Schneider's beliefs and background, see E. H. Robertson, *Paul Schneider, the Pastor of Buchenwald* (London: SCM Press, 1956).

comrade with makeup and put a wig on his head. Then he was laid out in ceremonial fashion, covered with flowers, in the garrison garage. After the family had taken tearful leave of their murdered father and husband, they were brought to the gate by the sadist Koch, who in fact had ordered the murder. At their parting, with tears in his eyes(!), Koch said, "Your husband was my best prisoner. Just when I wanted to inform him of his release, he died of a heart attack!"

FRITZ MÄNNCHEN, Dresden

58. The Last Days in the Cellblock

AT THE INITIATIVE of the management of the Gustloff Works—the fascists Tänzer, Siedeck, and Saupe—I was arrested for alleged sabotage on April 1, 1945 (Easter Sunday). I was brought to the gate by SS Sergeant Major Jakobs and jailed in the cellblock. In Cell 2, into which I was delivered, there were already one Pole and two Latvians. The cell was 39 inches wide and 6.5 feet long. Two of us slept on a wooden bunk; the other two slept on the cement floor. A rusty marmalade bucket was placed in the cell to take care of our bodily needs. Other than that we had two ragged and louse-ridden blankets as well as a straw mattress without straw.

We were awakened around 5:00 A.M. We were allowed at most two to three minutes to wash, empty the bucket, and clean up; otherwise we were beaten. Around 5:00 P.M. there was soup, followed by bread, occasionally with some marmalade on it and very rarely margarine. Often the SS bandits ate our marmalade or used our margarine to fry potatoes.

After six days I was transferred into Cell 3 and was forced to do domestic service. Thus I was able to find out who sat in the different cells.

In Cell 1 was a Russian woman who was strangled by the SS technical sergeant of the cellblock on one of the last days. I could hear quite clearly the cries and finally the death rattle. In Cell 4 lay four Dutch comrades; in Cell 5 were four Russians; likewise in Cell 6 were five Russian comrades who had starved down to skeletons. Cell 7 was occupied by five comrades from various nations. A cell in which two comrades sat was never opened. That was one side of the corridor.

The cells opposite were occupied mainly by SS men. In the first cell were two Ukrainian SS men; in the second, three Italians. Next was a comrade in strict isolation whom I saw only once through the slot in the door. In the night between Monday and Tuesday, all prisoners on this side as well as the comrades from Cells 5 through 8 were murdered by the SS beasts.

Although I of course did not see the murders with my own eyes, there was sufficient proof of them. During the night I heard muffled cries and death rattles in the corridor. In the morning all the cells mentioned were empty. All over the floor by the entrance gate and on the walls were fresh bloodstains that I had to wash off. Lying in the washroom sink were handcuffs covered with blood and scraps of flesh. Blood-soaked ropes hung in the supply room. I had to wash out two of the SS murderers' fatigues, which were soaked with fresh blood. I hung them out to dry in the second and third cells on the right side of the corridor. The collars of the jackets that the SS murderers had worn while committing their foul deeds were completely tattered. The underwear of the SS murderers was soaked with blood and still lay in the washroom on the day of our liberation. I likewise had to wash out four pairs of completely blood-soaked socks.

Very early in the morning of Wednesday, the day of our liberation, all torture equipment was packed into an open basket and taken away.

On the previous evening (Tuesday), I asked the SS master sergeant of the cellblock what would happen to me. He answered, "I don't know. I still don't have orders!" The first order the murderous bandits received on Wednesday said, "Stand at the ready!" After that the murderers hastily packed up their things. Two hours before the siren signal for the approach of enemy tanks sounded, the master sergeant had already disappeared. The other two SS murderers stood in front of the door and awaited orders. When the warning signal for approaching tanks sounded, the cowardly murderers ran as fast as they could. As they were leaving, the telephone rang about twenty to twenty-five times, but the fugitives paid no attention to it. Thus the final murder order, which probably was to be relayed by telephone, was no longer carried out. To this circumstance I owe my life.

When our comrades stormed the gate and the towers after the flight of the SS, the cellblock was broken open with pickaxes. And so we were liberated.

BRUNO FALKENBURG
Kapo in the Gustloff Works

59. SS Master Sergeant Sommer

That was a name that for years spread terror and horror in Buchenwald. When Sommer, too, was arrested in the course of the trial of the former camp commandant Koch, he had to admit to having carried out 150 murders in half a year. Today they can still be documented.

A chief form of amusement for Sommer was to strangle delinquents with his own hands. In other cases he satisfied himself with some form of injection: Air, chloral hydrate, or evipan were his favorite means.

Sommer was accustomed to summoning his victims to his room in the evening, where he then "did them in." He laid the corpses under his bed, upon which he immediately fell asleep, sleeping the sleep of the just, well satisfied with his successful day's work. In the morning the corpse carriers were requested to take away the corpse. They found it under the bed of Herr Master Sergeant.[2]

KURT LEESER, Aachen

60. MURDER METHODS OF SOMMER

DURING THE TIME I spent in the cellblock at Buchenwald, I became acquainted with a number of the murder methods of the cellblock overseer Sommer. They should be recorded in their full brutality for all later times.

To extort a confession this beast in human form did the following: He forced the prisoner to put his testicles first into a bowl of ice-cold water then into a bowl of almost boiling water. This procedure was repeated several times until the skin was inflamed and blistered. Then Sommer painted the testicles with iodine(!), causing excruciating pain.

The corridor of the cellblock between the rows of cells was locked with a barred door. Sommer would place the head of a prisoner between the wall and the barred door, then he would slam the door with full force so that the head was crushed.

In many cases Sommer suspended the prisoners with chains from the window bars, with their arms bent backward. Often he let the unfortunate victims hang in this painful position for three to four days. Then he threw a blanket over their heads and strangled them.

Sommer's "simplest" killing technique was to put a rope around the neck of a victim. With his own hands he hanged him from the heating pipes or a window bar. Sommer beat many prisoners to death with a three-edged iron bar. I know of one case in which Sommer placed an iron clamp over a prisoner's temples and screwed it together until the skull was crushed by the pressure.

Although giving prisoners lethal injections was a privilege of the SS doctors, Sommer also took part in this specialty of SS medicine.

FRITZ MÄNNCHEN, Dresden

---

2. Martin Sommer remained in hiding until 1950 and was not arrested until 1957. He was charged with committing 101 murders, tried in July 1958 by West German authorities, and sentenced to life. Walter Bartel, ed., *Buchenwald: Mahnung und Verpflichtung* (Berlin: Kongress-Verlag, 1960), 117, fn. 1.

61. IN THE BLACK CELLBLOCK

I AM A JEHOVAH's Witness. On February 10, 1938, I was delivered to Buchenwald concentration camp. After registration, we—like all Jehovah's Witnesses—were sent to the punishment company, where a fateful atmosphere prevailed.

However, fortune seemed to be on my side; I was a tailor and as such was urgently needed. So after a few weeks, I was sent to the SS tailor shop. But the work detail became my undoing. The facility was primitive, and it lacked the most necessary equipment and working materials. The boss was a civilian who repeatedly demanded a textbook on tailoring. I mentioned that I owned one. At the civilian's request, I had the textbook sent, addressed to the civilian. [The receipt of packages from home was forbidden during this period.] In the course of disagreements that the civilian had with SS members, the manner in which the textbook was obtained came out. This harmless violation of the unwritten laws of the camp order became my awful undoing.

On the evening of February 23, 1939, the entire work detail—it comprised thirty-four men—went to the whipping block. Those affected received between ten and twenty-five terrible lashes with a cane.

At the evening roll call on February 24, the senior block inmate handed me a note: "Appear at Signpost 2." After the end of roll call, the command sounded, "The designated prisoners to the red [signpost] at double time." The whipping block once again stood ready. We each received twenty-five lashes with a cane. After that we went into the infamous "black cellblock." That was the sleeping room in Barracks 3 that had been completely darkened. Every joint and every crack had been covered with paper. There was no heat. Because the room was hermetically sealed, considerable condensation formed on the walls, trickling down to create dank pools on the floor. I groped for these spots to sit down in, to alleviate somewhat the terrible burning sensation on my rear and the unbearable stretching of the skin.

One night three of our comrades broke out to get food. They were caught and sent back. Through new deliveries each day, the population of the "black cellblock" in the meantime had grown considerably. Among those punished in the black cellblock were comrades who had committed unbelievably trivial offenses. For the breakout of the three comrades, the entire population went to the whipping block.

We could wash ourselves only every two or three days and shave only every two weeks. Of course everything was done at high speed. We lost weight terribly. The room was completely bare; there were no blankets, straw, light, or water. In a corner stood two chamber pots for our bodily needs. We had to feel our way there.

Because of the feces, the air in the hermetically sealed room became suffocating and unbearable. We slept body to body, directly on the hard floor. Our shoes, covered with our caps, served as pillows; jackets had to substitute for blankets. We warmed ourselves with our own breath. We lay closely together in long rows in order not to freeze. No one dared change his position. Everything was done according to command. We could hold out thus for two or three hours before we were completely frozen. Then we would march again in circles until we became a little warmer. If anyone drooped, he was put in a corner. If he lay there for two days, he was taken away; most then died. Thus days and weeks passed. Dead and half dead were thrown out. A maximum length of punishment existed here no more than it did in the whole protective custody. I spent fifty days thus, but by then I was at the end of my strength.

On April 14, 1939, the door was torn open, and the SS appeared with the shout, "Everyone out!" Completely covered with filth, we stood in roll call square behind the comrades of the camp who had appeared for roll call. The daylight blinded us and caused us pain. SS Colonel Koch inspected us. No one dared move. The commandant judged each "sinner" of the "black cellblock." We were sorted out anew, and I had the good fortune to belong to the few comrades who that evening were allowed to leave the "black cellblock." The camp, with all its dangers, seemed to us like golden freedom.

On April 20 [1939], for Hitler's birthday, the "black cellblock" was finally dissolved.

OTTO LEISCHNIG, No. 2678, Pockau/Erzgebirge

62. Stories About the Whipping Block

DURING MY LONG IMPRISONMENT I had the most improbable good fortune of never having gone "to the whipping block," with the exception of a time at the Gestapo and police in Breslau. I nevertheless gathered many impressions as an unwilling observer and participant in many hundreds of whippings. I will describe here only three cases that are especially characteristic of the caprice and senselessness that often accompanied the severe flogging of prisoners.

One day the deputy commandant at the time, Rödl, stopped a wagon of the transportation detail that in his opinion was traveling too slowly. He brought the foreman, a Jew from Dessau named Leo Moses, to the gate for twenty lashes with a cane. Moses went to Rödl and explained to him that he had been in camp more than five years, had never been punished, etc. Then Rödl answered in his genuine Bavarian dialect, "Then you'll get only ten on the ass!" Once again Moses went to Rödl and reminded him that they had been at Sachsenburg together, which led Rödl to the following decision: "Then you'll get five!" And it remained at that.

The kapo of the lumberyard brought a basket of firewood to the wife of the camp doctor at the time, Ding, against the orders of the commandant. Since Frau Ding and Frau Koch were enemies, Frau Koch reported the affair to her husband, who then had the lumberyard kapo given twenty-five lashes with a cane. A few days later Frau Koch sent for a sack of firewood from the lumberyard. The kapo refused, expressly referring to his recent punishment. Koch had him whipped again the same evening because he had refused to obey an order from the commandant's wife!

For a long time in 1939–1940, it was customary for every whipping to be carried out in front of the entire camp. The prisoners designated for a whipping came to the gate after the evening roll call while all the other prisoners had to remain standing in roll call square. Each prisoner's name, along with the reason for and amount of punishment, was read over the microphone. Then the victim was strapped to the whipping block and whipped in front of the assembled men. The howls and cries of the unfortunate victims rang horribly in our ears. To cover it up somewhat, Rödl invented the following procedure: The roll call officer announced three to four cases on the microphone, the camp band played a march, and the comrades were abused to musical accompaniment. Such SS cultural offerings oftentimes lasted two hours or more.

STEFAN HEYMANN, Mannheim

63. "Shot While Attempting Escape"

HERE ARE SOME DETAILS from the secret autopsy reports of 1940 from Buchenwald concentration camp. SS Second Lieutenant Dr. Gutacker was at the time director of pathology and carried out the autopsies. SS Second Lieutenant Dr. Hübner of the Pathological Institute of the University of Jena was brought in as head physician, and an SS officer of the camp was present as a witness. Thus everything was conducted with genuine National Socialist order and thoroughness—namely, the concealing of actual conditions.

In June 1940 an epidemic of escapes appears to have prevailed in camp, for from June 14 to July 14, there were no fewer than thirty-four shootings! Nevertheless, if one looks more closely, one is astonished to see that it was not the strongest and the healthiest who harbored plans of escape but clearly the very weakest.

Of the thirty-four autopsy reports, twenty-eight (that is, 82 percent) include the introductory comment "poor" or "bad" to indicate the state of nourishment and health. We can pull out a random example: No. 622/40; personal data: Sally Cohen, former attorney. The autopsy report begins with the external observation, "Corpse of a sixty-one-year-old man in poor state of nutrition and health." A debilitated old man who wanted to escape and was therefore shot!

A grand total of seventy-eight prisoners were "shot while attempting escape" in the six months from June 14 to December 14. Nine additional prisoners committed suicide by hanging—most of them probably knew nothing about it until shortly beforehand. A typical case was the "escape" of the prisoner [Dr. Richard] Steidle, the former director of the Tirol, member of the Austrian federal government, and officer of the Heimwehr. He was told that in the evening he would not be allowed to go back into the camp and should therefore voluntarily walk through the sentry line. He refused. But that afternoon the SS pushed him so far that he walked toward the sentry slowly and calmly, his arms raised and a smile on his lips. The sentry—probably just as slowly and calmly—shot him down.

Then there was the case of [Dr. Walter] Gerdes, the son-in-law of the last Austrian federal president, Miklas, who was in protective custody only for that reason. One day he was sent to the stone quarry. But he had "luck": He was so severely beaten that he had to be sent to the prisoner hospital and there received convalescent duty. However, that displeased an SS hero, SS Sergeant Kubitz. So one morning he went out and for his own private pleasure fetched the prisoner Gerdes out of convalescent duty and took him to the stone quarry. There he "bumped him off" with his own hands.

Major Höffner had come into the concentration camp because his wife was Jewish and he was Austrian. People had said to him, "You must get yourself a divorce." He rejected that and continued to refuse when he was threatened. Thus happened what was bound to happen. Höffner was "shot while attempting escape."

The prisoner Humer was in the concentration camp only one full day. He had been police director in Munich and was known as a Democrat. Scarcely had he been admitted and assigned to the stone quarry detail when he was "shot while attempting escape."

GUSTAV WEGERER, Vienna

64. PUNISHMENT EXERCISES

IN THE LANGUAGE of the concentration camp veteran, the expression *geography lesson* [*Erdkunde*] meant what one could call punishment exercises— when one studied the earth. Countless times after evening roll call the entire camp had to perform hard exercises for the most trivial reasons. Either some blocks were alleged to be not quite precisely aligned with the man in front or on the sides or while marching in; or there had been noise during roll call; or the blocks did not stand as still as statues, hands sharply at the sides. Another time someone among the 10,000 had spit, or the command "Caps off! Caps on!" was not carried out briskly enough. For such offenses there were collective punishments. Again and again, under the supervision of SS men armed with whips and truncheons, men had to run at double time in rows of ten for hours, with only short pauses. We were ordered to lie down, duck walk, jump, roll and roll in pairs up and down the sloping roll call square. Block officers struck at heads and arms and with their heavy boots ran over the men lying on the ground, breaking their teeth and ribs. Block officers had a special eye out for the weak. Anyone who could not keep up with the double time run, stumbled, or even fell was tortured to death with kicks and blows.

In their daily inspections block officers often reported that they had found beds that were not sufficiently squared off or lockers that were not arranged quite perfectly. Then all inmates of the block concerned had to perform hard exercises. "Train your men yourselves!" was their slogan. That was an open invitation "to get rid of" prisoners who stood out, because of whom the entire block had been sentenced to punishment exercises.

For many years a long, high mountain of stone chips for road construction stood to the right of roll call square. Especially in winter it was selected as a favorite place for punishment exercises. In the deep snow one had to struggle up the pile, reaching the top with pounding heart and bursting lungs. Then the order was given to lie down, and one went sliding down the steep slope over the icy chips, scraping one's hands and face until they were bloody. In summer the other side of roll call square was popular, where there were deep trenches full of water from digging foundations for future buildings. It was merely a "joke" for many block officers to send a prisoner sliding down there with a punch or a kick. When he clambered out again, covered with water and mud, the game was repeated.

There were months when not a day passed during which work columns were not halted by the SS men. Either they had allegedly been too slow, or they had carried stones that were too small, carried too few boards, or something similar. Punishment exercises were performed immediately on the spot. That work was thus delayed was a matter of no concern; it was more a question of demoralizing the prisoners.

GUSTAV HERZOG, Vienna

Chapter Six
Sanitary and Health Questions

WHEN THE CAMP OPENED in July 1937, there was still no hospital. The first sick prisoners were housed in Block 1. Because of the murderous work system, the number of sick rose very quickly, so that soon all of Block 2 had to be set up as an infirmary. Only in summer 1938 was the construction of two sick barracks on the present grounds of the hospital begun. The first barracks contained the administrative rooms along with the internal and external outpatient department, the pharmacy, the dietetic kitchen, a small operating room, a radiation room, and a small sick ward. These facilities were all very primitive. In the second barracks were housed sick wards.

The prisoners employed in the hospital at that time were primarily professional criminals and antisocials. The conditions in the hospital corresponded to its staff. Fats and meat were skimmed off from the rations and sold on the black market. The treatment depended on whether the sick prisoner could pay or not. Whoever had nothing, died. Gold dental work was broken out of the mouths of the dead and made into jewelry that could be resold. In addition, the professional criminals made themselves popular with the SS because they used almost no medication for the sick. Prisoner doctors were not allowed to work in the hospital.

The camp doctor at the time was Dr. Ding (Schuler), an incompetent in medical matters. His skills were sufficient for carrying out the death orders of the SS.

All sick prisoners who were incapable of working but could not be admitted to the hospital received convalescent duty. Despite their often serious illnesses, they were occupied in the lumberyard with saws and other work. Every morning the medical supervisor and the convalescent prisoners had to report to the gate, where the deputy commandant checked their degree of illness. If it suited him, the deputy commandant declared a prisoner healthy. The prisoner then received beatings and kicks and was immediately sent to work in the stone quarry, from which he usually came back into camp a dead man. Commandant Koch in particular arbitrarily withdrew convalescent duty at every inspection and delivered prisoners to their deaths. Sometimes he sent a troop of block officers into camp for this purpose; they ordered all convalescent prisoners to the gate and drove them into the stone quarry with blows.

On the occasion of the assassination of the Nazi von Rath [November 1938], about 12,500 Jews were delivered into Buchenwald. They were plundered by both the SS and the professional criminals in the most shameless manner—if they were not beaten to death. The criminal prisoners employed in the hospital participated in these extortions, too, and drew the medical corpsman (SDG) of the SS into their dirty business. That finally led to the arrest of the corpsman, who hanged himself in the cellblock in winter 1939.

The antifascist prisoners made use of this scandal to replace the criminal order-lies in the hospital with antifascists. In particular, through the initiative of the Communist Landtag deputy Walter Krämer, conditions in the hospital changed fundamentally. From this time on the hospital became a main base in the camp's struggle against the SS, as well as an oasis of security for endangered prisoners. The battle for a better supply of medications began immediately and was success-ful, after a determined struggle with the SS doctors. Many medications were stolen from the SS infirmary, and eventually, through bribery of SS men, medi-cine was obtained from the outside with prisoners' money. All corrupt elements were removed from the existing personnel.

In the middle of this constructive work came the fight against the first great ep-idemic in Buchenwald, an epidemic of stomach and intestinal typhoid at the be-ginning of 1939. It cost hundreds of lives, among them the well-known Commu-nist Reichstag deputy Walter Stöcker. In summer, therefore, under pressure from the prisoner orderlies, all prisoners received vaccinations, the first that were ever given in a concentration camp at all.

In October and November 1939, the tragedy repeated itself with the Polish and Jewish transports into the so-called Little Camp. As a consequence of the unbear-able sanitary conditions, there arose a new epidemic of intestinal disorders that cost almost twice as many victims as the previous one. Only by pointing to the danger for the entire camp, including even the SS, were the German antifascists in the hospital able to get approval to treat the surviving victims of this hell, after weeks of struggle. At this time the SS invented a new crime, that of "friendship with Poles." Every sort of humane or comradely treatment of a Pole was horribly punished.

In 1940 a new sick barracks was erected. To improve the miserable conditions in the surgical department, in 1940–1941 the prisoners built Operating Room 2, which had an X-ray room. The SS did not provide a single brick for this new con-struction (the building was never even entered on the map!); at risk to their lives, prisoners had to steal every single piece of material from the work details. Even the interior furnishings and all the instruments were stolen—mostly from the SS infirmary. Among them was an entire operating room with instruments destined for Mauthausen concentration camp, which was not reclaimed by the SS Main Economic and Administrative Office until 1944.

The year 1939 brought a change in camp doctors. The SS Second Lieutenants Wagner and Hoven appeared, both still without their medical degrees. They had their doctoral dissertations written by prisoners: Wagner by the prisoner Grünwald, Hoven by the prisoners Wegerer and Sitte.

Wagner soon achieved a tragic fame, for he began mass liquidation by injections in Buchenwald. His victims were mainly Gypsies from the Burgenland [Austria]. Dr. Neumann arrived at the same time from the SS Hygiene Institute in Berlin. He practiced vivisections on prisoners. He cut pieces out of the livers of living bodies, causing all his victims to die in wretched pain.

Barracks 4 was also built and equipped then. At the same time the mass murderer Dr. Eisele came to Buchenwald. He took his victims off the camp street at random, gave them apomorphine injections, and amused himself with the effects (vomiting). He undertook unnecessary operations and amputations, after which he murdered his experimental subjects. Still living in the camp is the Dutch Jew Max Nebig, who was one of the few who could be saved. Eisele operated on Nebig's stomach without reason. After the operation Nebig was to have been given a lethal injection, but it was possible to save his life by telling Eisele that he had died. He was simultaneously transferred to the TB ward, which Eisele never entered.

All these horrible events led the German antifascist orderlies to take a stand on principle. The original intention was to withdraw from the work detail and thus leave the field to the criminal elements. We rejected this as avoiding responsibility and endangering the camp; on the contrary, we decided we had to take the bitter role of witness upon ourselves in order to save whatever could be saved whenever possible. This attitude was our guiding principle up to the day of liberation by the American army.

In the long run the determined antifascist work in the hospital could not be hidden from the SS. In October 1941 the two comrades responsible for the infirmary, Krämer and Peix, were called to the gate on orders of the commandant. They were locked in the cellblock. After six days both were transferred to the external work detail Goslar and after a few days were murdered there by a shot in the base of the skull from the infamous mass murderer Blank. If the commandant believed that the antifascist resistance was thus broken, he deceived himself. Into the place of the fallen stepped men of the same mentality, in particular the last and longtime kapo of the infirmary, Ernst Busse. But up to the end, the SS did not lose its distrust of the hospital, and the two leading comrades of the hospital, Busse and Kipp, stood on the final murder list of the week of liberation.

In the Hoven era the first transports went to Bernburg for gassing, under the documentary designation 14 f 13. For the most part they were Jews, but a few well-known political prisoners were among them as well.[1]

Without any sign of restraints, Hoven occupied himself with giving lethal injections to those prisoners the SS considered unfit for work. He did this along with SS Captain Dr. Plaza, who arrived later, and the longtime corpsman of the

---

1. The designation 14 f 13 was a code name for euthanasia killings by gas, as in the phrase *Sonderbehandlung 14 f 13.* See Wulf, *Aus dem Lexikon der Mörder,* 17, 88f.; see also "Todesarten der KZ-Häftlinge," in Weinmann, *Das nationalsozialistische Lagersystem,* lxxvii.

hospital, SS Master Sergeant Wilhelm. In the main these planned deaths could not be prevented, but it was possible to save many lives. Living witnesses to this are Paul Heller of Prague, Alfred Cahn of Cologne, Max Umschweif of Vienna, and Hans Lackner of Salzburg, among others.

After the antifascists' takeover of the hospital, the sick wards also admitted those healthy prisoners who were threatened with death transports or death sentences. In special cases, when there was no other choice, the endangered man was allowed to "die" and to live on under the name of an actual dead person. So it happened with three Belgians, twenty-six Russian prisoners of war, a German, and several foreign Jews. The comrades Eugen Kogon of Vienna, George Kraus of Berlin, and Leopold Hartmüller of Vienna, who were to go to Auschwitz for liquidation, were declared sick with TB and unfit for transport. The comrade Uitz of Vienna was even given an appendix operation to save him from a transport to the Vienna Gestapo that would have meant a death sentence. In a similar manner the Frenchman Povez as well as the Luxemburg comrades Nikolaus Simon and the physician Dr. Kong, among others, were saved. Many comrades who were designated for the infamous Night and Fog transports to Natzweiler (the most severe punishment camp) were taken into the hospital for protection. Of them only the physician Dr. Elmelick of Paris, the artist Harry Pieck of The Hague, and Professor van Lingen of Amsterdam can be named here. In an especially dangerous situation—during the struggle against Wolff, the senior camp inmate at the time and a collaborator—the infirmary literally saved at the last minute two Polish comrades, the physician Dr. Ciepielowski and Josef Duda.

In spring 1943 many Jews from the Gustloff Works were sent to the hospital and given lethal injections for the most trivial offenses. The reports came from the work detail officer, SS Master Sergeant Schmidt. Deputy Commandant Schobert turned the reported prisoners over to the murderous Dr. Hoven, who faithfully carried out each command to kill. Unfortunately, not all those condemned to death could be saved. But three Russians who were to suffer that fate for having stolen a drive belt *were* saved. The list of these and other comrades saved by various means contains several hundred names, which of course cannot all be given here.

The hospital was significantly involved in two situations created by the inmate leadership in 1943. At one time we granted convalescence against the will of the SS, and we examined prisoners designated for transport. From the same period dates the expansion of the German antifascist organization to an international level. In comradely, confidential cooperation with the spokesmen of all nations, the hospital accomplished its work and mission. In particular, convalescence was generously granted on the recommendations of the nationalities—against the futile protest of the SS doctor. Work was also successfully sabotaged by recording as sick those healthy skilled workers from the armaments factories.

In connection with the trial against the mass murderer Koch, Dr. Hoven was arrested in September 1943. He was held on charges of killing prisoners. His successor was SS Captain Dr. Gerhard Schiedlausky of Lebus on the Oder. He had a series of assistants: Dr. Roege of Berlin, Dr. Bender of Düren, and Dr. [Werner] Greunus, who became camp doctor in S III (Ohrdruf).

The last year of Buchenwald was marked by death transports from the east, from Ohrdruf, and from subsidiary camps like Wille [Berga/Elster] and Schwalbe [Tröglitz], etc. [See list of external details in Chapter Nine, §136.] Neither the camp nor the hospital was able to deal with the flood of mostly half-dead prisoners. As a solution to the catastrophic overcrowding, the camp doctor turned to tried and true practices [injections]. At the train station, in the bath, in the tents, and in the anteroom of the death block, Block 61, hundreds and hundreds of prisoners met their deaths at the hands of his tool, SS Master Sergeant Wilhelm. A letter from SS headquarters that arrived in the last month of SS splendor and demanded better treatment of prisoners sounds like bloody hypocrisy. Nevertheless, the letter ended this criminal practice in camp.

In conclusion, the special role of Dr. Hoven should be pointed out. Although he unhesitatingly carried out all murder commands from above, over time it was still possible to gain influence over him. For example, Hoven actively supported the politicals in the struggle against the greens in 1942, when the greens tried to seize power with the help of miserable informers. He also saved many a political prisoner from death by gassing. But he did it only in pursuit of all sorts of things for his private interests.

And another word on Dr. Ding (Schuler) must be added. He was informed at the time about the rescue of three English officers from death and consented to the action. Schuler knew that the war was lost for Germany and was trying to find a way to cover his rear.

This report can naturally provide only a faint likeness of the abundance of experiences in the hell of Buchenwald. A more extensive report would fill volumes and therefore must be saved for a later time.

OTTO KIPP, Dresden

66. THE JEWISH INFIRMARY

WHEN THE NUMBER of Jews in Buchenwald increased sharply through the so-called Rath action, the number of sick Jews also continued to climb. Block 2, which had already served as an infirmary, was made into an infirmary exclusively for Jews. Of course still fewer medications were allotted to the Jewish infirmary than was the case in the regular infirmary. The situation was especially unpleasant for Jewish comrades who had to be operated on and who were brought for this purpose in all sorts of weather from the main infirmary to the Jewish infirmary. Many of them acquired pulmonary infections and so forth in this manner.

From the beginning care of the sick was left entirely to Jewish orderlies and Jewish prisoner doctors. Although no prisoner doctors were allowed in the main infirmary, Jewish prisoner doctors were employed in the Jewish infirmary because the SS doctors naturally did not concern themselves with Jews. Care and treatment were very good considering the scarcity of supplies. The comrade Rudi Arndt should be given special mention here; under his direction the Jewish infirmary was expanded and newly organized. Many owe their life and health to his energetic initiative.

Of course the Jewish infirmary was a thorn in the side of the camp administration. They would have preferred to liquidate all sick Jews immediately—Koch's motto was, "In my camp there are no sick, only the healthy and the dead!" Therefore more frequent house searches were carried out in the Jewish infirmary. During one such house search Deputy Commandant Rödl found in the orderlies' locker a normal portion of butter, but one that to him seemed too large. For this reason he had all orderlies of the Jewish infirmary called to the gate and had each of them given twenty-five lashes on the rear with a cane. In this connection it must be stated that the distribution of food and rations in the Jewish infirmary was always carried out with exemplary correctness.

When the number of Jews in Buchenwald had greatly decreased because of releases for emigration, the Jewish infirmary was dissolved. The building was turned into a "normal" infirmary that admitted prisoners of all categories.

It should also be mentioned that corpses were taken away only at irregular intervals, so that often they lay around for days in the toilets or washrooms and sometimes had to be stacked up like piles of wood.

STEFAN HEYMANN, Mannheim

67. Hospital Ward 7

As an orderly in Ward 7 of the hospital, I had under my care comrades who were designated for liquidation by the SS. In the ward were ten beds; hardly any of the patients knew what fate awaited them. Since the room had barred windows, patients believed it was some type of jail. In the beginning I myself did not know what it was about. Only when I received the order to "transfer" a patient and had to bring him to medical corpsman Wilhelm in Operating Room 2 did the matter become clear to me. All of those "transferred" ended up in the morgue. Those who were in fact incurably ill were only rarely victims. Later SS doctors Hoven and Plaza also took part in these lethal injections.

The corpses were brought to the anteroom of Operating Room 2 and were taken away only after dark. Ward 7 was often "cleared" in this manner three to four times a week and was then refilled.

Later I became a corpse carrier. From this time I especially remember the corpses I had to carry from the cellblock to the autopsy room and the ones that were entirely disfigured as a result of poisoning by gas. The mass murderer Sommer would place a bucket with chlorinated lime in the cell of his victim, then pour water over it and almost completely seal the cell. The escaping [chlorine] gas then led to a torturous death by suffocation that lasted for hours. Other jailed prisoners were strangled with hand towels; murder by lethal injection was also common. All corpses from the cellblock showed signs of abuse.

LUDWIG SCHEINBRUNN, Vienna

68. The TB Ward of the Hospital

IN MARCH 1943 I arrived as an orderly in the TB ward of the prisoner hospital; at the time about fifty patients lay there. On the orders of the camp doctor, Hoven, the patients had to inhale coal dust. The medical corpsman, SS Master Sergeant Wilhelm, made visits to the room at least once a week and selected the weakest for "transfer." "Transfer" meant that the poor victims were taken out of the ward into another room, where Wilhelm gave them lethal injections. Of course we tried to give each patient the best possible report on his condition to save him from annihilation.

The following incident is typical. An assistant orderly was leading a patient to the bath when they encountered Wilhelm. Wilhelm shouted at the assistant orderly, "What are you thinking of, taking such a wreck to the bath! We make soap out of his kind!" Then he wrote down the number of the patient, who that evening was promptly "transferred." When in July the number of new admissions rose, the number of TB patients also rose rapidly, especially among the French. On the orders of the camp doctor, Schiedlausky, an additional twenty beds were placed in the overcrowded ward. At this time there were for the most part less serious cases in the ward, primarily one-sided cases that were treated with pneumothorax. Medications, above all codeine, were almost completely lacking. Since tuberculosis continued to spread, additional space for another 110 TB patients was created in the so-called Little Camp. In various wards of the inner section of the hospital, at least another 100 TB patients lay. An additional 120 cases of exposed tuberculosis were still in camp as the prisoners could not be admitted for lack of space.

But our ward served not only to heal the sick. Many comrades who were sought by the SS or the Gestapo to be sent on death transports were hidden in the TB ward and declared "unfit for transport." Others were given the names of dead prisoners. Only the following comrades can be named: the Dutch Jew Mayer

Nebig, the Dutchmen Jan Schalker and Fred Driessen, and Nickel Henkes of Luxemburg. These and many other comrades had their lives saved in this manner.

ALFRED KNIEPER, No. 6194, Höhr-Gunzhausen

69. DENTAL CARE FOR THE SS AND PRISONERS

PROPER DENTAL care for prisoners did not exist until mid-1939. The nursing staff of the hospital, who lacked any sort of dental knowledge, treated the comrades as they saw fit. As a rule teeth that caused toothaches were pulled—if the SS man could even find them. Not seldom healthy teeth were pulled. There were no injections with anesthetics at all. And since the medical personnel lacked any sort of professional training, most teeth were not pulled but broken off, so that in many cases remnants of teeth had to be removed later.

Only in June 1939 was an entirely modern dental clinic for prisoners opened in Block 7, although without professionally trained personnel. The first SS "dentist" was SS Sergeant Major Coldewey, who had not yet worked in a practice and conducted his first experiments on the prisoners. His lack of skill matched his sadistic tendencies. Before every treatment each prisoner had to perform punishment exercises and received kicks or punches. Of course he pulled teeth only without anesthetics. Almost none of his attempts at extraction succeeded, so that complications later ensued and larger operations became necessary. This incompetent sadist was in the SS Operations Department at the end of the war. Jews enjoyed his special favor. They were treated only at their own expense and at especially high rates, which he determined arbitrarily. When he discovered a gold tooth, he pulled it immediately, saying that the tooth could no longer be saved.

After Coldewey came dentists who were just as incompetent: Bublitz and Schwarzkopf.

Later, at Himmler's orders, all gold dental work was broken out of the mouths of dead prisoners before cremation and taken to SS headquarters. From there it was sent to the SS Operations Department with precise documentation (names and numbers of dead prisoners along with the weight were marked on receipts). There it was melted down into fresh gold. This stripping of corpses was done extraordinarily "correctly" and bureaucratically. Many pounds of gold were collected over the years.

Treatment by prisoner dentists was naturally completely different. In the dental clinic, which was transferred to the present hospital in spring 1941, the prisoner assistants saved many damaged teeth, illegally produced dentures, and attempted to treat toothaches, often with stolen medications. In the final days prisoners were no longer treated by SS men at all.

Dental clinics for the SS were established as early as 1938. In fact, there was one for headquarters and the Death's-Head unit and another for personnel of the SS tank division and their family members. Both clinics had modern equipment; the technical and auxiliary personnel was made up of prisoners. There was an enormous difference between the treatment of the officers and that of the men. Damaged teeth of the rank-and-file SS were simply pulled; they attempted to save those of the SS officers. Every artificial tooth for the officers was made of gold that came from the mouths of dead or murdered prisoners. Even in the creation of dental prostheses, there was a difference between officers and men: Bridges were produced only for SS officers. Of course corruption in the SS dental clinic flourished to the widest possible extent.

For example, SS Sergeant Roman Schulz of Ulm produced no fewer than three costly dental prostheses for SS Master Sergeant Schmidt of the prisoners' canteen. Only the last pleased Schmidt, who paid for it with an abundance of tobacco and cigarettes from the supplies of the prisoners' canteen. The treatment of SS Master Sergeant Schmidt depended on his delivery of meat and sausages from the prisoners' kitchen.

A special chapter was the treatment of female SS dependents. All "spouses" of SS men—and many had three or four at the same time—received free but just as costly dental treatment. Indeed, Saturdays and Sundays Sergeants Scholz and Robert Kus of Görlitz drove around the vicinity to treat private patients with supplies from the SS dental clinic—only in exchange for food and tobacco, of course. SS Master Sergeant Lothar Lenz also occasionally took part in such trips.

In the final months only those capable of making an appropriate payment were treated at all in the SS dental clinic. The director of the dental clinic, SS First Lieutenant Karl Abraham of Langensalza, definitely knew about this corruption and even participated openly in it. Among other things he had work done in the SS dental clinic for his private practice in Langensalza.

RUDI GLASS, Berlin-Köpenick

70. THE CONVALESCENT DETAIL

I WAS THE KAPO of the so-called convalescent detail. To it were assigned convalescent patients and the convalescent wounded—prisoners whose suffering was not so serious that they had to be admitted to the prisoner hospital. Also assigned to the detail for limited periods were recovering patients who had been released from the prisoner hospital.

The convalescent detail was considered a light work detail. In spring 1941 it was 100 to 120 men strong; the camp administration did not permit a larger number. Up to summer 1942 the convalescent detail was assigned to carry stones, clothes for the prisoners' clothing room, and dirt for the gardening detail.

By summer 1943 the number in the detail had reached 700. About this time SS Captain Schiedlausky arrived. He tried again and again to force down the number of convalescent patients. To this end he made numerous inspections himself and sent into regular work many who in his opinion were healthy. Our efforts were always directed at providing convalescent duty for as many comrades as possible. In so doing we provided convalescence to comrades who were not exactly sick. For example, the Russians had six to seven cases of extension of convalescence a day and about four cases of new convalescence. According to my estimates we helped approximately one-fourth of the prisoners through this method.

The greatest danger was always the inspections. On days when a strict inspection was to be held, we pulled out the healthy who were only pretending to be convalescing and replaced them with prisoners from the invalids' block. Thus we avoided the danger of discovery of false convalescence. The maximum number of convalescent patients we were able to obtain under Schiedlausky amounted to approximately 1,500. That was not very many, considering the high camp population at the end and the poor health conditions.

PIETER COOL, The Hague

71. MASS MURDERER DR. PLAZA

OLD SHAFTS and tunnels of a salt mine near Nordhausen were to be the basis for expansion into a large new armaments works. There the essential components of the German V weapons were to be produced. The shafts were of course inadequate in size and number. Thus at the beginning Herr Sauckel's cheapest labor force, the prisoners of the Buchenwald concentration camp, had to be used to expand the system. But this work had to be done at *caracho,* or else the commandant, SS Lieutenant Colonel Förschner, would not receive his medal. So in September and October 1942, about 15,000 prisoners were transferred out of Buchenwald concentration camp. In addition, the head camp doctor of Buchenwald, SS Captain Dr. Plaza, took over supervision of medical "care" at Dora camp.

The fruits of his labor were all too visible in Buchenwald. The corpses from Dora were sent by truck to Buchenwald until its own crematorium was erected many months later. On average a truck came with at least 100 corpses every other day. And what corpses! They were filthy beyond all measure, covered with lice, and wasted away, their average weight about 88 pounds (and shortly before they had been strong men). They were twisted together in clumps that could hardly be separated.

Dr. Plaza took no steps to improve the condition of those entrusted to his care. He probably never even saw them. Nor did he care about giving the men a chance to wash or about disinfecting those covered with lice.

From December to May the mortality rate was no less than 1,500 people per month, but often up to 2,000.

Autopsies were in principle demanded for all corpses, but for all practical purposes they could be carried out only in much-simplified form. Without exception they showed such a degree of deterioration that the slightest cold would have been enough to kill the man.

After a short guest appearance in Natzweiler, Dr. Plaza received the assignment to establish something similar in Ohrdruf (Commando S III). The result was similar. From Ohrdruf, too, corpse transports came to Buchenwald twice a week.

Even if we had not seen the signature on the accompanying documents, we would have recognized from the condition of the corpses that Dr. Plaza was at work again. But they looked a degree worse than those from Dora. Unfortunately, there are no confirmed overall figures on the dead from S III, but they probably at least equaled the numbers from Dora. Thus as a mass murderer Dr. Plaza also far outstripped SS Technical Sergeant Sommer.

[no signature]

72. The Health Certificate Doctor

DURING THE LAST year in which the hell of Buchenwald existed, the demands of the German armaments industry for labor power became ever greater. SS slave traders tried to capture new prisoners by all possible means in order not to lose this profitable business of trading in human beings. No wonder, then, that the doctors who had to examine each prisoner for fitness for transport became to an increasing extent merely health certification machines. They sent every prisoner into an external work detail just as long as he did not carry his head under his arm.

At Buchenwald a special doctor was employed to sort out those fit for transport. For the most part this selection immediately followed the admission examination, since it was very time-consuming. The manner in which these transport examinations proceeded can best be illustrated by the example of the transport doctor [August] Bender, who once "examined" 1,100 prisoners in two hours. Although almost all prisoners suffered from chronic undernourishment, Bender declared only twenty-six of these 1,100 unfit for transport.

We were able to create a certain counterweight against the murder methods of the SS doctors—which of course we could not alter—by taking numerous prisoners off the transport lists afterward. Certain comrades were reclaimed by the individual national committees. Often they were found and kept out of the transport only after several hours of searching. Sometimes it even happened that individual comrades were taken off the transport list after the transport had already been assembled in the cinema, where they were always locked in before marching out. In rare cases comrades were pulled out of transports while still in roll call square. There were countless tricks by which comrades were saved from transports to bad external work details, against the will of the SS.

JIRI ZAK, Pilsen

73. Captain Dr. Hofer

After the arrest of the camp doctor Hoven, who was involved in the trial of the former commandant Koch, Dr. Hofer of Salzburg became acting camp doctor.

This doctor was the only one who dealt with the prisoners in a decent way and really tried to relieve the lot of the Nazis' unfortunate victims. Nevertheless, the prisoners faced him with the greatest mistrust because he wore the hated Death's-Head uniform. They had undergone only the worst imaginable experiences with previous camp doctors.

A few days after his arrival, the chief of Section D III, SS Colonel [Dr. Enno] Lolling, had a conversation with Hofer at the SS infirmary. Hofer, full of pride, told him, "I am prepared to serve the camp as head camp physician, and I assure you that the number of dead will sink to a minimum, which has already started to happen."

Lolling's answer was, "Then you won't be head physician either!"

Dr. Hofer simply replied, "I request transfer to a field unit."

And so it happened, too, after only a few days. Never had a doctor shown so much understanding for the prisoners; he was a rare bird among the black murderers in white doctors' coats.

KURT LEESER, Aachen

74. The Crematorium

I was employed in the crematorium of Buchenwald concentration camp as of December 1941. According to my memory, Russian officers and men were delivered for burning in the crematorium from the beginning of November 1941. They were initially shot in slowly increasing numbers on the DAW grounds. They were officers, so-called commissars, party members, and Jews. This enumeration of those shot came from members of the SS who had participated. Papers were only seldom found on the dead.

As of December 1942 shootings occurred in the horse stable. According to my careful estimate, no fewer than 7,500 Russian prisoners of war were shot in the horse stable. It frequently happened that the prisoners of war who had been shot were still alive on their delivery into the crematorium. Indeed, sometimes they even rose up on the bier and spoke to us. Once a prisoner of war who had been brought in on a cartload of corpses spoke to me with the words, "Comrade, give me your hand." He was naked and bloody like all the prisoners of war who had been shot, and he had been sitting upon a pile of naked corpses. In such cases the SS beasts who stood at the ready sprang up and killed the victim with blows or a shot from a revolver. We knew in every case two to three hours beforehand via the political department that shootings were about to occur; however, we did not know the number.

The crematorium stood at first under SS Technical Sergeant Kott. After February 1942 SS Master Sergeant Pleissner was also assigned to the crematorium. At Pentecost in [May] 1942, SS Technical Sergeant Kott went to Ravensbrück and was replaced by SS Sergeant Helbig. In spring 1942 Master Sergeant Pleissner was replaced by SS Technical Sergeant Warnstedt.

As of February 1943, prisoners of war were no longer shot but hanged in the crematorium. They were driven into the courtyard of the crematorium in an SS truck, then led into the basement, where hooks for hanging had been attached to the walls. There were forty-eight such hooks. The prisoners of war only rarely put up a fight as they were led to the execution site; as a rule they were paralyzed by fear.

Women were also hanged in Buchenwald. Among these women were Poles, Russians, and even seven Germans.

Prisoners were also hanged, among them Englishmen, Canadians, Italians, and those from almost all European nations.

Corpses from Weimar were frequently transported into camp by the Gestapo. The corpses were packed into straw mattresses. I recall that in fall 1943 two older people (man and wife) were delivered and burned. Their articles of clothing were marked "Hirschmann, Arnstadt."

ZBIGNIEW FUKS, Kraków

75. CORPSE CARRIERS IN BUCHENWALD

BEGINNING SEPTEMBER 21, 1939, I was a corpse carrier for approximately two and a half years. During winter 1939 a tent camp was erected next to the present crematorium. Every day forty to fifty prisoners there died of cold or hunger; many others were poisoned by SS Master Sergeants Blank and Hinkelmann.

The camp doctor, SS Captain Dr. Wagner, often sent into the main infirmary Jewish prisoners who were lying in Infirmary Barracks 2 and whose recovery was taking too long. There they were given lethal injections.

SS Second Lieutenant Dr. Eisele simply cut off the limbs of prisoners who came into the infirmary for the treatment of small wounds. Or he "treated" them in such a way that they died immediately. And for approximately four to five weeks, he gave prisoners lethal injections just to be rid of them. I had to take away the corpses of the prisoners who had been killed. When I asked permission to be relieved of this duty, he threatened me.

Almost every day two to three people—prisoners and even civilians—who had been hanged or given lethal injections were taken out of the cellblock. Many foreign civilian workers, mostly Poles, were likewise hanged. We had to bring in the corpses from outside the camp at night. These last murderous deeds were all carried out by SS Master Sergeant Sommer. Every day we brought out of the stone quarry two or three prisoners who had been chased through the sentry line and shot by SS men. For these shootings, the SS man concerned received leave.

LUDWIG SCHEINBRUNN, Vienna

76. PATHOLOGY

I WAS DELIVERED into the camp on September 7, 1939. A month later I was employed as an assistant in the field laboratory of the SS men who had come to Buchenwald to study dysentery. The Little Camp was under the leadership of SS Master Sergeants Blank and Hinkelmann and the later senior camp inmate Wolff. An epidemic of dysentery had broken out there and spread to the entire camp. The camp was placed under a general quarantine; released prisoners were not allowed to leave. After the end of my job in the field laboratory, I was chosen as kapo for the newly created pathology department. The director of this department was SS Captain Neumann, who a little later was sent to Shanghai on the orders of the Reich government. His successor was SS Captain Gutacker, who, after the pathology rooms were equipped, carried out the first autopsies on dead prisoners.

The pathology department was created especially for the purpose of preparing autopsy reports and death certificates "in an orderly manner." They were filled out in duplicates of eight. The actual causes of death, which in most cases consisted of general exhaustion, starvation, collapse [*Kollaps*], pneumonia, and similar things, were of course not allowed to appear in the reports and diagnoses. Instead, causes of death were recorded as heart attack, circulatory failure, tuberculosis, sepsis, etc. Autopsies were also performed on all those who had been shot. Despite abundant evidence of abuse, a general empty formula went down in the reports: "No cause could be determined other than the effect of force reported above." The "effect of force" was in most cases a bullet hole from an infantry weapon fired at close range.

The next director of pathology was SS Sergeant Lewe, who was indeed trained in pathology but was a heavy drinker who did no work. All work in the autopsy room was performed for him by the infamous creature Stöckel, who above all held strictly to the policy of listing false causes of death. Stöckel was a previously sentenced homosexual criminal who had served time for seducing the son of the auto manufacturer Opel. Before his employment in the pathology department, he had been active as the right-hand man of the mass murderer Blank in the Little Camp. He had helped many prisoners develop fatal illnesses by having them bathe in the open air in frigid temperatures in a tub of carbolic acid solution, supposedly for disinfection. He was later executed by prisoners.

Beginning in fall 1940 SS Captain Müller worked in the pathology department. He was then called to the Obersalzberg [Berchtesgaden]. On orders from Berlin, Müller initiated the project of peeling off the tattooed skin from the bodies of dead or murdered prisoners, tanning it, and producing lampshades out of it. How many lampshades were produced from human skin I can no longer say precisely today. But on many occasions several hundred pieces of tattooed human skin, tanned in various manners, were sent to SS Colonel Lolling, the chief of Section D III of the Main Economic and Administrative Office of the SS in Oranienburg.

Lolling was the chief doctor of all the concentration camps in Germany until the end. Müller also gave Stöckel and Werner Bach the assignment of producing sheaths for pocketknives and other objects out of tanned human skin. Moreover, Lolling requested written instructions for the preparation of shrunken human heads, that is, human heads that were shrunk to the size of a fist, like those produced by the cannibals of the South Sea islands. There were reports from the information section of the American army about the methods of the South Sea islanders, which I sent to Lolling. In addition, the SS doctors themselves "prepared" a sizable number of heads here according to these methods.

Daily from the first day until about September 1943, corpses arrived with injection marks on the veins in the arms. The method of killing was easy to determine during the autopsies. They were frequently injected with air, which caused an embolism, or with carbolic acid, which had a characteristic odor that was easy to detect when the corpse was opened. We also saw evidence of evipan, strychnine, morphine, and other alkaloids; chloral hydrates were likewise used for murder. Often more than thirty such dead arrived in a single day. Corpses of strangled or garotted prisoners frequently came from the cellblock. In no case was the true cause of death reported.

The camp doctor, Dr. Wagner, wrote a dissertation on tattooing; it was notable that all those prisoners he summoned to be tattooed died the next day in the hospital. The tattoos were peeled off and tanned. All of Wagner's victims were given lethal injections. Several hundred original autopsy reports on liquidated prisoners were confiscated in the pathology department and were turned over to the American army.

After Müller was called to Hitler's headquarters, SS Captain Plaza became director of pathology. Plaza was completely incompetent in medical matters, in moral considerations completely depraved. After about a year of work in pathology, which consisted solely of fabricating falsified death certificates, he was made camp doctor in the external detail at Dora. He bears the main responsibility for the miserable deaths of 3,000 prisoners there in a very short period as a result of the horrible sanitary conditions and hunger. Because at that time the corpses from Dora were still autopsied and burned in Buchenwald, we could determine that all of the dead were severely undernourished and had died from intestinal diseases or general exhaustion.

The last camp doctor, Schiedlausky, conducted experiments with poisoned ammunition on about ten prisoners in summer 1944. The victims received flesh wounds from ammunition about which I have no precise information. They died under terrible torment, most after a short time; the longest death throes lasted seven hours.

GUSTAV WEGERER, Vienna

77. Death by Starvation in Buchenwald

Every prisoner knew that of those who died a "normal" death in Buchenwald concentration camp, the greatest number died of hunger. But there is also unimpeachable testimony to support this knowledge: autopsy reports prepared by SS doctors in the famine winter of 1940. Even though not every corpse was autopsied and even though autopsies were performed at random, the overall results nevertheless have some value as an approximate average, which most likely would only go downward [with more cases]. The numbers reveal the details:

Of ninety autopsies from February 13 to April 30, 1940, there were

sixty-three cases of poor or very poor nutrition	70%
fourteen cases of moderate or sufficient nutrition	15.5%
thirteen cases of good nutrition	14.5%

It should be observed that it already took a great deal for an SS doctor—at that time Dr. Gutacker—to describe a prisoner as poorly nourished.

At the beginning of May, the nutrition improved somewhat, as expressed in a slight improvement in the figures. From the end of May to the beginning of September 1940, seventy-five autopsies were carried out with the following results:

forty-four cases of poor or very poor nutrition	59%
fifteen cases of moderate or sufficient nutrition	20%
sixteen cases of good nutrition	21%

Since the physical decline of the prisoners became ever greater, the SS doctors also falsified the results on this question. Even in cases of thoroughly emaciated bodies, they designated the nutritional status as "good." Only when one had to as- sume an atrophied physical state for reasons related to a given illness (tuberculosis, diarrhea, etc.) was the truth to some extent entered into the reports. A statistical compilation for the period thereafter is thus useless for the reasons given above.

How severely starvation raged in German concentration camps, and not only in Buchenwald, can be seen from the accompanying letter of December 28, 1942, from the SS Main Economic and Administrative Office. In it objections are raised to the high death tolls among the prisoners. For the SS, concentration camps rep- resented only sites for annihilation; if an SS officer had to request a halt to the an- nihilation—for whatever reasons—then nothing better characterizes the extent of hunger in the concentration camps.

Up to the last days, indeed especially from the beginning of 1945, starvation raged. Again, there is documentary proof: the letter of March 17, 1945, from the camp doctor.

STEFAN HEYMANN, Mannheim

SS Main Economic and Administrative Office   Oranienburg
Section D Concentration Camps   December 28, 1942
D III/Az. 14 h(KL) 82.42. Lg/Wy   signed Pister Schobert
Secret Diary No. 66/42. 21st Copy

Regarding: Medical Duties in the Concentration Camps
Reference: None
Appendices: 1

To Camp Doctors of the Concentration Camps
Da., Sh., Bu., Neu., Bu., Rav., Flo., Lu., Stu., Gr.-Ro., Nied., Natz., Hinz., Mor., Herzog., Mau.
Copies to the Camp Commandants

In the appendix a compilation of current admissions and departures in all concentra- tion camps is transmitted for your information. It shows that of 136,000 new admissions, around 70,000 have been lost due to death. With such a high death toll, the number of pris- oners can never be brought to the level that the Reich SS leader has ordered. The chief camp doctors must work with all means at their disposal to substantially lower mortality figures in the individual camps. The best doctor in a concentration camp is not the one who believes he must stand out through unexcelled hardness but the one who keeps work capacity at the highest possible level through supervision and exchange at individual work sites.

Camp doctors must supervise the feeding of prisoners more than previously and, in agreement with the administrations of the camp commandants, submit suggestions for improvement. These proposals must not exist simply on paper; the camp doctors should follow through with inspections on a regular basis. The camp doctors must further con- cern themselves with how work conditions at individual work sites might be improved. For this purpose, the camp doctors must personally confirm working conditions by visiting sites.

The Reich SS leader has ordered that mortality be reduced unconditionally. For this reason, the above is ordered and reports on what has been achieved are to be made monthly to the chief of Section D III. The first report is due on February 1, 1943.

signed Klüder [?]
SS Major General and Major
General of the Waffen SS

Summary of the Months June–November 1942

| | Admissions | | | Departures | | | | |
	Deliveries	Transfers	Total	Releases	Transfers	Deaths	E^a	Total
June	10,322	2,575	12,897	673	2,903	4,080	243	6,899
July	25,716	6,254	31,970	907	4,340	8,536	477	14,260
August	25,407	2,742	28,149	581	2,950	12,733	99	16,363
September	16,763	6,438	23,201	652	6,805	22,598	144	30,199
October	13,873	5,345	19,218	1,089	6,334	11,858	5,954	25,235
November	17,780	4,565	22,345	809	5,514	10,805	2,350	19,478
Total	109,861	26,919	136,780	4,711	27,846	70,610	9,267	112,434

[a][*Erschossen*, or shot?]

Garrison Doctor of the Waffen-SS   Weimar-Buchenwald
Weimar   March 17, 1945

Regarding: Autopsies of corpses of dead prisoners in External Work Detail of
        Buchenwald—Leau
Ref.: Conversation of SS Brigadier General Pister with SS Colonel Dr. Lolling

To the Chief of Section D III
Oranienburg

On the occurrences that led to the autopsies on dead prisoners from the external work detail Leau, I give the following report.

The Leau work detail, which has existed since September 1944, is a very heavy work detail, since construction projects must be carried out in part underground. The demands on the prisoners are very high, and the composition of the prisoners selected for this detail was unfavorable insofar as it consisted to a large extent of middle-aged Poles from Warsaw as well as Frenchmen. Both groups were composed mostly of urban dwellers from intellectual professions who did not appear to be physically suited for such construction projects.

Shortly after the beginning of the detail, a series of suspected cases of dysentery were reported. However, a medical corpsman who was immediately transferred there could not prevent the spread of the disease, even with the help of the infirmary personnel. The fact remains that a number of deaths ensued, in particular among prisoners who worked below ground and who among other things did not see the light of day for weeks at a time.

Alarmed at the rising death toll, the head physician of the OT [Organization Todt] Construction Command Headquarters in Halberstadt called me to express the suspicion that it was a question of an unknown endemic. He proposed that some of these dead be autopsied. He expressed the opinion that these could be cases of frequently occurring *endarteritis obliterans* [*sic*], arterial spasms, which might be brought on by working conditions in a salt mine. In that case it therefore lay in the general interest to protect the prisoners from further injury.

For this reason, I consented to the performance of autopsies on some particularly striking cases of death among prisoners. This was done with the assurance that the matter would be treated confidentially, which in these procedures was the case anyway. For some time I heard nothing about the results of these autopsies. In the meantime I was able to improve the general hygienic conditions in the camp by arranging for brewer's yeast from the nearby breweries to be distributed. It was also proposed that the OT Construction Command acquire sunlamps for prisoners working below ground. In the monthly report of January 1945, a medical corpsman informed me that the result of autopsies on two corpses came out negative.

Just a few days ago, on March 3, 1945, I received a letter from the OT Construction Command. It informed me that the autopsies showed that a state of chronic hunger existed that could not be explained, however, since the prisoners received heavy labor supplements to their rations. Furthermore, in the letter the suspicion was expressed that there might be some sort of black market activity in the distribution of the available food supply to prisoners. I informed the director of the administration there—SS Major Barnewald—of the situation, suggesting this possibility. I was informed, however, that the OT Construction Command had taken the care of prisoners under its own administration. Therefore, if any sort of irregularities occurred, they did not come from our side. This was communicated to the task force [*Einsatz*] doctor of the OT in a letter of March 10, 1945, with the accompanying request to have him examine the conditions.

As far as I am aware, autopsies were performed on two corpses of the said detail about which a high degree of interest existed. In case further autopsies should be carried out, I request to be informed accordingly, to clear up the affair. For my part, I will in writing ask the medical corpsman responsible for the care of the work detail whether he is familiar with more cases than those studied up to now.

> The Garrison Doctor of the Waffen SS Weimar
> signed Schiedlausky
> SS Captain of the Reserves

78. Humans as Guinea Pigs for SS Doctors

I CAME TO Buchenwald on October 5, 1939, and worked at first as a medical orderly in the infirmary of the so-called Little Camp. As a result of the lack of medications and undernourishment, ten of about eighty sick prisoners died every day. When about twenty of the sick got diarrhea one day, the infirmary personnel were called to the gate and each received "twenty on the ass."

Later I worked in the prisoner hospital and had to watch with my own eyes how SS doctors killed people there. SS Doctor Neumann conducted studies of the liver using live subjects. With a specially constructed apparatus, he took sections out of the livers of live subjects, who without exception died from these experiments.

I was a witness when the infamous murder doctor Eisele quickly injected five Jewish prisoners with evipan sodium in Operating Room 2. The first one died immediately and was carried out on a bier; then came the next one, for whom it went the same way. Eisele continued until the last one was murdered.

One day thirty patients who could no longer walk were brought to Block 4. Eisele prepared them tea with a strong solution of chloral hydrate. Those who had weak hearts died immediately; Eisele gave lethal injections to the rest. This room and its methods were then taken over by Dr. Hoven, who murdered about ninety to 100 prisoners a week there. The above-named SS murderer continued this bloody handiwork for about one and a half years.

Later I went to Block 46. One day the kapo there, Arthur Dietzsch, suggested to the SS doctor Ding (Schuler) that the typhus patients be immunized with fresh blood, which the SS man cheerfully did. All six of the immunized comrades died a short time after these injections. In addition, other injection experiments were undertaken on prisoners that proved fatal 95 percent of the time. Such experimental injections were made with Luminal and Pervitin.

ARTUR GADCZINSKI

79. Experiments in Block 46

I HAVE BEEN in Buchenwald concentration camp since March 31, 1942, and went to Block 46, the isolation block for typhus patients, in 1943. The block stood under the direction of the kapo Dietzsch, who, following the example of the SS, terrorized and tormented the infirmary personnel as well as the patients. The additional food supplies allotted to the nursing personnel were not issued. They were requisitioned by Dietzsch in large quantities, not least for the female inhabitants of the "special building." Upon being remonstrated, he explained, "Otherwise the men would be too fat."

Kapo Dietzsch suggested to SS doctor Ding (Schuler) that typhus patients be injected with fresh blood. The patients all died after the injection. One time experiments were carried out with a poison that was to have been used in poisoned projectiles; six men were killed. Although in recent times sufficient numbers of typhus patients were available in the camp, healthy men were taken and used as "carriers," that is, immunized with typhus bacilli. The victims were without exception candidates for death.

JAN SCHALKER, Holland

80. VICTIMS OF BLOCK 46

On AUGUST 16, 1942, I was summoned from my place of work by a prisoner and brought to the infirmary. I was superficially inspected there and brought to Block 46.

Approximately sixty to eighty prisoners were already there. Most were professional criminals and antisocials, in addition to a few political and Jewish prisoners.

The first two months I was cared for decently, since at the time of my delivery to Block 46, I was in very poor physical condition.

A few times my blood was drawn for examination. About mid-October 1942 I was injected with typhus by SS Major Dr. Ding. SS Captain Dr. Hoven was also present, and he likewise injected prisoners. After four to seven days, I became very sick. My temperature climbed to 104 degrees F. This illness lasted about two weeks. I was cared for by a prisoner orderly with the first name of Kurt. This care was good. The course of my sickness was recorded daily.

During my sickness SS Major Dr. Ding and SS Captain Hoven appeared only once. They examined a few of the sick. After I had recovered, 20 cc of blood was taken from me three times at intervals of two days. About three days after my blood was taken, thirty prisoners were released from Block 46 at three times in groups of ten prisoners each. I belonged to the last group of ten. The ninety prisoners who remained in Block 46 were reassured by Kapo Dietzsch. I don't know what became of them. On Kapo Dietzsch's conduct toward sick prisoners, I would like to relate the following.

We were allowed to smoke at certain hours of the day. The political prisoner Habermann, who once smoked at a forbidden time, was struck with an iron by Kapo Dietzsch in such a way that he had to go around with a bandaged head for ten to fourteen days.

For the same reason, on two occasions he punished an entire wing of sick prisoners by withholding their rations for a day. On our release from Block 46, we received a month of convalescent duty. At that time Kapo Dietzsch also told us that we were not permitted to say one word about anything that we had seen in Block 46, otherwise SS Captain Dr. Hoven would send us back to Block 46.

JAN A. VAN LEEUWARDEN, Vlaardingen

Chapter Seven
Special Actions and Special Facilities

On October 18, 1938, I was brought into the punishment company, Block 11, as a "race defiler." We had to work fourteen hours a day, which was considered to be a "normal" workday. We always worked under a hail of punches and kicks. The pace was murderous; every trip had to be made at double time, regardless of how heavy the loads were that we had to carry. Two prisoners jointly carried a handbarrow with dirt or rocks. Use of a carrying strap was strictly forbidden and was immediately punished by twenty-five lashes with a cane. After "normal" working hours there were always an additional two hours of "punishment labor." For weeks at a time we worked under floodlights on roll call square. Almost every day, when we arrived in the block at 10:00 or 11:00 P.M. believing that we could rest, the loudspeaker announced, "Ten, twenty, thirty prisoners of the punishment company to the gate." The senior block inmate at the time, Paul Waitz (a pimp), and the kapo, von Jäger (a professional criminal), made our lives a hell. Even during the midday break we had to do punishment exercises—knee bends, double time, etc.

Every Sunday, on orders of Deputy Commandant SS Captain Hüttig, the punishment company had to stand at the gate from 10:00 A.M. until 5:00 P.M. Rations were withheld at the same time. Anyone who moved only slightly immediately received ten lashes with a cane, for which the whipping block was always placed at the ready. Going to the bathroom during this period was strictly forbidden. The torment this caused is unimaginable. But the German political comrades saw to it, at risk to their own lives, that each comrade of the punishment company secretly received at least a half quart of rations in the washroom during the evening.

After the start of the war, the policy toward the punishment company was sharpened still further. All work had to be done at double time amid punches and kicks; there was nothing else for us. Many comrades were chased over the sentry line and shot. Often the death candidates received especially heavy stones that even two comrades could hardly lift. Then they were chased around with them until they collapsed and were beaten to death by the SS.

After the so-called assassination attempt at the Bürgerbräukeller in Munich, three Jewish comrades were pulled out of the punishment company to be shot by SS Master Sergeants Blank and Warnstaedt. I myself escaped this fate only in the following manner: Blank called me to the front and asked me where I came from.

Upon my answer, "From Berlin!" he said cynically, "We already have enough from there!" and left me standing there. I will never forget those minutes of deadly peril.

Our block officer, Schmidt, was a special case. He had the sadistic habit of kicking a prisoner in the stomach or testicles before speaking to him. Every roll call cost three or four severely wounded if the count off did not go quickly enough, etc.

On March 12, 1942, I was finally transferred to a free block with other comrades who, like me, had already served more than three years in the punishment company.

ROLF BAUMANN, Berlin

82. The I Barracks

Hidden deep in the forest, across from the officers' houses, stood a large stone building—the so-called Isolation Barracks, or I Barracks for short. There the SS held especially prominent personalities they did not want to have come into contact with the other prisoners for one reason or another. Twelve SS men were stationed as a special guard for this building, which was surrounded by a 10-foot-high stockade.

Up to the bombardment of Buchenwald on August 24, 1944, a number of prominent people were locked up in these barracks. They included the former Social Democratic Reichstag deputy Rudi Breitscheid and his wife; Princess Mafalda of Hesse, a daughter of the Italian king, and her servant; and the Jehovah's Witness Maria Ruhnau. The building was completely destroyed by a direct hit from a bomb. Even the shrapnel protection trench to which the occupants had fled offered no safety. Out of the piles of upturned dirt, only the head of Princess Mafalda emerged, calling desperately for help. Across her feet, completely covered with dirt, lay Frau Breitscheid. Both were still alive.

Frau Breitscheid had received only minor contusions from the explosion and was sent away on a transport soon after the bombardment. Princess Mafalda had a terrible wound on her upper arm, which was amputated by the camp doctor, Schiedlausky. As a result of the loss of blood and the unprofessionally performed operation, as doctors later determined, Princess Mafalda died the next day. Breitscheid himself was covered with dirt about 18 inches deep. Whether he died of suffocation or was killed by the piece of shrapnel that struck him I do not know. In any case, he was already dead when he was dug out.

If the Nazi murderers maintain that Ernst Thälmann, the leader of the KPD, was also killed during this bombardment, that is a brazen lie. Thälmann was never in Buchenwald and was surely murdered by the SS criminals at another location.

The I Barracks were rebuilt and at the end occupied by fifty-four persons. At first—in any case only temporarily—the former federal chancellor of Austria, Schuschnigg, was there, as were the former mayor of Vienna, Seitz, and his wife and two others unknown to me. Prisoners were held there until just a few days before the liberation by American troops. Among them were the following: Fritz Thyssen, who claimed he had already been under arrest for four and a half years, at first in an insane asylum and then in Oranienburg (Sachsenhausen); Röchling; six members of the Stauffenberg family; a general Falkenhausen or Falkenberg (?); five ministers of the Hungarian "three-day government"; the wife of ambassador [von] Hassel; Frau Goerdeler and her children; the wife of General Lindemann; some wives of former labor union leaders and their children whose names I do not know.

At the end of 1944, the following event caused great excitement: A Fieseler-Storch [a slow-flying observation plane] circled the I Barracks several times. The female pilot could be seen clearly, waving from the cockpit. Since the rumor had circulated in camp that the inspector of the Luftwaffe, Galland, was in the I Barracks, I asked Thyssen whether perhaps the pilot was greeting Galland. Thyssen told me, however, that she was the test pilot Millert of Vienna, who was a friend of the jailed family of Count Stauffenberg. She was greeting her friends in this manner. For three days the bold pilot flew over, looped around, and then flew away. The plane was never seen again.

A few days before the arrival of the American troops in Buchenwald, all inmates of the Isolation Barracks were taken away in trucks, allegedly to Bavaria.

ARMIN WALTHER, Riese/Elbe

83. THE K COMPANY

AFTER THE OUTBREAK of war, the K Company was added to the punishment company. K prisoners were all those who were guilty of misconduct in the war but were not condemned to death because their "offenses" were too minor.

I will now try to describe a small excerpt out of my personal experiences in the K Company.

The K Company was a closed penal facility within camp. The designated blocks were surrounded with a double barbed wire fence and closed off. We were not permitted to have any sort of contact with the other prisoners, even when the workday was finally over. After the long and heavy workday, we fell into a leaden sleep on our straw mattresses in the overcrowded sleeping room (three men to every two beds). Even then the call often sounded on the loudspeaker, "Fifty prisoners of the punishment and K companies needed for unloading supplies (or carrying tree trunks). Report immediately to the gate!"

The punishment and K companies were composed not only of political prisoners but also of previous offenders. Some were also Poles whose only offense was that they had been intimate with German girls. If an even harsher level of treatment existed, then it was reserved for our Jewish comrades. The rather strong criminal streak in a portion of the population meant poor social relationships among comrades. Some of the senior block inmates and room attendants were a special case. For example, the prisoner Stelzmann was later revealed as an informer, as was the kapo Herzog, a former member of the French Foreign Legion.

The minimal privileges that other prisoners in camp had never came into question for us. Only once every three months were we allowed to write to our relatives and receive a letter from them. We were not permitted to make purchases in the canteen, were not allowed to have money, and were not allowed to smoke. We had to work on Sundays. We often had to perform punishment exercises, which cost a few lives each time. We were also cheated out of some of the food allotted to us. From the time we arose until we went to bed, we were beaten. When rations for the whole camp were withheld, we often received an extra one to three days without food.

In the beginning, as a matter of principle, all prisoners of the punishment and K companies had to perform heavy transport work for the building of barracks and houses. Later we all had to go into the stone quarry. We worked in the stone quarry twelve hours every day, with an additional three to four hours in the gardening detail. Day after day in the quarry, we had to pull fifty-two to fifty-four carts laden with about 1.5 tons of stones. We pulled them for a quarter of a mile up an incline of about 25 degrees, at double time and in wooden shoes. The return trip downward went at a run. All of us injured our feet but were not allowed to be treated in the infirmary. In addition there were constant beatings from SS sentries, kapos, and foremen. The kapos Vogel and Herzog and the foreman Adams in particular should be named here.

The break for the entire day amounted to half an hour—without food or drink. The majority of the comrades had diarrhea but were not allowed to go to the bathroom; their own pants had to serve as toilets.

Often as we pulled the carts uphill, the SS sentries would throw our caps 2 or 3 yards away. Then they would order us to fetch them. They used this trick to shoot down many prisoners in return for the pleasure of the leave and the premium they would receive as a reward.

Many sentries shot three prisoners a day. Another method of liquidation was "to finish off" [a prisoner], that is, torture a prisoner until he went insane, so he would run through the sentry line to put an end to his torment. Prisoners who fainted while working had water poured over them until they came to again and resumed their work. The dead were trampled upon by the Nazi stooge Herzog. Prisoners were also thrown over precipices in the stone quarry.

The punishment and K companies also had to provide the greatest number of prisoners to be infected with the typhus bacillus in order to obtain serum from their blood. Most of them died as a result.

Day after day at the close of work, each man had to carry a large stone out of the stone quarry. That finished many a man off.

That was the hell of the stone quarry at Buchenwald concentration camp. I was able to come out of it alive because of my professional skill and particularly because of the help of some antifascist comrades who freed me from the K Company through skillful intervention.

MAX PABST, Neu Schmiedefeld, Kreis Saalfeld

84. THE SPECIAL BUILDING

IN SUMMER 1943 there arose in Buchenwald, as elsewhere, a so-called special building, that is, a brothel. Through these means the SS attempted to corrupt the prisoners, to play them off against each other in that female prisoners were forced to surrender their bodies to prisoners in the name of camp order. Entirely aside from all the questions of morality, a visit to the brothel signified an acceptance of this Nazi tactic—and was recognized as such by the prisoners.

At first, supervision of the special building was in the hands of two female SS overseers who conducted themselves worse than whores. These SS women not only had their regular relationships with SS men: If a prisoner came with half a pound of butter or some other food, they would go to bed with him with equal enthusiasm. Indeed, they procured clients for the prisoner slaves of the brothel by creating propaganda for their building among the SS, although visits by SS men were of course strictly forbidden. If the overseers were sick, they forced prisoner women to be of service to their SS friends. Even SS officers did not shy away from a visit to the brothel and were frequently to be found there, though of course only late at night.

The women prisoners in the brothel were of course just as hungry as the other prisoners in camp, so prisoners who were able to "organize" sufficient foodstuffs were often accommodated outside the prescribed times as well. Especially among the criminally inclined, that led to the theft of foodstuffs, in particular the theft of packages. The prisoner leadership frequently had to use force to prevent it. One night it even came to a major brawl between the camp police and the criminals. The criminals had entered the brothel at night in a drunken condition and threatened the women, but the camp police quickly and thoroughly cleaned out this pigpen.

Over time the SS women overseers became so corrupt that they could no longer assert themselves against prisoners at all, so the camp administration relieved them and replaced them with SS men. But soon it was just the same with them. They misused the women prisoners in every way and of course very soon had lost all authority. To keep the operation somewhat honest, a camp policeman had to post watch there to make sure the SS men did not get involved with the prisoner women.

The special building was a swamp flower, a deplorable exhibition of the worst corruption and other sins, a true model of National Socialist enterprise.

CARL GÄRTIG, Kretzschen über Zeitz

85. MASS MURDER OF RUSSIAN PRISONERS OF WAR

IN BUCHENWALD as elsewhere, the SS murderers undertook one of the worst crimes of which one can accuse a so-called civilized nation: They systematically murdered prisoners of war who fell into the hands of the German Wehrmacht during military operations, even though these Russian soldiers were members of a regular army. But the fanatic hatred of communism ran so deep that the Himmler bandits did not shrink even from this brutal crime.

The cowardly murderers knew very well that they were committing a crime that they had to keep secret from the whole world, and they therefore sought to cover it up by all possible means.[1] They built a refined murder facility in the horse stable at Buchenwald, even installing a radio that they played so loudly that from the outside one could not hear the cries, death rattles, and groans of the victims of these cold and cowardly murderers. There is no word in the language of any people that could accurately characterize such a vile, cold-blooded crime.

The enclosed map of the horse stable shows all the details of this murder facility, one that could only have sprung from the mind of a perverse sadist. [The map does not appear in this version.]

The attached letter from the SS Supreme Command [below] clearly shows that this Himmler guard ordered the murders of these defenseless prisoners of war. But death still did not satisfy this brood of criminals. The victims had to work for their murderers until their already pronounced death sentences were carried out, until their bodies were so weakened that they could no longer turn a profit. Only then would the executions finally take place. Without the original of this letter [from the SS Supreme Command] in black and white in front of him, no normal human could believe that such a thing was still possible in the twentieth century. But this horrible crime against about 7,200 Russian prisoners of war who were

---

1. These shootings were in violation of the 1907 Hague and 1929 Geneva conventions concerning the treatment of prisoners of war. In a decree of June 6, 1941, known as the *Kommissarbefehl*, Hitler ordered that captured Soviet army political officers should be shot on the spot or liquidated later. See "The Kommissarbefehl and Mass Executions of Soviet Prisoners of War" by Hans-Adolf Jacobsen in Krausnick et al., *Anatomy of the SS State*, 505–534.

murdered on Himmler's orders in cowardly, back-stabbing fashion at Buchenwald will never be forgotten!

KARL FEURER, Munich

The Reichsführer SS   Oranienburg,
Inspector of the Concentration Camps   November 15, 1941

Pol. File 14 fN14/L/Ot.
Secret Diary No. 213/41

Re: Execution of Russian Prisoners of War
Attachments: None

SECRET!

To the Camp Commandants
of the Concentration Camps
Da., Sch., Bu., Mau., Flo., Neu., Au., Gro., Ro., ...
Copies to Camp Doctors, Protective Custody Camp Leaders &
Administrations

The Reich SS leader and chief of the German Police has declared himself in agreement in principle on the following. Execution can be postponed for those Russian prisoners of war transferred to the concentration camps for execution (in particular commissars) who, on the basis of their physical fitness for work, can be utilized in the stone quarry. For this measure, the agreement of the chief of the Security Police of the SD [Sicherheitsdienst] must be secured in advance.

On this matter it is ordered:

On the arrival of execution transports in camp, the protective custody camp officers and the camp doctor should select Russians who have the bodily strength and are suited for work in the stone quarry. A list of names of the selected Russians is to be provided in duplicate to this office. On this list the camp doctor must note that there are no medical reservations regarding the prisoners' suitability for work. After agreement has been obtained from the chiefs of the Security Police and the SD, the Russians' transfer to a quarry camp will be ordered from here.

signed Klüder [?]
SS General and
Major General of the Waffen SS

---

86. COMMANDO 99: THE HORSE STABLE

THE OFFICIAL murder site for the Russian prisoners of war was the horse stable; the SS called the work detail itself Commando 99. Only one prisoner was employed in the commando, the Russian White Guard officer Kushni-Kushnarev, who was also active in the camp as an informer. He died in camp of typhus one day.

When the unsuspecting victims came into the stable, the directing officer of the murder detail said something like the following: "You are in a collection camp [*Sammellager*]. To avoid the danger of infection, you must first be disinfected, examined, and bathed. Take off your shirt first, then your pants; place your shoes in front of them, and put the identification marker into the shoes so that there will be no confusion."

This address was translated by Kushni-Kushnarev, who walked among the new admissions the entire time and tried to overhear their conversations. When through skillful questioning he discovered a commissar or party member, he immediately reported it to the SS officer, which without fail led to a death sentence. This criminal informer had many hundreds of lives on his conscience.

Then began the interrogation, during which a number of prisoners of war unsuspectingly gave their correct names and titles. During interrogation SS murderers in white coats walked through the ranks and thus simulated medical examinations.

After six men had been questioned, the order was given, "The first six to the baths." At the same time one loudspeaker that played very loud music was turned on, while through the other different names and numbers were called, likewise quite loudly. Simultaneously, the bloody tragedy was taking place in the back rooms.

The victims chosen for "bathing" walked into a small room that had a sound-proof wall and door. The room was equipped as a shower room, with tiles on the floor and eight shower heads on the walls. The door had a slit about 1 foot wide and 1 inch high. When the victims of the SS were in the shower, an SS man shut the door firmly and shot the unsuspecting victims down with an automatic pistol.

When they all lay on the floor, often not fatally injured, they were thrown into a truck outfitted with a special zinc-lined body. The showers were turned on, the blood was washed away—and the next ones could come in to "bathe." In this manner 500 men were "bathed" between 9:00 P.M. and 5:00 A.M.

In the beginning the SS murderers used a machine they later got rid of because it did not work quickly enough. On a wooden stand was a measuring stick (to measure a person's height); attached to it was a firing pin at the level of the base of the skull. When someone stepped onto the stand, the pin hurtled out and shattered the nape of the neck or the skull. With this, too, many were not struck a fatal blow but were nevertheless taken to the crematorium in a truck full of corpses. At the crematorium many of the still-living victims of the sadistic SS bloodthirstiness received a mercy blow from an oak club, which immediately smashed the skull. Sometimes it also happened that one who was still alive jumped out of the corpse truck and tried to run into the woods naked. He would then be shot down by the sentries stationed there.

When the transports were too large, the prisoners of war had to undress in front of the horse stable in the open air. They were led in a large unit to the riding hall, where they had to line up and were mowed down with a machine gun. The bloodstains were immediately covered with fresh sawdust and the next victims brought in. Of course these brutish SS murderers were always drunk throughout the drama. Alcohol in unlimited amounts stood at their disposal.

The victims were not always completely unsuspecting. Occasionally a prisoner would sense his impending doom and would run naked out of the stable—and directly into a sentry line that was drawn up around the horse stable. In one case the Ukrainian SS men did not shoot; after that only Reich German SS men were stationed as sentries.

A typhus epidemic once broke out in the murder detail, its members having caught the disease during their bloody work. Twenty-two murderers were alleged to have died of it.

Civilians, too, were liquidated in the horse stable. One day a bus from the Apolda Transit Company arrived with well-dressed civilians and a few officers. Amid cheerful, excited conversation, they went into the horse stable. It was around 4:00 P.M. Softly the sentry line drew close, and two hours later the crematorium received new victims.

For their murderous deeds, all members of Commando 99 received the Military Service Cross.

KURT LEESER, Aachen

87. Living Humans Among the Corpses

In my service as a mason during the building of the new crematorium, I could observe things that probably are still not known.

As long as the new ovens were not yet finished, the old one was still used. Between the old and the new ovens was a wall of boards. After the first new oven was ready, the wall was moved between it and the second new oven still under construction.

At this time many Russian prisoners of war were murdered by shots to the base of the skull. When the murderers arrived with a truckload of victims, the bodies were delivered directly into the basement through a built-in chute. Every time the

Nazis let bodies slide down into the cellar, a loud howling and groaning arose—proof that many of the victims were not yet completely dead, since they returned to consciousness when they struck the cement floor of the cellar. Whether these still-living, unfortunate victims of the murderous beasts were then beaten to death or were sent into the ovens while still alive, I don't know.

When we built the chimney of the crematorium, I once saw three and another time two Russian soldiers standing, alive, in the courtyard. They were led into the crematorium—and then I saw nothing more of them again.

PHILIPP KOHL, Frankfurt/Bad Vilbel

88. EXECUTIONS AT BUCHENWALD

IN THE EARLY YEARS of Buchenwald's existence, many hundreds of prisoners were indeed shot by the SS murderers or killed in other ways, but only two public executions were carried out. Two prisoners who had beaten an SS man to death were hanged—hanged before the eyes of all the prisoners.

The SS murderers carried out the next executions for the most part secretly in a room of the dog kennel. These were almost exclusively cases of Polish workers who had been deported to Germany and had entered into intimate relationships here with German women. In these cases denunciations without supporting evidence were frequently taken as proven facts. Many people in the vicinity of Weimar and Buchenwald came to these executions. When a case of alleged or actual relations between a Pole and a German became known in the tiniest village or in a larger town, the SS drove out from Buchenwald with a portable gallows and hanged the Poles. Two Polish prisoners served the SS as executioner assistants on these expeditions. It is no longer possible to determine exactly the number of those the SS murdered in this way, though probably at least 250 to 300 people a year lost their lives in this horrible manner.

For a time beginning in 1943, the SS conducted hangings in roll call square, executing those who had escaped or had only attempted escape. These took place on the express orders of Himmler, who hoped to put a stop to the rash of escape attempts. But all the public executions were of no avail; on the contrary, hatred and defiance grew, and resistance against the murderers became ever stronger. When the SS noticed this effect, they stopped all public executions, and instead the victims of the Nazi hangmen were hanged in the crematorium by the kapo there and by SS Sergeant Hübner. The exact number of these victims, who were often reported as "transferred," can no longer be determined either, but it would probably be at least equal to the numbers in previous years.

The prisoners succeeded in compiling a complete list of all those executed only for the last year, 1944–1945; it is appended to this report [not included in this edition]. According to the list, 287 comrades were hanged in the final twelve months before the liberation of Buchenwald. Even by the most conservative estimate, the number of people Himmler's SS hangmen hanged at Buchenwald would be at least 1,100.

Prisoner Records Office

89. LIST OF SECRET SERVICE OFFICERS

Two original lists of the roll call officer of Buchenwald concentration camp are available. They read as follows:[2]

Sept. 9, 1944

Determine where the following prisoners are working:

8511	Allard, Elise Albert	born	7/14/16
13092	Benoist, Robert		3/20/95
7864	Bougennec, Jean		7/25/12
12817	Debal, Julien		5/02/16
8870	Defendini, Ange		12/04/09
8051	Garry, Emile		4/02/09
14185	Geelen, Pierre Albert		6/24/16
14930	Hubble, Desmond		1/29/10
12463	Kane, Gerard		8/10/11
15374	Leczia, Marcel Rene		1/01/11
9636	Macalister, John Kennedy		7/09/15
9161	Mayer, James Andreas		4/19/20
9992	Pickersgill, Frank Herbert		5/28/15
8945	Rechemann, Charles		8/24/12
8738	Sabourin, Romeo Josef		1/01/23
7898	Steele, Arthur		4/06/21

In parentheses behind all names: under arrest

<table>
<tr><td>Roll Call Officer of</td><td>Order to report</td></tr>
<tr><td>Buchenwald Concentration Camp</td><td>at 3:30 A.M.</td></tr>
<tr><td>WERLE</td><td>at Signpost 3</td></tr>
</table>

---

2. The original lists were not alphabetized.

Oct. 5, 1944

Determine where the following prisoners are working:

Avallart	Jean	12/17/08	Construction Detail 3	7859
Barret	Denis John	11/23/16	"	10449
Chaigneau	Jacques	2/18/23	"	10375
de Seguier	Jean Marie	3/27/18	"	11491
Evesque	Jean	12/16/09	"	7795
Gerard	Andre Leon Rene	6/22/11	"	7582
Heusch	Henri	11/29/09	"	10381
Keunen	Marcel	5/30/11	"	10062
Lavallee	Jean	10/11/13	"	10045
Loison	Yves	3/14/21	"	7638
Mulsant	Pierre	7/13/14	"	13474
Peuleve	Thomas Henri	1/29/16	"	12332
Prager	Henri	3/03/97	"	8144
Vellant	Paul	12/27/07	"	10253
Wilkinson	George Alfred	8/31/13	"	7740

Above-named prisoners report on 10/5/44 at 6:00 A.M. to the roll call officer. Behind the name *Peuleve* is marked in pencil: *Hospital*

90. LIST OF ALLIED AVIATORS

[List of names of 168 Allied aviators, omitted in this edition. Lists include names, ranks, and serial numbers of eighty-two U.S., fifty British, twenty-five Canadian, nine Australian, and two New Zealand aviators who were held in Buchenwald for a few months in fall 1944.]

91. SHOOTING OF AN ENGLISH AVIATOR IN AROLSEN

[Item appears to be missing in the translator's copy of the original manuscript.]

92. MASS MURDERS AT THE BERNBURG SANATORIUM

BECAUSE THE annihilation of prisoners, in particular the Jews, did not go quickly enough for the SS murderers, they assembled so-called death transports after 1941. For the first of these, the names of prisoners destined for transport were read out at morning roll call, and they were immediately loaded into a truck. In the evening or the next day, the clothing and underwear of the murdered men returned. They were gassed in the sanatorium and nursing facility at Bernburg/Saale, under the supervision of the head doctor there, Dr. Imfried Eberl. The SS had given the murder action the file designation *14 f 13*. The following excerpt from a report (of March 19, 1943) by the garrison doctor, Hoven, about the subsidiary camp at the Junker Works at Schönebeck/Elbe characterizes Dr. Eberl.

> Contracting with doctors and negotiating with cemetery offices have often led to insurmountable difficulties. … I therefore made contact with the chief doctor at the sanatorium and nursing facility in Bernburg/Saale, Dr. Imfried Eberl, P.O. Box 252, tel. 3169. He is the same doctor who carried out the 14 f 13. Dr. Eberl showed an unusual understanding and willingness. All the corpses of prisoners from Schönebeck and Wernigerode were transported to Dr. Eberl in Bernburg and were immediately burned there, even without death certificates.

And such criminal mass murderers call themselves doctors at a health (!) facility! Sending prisoners to the gas chambers was purely a business affair for the SS bandits. Two letters from this correspondence are reproduced below. The cold, businesslike style hardly sugests that both transports sent hundreds of unfortunate people to a horrible death by asphyxiation.

OTTO KIPP, Dresden

Buchenwald Concentration Camp   Weimar/Buchenwald,
Camp Doctor   February 2, 1942

Re: Jews incapable of working in Buchenwald Concentration Camp
With reference to: Personal conversation
Appendices: 2

To the Sanatorium and Nursing Facility
Bernburg on the Saale
P.O. Box 263

In regard to our personal conversation, submitted for further action are two copies of a list of all Jews held in Buchenwald concentration camp who are sick and unable to work.

The Camp Doctor
Buchenwald Concentration Camp
signed Hoven
SS Colonel of the Reserves

Sanatorium and Nursing Facility   Bernburg,
Bernburg   March 5, 1942

Gesch.Z.:Be Go/Pt.

To the
Concentration Camp
Buchenwald at Weimar
Attention: Camp Commandant
Re: Our letter of March 3, 1942
Concerning: 36 Prisoners, 12th Shipment of Feb. 2, 1942

In our letter of the third of this month, we asked you to place the remaining thirty-six prisoners at our disposal on the occasion of the last transport of March 18, 1942.

As a result of the planned absence of our head doctor, who undertakes the medical certification of these prisoners, we ask that these prisoners, along with their files, be turned over not on March 18, 1942, but instead on the transport of March 11, 1942. The files will be returned on March 11, 1942.

Heil Hitler!
Godenschweig

93. SPECIAL ACTIONS IN BUCHENWALD

IN ADDITION to the normal new admissions to Buchenwald, which were delivered almost every day by the Gestapo or the criminal police offices, there were the so-called actions. These were composed of certain groups that were captured and brought into the camp in specific actions ordered by Himmler's men. In the beginning these actions were carried out only in Germany, but they later reached throughout Europe. Below we list the most important actions sent to Buchenwald.

Name of Action	Date	Number	Citizenship
Shirkers	May 1938	ca. 4,000	Reich Germans
Jews	June 1938	500	Reich Germans
Prisoners of the Viennese police	Sept. 1938	400	Austrians
Rath action Jews	Nov. 1938	9,815	Reich German Jews
Militarily unworthy	Sept. 1939	ca. 500	Reich Germans
Hostages	Sept. 1939	756	Czechs

Name of Action	Date	Number	Citizenship
Protectorate Jews	Sept. 1939	ca. 500	Czechs
Poles	Oct. 1939	4,098	Poles
Snipers	Oct. 1939	123	Poles
Polish minority	Oct. 1939	181	Poles
Jews from the Vienna nursing home	Oct. 1939	ca. 200	Austrian Jews
Immigrant Jews from Poland	Oct. 1939	ca. 2,000	Germans and Austrians
Hostages	Oct. 1940	366	Dutch
Jewish action, Amsterdam	Feb. 1941	730	Dutch
Prisoners of war	Oct. 1941	ca. 3,000	Russians
Civilian workers (Ukraine)	Fall 1943	5,394	Russians
Ocean Spray and Spring Wind action from Compiègne	1943–1944	19,234	French
Night and Fog action from Brussels	May 1944	2,332	Belgians
University of Oslo	Jan. 1944	349	Norwegians
Warsaw uprising	Aug. 1944	4,560	Poles
Budapest Jews	Summer 1944	6,115	Hungarians
Iron Bars action	Aug. 1944	ca. 750	Reich Germans
Danish police	Sept. 1944	1,953	Danes
Polish Jews	Jan. 1945	5,745	Poles

After the Nazis had to evacuate a number of concentration camps as a result of the advance of the Allied armies, prisoners from these camps were brought to Buchenwald. They were thoroughly undernourished and completely debilitated. This last "action" of the collapsing Nazi regime in Germany was comprised of the following transports.

Date	Number	Type of Prisoner	Origin
12/24/44	916	Polish Jews	Kraków
12/25/44	1,913	Hungarian Jews	Budapest and Vienna
1/17/45	263	Various	Cologne and Aachen
1/17/45	2,740	Polish Jews	Czestochowa
1/20/45	1,446	Polish Jews	Czestochowa
1/22/45	2,224	Jews of various nations	Auschwitz
1/23/45	917	Jews of various nations	Auschwitz
1/26/45	3,987	Various	Auschwitz-Monowitz
2/03/45	291	Various	Küstrin
2/05/45	285	French and Belgians	Prison Gross-Strehlitz
2/07/45	250	Various	Küstrin
2/10/45	6,805	Various	Gross-Rosen
2/24/45	464	Russians	Gross-Rosen
2/26/45	290	Various	External detail Gross-Rosen
3/05/45	580	Various	Gross-Rosen
3/07/45	905	Mostly Jews	Gross-Rosen
3/12/45	399	Mostly Poles	Gross-Rosen
3/30/45	280	Various	External detail Natzweiler

94. THE SHEEP PEN

ON JUNE 15, 1938, 500 Jews came to Buchenwald, primarily from Berlin and Breslau. After the usual tortures during the admissions process, they were housed in a wooden building in the so-called sheep pen. There were neither tables nor chairs, nor of course any beds. Prisoners slept on bare ground covered in a makeshift manner with pine branches. Since there was no water despite the warm season, prisoners often paid 1 mark for a swallow of water.

Professional criminals, who constantly beat us, were assigned as room attendants. For every five men there was one loaf of bread, along with half a liter of food every day. The room attendant stole most of the rations and then sold them to the prisoners. Wake up was around 3:00 A.M. About 5:00 A.M. came roll call, which often lasted until 7:00 A.M. Because of the poor-quality shoes, the walk to roll call square through the mire often took an hour. We all had injured feet. We had to eat in the open air in all sorts of weather. About 5:00 P.M. we returned from work and went to roll call. Then began the dreaded night shift, which lasted until the onset of darkness. Many of us, however, worked on construction of the stone barracks under floodlights until 11:00 P.M. Punches and kicks belonged to the daily routine.

A large number of comrades died of exhaustion. Many fell into open latrines while using the toilet and drowned there. Many despaired. They ran into the so-called no-man's-land—a 5-yard-wide strip of ground in front of the barbed wire—where they were immediately shot; others hanged themselves. After two months 150 comrades were already dead, and almost all the rest of us were incapable of working. We were forbidden admission into the infirmary or even treatment there. At risk to their own lives, the German political prisoner orderlies treated us against the express orders of the SS administration. Indeed, it was forbidden for all prisoners even to speak to us.

The second deputy commandant at the time, Hackmann, had threatened camp inmates during a special anti-Jewish pogrom: "Whoever takes anything from Jews dies!" Two days later Hackmann demanded that we "contribute" money toward the purchase of books. About 8,000 marks were collected, which disappeared into his bottomless pockets. Two weeks later came a new demand for a "fund for the poor," with the same result. That, too, was absorbed by the SS officers. For two months we were in the hell of the sheep pen. Only at the end of August [1938] were we finally moved into a wooden block.

WILLI TICHAUER, Berlin

95. THE RATH ACTION OF 1938

On NOVEMBER 8, 1938, the German consul in Paris, von Rath, was shot, allegedly by the Jew Grünspan. With the help of the SS and the Gestapo, the Nazis used this incident to stage a pogrom against the Jews and to drive tens of thousands of Jews into the concentration camps. Such an action was already prepared for long before the "murder": In mid-October 1938 five large wooden barracks had to be erected in roll call square in Buchenwald. They were finished "just in time."

Two days after the incident in Paris, the first Jews arrived in camp. The transports always arrived during the night, primarily from Silesia, Berlin, Frankfurt on the Main, and of course above all from Thuringia and the Hessian provinces. In addition to bankers, industrialists, professors, doctors, and artists, there were masses of Jewish artisans, mine workers from Upper Silesia, Hessian rural populations, etc.

Even the road from the train station to the camp was a form of torture without equal. It had to be traveled at double time under constant blows from sticks and lashes from whips. Because people were arrested without regard to their age, one could see seventy- to eighty-year-old men next to ten-year-old children. Those who fell behind were shot down along this death road. Those who survived were forced to drag the blood-soaked corpses along with them into the camp. At the gate the masses jammed together—about 1,000 always arrived in camp at the same time—because the SS refused to open the large barred gate, instead opening only a small side entry for each individual. The block officers stood next to the entry and beat every new arrival with iron bars, whips, etc. so that virtually every incoming Jew had contusions or wounds on the head. Many weaker men were trampled to death in the throng.

No language has the words to describe the scenes that then took place in roll call square. Before everyone's eyes the SS men plundered in the most shameless fashion those who had been beaten to the ground, murdered, or trampled to death, stealing watches, rings, money, and other objects of value out of their pockets. Selected professional criminals provided worthy assistance in this business. There was one interesting scene when a man who had been pushed through the gate collapsed under kicks. He sprang up, tore off his coat, and ran up to Deputy Commandant Rödl, who was standing nearby. "You can shoot me," he told Rödl, "but I will not let you beat me!" At the same time he pointed to the medal "pour le mérite" that he wore around his neck. After he explained to Rödl, who knew nothing about it, what sort of order it was, he introduced himself as the World War I aviator [Kurt] Wolff. Rödl took him along and released him the very next day.

As a result of the horrible experiences of these first nights, which were repeated again and again until the camp was overflowing with inmates, about seventy Jews went insane. They lay in chains on the cement floor of wooden barracks that had previously served as a washhouse. In groups of four they were gradually taken to the cellblock, where Sommer beat them to death.

In the five hastily built emergency barracks, through whose holes and cracks an icy wind whistled, 12,500 people were jammed together. They slept on wooden bunks four levels high, without straw mattresses or blankets. One could sleep only on one's side, since there was hardly enough for one-fifth the people. Sanitary facilities like toilets and washrooms were not available at all. Two latrines were erected in great haste, during night shifts; after a few weeks a third was added. Because of lack of space, no more latrines could be installed. When one day all inmates of Barracks 1a to 5a fell sick with diarrhea after eating cold whale meat, the barracks camp, which was separated from the rest of the camp by a barbed wire fence, offered a terrible sight. Even the no-man's-land in front of the barbed wire, which could only be entered at risk to one's life, was covered with excrement. During the night the tower guards had in fact shot several people. The interior of the barracks, too, was completely covered with excrement. In their weakness many fell into the open latrines, next to which a mountain of hats, clothes, and underwear full of excrement piled up.

Every day several desperate men committed suicide by running into the electrically charged fence, or they plunged into latrines in which they suffocated miserably. When a Frankfurt Jew slashed his wrists and a Jewish doctor attempted to sew up the wounds (albeit with ordinary thread), the deputy roll call officer Petrick, who had the appropriate nickname "Hex," arrived to prevent any sort of aid. A man from Breslau named Silbermann had to watch while his brother was gruesomely tortured to death by SS Sergeant Hoppe. Hoppe trod on the unfortunate victim until he collapsed, covered with blood. Then the sergeant tied him to a post with ropes, until life eventually drained out of the man as the blood flowed from his many wounds. The surviving brother went insane at the sight of this martyrdom, and that night he caused a panic by raving and crying out, "The barracks are burning." Hundreds jumped out of the upper bunks onto the lower ones, and the bunk beds collapsed. Although SS men shot into the mass and the green SS collaborators struck at the prisoners with truncheons, it was almost impossible to restore order. Deputy Commandant Rödl construed this incident as a "mutiny." He ordered seven Jews to be brought out of the menacing barracks and had them handcuffed to one another. Then the three brutal block officers turned trained dogs on these unfortunates until all seven were completely torn apart.

Since there was no water and coffee was intentionally rarely given out at all, the thirst was unbearable and drove many insane. Twenty-nine men who lost their minds during this horror-filled time were summoned to the cellblock by Sommer and beaten to death with a triangular iron bar.

The prisoner leadership installed by the SS consisted at first only of professional criminals. They had "operated" on the Jews in the manner described above by robbing them of everything. These real criminals threw their Jewish victims into the latrines or drove them into the barbed wire fence to cover up traces of their crimes. One night thirty-one Jews died thus. The professional criminals even exploited the terrible thirst, often demanding 100 marks for a half-filled cup of coffee. The SS camp administration had a corporal named Jansen who constantly carried a truncheon with which he indiscriminately beat those around him. In any case he allowed many a blow to be bought off for a gold watch or ring, fountain pens, large sums of money, etc. Besides him, the SS Sergeants Chemnitz and Uhlemann in particular also "operated."

When the network of corruption among the SS and the professional criminals became a danger to the SS men themselves, they dismissed the greens and replaced the prisoner camp leaders with Austrian police prisoners. Conditions improved thereby: The distribution of food was carried out more correctly, and temporary sick wards were built. What two doctors, Dr. Margulies and Dr. Gerö, accomplished borders on the inconceivable. With the active assistance of political prisoners from the hospital, they illegally smuggled in medications and instruments. The camp doctor, Dr. Ding (Schuler), forced the Jewish doctor, Dr. Kriss, to gather for him material on hereditary diseases among Jews, which involved hundreds of men who had to stand in line miserably for hours in icy cold weather. Of course SS bandits could not be prevented from entering the barracks night after night to perform terrorist acts.

As a result of overcrowding, two barracks collapsed one icy cold night. Everyone was then shoved into the other three barracks. Prisoners who could not find the entrance quickly enough in the terrible throng were struck down by the SS murderers. I myself was beaten up by Jansen because I made no report on the incident.

The SS robbers used the Rath action as an excuse for the most shameless extortion of all sorts. One day, for example, it was announced over the loudspeaker, "All millionaires to the gate." Their signatures were demanded for large donations of money (a total of several hundred thousand marks!). Indeed, all Jews were suddenly allowed to write, although only to send for money—allegedly to pay for the travel home of poorer comrades. Automobile and motorcycle owners were also summoned and required to turn their vehicles over to SS officers. But the Nazis from Weimar also wanted to bring in a catch. To do so they used a good intermediary in the form of SS Master Sergeant Michael, who bought all the useless merchandise (nose drops, old books, magazines, hairpins(!), pins, etc.). He disposed of them in infamous coupled sales, combining them with a few cigarettes or some edibles and selling them to Jews at fantastic prices. Michael and his accomplices carried money out of the barracks camp in baskets!

After only about three weeks the first releases began. The words announcing them have become world famous: "Attention Barracks 1a to 5a! The following Jews to the gate with all their belongings!" The camp's prisoner leadership now assembled lists of Jews who were to be given early release. They included first of all the weak and old men; next followed World War I veterans, of which several hundred were in camp, to the surprise of the SS murderers.

Only those who had money for the trip home were released. For this purpose a so-called travel fund was created to provide travel money for impoverished Jews. Into the fund flowed the profits from canteen purchases as well as the donations of rich Jews. This fund, kept in a blue suitcase, had to be brought to Deputy Commandant Rödl and Roll Call Officer Strippel every day when another famous announcement was heard, "Herzog to the gate, with the diamond case!" Although the evening before I had always collected contributions against receipts—often tens of thousands of marks—by morning the case would be empty. One night it was finally stolen by a professional criminal, who even received a prison sentence for the crime.

Even Jews coming up for release were thoroughly milked. Under all kinds of pretexts—broken crockery, dirty hand towels (none were ever issued), shoe shining, etc.—20-, 50-, and even 100-mark notes were pocketed by the SS bandits employed in the release.

By the time the Jewish camp was dissolved on February 13, 1939, 600 men in the five barracks had been murdered. The 250 or so action Jews not yet released moved into the large camp. Thus one of the bloodiest and most horrible chapters in the history of Buchenwald came to an end.

GUSTAV HERZOG, Vienna
FRITZ MÄNNCHEN, Dresden

96. The Action Against Dutch Jews

AFTER THE GENERAL strike against the German occupation methods in Holland, the Gestapo and the SS rounded up all Jewish workers in Amsterdam and Rotterdam. On February 28, 1941, 389 of these Dutch Jews, victims of the worst fascist terror, arrived in Buchenwald. They were immediately placed in the harshest work details. They bore this rather well at the beginning, since most were accustomed to heavy physical work. But soon the effects of insufficient nourishment during such heavy work became noticeable. And because the Dutch were not used to the raw climate—cold, fog, and rain—they were soon seized with respiratory infections and diarrhea, which combined with a rapid decline in strength.

Since the Dutch Jews had fought as antifascists, the whole camp strongly supported them. As a result, this transport was probably not liquidated as rapidly as the SS administration had ordered. On the orders of the infamous Dr. Eisele, a ban was therefore placed on infirmary treatment for Dutch Jews. The comrades from this transport who were in the hospital at the time were put back on the camp streets. Or if this was not possible for health reasons, Eisele gave them lethal injections. Because of the ban on infirmary treatment, unbearable conditions soon arose, even though many were nevertheless illegally treated with very primitive and insufficient means. But soon the stench of festering, putrid wounds was no longer tolerable.

The senior block inmate of Block 16, Herzog, therefore went to Dr. Eisele and asked him to receive at least the worst cases. Eisele let two such cases be brought to him; one of them was the comrade Amerongen of Amsterdam, who had a constantly festering, fist-sized wound on the right heel. Without hesitation he ordered them, "Go back to the work detail!" The sick comrades thus had to be hidden, always under considerable danger. Many, among them Amerongen, died under great torment.

Since even these measures did not lead to the rapid liquidation that had been ordered, all surviving Dutch Jews (341) were sent to Mauthausen, where, in a few days in the stone quarry, they were murdered by the professional criminals who were in power there, along with the SS. A single Dutchman from this transport survived the liquidation action—Max Nebig, who at risk of death was hidden in the TB ward by comrades of the hospital and was thus saved.

MAX NEBIG, Amsterdam

97. The Murder of Dutch Jews in Mauthausen

THE STONE QUARRY at Mauthausen, named the "Viennese Trench," was fenced in on only three sides to save on sentries. On the open side was a trench 60 to 75 feet deep. In the fence was a gate, the so-called death's gate, through which prisoners were chased over the sentry line and mowed down one after another with machine gun fire. In 1941 a transport of about 400 Dutch Jewish prisoners came from Buchenwald concentration camp to Mauthausen. The transport arrived around midnight. The Mauthausen prisoners were not allowed to leave the barracks; fifty of the arriving Jews were driven naked from the bath into the camp and chased into the electric fence. All the others went into a block.

A political prisoner, George Glas of Landshut, was the clerk in this block. The first deputy commandant (he came from Dingolfing in Lower Bavaria) and the second deputy commandant, Ernstberger, declared to the prisoner clerk that the block had to be empty in at most six weeks. The clerk answered that he wanted to have nothing to do with such things and would rather resign from his post than attack prisoners in any way. He was immediately dismissed, received twenty-five—perhaps even thirty-five—lashes on the buttocks and back with a cane, and was transferred into the sock-darning work detail, which was essentially designated for liquidation by injection, "according to need." It was possible to save the comrade by transferring him to another camp. A "green" (professional criminal) replaced Glas as block clerk.

On the second day after their arrival, the Jews were chased to "work" in the stone quarry. They were not allowed to go down the 148 steps that led to the bottom of the quarry but had to slide down the sloping sides on stone rubble, which already killed or very seriously injured many. Boards to carry stone were then laid over their shoulders, and two other prisoners were forced to hoist an extremely heavy stone onto the Jews' boards. Then the prisoners went up the 148 steps at *caracho* [double time], these heavy stones on their shoulder boards. At times the stones fell straight back, so that some prisoners had their feet chopped off or suffered other severe injuries. If a Jew's stone fell down, he was beaten horribly and the stone loaded on again. There were tortures, tortures that cannot even be described. Already on the first day of "work," many Jews chose suicide out of despair, plunging from the top into the 80-foot-deep hole, to remain lying there, crushed.

On the third day the "death's gate" was opened. Terrible beatings of Jewish prisoners began, and they were driven over the sentry line to be shot down into piles by tower guards with machine guns. Already by the next day Jews no longer jumped into the depths individually: They joined hands, and the first one pulled behind him nine to twelve comrades into a horrible death. It took not four but scarcely three weeks before the block was empty. All 600 prisoners met their deaths through shootings, beatings, and other tortures or through suicide.

It should also be mentioned that civilian employees of the Mauthausen stone quarry requested that death by jumping be prevented because the scraps of flesh and brains that stuck to the rocks offered a gruesome sight. Then the stone quarry was "cleaned" with water hoses, and prisoner guards were stationed to keep prisoners from jumping. The remaining Jewish prisoners were beaten over the sentry line and into death. When new transports of Jewish prisoners arrived, the SS joked about it, saying that a new "battalion of paratroopers" had arrived.

ADAM KUSZINSKY, Poland
LUDWIG NEUMEIER, Germany

98. November 9, 1939, and Its Consequences

On the night of November 8–9, 1939, an alleged assassination attempt on Hitler was made in the Bürgerbräukeller in Munich. In the early morning hours of November 9, all Jews were suddenly summoned out of the work details and locked into their blocks. After a short time each block had to report, block by block. The block officers Blank, Jänisch, and Warnstaedt randomly selected twenty-one strong young Jews, exclusively Austrians and Germans. A seventeen-year-old youth who had just come from the post office was taken along without further questioning. All twenty-one comrades were led out the gate to the stone quarry and were shot at close range there or along the way.

All Jews were locked in their blocks for the next five days. The windows were darkened; there was not a bite to eat, not a swallow to drink. The solidarity of the Aryan prisoners was immense. At risk to their lives, they came at twilight or at night and brought us whole vats of food and drink.

During the next few days, the most horrible feeling for us was the uncertainty about our fate. At any minute the murderers could come back and fetch the next victims. After three days of complete fasting, each Jew received half rations for the next two days. Just as the punishment measures against the Jews were to end, the theft of a pig was discovered. We had to stand in roll call square until 10:00 P.M. in our weakened condition. Finally, the sadist Koch declared, "Until the thieves are found, the entire camp will get nothing to eat!" Everything possible was done to find the thieves. Clothes were inspected for spatterings of blood; shoes were checked for traces of sawdust; endless interrogations took place—all in vain. The pig had actually been stolen by some SS men, which came out only after some time had passed. For four long days the entire camp received nothing to eat; for four additional days there were again only half rations.

Thus the Jews had suffered through seven days of complete fasting and six days of half fasting. Because at the same time the quality of food began to decline throughout the camp, hundreds of Jews never recovered from this starvation diet. At least 250 to 300 comrades died of the immediate consequences of this torture.

STEFAN HEYMANN, Mannheim

99. THE DANISH ACTION

IN OCTOBER 1944, 1,700 Danish policemen were brought to Buchenwald. All were from the active service and most were therefore strong young people, well nourished and in good physical condition. Within about four months of their arrival in Buchenwald, sixty men from this group died; that is, 3.5 percent, or 10 percent calculated at a yearly rate—and that among strong young men.

Autopsy reports still exist for fifty-four; from them we take the following figures.

Within the first weeks up to November 20, 1944, reports on over nine cases of death are available. The reports show:

six cases (67 percent) of good or very good nourishment
three cases (33 percent) of moderate condition
no cases of poor condition

In the following period the picture changed; the later forty-five autopsies report the general condition as follows:

eight cases (18 percent) of good condition
no cases of moderate condition
thirty-seven cases (82 percent) of poor or very poor condition

Thus two to three months of Buchenwald altered the general condition of the prisoners.

In forty-five cases (83 percent of all cases) we found the cause of death given as septic processes (infections, erysipelas, etc.). These represent a small piece of evidence about the hygienic conditions in Buchenwald (where air and soil are almost saturated with staphylococci). Commentary is superfluous here.

[no signature]

100. Prominent Personalities in Buchenwald

IN ADDITION TO the "ordinary" prisoners, there were always a lesser or greater number of well-known political personalities or artists in Buchenwald. In the following list a number of such well-known personalities are named. However, the list can make no claim to completeness, since some of the prominent prisoners were in constant isolation and did not come into contact with other prisoners.

The list contains the following names:

Germany

Rudolf Breitscheid	Reichstag deputy (SPD) and wife
Kurt Eisner	son of the former Bavarian prime minister
Frau Dr. [Carl] Goerdeler[3]	wife of Leipzig mayor Dr. Goerdeler
Colonel General [Alexander von] Falkenhausen	
Frau [Ulrich] von Hassel	wife of Ambassador von Hassel
Ernst Heilmann	president of the Prussian Landtag caucus of the SPD
Frau General [Fritz] Lindemann	
Princess Mafalda of Hesse	daughter of Italian king

---

3. Several of these figures (Goerdeler, von Hassel, Lindemann, and Stauffenberg) were involved in the July 20, 1944, assassination plot against Hitler. Their families were arrested under the Nazi practice of *Sippenhaft* ("kith and kin" arrest). See Bundeszentrale für Heimatdienst, *20. Juli 1944, Dokumente und Berichte* (Freiburg: Herder, 1961), 184–189.

Theo Neubauer	Reichstag deputy (KPD)
Ernst Röchling	industrialist
Werner Scholem	Reichstag deputy of the KPD
Family of Colonel [Claus Schenk, Graf von] Stauffenberg	
Walter Stoecker	Reichstag deputy of the KPD
Fritz Thyssen	industrialist
Herbert Volck	nationalistic author

Belgium

Paul Soudan	Labor minister

France

Alfred Balachowsky	professor at Pasteur Institute
Pierre Bloch	former justice minister
Leon Blum	French prime minister and wife
[André] Challe	general
Alfred Nakache	world-class swimmer
Marcel Paul	deputy
Paul Reynaud	French prime minister
Robert Waitz	professor at University of Strassburg

Austria

[Dr. Ludwig] Bechinie	security director of Salzburg
[Dr. Walter] Gerdes	son-in-law of federal president [Wilhelm] Miklas
Fritz Grünbaum	cabaret performer and librettist
Höffern	major
[Hermann] Leopoldi	singer
[Fritz] Löhner-Beda	author and librettist
Paul Morgan	cabaret performer
[Dr. Kurt] Schuschnigg	former federal chancellor
[Karl] Seitz	former head mayor of Vienna
[Richard] Steidle	leader of Heimwehr
[Josef] Trummer	prison director
[Dr. Robert] Winterstein	former justice minister

Czechoslovakia

[Petr] Zenkel	mayor of Prague

[no signature]

Chapter Eight
The Antifascist Struggle Against the SS

AT THE VERY BEGINNING Buchenwald concentration camp was controlled entirely by the criminal elements—the so-called greens—but that changed in December 1938. The greens had so corrupted the SS men through their joint black market activities that no block officer dared to appear in camp anymore. Therefore Commandant Koch had to swallow a bitter pill—for better or worse—and appoint politicals ("reds") as camp functionaries. But the greens attempted again and again to recapture power. Finally, at the beginning of 1942, they believed themselves capable of winning a major coup.

At that time the greens had two personalities on their side who were well suited to leading such a struggle. Deputy Commandant Plaul, a fanatic hater of the reds, was predestined to collaborate directly with criminals because of his unbelievable corruption. The greens themselves had one in the person of the kapo of the construction office, Ohles, a scoundrel who shrank from nothing to reach his goal. Ohles built up an elaborate and clever system of seventy-six green informers that worked in the following manner. In a pipe tunnel under the office, a secret short-wave radio was set up. The electricians of the construction office sat there night after night and listened in on foreign news. The following morning they passed on the news to green camp informers. These greens had to spot a group of well-known reds standing together somewhere and then they would make an immediate report to Ohles containing information from these news broadcasts, thus giving the impression that it was actually the reds who had been listening to the radio illegally.

When Ohles had enough reports, he took them to Plaul. They were checked in the political department, where of course foreign radio stations were also listened in on for police reasons, and confirmed in full. So Plaul took action: He removed fifty of the best-known politicals from their functions, placed them in the punishment company, and feverishly worked toward their complete liquidation.

In the meantime, however, a political comrade in the electricians' detail discovered this secret radio. He informed some trustworthy people, and I had the opportunity to mention it in a conversation with Commandant Pister. I did this because plans had been made to send the comrades of the Special Section of the punishment company to the stone quarry the following day, obviously to shoot them there. Pister promised a new investigation, which of course confirmed the accuracy of my information. After that the Special Section was dissolved. Plaul and his buddy, the roll call officer Petrick, were transferred to another camp some time later at Pister's initiative.

The aftermath was a bitter defeat for the greens. Through his criminal conduct, Ohles, who in the meantime had become senior camp inmate, had made enemies everywhere, even within his own faction. Many green comrades who did not want to go along with his actions had been sent into the punishment company because of vicious lies and denunciations from the Ohles gang. Now one pillar after another of this clique of criminals collapsed. One informer after another was sent into the punishment company, where his fate was usually as follows: A placard with the words "I am an informer" was hung around his neck, and he had to stand on a chair. He was beaten and kicked from all sides; in the morning his corpse was brought to the crematorium.

Ohles himself was brought down when he signed copies of a notice from the deputy commandant that was to be posted in all the blocks: "For the validity of the signature, Ohles." Because of this trivial incident, Deputy Commandant Florstedt, who was waiting for a favorable opportunity, started a quarrel and removed Ohles from office. A few days later he was in the punishment company. On the day after his arrival, the commandant asked me how Ohles was doing, to which I answered, "He is dead; he fell down the stairs." Pister only smiled at the news.

The electrician of the construction office, Ohles's most important supporter, was eliminated after he came through the gate into camp drunk one evening and called to the labor service officer Bergt with upraised hand, "Heil Hitler, Comrade Bergt!" For that he was sent into the punishment company, where he suffered the fate of other criminals.

From this time on, the backbone of the greens in Buchenwald was finally broken, and the path was clear for the antifascist trend in Buchenwald concentration camp.

FRANZ EICHHORN, Weimar

102. Origins and Development of the Camp Police

IN PAST YEARS every prisoner suffered under the brutality of the SS. Almost every man knew about the black market operations the SS administrators conducted using the property of the prisoners and the camp. To have the SS in camp as little as possible, the prisoner leadership reached the decision in June 1942 to push the SS camp administration toward the formation of a camp police. After a lengthy tug-of-war, approval was finally obtained. An increase from the original twenty men to thirty was achieved soon afterward.

The camp police had the following tasks. Order and discipline had to be maintained in camp. At night they guarded the food store, the various supply rooms, and other places in which we prisoners had an interest. It was of equally great importance that the SS patrol no longer went through the camp at night, as fellow prisoners were thus spared its terrorism. An additional improvement for the camp inmates was keeping the SS away from the new arrivals in camp. After the camp police took over the task of bringing these prisoners into camp, they were spared the SS persecution they previously had to tolerate. The camp police also assisted day and night in the struggle against epidemic diseases, preventing the decline of sanitation in the Little Camp through increased awareness and by holding its prisoners to strict standards of washing and personal hygiene.

I would like to stress that in cases of theft or break-in, no reports were passed on to the SS, even though the SS had ordered me to do so. A prisoner who had committed an offense was turned over to the comrades of his nation, who called him to account. In various cases that was not exactly easy, as one had to reckon that the SS would find out. It was then a matter of making clear to the SS men that the prisoner would be strictly punished—which was never actually the case, though. Quarrels came about now and then, which could not have been avoided in a camp with 40,000 to 50,000 inmates of the most varied personalities. Nevertheless, I would like to state that we were able to maintain order and discipline without using the methods of the SS (beatings, etc.). "Beating is the most primitive form of discipline, and we therefore reject it"—that was the policy of the camp police.

Corresponding to the military and political development outside the fence was the development on the inside. The closer Nazism headed toward the abyss, the more the camp filled with new prisoners and thus posed ever greater tasks for us. We had long wanted to include foreign comrades in the camp police. Taking advantage of the new situation, we tried again in August 1944. The SS camp administration rejected our proposal several times but was finally convinced of its necessity due to language difficulties, since all nations of Europe were represented in the camp. French, Germans, Belgians, Luxemburgers, Russians, Poles, Czechs, Yugoslavs, and Italians were now incorporated into the camp police, and the ranks increased to around 100 men.

After we had accomplished this expansion, we were able to intensify the antifascist work that lay close to our hearts. Under difficult conditions, while concealing our illegal activities from the SS, we performed our work. Then as before, we preached order and discipline, held speeches in the blocks, and made our contacts. We held the conviction that unless we kept strict order and kept in touch with all prisoners, the main task before us—freeing ourselves from the claws of the Nazi bandits—would not be possible.

We took over the security of the camp. Because the tension of the situation had mounted, sentries patrolled all important parts of camp day and night in order to observe every movement of the SS and keep the antifascist leadership informed at all times. Thus we of the camp police are proud of having been among those who formed the antifascist front and of having stood with weapons in hand at the outbreak of the struggle against the SS on April 11, at the approach of American tanks and the liberation that came with it.

KARL KEIM, Stuttgart
Kapo, camp police

103. TASKS AND FUNCTIONS OF THE MEDICAL CORPS

WITHIN THE FRAMEWORK of the general camp policy of building illegal organizations into existing camp institutions, the attempt was also made to influence the SS to create new camp institutions. When Allied air raids intensified at the time of the camp's turn [toward control by the reds] in 1943–1944, the gentlemen of the SS became alarmed. They expressed their intention to set up a medical corps formed of longtime political prisoners who would be provided with passes to cross the sentry line. To prevent attempts at escape, reprisals against the entire camp were threatened. The task of this corps was to march out of camp at the first alarm and station itself outside the sentry line to be fully prepared for action in case of an air attack on the camp and its vicinity. It was clear to us that this new camp institution should be used to build an illegal corps with specific tasks. Out of the ranks of the political prisoners, sixteen willing antifascists were chosen; they marched out over the entire area of the Ettersberg, acting as a reconnaissance troop of the SS organization. The troop was equipped with gas masks and captured Soviet helmets. Working unobserved, they had the opportunity to determine all changes and new facilities throughout the camp's reaches. They could report to the proper authorities the installation of munitions depots outside the camp, trenches with foxholes in an expanded sentry line, and changes in the strength and equipment of the SS units.

Its proper function as a medical corps was fulfilled for the first time after the bombardment of the factories at Buchenwald on August 24, 1944. Because at this time prisoners had to remain at their work stations even during air raid alarms— and because some of the sentries fired on the prisoners—this attack cost 364 comrades their lives. The medical corps itself had two fatalities: the Austrian comrade Roman Felleis and the German comrade Otto Pohle. In addition to bandaging the wounded and removing the dead, the medical corps also took part in securing military supplies for the camp. At that time the exchange of Russian helmets for German ones began, so that it would be easier to deceive the SS in case of an action. The military work was intensified more and more.

The next great period of activity was brought about by the great Soviet offensive, which forced the fascists to evacuate all camps in the east. Then prisoners came in the thousands, after days of marching on foot in the cold of winter or being loaded into open railroad cars without food. They arrived completely exhausted, hundreds of them frozen and starved to death. To prevent the SS beasts from tormenting these pitiful creatures still further or abusing them in their usual way, the medical corps was assigned to the infirmary. They helped unload the weak as each transport arrived at the railroad station; cared for the sick and the wounded, transporting them to the infirmary; and loaded corpses onto trucks to be taken to the crematorium.

Because of further developments in the military situation, the illegal work was intensified even more. Around this time the auxiliary medical corps and the stretcher corps were formed. These additional organizations were composed of antifascist activists of all nations. Everyone was issued bandaging materials and medications as well as special kits for surgical procedures. Gas masks were removed from the gas mask pouches and replaced with military gear, as the medical corps acted as an assault detachment and could not carry backpacks.

In the final critical days, the medical corps was in a state of constant alert. In the action [of April 11, 1945] these groups played an active role at various points. After turning over its weapons to the U.S. Army, the medical corps viewed its task as having been fulfilled, and the individual members returned to their nursing duties.

HELMUT THIERMANN, Werdau/Saxony

104. THE CAMP FIRE DEPARTMENT

In SUMMER 1942 a camp fire department was assembled out of about twenty comrades who volunteered from various camp work details (tailorshop, cobbler, supply rooms, etc.). The reason for having prisoners trained in fire fighting was so that the existing SS fire department could be deployed elsewhere.

At first training was carried out under the supervision of an SS man. In spring 1943 the fire department was expanded as a result of the increase in aerial attacks on Germany. Once again twenty comrades were assembled from various work details, but then we conducted their training ourselves, since in the meantime we had two fire trucks put at our disposal. Unfortunately, right at the beginning of this training, we had a regrettable accident in roll call square in which one comrade was killed and five comrades were seriously wounded. During summer 1943 we also began training the fire department in antifascist ideals.

Up to the time of the air raid on Buchenwald, we had to move out more and more often during air raid alarms. Day and night the majority of our comrades were outside the camp. During the attack on August 24, 1944, the fire department had casualties of three dead and ten seriously injured, as well as a large number of lightly injured. Because the water supply was interrupted by the attack on Buchenwald, in the days thereafter the fire department tried to make certain that water was available at least for the kitchen and the hospital.

As early as spring 1944, an additional so-called room attendants' fire department was formed; once trained, it had to perform the same tasks inside camp as the camp fire department. After August 24, 1944, it was integrated into the [fire department] work detail, its strength thus reaching fifty-five men.

HEINZ MÜLLER, Kapo

105. THE ANTIFASCIST INFORMATION SERVICE

FROM THE FIRST DAYS onward, the antifascists in camp considered it urgently necessary to get news from foreign broadcasters in order to form an accurate picture of the situation in Europe. The SS tried to gain influence over the prisoners through German radio propaganda. Because the radio was not only one of the most important sources of news but also an opportunity for the SS to influence prisoners, it was all the more important to maintain a counterweight in the form of foreign news. The antifascists' effort to organize this illegal news service was of course extraordinarily difficult and dangerous.

In the early days most foreign broadcasts were listened in on in the construction office, and the information was passed on. The construction office had one of the few shortwave receivers, and at that time there were several good antifascists in the office who risked their lives to listen in on foreign stations and pass news on to their comrades in camp. The comrade who actually listened in passed on the news to only one or two comrades, who then made it accessible to a larger circle. In this manner there was a certain guarantee that the identity of the individual illegal listener would never become known to the SS. In fact in no case was a comrade caught or even punished for listening in on a foreign broadcast.

As conditions worsened in the construction office and listening in was hardly possible any longer, the antifascist comrades of the electricians' work detail were assigned to listen in on foreign broadcasts. In one workshop these comrades built an apparatus that was externally disguised as a standard AM radio set but that in fact could receive all foreign stations, in particular on shortwave. With this apparatus all news from abroad was received and transmitted to the camp in the manner described above. Thus it was possible for the antifascists in camp to be precisely and accurately informed about all events in the world. Through the illegal receiver they always had an opportunity to counteract Nazi propaganda.

A further source of information consisted in the collection of news out of Nazi-influenced newspapers. Even though there was no important news in the large German Nazi newspapers, there were nevertheless a number of papers that published anti-Nazi news. These included all the newspapers from occupied territories, where censorship was carried out somewhat more loosely, and likewise newspapers from German border states, in which interesting news often appeared because the border population could easily inform themselves by reading foreign newspapers. All these newspapers came into camp because the camp administration had allowed subscriptions to "hometown" newspapers. Of course for the Buchenwald antifascists, these newspaper reports were also an important source of information that they successfully used to fight the lies of Nazi propaganda. This news was spread by passing either entire newspapers or specific clippings from block to block. For the transmission of news in this form, too, only small groups came together and in turn informed a larger circle.

Finally, oral information from civilian workers and new admissions should be mentioned. But news from these sources was always cautiously received, since it very often proved to be untrue and therefore was taken only as an expression of a particular opinion among the people.

Just as unreliable was the news that was spread by illegal listeners inside the camp. For when a prisoner had the chance to be alone in a room with a radio receiver for a few minutes, he of course immediately tried to catch any foreign broadcast he could. This obviously meant that misunderstandings and garbled messages were part of the daily routine. But such news, called *Bonken* [rumors] in camp slang, was very widespread.

OTTO HORN, Vienna

106. THE CAMP BAND

ON ORDERS of the deputy commandant at the time, Rödl, the camp band was formed at the end of 1938. It was made up mainly of Gypsies with guitars and harmonicas who played a thin and shabby sort of music. After a while a trombone was added, and later a drum and two trumpets. All instruments had to be supplied by the prisoners themselves. During the day members of the band had to work in the lumberyard or in the carpentry shop, so no time remained for practice. It was horrible to watch the Gypsies play their cheerful marches while exhausted prisoners carried their dead and dying comrades past them into the camp. Often the band also had to play during the so-called counting out loud— that is, when prisoners were whipped.

The band had to bear the brunt of the suffering when the prisoners learned camp songs, which were practiced over and over again. And when their stomachs had contracted from hunger, when their arms and legs were frozen from cold, when their entire bodies were sore from the exertions of work—the songs still had to be sung. And not just once—no, often for hours at a time. The block officers would walk up and down through the ranks, checking to see if each prisoner was singing. Anyone who was caught catching his breath immediately received a blow on the head with a truncheon, if not a report that would lead to punishment. Thus singing, which lifts the souls of free men, became a terrible torment for us.

In 1940 Deputy Commandant Florstedt ordered that a proper brass band be created, the costs to be taken over by the camp administration. But when the instruments that were ordered arrived, Florstedt came upon a simpler solution: "The Jews must pay for the music!" And so it happened. Besides that, Florstedt immediately appropriated the new instruments for the SS band; they were given back to the camp band just a few days before our liberation.

The comrades of the band were then faced with heavy work and hours of practice. But practice was only another form of torment, since the block officers chased away their boredom by staying in our practice room. They had us play one hit song after another. No wonder that in this apparently easy work detail, six comrades had to leave because of weak lungs and TB and one comrade died of tuberculosis of the larynx.

To make a better impression on visitors, in 1941 the band was outfitted with uniforms stolen from the Yugoslavian royal guard.

The band did not play an important role—at least as far as the SS was concerned. It took part in many functions that, under the cover name of a "concert," were occasions to spread well-concealed antifascist propaganda. Moreover, I had assembled a string orchestra of eighty-four comrades, with whom I could perform good concerts in the cinema hall. Through the creation of the band, many a good worker was diverted from the German armaments production.

VLASTIMIL LOUDA, Prague

107. THE ARTS IN BUCHENWALD

THE ARTISTIC ENDEAVORS of the prisoners of Buchenwald concentration camp are as old as the camp itself. As early as 1938 there arose spontaneous Sunday affairs that had a clearly antifascist character. These small cabaret afternoons reached particular heights when the Jewish actions of 1938 brought a number of prominent artists into camp. Music, too, came into its own, despite all the obstacles that stood in the way for musicians in particular. Imagine what it would be like to play intricate violin pieces with stiff fingers after ten hours of hard labor. What sort of special dangers one encountered can be seen from the following example. In 1939–1940 there was a Jewish string quartet. One day all of its members were called to the gate and punished because they had played German music.

In 1941 the SS opened the camp cinema, a profitable venture. The SS probably calculated that prisoners who were starved for any sort of culture would gladly pay 10 pfennigs to see something other than the camp, even if it was only Nazi films. At the same time we began again on a small scale. The "literary evenings" in particular should be emphasized; organized by a small circle of political prisoners, they featured new and always militantly antifascist programs.

In the meantime the camp orchestra was also considerably improved, and it became a custom to have orchestra concerts in the cinema hall on days no film was shown. These orchestra concerts were eventually changed into variety shows [*Bunte Abende*] in which musical pieces and short skits were performed. After summer 1943 such "variety shows" were put on at least every six to eight weeks.

Up to that point, corresponding to the composition of the camp, the German element had predominated in all these functions. But after 1942 and 1943, the arrivals of mass transports of foreign prisoners created new conditions. These groups, too, had artistic impulses. At first concerts with special interludes, the so-called block concerts, were staged. Soon antifascist elements took them over and turned them into their own instruments, which was all the more possible because the danger of betrayal in nationally homogeneous blocks was slight. Above all the Russians, French, and Poles brought their programs to a high level.

In winter 1943–1944 the staging of concerts in the cinema hall was newly organized. A committee with representatives from all nations took over the organization of the programs, arranging them according to guidelines the antifascist prisoners deemed necessary. They always managed to find the right language to make clear to the prisoners what had to be said and yet would not arouse suspicion among the SS.

The committee did not limit its work to the concerts in the cinema hall. It also carried on illegal, directly antifascist work through the arts, putting together completely harmless performances as a cover. The greatest show of the harmless sort was a performance of Shakespeare's *As You Like It*.

The French group deserves special praise for its exemplary work. Among other things the French ran a writing contest that won great approval and success. They also arranged an exhibition of graphic art created in Buchenwald.

After the bombardment of August 24, 1944, a memorial service was arranged. Shortly afterward the International Committee underwent a crisis. After the Gestapo arrested a number of prominent political prisoners, an acute danger to the camp arose. Literally overnight, a strongly political program that had been prepared had to be replaced by a harmless one. That it was successful is proof of the breadth that the work in artistic fields had already reached. Performances in the cinema hall continued until the building was taken over for other, more urgent purposes.

The work in the blocks went forward at the same time. In this connection the Polish youth group deserves special praise. In the last days before the evacuation, it presented a good and clear program. Short, distinctly educational skits performed in the Jewish blocks should be remembered as well. Up to the last days of the camp, the tradition of chamber music was continued. Out of the first dilettante string quartet, two quartets of high artistic quality were created, performing in the cinema hall with great success.

A report on the artistic activity of the prisoners in Buchenwald concentration camp would be incomplete without mention of the literary and musical works created in camp. The camp orchestra premiered a considerable number of orchestral pieces composed by its members or by other prisoners. In the field of literature, in addition to short-lived skits and poems, some works of lasting value emerged from the camp experience. Poems, short stories, and novels, popular as well as scholarly works, were drafted and either partially written or completed here. If a collection of all these works could be published, there would be no better monument to the unbending will of the antifascists of Buchenwald concentration camp.

BRUNO APITZ, Leipzig

108. The Prisoners' Library

AT THE BEGINNING of 1938, a prisoners' library was opened. The stock of 3,000 books was to a large extent assembled by the prisoners themselves. The prisoners had books sent from home or donated the funds for new purchases. SS headquarters supplied Nazi literature out of funds the camp administration took from prisoners in the form of "donations." Out of the many tens of thousands of marks, headquarters procured only 1,009 books; the administration itself supplied only 246 books, of which there were sixty copies each of Hitler's *Mein Kampf* and [Alfred] Rosenberg's *Mythos* [*Myth of the Twentieth Century*]. In the end the holdings on the shelves amounted to 13,811 books; 2,000 unbound works could not be put on the shelves because of a lack of bookbinding materials.

Adventure and crime novels were for the most part read by the SS. Adjutant SS Captain Schmidt, for example, read thirty-eight such books in one month alone. Typical of the mendacious SS propaganda, two incidents are worth special mention. When the first military commission toured the camp, it paid a visit to the library. During the visit, a major asked Deputy Commandant Florstedt, "Who built up the collections?" The deputy commandant answered, "We left that to the prisoners." To this the major replied, "Then they must be intelligent people. What will happen to these men? Surely these people will be needed on the outside?" The deputy commandant said only, "These prisoners will soon be released at my recommendation."

Shortly before July 20, 1944, a commission of recipients of the Iron Cross under the leadership of a colonel toured the library. During the visit he declared, "Works such as those found in this library are hard to come by even on the outside. There are books here from Schlieffen, Clausewitz, and Moltke." When he picked up the list of borrowed books, he asked Deputy Commandant Schobert, "How is it that so many military and political books are loaned out?" When the deputy commandant gave no answer, the colonel declared, "I will give a lecture on that on the outside."

After the outbreak of war, all foreign-language books from countries at war with Germany were to have been destroyed. Because a prisoner told the administrative officer that these were mostly textbooks, they were allowed to remain in the library under the condition that they not be loaned out. After a few weeks, however, they were loaned out again.

In addition to the books on the shelves, we had also a number of illegal, banned books that, for security reasons, could only be given to a small circle to read.

ANTON GÄBLER, Duisburg

109. SPORTS IN BUCHENWALD

ALTHOUGH THE CONDITIONS for pursuing sports at Buchenwald were not exactly rosy (workdays were long and hard), some people, particularly the younger ones, felt a need to play sports. Sports facilities, equipment, etc., were not available at all. Nevertheless, in a short while there was not only a ball but also a field, if one could call it that. Soccer dominated the field. Soon the square by the canteen was too small, so another playing field was created and in the very spot where the Little Camp stands today.

All types of sports now appeared: soccer, handball, volleyball, rounders. Thus ever wider circles were drawn into sports. If at first many were against pursuing sports, now they could see that sports brought many prisoners a needed diversion.

As on the outside, championships were played in Buchenwald, too. Several teams were formed to take part in them. For a time there were twelve teams; in the beginning there was even a Jewish team, but it was later forbidden. Most teams appeared in flawless uniforms, even proper soccer shoes—one simply had to wonder where it all came from.

When the camp became overcrowded, the sport field had to make way for new barracks. Nevertheless, still another push was made for a new sport field, which was created in the forest near the gardening area. Sports were still played there for a while, then the gardening detail took over the field, sowed it, and harvested little—but we had been allowed to enjoy the sport field for a time.

Even in the period of "organized" [i.e., illicit] sports, prisoners still played sports on the side, above all deck tennis, in which old and young participated. There was also a group of athletes who practiced gymnastics on the beam and bars (in the cinema hall). In 1943 boxing appeared in camp, and one must say that it stood in high regard. Boxing contests were held in the woods or in the cinema hall until they, too, were forbidden. Volleyball, which the Czechs had long since played, became popular among the masses, too. At the end a game surfaced that in the main foreigners played: basketball.

WILLI SEIFERT, Plauen

110. ARRESTED BY THE WEIMAR GESTAPO

On October 30, 1944, the Gestapo in Weimar tried to liquidate antifascist solidarity in Buchenwald. There were two informers in camp, Strand and Duda, who had given the Gestapo false information. On the basis of their statements, a number of leading antifascists, among them the senior camp inmate Erich Reschke, were brought to the Gestapo prison in Weimar. Of the methods of torture practiced there, only one example follows.

Comrade Wegerer was brought with his hands shackled behind his back into a cell just 2 cubic yards in size, where the temperature was about 50 degrees. Wegerer remained in this cell without water or food for five days and then was brought into interrogation. The tormenting thirst in this torture cell was indescribable. Other comrades were housed in similar cells. Comrade Bleicher had to strip to the waist during the interrogation; then the Gestapo beasts burned holes into his skin with cigars. But despite these torture methods, none of the comrades confessed, so no danger thus arose for the antifascists in camp.

When the Gestapo saw that they could not extort a confession, they took their prisoners to the Gestapo prison in Ichtershausen. On April 9, 1945, the prisoners were evacuated from this prison because of the approach of the American army. On the transport two comrades succeeded in escaping.

GUSTAV WEGERER, Vienna

111. THE CASE OF WOLFF

One of the most infamous chapters in Buchenwald's history was that of the first lieutenant and, for a time, senior camp inmate Wolff, son of a Jewish doctor from Silesia. During World War I he served mostly on the general staff, for a time on the staff of Prince Eitel Friedrich [of Prussia]. After the war he went into the Reichswehr, from which he later had to resign because of the racial laws. His first marriage to a rich woman lasted as long as the money. His second marriage almost got him into the penitentiary because he had procured his wife for a rich playboy. But Wolff received only a light jail sentence, after which he went into a concentration camp. First he was at Dachau and then went to Buchenwald with the Jewish transport of 1938.

Here he became a senior block inmate, along with other Jews, on January 30, 1939. In this capacity he made numerous black market deals with the then deputy commandant, Hackmann, thus gaining the trust of the headquarters staff.

In 1942, when the greens began their great informer action against the political prisoners, Wolff stood on the side of the reds, since he had reason to fear his criminal "friends." Even after the criminals' [false] denunciations were revealed, mistrust of antifascist prisoners did not disappear. In this situation the prisoners nominated Wolff as senior camp inmate because as a former Reichswehr officer, he appeared to be above suspicion politically. The SS administration accepted the nomination immediately.

But as senior camp inmate, Wolff severely misused the trust the prisoners placed in him. Wolff had homosexual tendencies and fell completely under the spell of a ravishing Polish youth. Polish fascists used this youth to influence Wolff, and he thus sunk to an increasingly dangerous position of hostility toward the antifascists, about whose organization he knew many details. It even went so far that Wolff became an informer for the SS. But all his efforts to inform failed. When, for example, the comrade Brand of Magdeburg was to be released, Wolff declared that he would prevent his release by reporting on Brand's political activity. Only under the threat of having his homosexual offenses reported did Wolff give up on this dirty trick.

As his activities became ever more dangerous, the antifascists had to render Wolff harmless in the interests of the whole organization. Through circuitous routes, the SS was informed that Wolff was fighting on the side of the Poles against the Germans. That led to his dismissal and transfer into a heavy work detail, where he died after a few weeks.

HANS EIDEN, Trier

112. SS INFORMER STELZMANN

STELZMANN, A POLITICAL PRISONER who had received long sentences in prisons and concentration camps, turned into a Nazi henchman while he was at Buchenwald. He stole food rations from prisoners of his block and sold them, and he personally beat to death about ninety to 100 prisoners. The former senior camp inmate Wolff had made him senior block inmate of the K Company, in which all so-called war criminals were housed under especially severe conditions. Later he was made senior block inmate of the security prisoners.

It took a long time before the German antifascist leadership succeeded in bringing Stelzmann down and liquidating him. He was initially reported for his black marketing of food rations and prisoners' valuables. But SS First Lieutenant Gust rejected Stelzmann's dismissal on the grounds that he had made himself very useful. So it was attempted in another manner: Stelzmann was a sheet metal worker. The German Armament Works (DAW) needed skilled workers. The senior camp inmate Reschke proposed him for work in the DAW. But Deputy Commandants Schobert and Gust rejected the proposal. In January 1944, with the help of criminal prisoners, Stelzmann made a large black market deal in which property from the disinfection room was stolen. The antifascists were successful in making it clear to the SS administration that Stelzmann had thus also stolen from the SS, and so they finally won his dismissal. On the following day Stelzmann was found beaten to death in the Little Camp.

FRANZ EICHHORN, Weimar

113. How Informers Were Eliminated

THE FIRST GREAT INFORMER in Buchenwald, who had many hundreds of human lives on his conscience, was named Knigge. He was an antisocial. At the slightest offense he made a report and snooped around the entire camp with a pass provided by Deputy Commandant Rödl. Once he remained in Block 4 at twilight during roll call. I found out about it and went down right away to give him a proper beating. One day SS Master Sergeant Köhler, the gate sentry, let the radio play somewhat longer than was permitted. Knigge appeared at the gate first thing the next morning and made a report against the SS man. I found out about this and told Commandant Koch right while I was shaving him that it had come so far that prisoners were allowed to make reports against SS men. Koch was very ticklish on this point. When he had convinced himself of the accuracy of this news, he ordered that Knigge be gotten rid of. Since the SS failed to do so, the prisoners themselves took care of it.

Pospisil, a Czech journalist and just as dangerous an informer, was brought down in a similar manner. He had particular designs on the German antifascists and worked closely with the greens. When I met Pospisil alone in the woods one day, I boxed him on the ear a few times, after which he angrily said, "You apparently don't know what high-ranking people are on my side!" When I told Commandant Pister about this conversation and the incident leading up to it, he immediately let the informer drop. Pospisil lived only a few more days.

A particularly dangerous individual was the Russian White Guard general Kushni-Kushnarev, who became a collaborator with the SS murderers out of political conviction. In particular, Kushnarev had actively supported the mass murders of Russian prisoners of war in the horse stables. He had served the bestial murderers as a translator and gave the prisoners of war instructions that ultimately led to their deaths. Since he was indispensable to the SS in every way and since he was also recognized internally, especially by other Russian prisoners, as an acknowledged Nazi agent, his elimination was very difficult. It succeeded when one day he developed a fever from the flu, which the infirmary orderlies declared to be typhoid fever. Two days later he died in the infirmary.

These are just some examples, but they show how prisoners in Buchenwald eliminated their enemies.

FRANZ EICHHORN, Weimar

114. A Criminal Executed

HERMAN KRAUSE WAS an old political prisoner who had served sentences of many years in prisons and concentration camps. In Buchenwald he became demoralized and finally met an inglorious end. He burglarized the disinfection room and the supply room and stole prisoners' property—articles of clothing and personal valuables. He swindled a French professor out of a diamond ring, a gold watch, 300 Dutch guilders, and about 500 dollars by assuming the name of an antifascist in the supply room. He sold the stolen goods to the SS.

Because he had become a danger to the antifascists in camp, he had to die. When he once again attempted a theft, he received such a severe beating that he died of the consequences.

WALTER BARTEL, Berlin

Chapter Nine
Conditions During the War

115. THE LITTLE CAMP AT BUCHENWALD,
WINTER 1939–1940

IN OCTOBER 1939 a portion of roll call square at Buchenwald concentration camp was separated from the rest of the camp by a double barbed wire fence; it was designated for the reception of prisoners. In this so-called Little Camp, four large tents were put up that contained only wooden bunk beds with four levels. After a wooden barracks was erected and a latrine excavated, the Little Camp was ready to receive prisoners (principally Poles and Austrians). A total of 1,700 men were housed there.

They went to work daily in the stone quarry, from which they had to carry stones to the watchtowers around the camp. The road there led through a sentry line, along which every second sentry held a weapon at the ready. The remaining guards stood there with truncheons and struck every prisoner who walked or ran by, without regard to what part of the body they hit. Every day several prisoners who could no longer bear the torment of being driven along and beaten ran through the sentry line and were shot. According to the official designation, they were shot "while attempting escape."

The "compensation" that was given to the prisoners for their slave labor looked approximately as follows.

1. Housing in tents. The wooden bunk beds had neither straw mattresses nor any other sort of padding. The prisoners lay on bare wood; each had only a blanket at his disposal. There was no floor in the tents; when one climbed out of the bunk bed, one had to wade in mud almost up to the knees.

2. Clothing, consisting of prisoner's uniform (jacket, pants, cap, shoes) and underwear (shirt, underpants, socks), which was very seldom changed; no overcoats, no sweaters, no gloves.

3. Food, consisting of 7 ounces of bread at the beginning; later 6, 4, and even 3 ounces, without any extras (margarine, syrup, sausage, etc.), which were available for the rest of the camp; camp soup in the amount of a quart, later three-fourths of a quart—from which, however, the entire content of potatoes or vegetables was taken out before it was sent to the Little Camp to be distributed.

4. Hygiene. There was the above-mentioned latrine, which did not correspond in the slightest to the demands of health, and a wash facility in the open air, which was "unusable" by the first frost. The sick were cared for in the outpatient department of the prisoner hospital. But care could be granted only to a few prisoners of the Little Camp, since the SS administration ordered that a limited number of prisoners could be held back from work for the purpose of sick care. In the so-called sick barracks, there was inpatient care, which in essence consisted only of allowing the sick prisoner to die in peace, since neither medication nor sufficient food was at hand.

The consequences of the conditions described soon became apparent. The prisoners, insofar as they remained alive, rapidly became weaker and less capable of resistance. As early as the second half of October, an epidemic of dysentery broke out. It spread so rapidly that the SS administration was forced to pull the prisoners of the Little Camp completely out of work details and impose a quarantine on the Little Camp.

It would, however, be wrong to suppose that with the end of the murderous work in the stone quarry, the lives of prisoners in the Little Camp became any easier. The SS administration was tireless in thinking up new torments to fill up the compulsory free time that had arisen. Its representatives were Camp Commandant SS Colonel Koch, Second Deputy Commandant SS Captain Hüttig, and the officers in charge of the Little Camp, SS Sergeants Blank and Hinkelmann.

The entire life of the Little Camp took place on roll call square. To get morning coffee the entire population had to stand in the square, receiving coffee that had become cold after an average wait of two hours. The midday soup was distributed the same way, just as bread was to be had only after hours of standing. The rare exchange of underwear took place on roll call square. The prisoners had to take off shirts, underpants, and socks in the open air, even in the most bitter cold, to receive fresh underwear. The roll call that took place two or three times a day took at least two hours each time.

But SS Sergeant Blank was not satisfied with all this. As "punishment," for what reason no one knew, he ordered the prisoners not to return to their tents afterward but to stand the rest of the day in roll call square. The torment involved in standing without interruption can scarcely be imagined by those who do not know something similar or have not experienced it themselves.

Now and then SS Captain Hüttig provided popular entertainment. He had the "whipping block," an apparatus for the execution of punishment by whipping, brought into the Little Camp. He came with a number of block officers and had twenty-five lashes with the cane given to every tenth prisoner chosen at random. In a case where a prisoner offered to receive the punishment in place of his brother, who had been selected at random, SS Captain Hüttig showed his appreciation by having both brothers whipped.

SS Sergeant Hinkelmann derived special pleasure from setting out a kettle half-filled with soup in roll call square to watch the hungry prisoners crowd around the kettle to receive some soup. Then he would fall upon the entire group with a truncheon and beat their heads bloody.

As the season advanced, it became ever colder, but conditions in the Little Camp did not change. Each prisoner received one blanket, although the camp possessed enough blankets to be able to give out at least one additional blanket per man. Of course to retain some degree of warmth prisoners could not undress. They slept in their clothes and were accordingly afflicted with vermin to a higher degree.

Food became ever scarcer; the bread rations were decreased; the soup was almost filtered in order not to allow one little piece of solid food into the Little Camp. The quantity was reduced to less than 1 quart. Even this "food ration" was not given to the prisoners every day because SS Colonel Koch liked to impose days of fasting to punish the camp for any alleged infraction. The Little Camp was allowed not only to faithfully observe all fast days of the entire camp but also received its own additional ones by order of SS Sergeant Blank. This grew to such an extent that, for example, in the month of November 1939, the Little Camp had a full twelve fast days. Thus on only eighteen days of the month was the prescribed food ration received.

To what extent men became brutalized through these barbarous methods can be seen from the way food rations were obtained, which soon became customary. When a new victim died in the tent at night, it was kept secret. The dead man was dragged by two comrades, or carried on their backs, to the bread distributor. The bread ration for the dead man was given to his comrades, who thus received double rations. After the successful receipt of bread, the corpses were simply left lying on the ground next to the food distribution point.

The amount of clothing remained at whatever had been issued in the month of October. Even in periods of the greatest cold, in the months of December and January, neither overcoats nor pullovers, scarves, earmuffs, or gloves were made available. Outpatient treatment in the prisoner hospital had ceased with the imposition of the dysentery quarantine; frostbite on the feet and other sorts of illnesses inevitably led to the death of those afflicted.

Every day at morning roll call, one could count fifteen, twenty, or twenty-five corpses that had been delivered by the sick barracks during the night and left lying in the snow. SS Colonel Koch responded to a daily report on the number of dead in the Little Camp with the words: "This is going too slowly for me. Couldn't we let the men work?"

No, one could not let the men work; the fear of dysentery was still too great. But there were other means. At the beginning of December, the increasing number of lice in the Little Camp (fifty lice on one man was not atypical) appeared threatening to the camp administration. A complete disinfection of the Little Camp was ordered. On December 8 the action was carried out, and a very beneficial bath was granted to the inmates of the Little Camp. But clothing was held back for two days for the purpose of disinfection, and the prisoners were given other clothing— summer clothing of thin cotton twill. Of course the blankets also remained at the disinfection station; replacement blankets for the interim period were not provided. A night full of torment followed, in which no one could sleep because of the cold. In the morning on the way to roll call, one could see the disturbing results of this night. There lay six neat, orderly rows of ten each and seven pieces left over: sixty-seven dead in the snow, a number that probably would have satisfied SS Colonel Koch.[1]

The standard of living of the Little Camp inmates was undercut still further in the case of a special group of more than eighty Polish prisoners. They were generally called "snipers," although no one knew whether it was really a question of that. These prisoners were locked into a cage and received a food ration half that described above. Accordingly, they starved one after another. At the beginning of January, when about twenty of these snipers were still in the camp, the procedure was cut short, and one day the remaining prisoners were poisoned.

The extermination plan toward the prisoners of the Little Camp (as revealed in the words of SS Colonel Koch, quoted above) was not carried to its completion. For reasons not precisely known, the camp administration decided to dissolve the camp in mid-January 1940 and transfer the surviving remnant into the general camp. Of the 1,700 men who had occupied the Little Camp in October, only 600 were still alive in January. But when they left the Little Camp, they were in such a condition that the majority of them no longer appeared capable of survival. The average weight of the prisoners on leaving the Little Camp was well under 85 pounds. The generous granting of convalescent duty by the prisoners' hospital could no longer save the majority of those weakened in this way. In rather quick succession several hundred of these prisoners died.

After the prisoners' hospital had exhausted the possibilities of convalescence to the maximum extent for those who remained alive, it had to release them from its protection. The prisoners were put back to work. In fact, they were again assigned to the stone-carrying detail, which had already demanded so many victims in the fall.

What the immediate consequences of life in the Little Camp did not complete was eventually accomplished by work in the heavy work details of Buchenwald concentration camp. Out of the original 1,700 men, an estimated forty are probably still alive today. After their long hoped for and now finally achieved liberation, they can lay witness to the horrors that they experienced.

The testimony contained in the above report I have given to the best of my knowledge and conscience and can vouch for its truthfulness at any time.

FELIX RAUSCH, Prague

---

1. The SS commonly called their prisoners *Stück,* a term farmers use to designate the number of animals (or head) in a herd. For an example of this SS slang for prisoners, see Michel and Noucera, *Dora,* 55, 83, 151.

116. POLES IN THE LITTLE CAMP, 1939

On October 15 and 16 [1939], about 4,500 Poles were brought to Buchenwald. Even during unloading we were worked over in the most brutal way, with blows from rifle butts and kicks. Then began our Way of the Cross from Weimar to Buchenwald. Men, women, and children threw stones at us and shouted, "Strike them dead, the Polish pigs, the snipers!" Approximately 200 yards beyond the station, the infamous mass murderer Koch, who along with Rödl and Florstedt had come to our "reception," began a devilish game. He commanded, "Hands up and sing German songs!" Waving a revolver, he drove his car through our ranks. Whoever stepped to the side and thus stepped out of the ranks was immediately shot. Behind this parade of misery drove several trucks on which the murdered were thrown, as well as those who as a result of the inhuman abuse were no longer capable of marching further.

When the camp gate closed behind us, we had to take our number at a table in the reception. As a prisoner approached the table, he received a blow in the back with a rifle butt; a kick sent the unfortunate prisoner back into the ranks again. Then it was off to the bath, where we had to undress stark naked. After the bath, the SS drove us naked on a cold and rainy day into the deep mud in front of the bath. There we had to wait until the clothing was finally issued. Then we went into the so-called Little Camp.

Four tents and a wooden shed stood there, surrounded by a tall barbed wire fence. One part of the fenced-off space served as our roll call square; into another part the dead were thrown. On the southeast portion there was a special fenced-in cage in which 123 Poles from Bromberg were housed. They were tortured to death with unspeakable torments. Not far from it was the latrine: a trench over which two planks were laid. Not seldom our camp officers, the mass murderers Blank and Hinkelmann, sprang over to it and knocked into the trench those comrades who happened to be sitting on the planks; they drowned miserably.

After about a week the majority of our transport (mostly so-called ethnic Germans) was transferred into the large camp. To those of us who had to remain in hell, the commandant said with a sneering grin, "You will all have to kick the bucket here." We were now divided into companies of 100 and had to march in this formation to roll call, which often lasted the entire day. Anyone who stirred was beaten to death or worked over with truncheons until he collapsed unconscious. A total of 487 Poles remained in the Little Camp.

Almost every day Deputy Commandant Rödl visited us with his sidekicks; he always brought the "whipping block" along. Comrades were pulled out indiscriminately, strapped to the whipping block, and whipped until the flesh fell off in scraps. When one SS executioner became tired, he was replaced by another.

For refreshment we received at first ice-cold coffee after we had stood on roll call square for several hours. The midday rations were brought into the camp at nine in the morning but issued only in the afternoon, of course completely cold. Each man received only three-fourths of a quart; there were no spoons. In addition there were two to three fast days each week. If a single person stirred during roll call or collapsed of weakness, the command was immediately handed down: "Today there will be no slops [*nichts zu fressen*]!" Our food then ended up in the pigsty. In November there were a total of seventeen hunger days for us.

On November 14, 120 Poles from the Little Camp were dragged into the stone quarry. The majority were immediately beaten to death in the stone quarry; only a few came back in the evening, bleeding from many wounds.

On December 16 we were deloused because millions of lice afflicted our emaciated bodies as a result of insufficient opportunities for washing. In 18-degree cold we had to undress in roll call square, went naked into the bath, and returned again naked. In any case not all came back; many remained dead in the bath or died on the way. In roll call square we received light summer clothing. While we were in the bath, our sleeping bunks were "cleaned." That was done by simply pouring water over the boards, which of course froze immediately in the extreme cold. When we returned to our tents, all the sleeping places were covered with a thick crust of ice. The next morning sixty-seven dead lay in roll call square.

Amidst these unspeakable torments and the starvation, dysentery began to rage among us. Each day demanded new victims, who had to be laid out in rows next to the tents. At the beginning of the camp, the four tents were filled to overflowing, but we were so decimated by the end of December that all inmates of the camp scarcely filled half a tent.

At the end of December a well-known Upper Silesian freedom fighter, Wawrzyniak, a gardener from Nowy-Bytom, was brought to us out of the large camp. The murderer Blank summoned him and told him that he should hang himself, since there would be no way out for him any more. The comrade did not do it. On the next morning he was brought to Blank, who murdered him with an injection.

At the same time a so-called infirmary consisting of two iron beds was created. Anyone who was not dead after three days was thrown back on the street, where a sick person could not remain alive.

In mid-January 1940 the evacuation of the Little Camp began at the urging of the prisoner orderlies in the hospital. But the SS delayed the move so long that only at the end of February were the last 110 Poles and Jews allowed to leave the Little Camp. We joined our comrades in the large camp, where new sufferings awaited us.

BRONISLAW SZEJA, Kollowitz
TEODOR MIKLASINSKI, Praszka

117. The "Tent Camp"

IN SUMMER 1944 all blocks of Buchenwald concentration camp were overfilled. Two thousand French prisoners arriving from Compiègne had to be housed in an empty square surrounded by barbed wire. After two days the SS made available five tents with a capacity of 200 men each; the administration then felt relieved of all further responsibilities. In the so-called tent camp there were no beds, blankets, seating, any sort of water to drink or wash with, no underwear, latrines, drainage system, medications, dishes, or spoons. In short, it was the most primitive of living conditions. From the very first day, the specter of an epidemic hovered over the tent camp. The prisoner leadership worked feverishly to create more bearable conditions in the tent camp. With materials stolen from the SS warehouses and by using illegal labor services, a water supply, latrines, a sewage system, and a bread storage facility were built. Likewise blankets, dishes, and spoons were gathered from all over. An outpatient clinic began to function; drainage trenches were dug; the roll call square in the tent camp was paved (lime was spread on the entire surface again and again).

The prisoner camp leaders sent trustworthy prisoners of all nationalities into the tent camp to act as room attendants. Their task was the following.

1. Distribution of food, coffee, and drinking water, which was unusually difficult in the heat of midsummer.

2. Organization of the most urgent hygienic facilities, such as cleaning the site and the latrines; ensuring that every chance to wash and disinfect was indeed used; rodent control; and the organization of the most urgent work on drainage, paving, etc.

3. Organization and execution of the fastest possible registration process and closing down of the tent camp by transferring the prisoners into the mostly more bearable conditions in the subsidiary camps.

4. Identification and support of the antifascist fighters and their transfer into the large camp. The best of them were grouped together as prisoner camp leaders in the subsidiary camps or were given recommendations to the already existing antifascist prisoner camp leaderships. Nazi informers, Gestapo agents, and the prisoners who had made themselves into murder instruments of the SS in other camps also had to be identified.

Tens of thousands of prisoners of all European nationalities as well as American, English, and Polish prisoners of war, soldiers, and officers went through the tent camp. The population soon after opening stood at 7,000 to 8,000 prisoners. Among them were numerous children of three years and up. These prisoners were poorly clothed and insufficiently nourished; most had no blankets and in scorching heat no water for drinking or washing. (At the beginning, after completion of the water pipes, water flowed only on Sunday mornings, later on up to an hour every day.) In pouring rain that lasted for weeks, dressed in insufficient, worn-out clothing, barefoot prisoners sank into the softened clay soil. These poor souls were simply vegetating here. Many room attendants broke down physically after a short time.

Typhus, typhoid, and dysentery epidemics were contained and not allowed to spread to the entire camp and neighboring villages and towns. The number of dead was kept to a minimum, measured against the indescribable conditions. These were exclusively the accomplishments of the prisoner camp leaders. They were helped by the thousands of antifascist fighters passing through the tent camp, who worked together with the camp functionaries with exemplary discipline.

The five tents were augmented by a barracks put together from stolen boards by the end of August [1944]. In the fall they were replaced by Blocks 65, 66, and 67, built next to the tents. The tents were gradually torn down. The last one disappeared at the beginning of January 1945.

KURT MELLACH, Vienna
PAUL SPRINGER, Vienna

118. Children in Buchenwald

THE LAMENTABLE FATE of children of our day is that they have had to experience all the horrors of these times. Many thousands of children, together with their parents, were deported into German concentration camps, where they experienced much that was unknown to children of other eras.

From the reports of the children, it must be concluded that their most painful basic experience was the separation from their mothers. The saddest event for some was the murder of their fathers before their own eyes. Many know enough to report that their mothers, brothers, and sisters met their ends in the gas chambers of Auschwitz, that they have become homeless orphans. They tell about their experiences objectively and precisely, observing in the process that the worst did not occur to them in Buchenwald. Here there were blocks (for example, Block 8) where a number of them enjoyed instruction under the supervision and guidance of prisoners. The most difficult part, especially for the Jewish children (the overwhelming majority of the children in the camp), was the last period immediately before the liberation. They report that they arrived here from evacuated camps under the most unfavorable conditions and were housed in overfilled barracks. When the camp administration wanted to evacuate Jewish prisoners, the children were overcome with feelings of panic. Many hid in sewers, where they suffered extreme privations for days at a time.

The children's psychological reactions to their camp experiences vary according to their psychic constitutions. One says, "I will never forget it, and I will hate the fascists for the rest of my life." Another says, "For a year I have dreamed about bad things, but if sometime my mother wakes me up and calls to me, 'Good morning, my son!' then I will no longer remember the bad things."

From the numerous reports we have from the children, it emerges clearly that they faced their fate powerless and uncomprehending, experiencing both the sinister and the horrible. Many make the touching pledge to fight against fascism and the fascist perpetrators in the future. But one hears—if only occasionally— other voices that desire and proclaim no retaliation. They emphasize that "we must remain civilized humans under all conditions, although the fascists wanted to make us into animals."

The number of child inmates in Buchenwald concentration camp is estimated at about 900. The age group between fourteen and eighteen makes up about 85 percent of the total number of children. The youngest, a three-year-old child, is Polish.[2]

Since the liberation the children's situation has improved considerably. Now they are living in bright, comfortable, and well-equipped spaces under the supervision of doctors and teachers. Their meals have improved; they receive treats from the American headquarters. Their state of health is on the whole satisfactory, although some individuals suffer from TB.

DR. JONAS SILBER, Metz

119. THE FIRST RUSSIAN PRISONERS OF WAR

IN THE MIDDLE of October 1941, it became known that Russian prisoners of war were to be delivered to Buchenwald concentration camp. The whole camp was in a state of tension about what the SS would do now, since they had always pursued a constant campaign of vulgar incitement against the Russians. Finally, one Saturday afternoon, the report circulated: The Russians were coming! Almost the entire headquarters staff, with all the familiar executioners and murderers—foremost the infamous Deputy Commandant Plaul—were assem-

---

2. The child, Stefan Georg Zweig, son of attorney Zacharias Zweig of Kraków, was smuggled into camp in his father's rucksack (*KL Bu*, 43–44). This incident provided the basis of the plot for Bruno Apitz's classic East German novel on Buchenwald, *Nackt unter Wölfen* (Halle: Mitteldeutscher Verlag, 1958).

bled at the camp entrance. They showered the arriving prisoners of war with insults and curse words. The Russian prisoners of war arrived in the camp completely exhausted and emaciated into skeletons. They were ragged and torn after months of marching hundreds of miles, during which they had received almost nothing to eat. How many of them had fallen on the way I do not know, but according to the testimony of those arriving, it was very, very many.

Some of the comrades came through the gate dead or dying. The SS intended to fool us into believing that Russians were poorly fed and clothed. They were able to deceive the German population in this regard because of the months the Russians spent marching all the way across Germany. But with us prisoners, our executioners got the opposite of what they wanted. A spontaneous solidarity action of all antifascists in camp immediately developed to an extent never before experienced. Each ran to his block to fetch food or cigarettes; many surrendered their last little piece of bread.

Deputy Commandants Florstedt and Plaul found in this demonstration of solidarity an excuse to act against the reds they so hated. The three antifascist senior block inmates they had selected as victims (Karl Wabbel, Kurt Leonhardt, and Josef Schuhbauer) accepted their punishment knowing that they had acted correctly. The three senior block inmates were dismissed, received twenty-five lashes with a horsewhip from the infamous executioner Sommer, and were sent to the punishment company, where they had to work in the stone quarry. The punishment was performed the next morning, a Sunday. Just before, the [SS] criminal gave a speech to the entire camp in which he said "that the gentlemen of the red category had considered it proper to bring their sympathy for the Bolsheviks to expression."

But since almost the entire camp had participated in this solidarity action for the Russian prisoners of war, all prisoners were punished by a day without food. If on other occasions punishment had been received with hatred and bitterness, this time the entire camp bore it in the consciousness of having acted in an antifascist manner.

JOSEF SCHUHBAUER, Ulm

120. The Illegal Organization of the Russians

THE FIRST 3,000 Russian prisoners of war arrived in Buchenwald in September 1941. Not until March 1942 did the first captured Soviet civilians arrive, those who had been deported by force to work in Germany. The civilians were imprisoned under a variety of pretexts: one because of sabotage in industry, another because of political work in the prisoner of war camps. The majority, however, were brought for having attempted escape from prisoner of war camps, factories, agricultural enterprises, etc. The escape attempts had been carried out in both large and small groups, at times even by groups of armed men.

In the months of March, April, May, and June 1942, more than 6,000 Soviet civilians were delivered. As a rule they were brought in as emaciated and half-starved figures who had been dragged along for months on the back roads of the east, to display them before the German people as Asiatic hordes of inhuman appearance.

Especially difficult was the situation of the Russian prisoners of war. The first unit, 2,500 men, came from Camp 310, the next of 2,000 men from Camp 307. Somewhat later 4,000 men came in a completely exhausted condition from the Ukraine. Of them, 417 men died on the stretch from Weimar to Buchenwald alone. The political prisoners received the Russians with the greatest warmth, showering them with gifts of food, smoking materials, etc. For this the camp was punished by three days without rations.

The prisoners of war were cut off from the rest of the camp by a barbed wire fence. The area was provided with a plaque reading "Prisoner of War Camp," to counter any possible complications because of their being housed in a concentration camp.

In February 1942 a large number were sent on transport to Sachsenhausen, where 4,200 men met their deaths. At the end of 1942, only 1,200 prisoners of war were still left in Buchenwald. Some of the remainder were beaten to death; some died of hunger and disease. Approximately 100 men were delivered into the infamous Block 46. They suffered a painful death through medical experiments. In the camp hospital many prisoners of war were murdered through injections by the SS bandit Eisele.

The career of each Russian began in the stone quarry, but they also had to work in other heavy work details. Indeed, there were even quotas set for the number of Russians to be liquidated in the individual work details. The weak were dragged to work on litters, were beaten to death there, and were sent directly to the crematorium from the work site. Even medical assistance was for a time denied them, regardless of their horrible wounds or diseases.

In the first Russian barracks, there were neither tables nor benches nor beds. They slept on the bare floor, without mattresses or blankets. The Russians worked at times from four in the morning until eight in the evening, with a daily ration of only 5 ounces of bread and three-fourths of a quart of thin soup.

Russians were beaten mercilessly. The SS found willing helpers among the greens (criminals). Thus, for example, the criminal murderer and sadist Mückenheim, kapo of the excavation detail, had forty-seven Russians on his conscience. A senior block inmate beat to death a Russian who had soiled the corridor because he had diarrhea. Numerous such examples could be added.

The Russians were clothed in cotton twill, often without any head covering. Their footwear consisted of wooden shoes, so-called Dutch shoes, which had sharp corners, so that even after a few hours the ankles and heels were worn bloody.

The environment for political work in the camp was of course extremely dangerous. For every word directed against fascism, there stood a death penalty. In summer 1942 our illegal political organization was born. It was formed in the days in which politics could only be whispered from ear to ear. Not everyone dared to participate in such perilous and difficult work in those dangerous times.

The first steps were taken by three men: Vasili Azarov, Adam Astachov, and Vladimir Orlov. The network was then extended from this center to another ten persons. During its development the organization went through several stages. In the first period there were tasks of welfare: help for comrades, improvement of food, and convalescent detail. Recommendations were made to work details for the purpose of sparing our best comrades and preserving them as fighting units for the future. The second task was fostering the cohesion of the Russians, raising the Soviet spirit, and breaking the stifling atmosphere that had worked against the successful collaboration of Russian comrades. It included strengthening international friendships with other peoples, showing through proper personal conduct and leadership the true face of Soviet man, and informing foreigners of the truth about our Soviet state. For this purpose, articles were written and spread among Russians and non-Russians. In the area of sabotage of armaments, much valuable work was accomplished.

In May 1943 the political center was expanded by two additional members: Vasili Schuk and Gregor Kradmanen. In this period the organization faced a whole series of new issues: establishment of connections to external work details, cultural work with the masses, and joint antifascist actions with other nations. To establish contact with comrades working outside the camp, responsible persons were appointed who carefully chose men with special tasks who were to be sent along on all transports. Our cultural programs emphasized concerts of a purely Soviet nature. Russian comrades also participated in international concerts for the camp. In this area Russians achieved great successes, substantially raising their prestige in camp. We maintained contact with the international center through a Czech comrade. In this period our organization completed the consolidation of the majority of the Soviet civilians and prisoners of war into a unified group.

On March 12, 1945, the active cadre gathered together in Block 7. It drew up a concrete plan for work in the immediate future. During these discussions the Gestapo feverishly searched for traces of our illegal organization in camp, but in vain. At this meeting a new political center was elected that vigorously engaged in managing the new tasks brought before it.

[no signature]

121. UKRAINIANS AND RUSSIANS IN BUCHENWALD

AFTER THE OCCUPATION of the Ukraine by Nazi troops, many Ukrainian men and women were deported to Germany for forced labor. Granted, a number of them also went voluntarily because of skillful nationalistic propaganda by middle-class Ukrainians who had entered the Ukraine along with the Nazi army. This propaganda had an effect, especially in the rural areas. Many Ukrainians believed that they could establish an independent Ukraine with the help of German fascism.

When therefore the SS bandits sought collaborators against Russian troops in prisoner of war camps, it was above all Ukrainian soldiers who volunteered, along with Georgians and Tartars. They were organized into units and sent into various concentration camps, where they were trained both ideologically and militarily, as in the Prussian military drill. In Buchenwald, too, there were about 400 "volunteers" for the fight against the Soviets.

But the Ukrainians soon noticed that the Nazis were not really interested in helping them. For German fascism, it was solely a matter of exploiting the resources of Ukrainian soil and its work force in the interests of the German war effort. Escapes by Ukrainian workers from German factories continued to increase. However, recaptured escapees were not brought back to their factories but sent straight to the concentration camp.

As these prisoners were admitted, something remarkable happened. When Ukrainians arrived in camp, they of course had no hint of the conditions that prevailed in Buchenwald. Because they saw only SS men and German prisoners, during the admission formalities, they believed they could improve their situation by presenting themselves as Ukrainian nationalists. They energetically denied any connection with the Soviet Union. After a few days in camp, they noticed that the sympathies of all the prisoners were on the side of the Allies—that is, on the side of the Soviet Union. Then they declared themselves to be convinced Soviet citizens, Communists, or Komsomol members. Obviously, the entire camp regarded them with a certain mistrust because of this rapid change of opinion. It was all the more so because more often than not papers were found in their effects revealing their activity as informers or involvement in other active collaboration with the Nazis.

Some of them who arrived later had even received German decorations for killing Russian soldiers. Russians and Ukrainians were awarded special medals for every twenty-five Red Guards they could prove they had murdered. Among the Ukrainians there were those who had received this order three times(!).

The prisoners' mistrust of the Ukrainians in most cases turned out to be only too justified. Since as a result of their pasts they received no support, an extraordinary number of the Ukrainians became thieves. They stole from their comrades in the block, from the kitchen, or from the food warehouse. They even created organized bands of thieves with preassigned roles who carried out raids in the camp. It was at its worst in the final days, when they fell upon the ration carriers of the individual blocks, stole the rations, and so robbed hundreds of comrades of what little bit of food they were rationed.

Quite the opposite of these elements were the Russian comrades in camp, especially the prisoners of war. Captured soldiers, who above all in the early days had come to Buchenwald completely starved and enfeebled, conducted themselves in a disciplined and comradely manner, despite their horrible suffering. This is all the more remarkable because at the beginning they had to withstand terrible suffering. They were constantly kicked and beaten by SS bandits. They were often tortured to death through the most brutal abuse by the criminal prisoners, whom the SS appointed as "Russian kapos." The specter of death by execution in the horse stable hovered constantly over them. Despite all these sufferings and tortures, the Russian prisoners of war organized themselves in a comradely manner from the first day and through their irreproachable behavior won the sympathies of all antifascists of the camp. They never engaged in theft from comrades or raids.

In 1943, Russian civilian workers who had attempted to escape their workplaces were also delivered into camp. They immediately found strong support from Russian prisoners of war who had already been in camp a while. Russian civilian prisoners attempted again and again to work on the Ukrainian prisoners ideologically and support them materially, to improve the poor image that every prisoner must have had of the Ukrainians. But that was successful in only a few cases. The Russian civilian prisoners—aside from a number of unclean elements—distinguished themselves positively from the Ukrainian prisoners.

After liberation of the camp, the same picture was revealed: on the one hand discipline and order, on the other plunderers and thieves. It is unfortunate that the ideological indoctrination that foreign comrades undertook to improve relations was effective in only a few cases.

WALTER BARTEL, Berlin

122. ATROCITIES AGAINST RUSSIAN PRISONERS

THE SS CREATED especially unbearable conditions for Russian prisoners. The first transport of Russian prisoners, numbering almost 300 men, arrived in Buchenwald in May 1942. Later, additional prisoners arrived in larger and smaller groups. The causes of arrest were various: Bolshevik propaganda, sabotage in factories. The largest number of prisoners were delivered because of escape from prisoner of war camps, armaments factories, and railroad and agricultural enterprises.

When Russian prisoners were delivered in very large numbers in summer 1942, the SS placed them in the most difficult work details, such as the X detail, the stone quarry, etc. The clothing room received special instructions from the SS that no winter clothing be given to the Russian prisoners. The only footwear issued were Dutch wooden shoes, which soon rubbed the feet bloody and caused unbearable pain.

In winter 1943 a large number of Russian prisoners were placed for the first time in the X detail, which lacked the needed number of tools. The SS forced many prisoners to remove stones from water ditches with their bare hands and stack them in large piles. After several such piles were completed, the prisoners had to carry the stones elsewhere.

The work in the stone quarry was especially difficult. There the prisoners had to push a cart piled high with stones up a steep ramp. A number of prisoners were yoked together in front of each cart with a long iron chain and a pole. They had to pull a cart weighing several tons up the steep ramp almost at double time. If one of the prisoners collapsed of weakness, the SS men beat him with thick truncheons. When the X detail and the stone quarry detail returned to the camp in the evenings, they had to bring along their dead. They laid them down at the entrance gate in front of the cellblock to be counted.

In mid-1942 Russian prisoners received a daily ration of 5 ounces of bread and three-fourths of a quart of soup. All other supplements available to non-Russian prisoners were kept from the Russians. If anyone became sick, before he could be examined in the hospital, he had to appear before the labor service officer, who arbitrarily accepted or rejected the claim to illness.

During work the prisoners were driven on with truncheons. The SS told the kapos and the foremen, "The Bolshevik pigs are allowed only to work and die." The mortality figure among Russian prisoners in 1942 amounted to fifty to sixty a month.

This brutal treatment of the Russian prisoners awakened in them a will to fight. They gathered themselves into an illegal resistance organization that eventually expanded to such an extent that it was in a position to lead the Russian prisoners in a breakout through the barbed wire fence on April 11, 1945, to carry on battle against the SS.

Committee of the Russian Prisoners
in Buchenwald Concentration Camp

123. ACTIVITIES OF THE CZECHOSLOVAKS

IT WAS NO SENSATION that the American troops encountered 5,000 dying men upon their arrival at Buchenwald, considering the well-known Nazi methods. What is remarkable is that it was possible to snatch 21,389 men from the claws of the SS, saving them from evacuation—that is, from probable death. (Unfortunately, that has not been mentioned in Allied propaganda up to now.) It is just as remarkable that immediately after the flight of the SS, the national committees together took over the camp, provided for order and discipline, and protected the camp from the outside with arms. This was no accident. It was the result of years of illegal work by the national committees in Buchenwald. Here only the activity of the national committee of the Czechoslovaks in Buchenwald concentration camp will be dealt with.

As early as 1939 the Czech sector in the camp was strongly represented in constantly increasing numbers. At first it was Czech Jews, then antifascists, and finally Czech citizens of all sorts. Collaboration with the German antifascists also developed very early. Through it, we made an effort to come into all branches of the prisoner camp leadership and were successful with the help of the German comrades. We had Czech antifascists in the camp records and labor records offices—the two decisive offices for life in camp. The entire assignment of labor for Buchenwald concentration camp, as well as the transport department, also stood under the direction of Czech comrades.

Similarly, there were numerous Czechs active in the political department, primarily as translators in the reception of new prisoners. (On our work with new admittees we give more information below.)

While there were already Czech comrades as room attendants in many blocks, only in the final period did we convince the SS camp administration to appoint Czech comrades as senior block inmates. The senior camp inmate Hans Eiden was able to appoint Czech senior block inmates to Blocks 51 and 66. Likewise, our countrymen were represented in the camp police and in the camp fire department. There were Czech prisoners in all supply rooms and camp workshops as well, which was of great significance, especially for the material support of our comrades.

Of special importance to us was our collaboration with the prisoners' hospital. Here above all, the German antifascists Ernst Busse and Otto Kipp always held to the policy of international solidarity even in difficult times. Here our sick comrades were helped in the most generous manner. But still more important, by having them "submerge" in the hospital, it was possible to save endangered comrades whom the SS had threatened with death. They would either be reported as not fit for transport, or they would have their names exchanged for those of dead prisoners, in effect making them dead to the SS. In-block convalescence was generously granted not just to those who actually deserved convalescence but also to comrades who were temporarily withdrawn from their normal work details because they had to perform political work.

When new arrivals came into camp, we tried to seek out our countrymen and establish contact with them. (In the last months it was often several thousand a day.) That happened as early as the disinfection station, through which all new admissions were channeled. We had Czech comrades in this work detail who started conversations with all newly admitted Czechs and asked the reasons for their arrest. That was very important. Many presented themselves as friends of the Nazis in the disinfection station, where they could not yet know much about the camp. At the end of the admissions procedure, however, after they had detected the atmosphere that prevailed at Buchenwald, they already presented themselves as convinced Communists. These people were of course treated with particular caution.

After the bath they went to the clothing room, where likewise Czech comrades had the opportunity to speak to them. Finally, they went to the Personal Property Room, where the interpreters of the political department sat and took down the personal information from each new admittee. Since almost all these interpreters were Czechs, they could question each newly arriving Czech thoroughly and give us much valuable information. In addition, the contact man [*Vertrauensmann*] of the national committee received from them an admissions list of all Czechs. In many blocks, particularly in the so-called admissions blocks, we had Czech room attendants who immediately cared for their countrymen. Thus after a short time we always had a fairly precise picture of the Czech admittees. Moreover we very often received from the admittees valuable information about the situation in our homeland, on conditions in the protectorate, etc., so that we were well informed about everything that especially interested us.

The result of these determinations was transmitted to our comrades in labor records, who then assigned prisoners to work details, each according to his suitability. We directed particular attention to sabotage in armaments work because the majority of prisoners were employed in the German war industry. Once an entire transport of antifascist workers from the Skoda Works in Pilsen was sent to the Gustloff Works, where these comrades carried out successful sabotage. For example, in certain production areas hard metal was exchanged for soft metal, or unskilled workers were given instructions so that the objects they produced were unusable but in such a way that the mistake could not be discovered immediately.

Material support in camp also played a great role. Up to the end we Czechs still received numerous packages from the homeland—almost the only group in Buchenwald allowed to do so. We could thus support not only the impoverished and sick Czech comrades and the many Czech children but also impoverished comrades of other nationalities. In particular we regularly aided Russian prisoners of war and children in Block 8. Warm clothing was distributed in this manner as well. Furthermore, the Czech antifascists regularly received cigarettes, even beyond what was normally distributed.

The leadership and the execution of these tasks lay in the hands of the Czech committee, which was composed of the following comrades: Hrsel (chairman), Tymes, Helecek, Dr. Dufek, Dr. Neumann, Dr. Polansky, Frank,[3] and Priester. Neumann, Frank, and Priester were our representatives in the International Camp Committee because they had already maintained contact with the other nationalities while doing so was still illegal.

But the committee also had political and in the last period military tasks. We assembled in small groups and discussed political and military events of the day. We were not entirely dependent on German news but were also supplied with news from foreign broadcasts, a situation we owed primarily to our comrade Jonas. The creation of national unity through the National Council in London [April 3, 1945] gave our work in Buchenwald a new impulse. It led to the creation of the above-named national committee, which after liberation by the American army was unanimously confirmed in office in a meeting of all Czech prisoners in Buchenwald.

Our military preparations for the final confrontation with the Buchenwald SS murderers of course had to proceed strictly illegally. Even reliable antifascists who had not served in the military and were therefore not suitable for this task learned nothing about it. On the day of liberation, April 11, 1945, we had 100 men in the Czech brigade and two squads of medical corpsmen. For weapons we possessed two heavy machine guns, four automatic weapons, numerous other weapons, and a few hand grenades. Unfortunately, during the bombardment on August 24, 1944, an illegal cache with 100 hand grenades was blown up.

All this work, which can only be briefly described, was the preparation for our success on April 11, 1945. Of course many prisoners were surprised at the results of our illegal work. For years they did not worry about antifascist work but only about their own stomachs. We were of the view that in the future, too, these people should occupy themselves only with their private interests.

We Czech antifascists had become well acquainted with one another during the years of our often dangerous and difficult work in the struggle against the common foe. But we were firmly convinced that this collaboration would continue just as smoothly and as well in the period of legality as it had in illegality.

National Committee of Czechoslovaks

[Reports of some of the national committees that follow have been abridged slightly, since many of them repeat the same themes and incidents mentioned above.]

———

3. Josef Frank was in Buchenwald from 1939 to 1945. He later rose to a position of power in the postwar Czech Communist party, eventually becoming party secretary. Along with Rudolf Slansky, he was purged in 1952 in a public trial that had strong anti-Semitic overtones; like Slansky, he was executed later that year. See Jiri Pelikan, ed., *The Czechoslovak Political Trials, 1950–1954* (Stanford: Stanford University Press, 1971).

124. Report of the Dutch Committee

I**T IS CERTAINLY REMARKABLE** that on their arrival in Buchenwald concentration camp, the American troops did not encounter a state of chaos. The inmates of the camp were united into an international organization of antifascist forces. It is just as remarkable that one could still encounter here people full of energy, vitality, and the courage to resist, after up to twelve years of imprisonment in Nazi prisons and concentration camps under the most difficult conditions.

To make this amazing fact understood, we must give a short history of the extremely difficult and dangerous illegal work and the painstaking preparations. ...

In 1941 about 150 Dutch hostages [prominent prisoners] were delivered here. Because of their preferred treatment, however, they experienced little of the actual camp life, and after a short time they were released again.

But the Dutch street people [*Gauner*] delivered in the same year were put into the prisoners' camp and had to take part in the hard camp life with the other prisoners. In April 1942 another 300 Dutchmen came, among whom were a great number of Communists. After a few days eighty-five men from this group went to Gross-Rosen concentration camp. All were liquidated there.

In the early days there were tense relationships between the various Dutch political groups. The constant efforts of the more responsible elements in the various groups gradually led to an improvement of this situation.

The German and Austrian prisoners established contact with the Dutch and drew Seegers, Pieck, and Schalker Jr. into collaboration. Through the collaboration of the three named above, it became possible to place a number of Dutchmen into better work assignments, where in return they were able to accomplish much good for the other Dutch prisoners.

Our activity consisted of, on the one hand, improving the living conditions in camp and, on the other hand, engaging in a constant struggle against chauvinistic elements among the prisoners. They did not understand the measures agreed upon and attempted to belittle the service of the German Communists. It must be emphasized again and again that the German Communists fought against Hitler even before the long years of arrest, long before most Dutchmen recognized a danger in Hitler and his National Socialism. One should not put these Germans on the same level with the National Socialists. ...

In June 1944 our work was continued on a broader basis through the formation of a Dutch committee. The committee was composed of representatives of the Antirevolutionary party, the Progressive Democrats, the Catholics, the Social Democrats, the Communists, and the nonparty elements. Over the course of time, the following took part in the work of the committee: Captain Dr. van

Lingen, Lieutenant Ramshorst, Joukes Sr. (an engineer), Joukes Jr., Head Mayor Ritmeester, Treurniet, Staal, Bouwman, Hemmerswaal(?), van Vuuren, Aalders, Pastor Sprenk, Varewijk, Seegers, Bestiansee, Haken, and Pieck.

Besides trying to improve the living conditions of the Dutch in camp, we discussed the future tasks of the Dutch people, so as to put the unity we had achieved here to work for the benefit of our nation.

After such committees were formed in almost all national groups, the first illegal discussions of representatives of these nations took place in 1944. … Under the leadership of the German comrades, representatives of France, Austria, Czechoslovakia, Russia, and the Netherlands took part in these first international discussions. For conspiratorial reasons, only a few members of the committee could be involved. After Belgium, Spain, Italy, and Yugoslavia joined us, we were soon forced to divide into a West and an East sector. We held discussions primarily on the political and military situation and on certain conditions in camp, in which the illegal reception of broadcasts from the assembled nations played an important role.

The ever increasing crisis in Germany and certain conditions in camp soon made the creation of a military apparatus necessary. Persons standing outside the International Camp Committee were entrusted with this task. For the Netherlands, Haken and van Lingen participated in this work. To disguise the illegal structure of this military organization from the SS, the camp police, fire department, fire patrol, rescue squad, medical corps, and stretcher squad were formed. The active direction of this organization took place in a dugout near Block 32, which was constructed under the guise of an air raid shelter for the fire wardens.

Thus it was possible always to take the right measures at the right moment. It should be mentioned in particular that through the systematic delay of the evacuation measures the SS planned, thousands were saved from being carried off to an uncertain fate. It was also possible to hide forty-six political comrades in camp— among them five Dutchmen who were to be turned over to the executioners—and thus save their lives.

At last we saw the right moment to strike, to give the advancing Americans the aid intended for them.

For all these reasons, upon their arrival the American officers found the entire camp committee assembled at the gate to receive them. Instead of an anarchic, disorganized mass, they found a well-disciplined organization and a large number of determined, purposeful fighters against Hitler, his SS, and the National Socialist criminal regime.

We, as representatives of various political directions, declare that this report of the Dutch committee on the illegal preparations for international antifascist collaboration in Buchenwald concentration camp corresponds to the actual factual conditions, and that this collaboration of all political directions of all nationalities has led to the positive results named in the report.

Signed for the:

Antirevolutionary party DR. D. VAN LINGEN	Social Democratic party A. TREURNIET
Progressive Democratic party G. RITMEESTER	Communist party L. SEEGERS

125. Yugoslavians in the Antifascist Struggle

W E YUGOSLAVIANS were the last nationality to arrive in Buchenwald at the end of 1943 and 1944; we came out of various concentration camps in Italy and prisons in Croatia. Most of us were captured in our homelands as active antifascist fighters, and as such we had clear ideas of the political and organizational principles of the antifascist struggle. Thus for the most part we were already internally organized. The German comrades, the oldest antifascists in camp, included us in the international antifascist front. They were particularly familiar with all the essential camp tasks and methods of struggle. It was they who initiated and organized this struggle.

Of course honest and serious-minded antifascists of all nations recognized very quickly that this struggle must have an international leadership. Its success depended on the suppression of all chauvinistic tendencies. The German comrades did not allow the SS to turn them against the foreigners. The foreign antifascists did not allow political agitation to be turned against all Germans, regardless of whether they were fascists or antifascists. Unity and solidarity of the antifascists of all nations was our slogan against all attempts to divide us. ...

The fulfillment of our military task—breaking out of the camp and disarming the SS—by the various national units proves our axiom: Only honorable, serious-minded antifascists, cleansed of all chauvinistic nationalist elements, can successfully achieve the common mission in the struggle against fascism.

The Yugoslavian Committee

126. Annihilation of Yugoslavians in Buchenwald

T HE MAJORITY of Yugoslavians who were brought to Buchenwald concentration camp were destroyed through the murderous methods of the fascist bandits. I myself was brought to the camp on August 17, 1941, with nineteen comrades, of whom only seven are alive today. In 1943, 1,600 Yugoslavians who had been held as political prisoners in Italy arrived in Buchenwald. Of these, 600 immediately went to Dora and 320 to Laura. By summer 1944 over half the comrades in Dora had already died; later audits were no longer possible because the camp had been separated from Buchenwald. Of the comrades transferred to Laura, only twenty-five were still alive in summer 1944; they returned to Buchenwald in a condition of complete starvation.

The situation was similar for Yugoslavian prisoners of war who were brought into the concentration camp against international law. In spring 1944, 450 Yugoslavian prisoners of war, with the exception of three comrades, were transferred to S III (Ohrdruf). When this camp was evacuated and the inmates brought back to Buchenwald, only twenty-six were still alive, of whom sixteen had to be admitted to the hospital immediately for TB and malnutrition.

Finally, 250 Yugoslavians were likewise sent to S III in December 1944; we never again heard anything about them.

But the Yugoslavians who remained in Buchenwald also had to withstand much. A larger percentage of them remained alive thanks mainly to the German antifascist comrades; to a large extent they protected our countrymen. Unfortunately, they could not prevent the hanging of two Yugoslavian antifascists, the brothers Lacen from Vrevalde.

VICESLAV FIGAR, Kocepje

127. THE STRUGGLE OF BELGIAN ANTIFASCISTS

W E HAVE DECIDED to describe in this report the antifascist struggle of the prisoners in Buchenwald so that the entire world will recognize our strength, unity, comradeship, and international solidarity. ...

Soon after their arrival the Belgian comrades united in a secret organization. They formed a steering committee of antifascists who had already proven their bravery and ability in the antifascist struggle in Belgium. Our work was made easier for us because most of us had already become acquainted with one another in Belgium when we had worked together in the "national struggle against fascism." Later we joined the International Committee of all antifascists. ...

Our tasks among the Belgian prisoners consisted of the following:

1. Solidarity and material support. Needy comrades were supported with food and money for canteen purchases. We were able to "organize" shoes and clothing for needy comrades. Packages sent by the Belgian Red Cross were justly distributed to all, but especially to the sick.

2. Care of the sick. We were able to place a number of Belgian comrades as orderlies in the hospital. Together with German comrades, they often stole valuable medications from the SS at risk to their lives. Our comrades withdrew many good Belgian antifascists from the transport examinations by the SS doctor and thereby prevented them from being sent to bad work details.

3. Cultural work. The International Committee sponsored Sunday concerts and theater performances in which the antifascist spirit of struggle was awakened and

strengthened by appropriate presentations. Even athletic contests were held. In all these performances Belgian comrades always participated. Christmas and New Year's were celebrated with appropriate Belgian festivities.

4. Occupation of camp functions. In 1943 the criminals, who up to that point had occupied camp functions, were overthrown by the German Communists in a heroic struggle during which many good Communists even lost their lives. The German Communists immediately used their occupation of camp functions to demonstrate international solidarity. ... We Belgians were represented in all camp work details with the help of the German Communists and thus had more opportunities for supporting our countrymen than previously.

Among the numerous proofs of international solidarity, one in particular deserves to be emphasized. The SS condemned to death three Belgian comrades. With the help of responsible German comrades, the hospital reported them dead, and at the last minute they were able to disappear unharmed into an external work detail under false names. All three comrades are living testimonials to the splendid conduct of our antifascist struggle!

5. Struggle of the antifascists. We regularly received news from foreign broadcasts that responsible comrades listened in on at risk of death. The news was passed on to reliable comrades. We conducted systematic sabotage in the German war industry. In many cases parts necessary for production disappeared. But in the course of this work, we discovered cowards in our ranks, even some SS collaborators who of course were isolated and had to be removed from the community. That occurred as well in other cases, when Gestapo agents and traitors were occasionally delivered into camp in transports of new admissions.

6. Military preparations. When the military events at the front reached a head, our military organization, which had long existed under international direction, prepared itself for all possibilities. It prepared four military plans under the following headings: offensive, defensive, evacuation, and takeover of the camp with the help of Allied troops. This strategy succeeded because of our long years of preparatory work.

7. Liberation of the camp. When the SS suddenly fled the camp grounds at the approach of the American tanks, our armed troops proceeded to storm the watchtowers. We occupied them and disarmed the SS men we found there. At the same time prisoner patrols scoured the forest in the vicinity of the camp and the neighboring villages and secured the grounds until the arrival of the American infantry.

The Belgian shock troops under the leadership of Comrade Mathieu Bielen played an important role, since it was formed for the most part of Belgian partisans who were accustomed to fighting. A group led by comrade Henri Flinker of Liège and Walter Petters of Antwerp made a particularly lucky catch in the person of a Belgian SS man who carried with him valuable and important lists of addresses of foreign SS volunteers.

The Belgian Committee

128. Austrians in Buchenwald

In September [1938] the first Austrians arrived in Buchenwald. At almost the same time, about 400 police prisoners arrived from Vienna and about 1,200 Austrians Jews arrived from Dachau. A large portion of the police prisoners were released again; only a few of them are still alive today. At the beginning of the war, many suspected antifascists, primarily Social Democrats and Communists, were arrested. After September 1939 they were continuously delivered to Buchenwald.

The antifascist elements among the Austrian prisoners immediately recognized the need for a close association. At first they organized themselves, then they joined with the German antifascists, which they could do easily because there were no language difficulties to overcome. Our tasks were of two sorts: safeguarding life in a broad sense and continuing antifascist propaganda activity among all Austrians.

In the matter of safeguarding life, the struggle against the SS camp administration and its collaborators in camp was the most important task. At first it was only occasionally possible to save Austrian antifascists from liquidation by the SS and Gestapo. But by 1944 and 1945 many comrades were kept alive, primarily with the help of the antifascist hospital orderlies. Lackner, Kogon, Hagmüller, Uitz, Powatz, and many others need only be named. A great many were saved from transport to bad external work details. ...

For us Austrians, a special difficulty in antifascist work was the question of our future state. A great many antifascists were of the opinion that Austria must join in a federation with a truly democratic Germany (this opinion was held mostly by German comrades). The majority, however, even among the German comrades, favored an independent Austria. After long discussions, and especially after the conference of Allied foreign ministers in Moscow, a common policy was established. Under the flag of an independent Austria, all antifascists united in the common struggle.

In the same year the International Committee was also created. It brought together under unified leadership all the nations represented in Buchenwald. ...

A special chapter in the history of our antifascist struggle was the creation of a military organization to allow us to actively defend ourselves against the SS. Comrades who had performed military service instructed younger comrades in the most important military issues (the handling of weapons, study of terrain, etc.). The Austrian comrades had an important share in the work of obtaining weapons and building up the organization. It should be emphasized in particular how correct the selection of antifascists in the military apparatus was, for in all the years of preparation, not a single case of betrayal occurred. In fact the Gestapo and the SS never found out about the actual international organization of antifascists. During all our work we never forgot the special difficulties of our Jewish comrades. We repeatedly rescued them from the claws of the SS, hid them, illegally "Aryanized" them, or even put them in the records under false names. The growing influence of our antifascist struggle revealed itself in that all important prisoner functions were occupied by convinced antifascists. The few functionaries of other tendencies (for example, the criminals) no longer dared to act against this united front. Thus the liberation of Buchenwald is no miracle but only the expression and result of the organized common struggle of the antifascists of all lands.

The Austrian Committee

129. The Polish Secret Organization

The FATE OF the Poles in Buchenwald was almost as difficult as that of the Jews. At times the Poles were treated even worse. But at least the possibility existed of improving the lot of some, if not that of the entire group. This was because the organization of the camp rested on the method of involving prisoners in supervising and organizing the camp. ...

...In 1942 the strongest group of German political prisoners, the Communists, seized internal power in camp after a difficult struggle with the greens. It took over the task of maintaining internal order and work discipline. Under these conditions the secret Polish committee was founded on October 5, 1943. The decision was made to establish contact with representatives of the German group to open up the possibility for intervention on behalf of the Polish comrades with their help.

On this committee sat Dr. Marian Swiderek, docent at the University of Warsaw who was later released through the efforts of his wife; Stefan Szczepaniak, president of the Federation of Poles in Germany; Stefan Taberski, master tailor from Rybnik; Paul Kwoczek, chairman of the Association of Polish Scouts in Germany; Dr. Marian Ciepielowski of Kraków; and Ignaz Szymala, government official. The last-named had already made contact with the leading comrades of the hospital, Ernst Busse and Otto Kipp. At the same time contact was made with the leading member of the Polish Communists, Henryk Mikolajczyk, an orderly in the hospital. The Polish Communist group, which was separately organized, had long maintained contact with the German group. It was too small, however, to find a greater response in the larger group of Poles. Comrade Mikolajczyk declared himself prepared to collaborate, and the committee began to function.

The first task of the committee consisted of taking newly arrived Poles under its protection and providing assistance for the valuable elements. It attempted to prevent all those who still showed some vital energy and capacity for social life from being sent to difficult external work details. It also intervened in the admission of prisoners to the hospital, arbitrated conflicts between Poles and other groups, and protected against informers sent into the camp by the SS. Finally, it combatted the display of too much enthusiasm in work at the armaments factories.

Whenever Poles were among the new admissions, the committee made contact with them. Bread and cigarettes were collected in the Polish blocks, and deals were made to provide access for the greatest possible number to the lighter work details and to retain as many of them as possible in Buchenwald. As a rule new admissions were specifically designated for further transport into the heavy external work details. Gradually, it was possible to place representatives of the Polish group in the most important camp work details (records office, labor records, camp police, etc.). Among the senior block inmates, Vladek Nowak was the representative of Polish interests.

In 1944 the committee decided to expand its membership as a result of the relaxation of tensions that had developed between groups and the expansion of its duties because of the delivery of masses of new Polish prisoners. It co-opted Vladek Szczerba (a teacher), Vladek Oszrowski (a military specialist), and Vaclav Czarnecki (a journalist) as new members. The committee now called itself the Provisional Committee of Polish Reconciliation and included all political groups of Poles in Buchenwald. In addition, Teofil Witek later joined the committee.

At the beginning of 1945, a so-called contact-man system was created in all Polish blocks; the contact men [*Vertrauensmänner*] were the room attendants in each block. The placement of Polish room attendants in the so-called Little Camp was especially important in order to establish contact with the Poles among the new admissions and make the necessary organizational arrangements in the short time they remained there: All new admissions went through the Little Camp and immediately left on mass transports to external work details. The contact man for the room attendants in the Little Camp was Emil Niemirowski. The committee augmented by the most important contact men was represented in the International Committee by Henryk Mikolajczyk.

Outside this organization an illegal military organization began its activity under the command of Colonel Bierowski and another group from the Polish Workers party under Henryk Mikolajczyk. The military organization established contact with former officers, noncommissioned officers, and soldiers and registered them to prepare for an armed confrontation with the SS. These preparations took on a more intensive character after December 1944. The military organization had at its disposal a certain arsenal of weapons that were in part stolen from SS warehouses and in part even purchased from the SS.

As the American army approached, a special detachment of 100 men from all nations was formed. These prisoners received weapons and were to remain in camp in case of an evacuation, in order to defend the sick and the inmates unfit for transport who remained behind against any sort of liquidation attempt by the SS. This company of 100 was prepared to fight to the last breath.

Although the SS attempted to deny it, evacuation was eventually ordered. The internal camp leadership sabotaged these orders and attempted to gain as much time as possible. Jews were designated for evacuation first; only somewhat over half of them went. The others were hidden by the prisoners without respect to their nationality. Of 5,000 non-Jewish prisoners who were locked into the German Armament Works grounds for the next transport, over 2,000 returned to the large camp with the help of the camp police who were to guard them.

Finally, on April 10, 1945, 9,200 prisoners marched out, of whom about 5,000 were Poles. Almost all members of the Polish military organization were evacuated, a mere fifty members of this organization remaining in camp. The Polish military organization received the assignment of escaping en route by attacking and disarming the SS guards at a favorable opportunity. According to American radio reports, it seems this plan was successful.

After liberation from the SS, the Polish committee, of which several members had marched out, was reconstituted and expanded. To the remaining members were added Tadeusz Sulowski, Piotr Kalinowski, Colonel Bierowski, Milanowiscz, Jakuvowski, and three representatives of the Polish Jews: Frankiel, Landau, and Werber. Stefan Szczepaniak became chairman, and Henryk Mikolajczyk and Tadeusz Sulowski were elected as delegates to the International Committee.

The first task of the committee consisted of gathering all Poles of the camp together into purely Polish blocks and placing Polish senior block inmates there. Then a list of all Polish citizens in the camp was made, as well as a list of all Poles who had passed through Buchenwald concentration camp. Self-help and sanitary measures were also organized. Because hundreds of men and women who had been brought to the vicinity of Buchenwald as civilian forced laborers soon reported to the committee, the committee took over the organization and protection of these Polish men and women. Thus in the first days after liberation, 500 items of women's clothing were issued to Polish women from the SS warehouses.

The Polish Committee

130. Labor Records and Transport Protection

Labor assignments for all prisoners in Buchenwald itself, as well as in the subsidiary camps, were the domain of the labor assignment officer, SS Captain Schwarz. He was a cold-blooded beast for whom the prisoners represented only commodities. That the transport and assignment of labor had cost thousands their lives was a matter of no concern to him. His immediate SS underlings were the labor service officers Weyer and Zinneke, both compliant creatures.

On the prisoners' side, the labor records office directed the assignment of labor in and outside the camp. And today one can confidently state that the actual assignment of prisoners was never really determined by the SS but always by the prisoners. Only once did Schwarz make the attempt to put together a transport of 1,000 prisoners himself. After he had let almost the entire camp stand in roll call square for half a day to check the rolls, he was lucky to assemble about 600 prisoners. From then on he cheerfully left all questions of work assignments to the comrades of labor records, primarily comrades Willi Seifert and Herbert Weidlich. These two comrades represented the antifascist line toward the SS so skillfully that they had the full confidence of the labor assignment officers. Yet despite that, they represented only the interests of the prisoners.

The most important area was of course labor placement. The following considerations were determining factors.

1. Comrades who were urgently needed for antifascist work in Buchenwald concentration camp were not allowed to go on transports. They were to be placed in those work details that allowed them sufficient time for their political work. Since it was not possible to do this for all comrades, "convalescence" was often granted with the help of the antifascist comrades of the hospital.

2. To the armaments factories only those comrades were sent who could guarantee the execution of the necessary sabotage in the war industry. They had to be skilled workers and faithful antifascist fighters with conspiratorial experience. Yet the required skilled workers were either not put at the disposal of the SS at all, or unskilled workers or workers from other categories were substituted for the requested skilled workers. Here is one example of many: The Reichsbahn railroad repair shop Schwerte urgently requested a boilermaker for locomotive repairs. Because roofers were requested in another external work detail at the same time, all available boilermakers in camp were sent to work as roofers, while for months Schwerte advertised in vain for boilermakers. There were of course none left here.

3. In the last months external work details continued to grow and played an increasingly important role in labor assignment. Insofar as important armaments factories were involved, reliable antifascists were sent who were in a position to organize sabotage work in the external work details. But to these subsidiary camps went above all those elements the prisoners remaining in camp considered undesirable for various reasons. There were those who both in freedom and in camp had served the SS or Gestapo as informers and denouncers against their fellow countrymen. In addition, there were all those men who were not in camp for political reasons but for criminal or actual antisocial behavior. Finally, there were those elements who had demonstrated antisocial conduct in the camp itself: bread thieves, black marketeers, hoarders, etc.

All these negative elements were selected by the national groups, which also identified the positive elements who under no condition were to go on transports. To be able to carry out this work correctly, a special department was created to assemble the transport lists on the basis of suggestions by the national committees. Of course the overriding goal of the antifascists of all lands was to make the camp capable of fighting in the final showdown.

A few additional words should be given on transports to the external work details. Often, above all when firms required skilled workers, engineers of the firms concerned came and selected prisoners for their factories themselves. In such cases it was almost impossible to strike a comrade off the transport list. But that, too, occurred in a few very important cases. If a special request nevertheless came from the firm, then the prisoner was simply unfit for transport or had just died.

There were two types of prisoners that the camp administration ordered not be sent into external work details under any circumstances. One group was the so-called DIKAL prisoners ("DIKAL" was a note the political department made on a prisoner's index card; it meant, "not to be sent to any other camp" [*"Darf in kein anderes Lager"*]). The others were so-called escape mark prisoners (those who had already escaped from a camp or prison and who wore a red dot with white border on their backs and chests). Nevertheless, we sent such prisoners away as well. When a dispute once broke out because of the dispatch of some DIKAL prisoners, we made use of the constant tension between the camp administration and the labor assignment officer. We pointed out that the command to assemble a new transport was given with so little notice that there was insufficient time to check for marks on the index cards of all the prisoners who were sent. The result of the conversation was that Deputy Commandant Schobert called the labor assignment officer Schwarz an asshole. With that, our part in the matter was resolved.

It was more difficult with escape marks. One day eighty-five escape mark prisoners were summoned. As punishment for their escape attempts, they were to receive twenty-five lashes with a cane. But only about twenty of them were still left in camp. All the others had been sent to external work details in order to save them. A portion of them had probably already escaped again, which was more easily done from an external work detail. The storm that arose out of this incident also passed, and we saved sixty comrades from a beating.

It should be obvious that not all the prisoners understood the principles according to which we acted and had to act in the interests of the entire camp, for not all prisoners could be initiated into the secret antifascist work. But to prove that we acted correctly, we have 22,000 Buchenwalders alive today as witnesses.

JIRI ZAK, Pilsen

131. SS CONSTRUCTION COMMAND IN RUSSIA

As EARLY as August 1941, SS Corporal Crawenbrock from the Construction Office at Buchenwald was ordered to the Central Building Headquarters for service in occupied territories in the east. Soon after, we in the Construction Office received an organization plan for prospective building offices. It carried the official title "Construction Command of the Waffen SS and Police." The following offices were created: Moscow (situated in Minsk), Leningrad (situated in

Riga), Tiflis (situated in Kiev), Kiev, Riga and Pskov, Astrakhan, Baku, Voroshi-lovgrad, Rostov, Voronezh, etc. For the Construction Command in Moscow and for the Central Construction Office at Astrakhan, SS Captain Drosch and SS First Lieutenant Schlachter had already been appointed. This plan was announced in October 1941, at a time when the majority of the cities named had not yet been occupied.

After the battle for Stalingrad, the names of the construction inspections were changed. Now they were called "Russia-North in Riga," "Russia-Middle in Mohilev," "Russia-South in Kiev," and "Caucasus in Voroshilovgrad." Even when the German troops had been driven back over the Dnieper, these desk officers did not want to give up their good positions. They continued to maintain offices in cities located closer to Germany.

In general, corruption and malingering was especially pronounced among the SS men of the Construction Office. A typical case was SS First Lieutenant Hünefeld (SS No. 7168), whom not only the prisoners but also his SS subordinates recognized as a ruthless egoist and a malingerer. The building of the railroad from Weimar to Buchenwald serves as one example of his conduct. To provide the prisoners an "incentive" to work and to give the sentries an interest in faster work, 1.5 million cigarettes and quantities of schnapps were placed at their disposal. Hünefeld gave only a small portion of these cigarettes to the SS men of the Construction Office, keeping the rest for himself. The schnapps he drank up by himself with his friends. The prisoners as well as the sentries were cheated out of the distribution.

Another "standout" among the SS was Second Lieutenant Walter Frey of Enningen near Reutlingen. He constantly threatened to have every prisoner shot. At the slightest mistake he would threaten to bring charges of sabotage against a prisoner. When the defeats of the Nazis became ever greater, he crept anxiously through the rooms. His cowardice was especially evident during the air raids on Buchenwald. While the prisoners tried to rescue whatever was possible from the burning ruins of the Construction Office, he lay upon a pile of bricks wrapped in a blanket, looking gray and crestfallen and wailing ceaselessly. He needed two weeks of vacation to recover.

MARTIN MAY, Frankfurt

132. Railroad Construction to Buchenwald

IT IS A well-known fact that the Nazis irresponsibly wasted billions of marks of public money. A particularly brilliant example along these lines is represented by the building of the railroad from Weimar to Buchenwald. On March 18, 1943, Himmler gave the order for the construction of this railroad, with the proviso that the test run must under all circumstances take place on June 21, 1943. To characterize this absurd [*bahnwichtigen*] demand, the following should be mentioned.

The length of this stretch amounted to about 10 miles. The composition of the roadbed was clay with a large mixture of crushed rock. The difference in altitude between the Weimar railroad station and Buchenwald concentration camp amounted to about 930 feet. It must be clear even to a layman that not even a makeshift railroad could be built in so short a time. The appointed construction director, SS Second Lieutenant Bertram, indicated from the very beginning the impossibility of completing the stretch in the time that was set. The response from Berlin was to give overall direction of railroad construction to the infamous slave driver and abuser of men SS First Lieutenant Alfred Sorge, a man who had become infamous for his slave-driving methods after several years at Sachsenhausen concentration camp. Moreover, Sorge brought with him two of his henchmen, SS Master Sergeants Baumann and Sohn.

In twelve-hour day and night shifts, including Sundays and holidays, the prisoners were driven on by the bloodhounds of the canine patrol. Under a regime of constant beatings, a murderous work began at a frantic pace, the likes of which had never been seen. Hundreds of prisoners lost their lives because of this hectic pace. The number of daily accidents amounted to several dozen. But that never caused the SS bandits headaches; the main point was and remained that on the evening of June 20, the construction of the railroad would be "completed."

According to plan, the first test run took place in the presence of SS Major General [Dr. Hans] Kammler (an engineer) and a large number of Nazi bosses. There was a hail of promotions and medals. The SS members and the civilian workers employed in the railroad construction celebrated a comradeship evening with beer and schnapps. In addition, they received salary bonuses. The prisoners also had "a good day": They were finally allowed to bathe again.

Dr. Kammler never found out how the roadbed looked after the test run. Most of the escarpments had crumbled; the earthen dams had slid. With the exception of one test train that consisted of a locomotive and one car, no other train came to Buchenwald for half a year. For economic reasons, not the entire stretch but only those parts that had collapsed were rebuilt. Indeed, with this repair the roadbed lasted until February 1944, after having been in use for about four to six weeks. But then when the snow began to melt, there were new landslides that again made large-scale renovations necessary. The railroad was finally really ready for operation only in late summer 1944.

A special chapter should be devoted to the private businessmen—all good Nazis, of course. Their work was given to them by oral contract. The required written bids and the ensuing contracts were completed nine months after the beginning of the work, "as a matter of form." Of course all the Nazi firms made enormous profits during this railroad construction. The waste of public monies was enormous. Unfortunately, precise figures can no longer be determined because the records were completely destroyed during the air raid of August 24, 1944. Finally, it must be observed that the maintenance of the railroad roadbed that had been built unprofessionally consumed relatively large amounts of money and manpower.

THEO ECKERT, Cologne

133. MURDERS IN BUILDING THE GUSTLOFF WORKS

DURING THE BUILDING of the "Buchenwald Works," Works No. 2 of the Gustloff Works, I saw the following.

Two SS sergeants—whose names I don't know—drove a prisoner up and down a hill of piled up earth in the woods behind the Wiesehalle, beating him with truncheons, until he collapsed in exhaustion. SS sentries standing in the woods nearby motioned to the sergeants to drive the prisoner toward their guns. That was not very difficult, as the prisoner himself wanted to end his torment and ran into the SS sentries' guns. They cold-bloodedly shot down the tormented creature.

For a second prisoner it went likewise. Thus in one afternoon the SS sentry had lying next to him two victims, whom he kicked with his boots after shooting them.

I observed Sergeant Schmidt, who comes from Apolda and is the son of a tavernkeeper, in the following cases.

1. With his pistol he shot a Pole whom he had struck for one reason or another after he bent over to get his shovel to resume work.

2. A Russian who had irritated Schmidt had to bend over at the corner of a wall in the newly begun Hall 10 of the Buchenwald Works. Schmidt struck the Russian with a truncheon, which he had to grip with both hands so that he could strike him several times on the top of the skull with full force. After that the Russian stirred no more.

3. Schmidt threw another prisoner into a trash container filled with water and forcibly held him underwater until the prisoner drowned.

4. Schmidt had singled out a young, fourteen- to fifteen-year-old Russian who had eaten tree bark out of hunger. Schmidt had a rope in his hand and intended to hang this Russian. But to torture him properly first, he tied the rope securely to the construction scaffold. The youth had to slip his head into the noose. The youth begged and pleaded with him, called for his mother, and in fear of death threw himself on the ground and grabbed the knees of the SS sergeant. Then Schmidt drew his pistol and grabbed the youth's head so that he had to stand up.

Schmidt smoked a cigarette and enjoyed himself. This bestial treatment I observed lasted over half an hour.

MAX PABST, Neu Schmiedefeld

134. SLAVE LABOR IN THE GUSTLOFF WORKS

THE DEGRADING slave conditions that prevailed at the Gustloff Works are shown by the following copy of the "Guidelines for the Prisoners at the Gustloff Works." These guidelines were issued by Camp Commandant Pister but were worked out by the Nazi directors of the Gustloff Works. They are an eloquent document showing that Nazis who did not belong to the SS consciously applied the same murderous methods toward prisoners as the SS executioners themselves. This shameful document has the following text:

1. After November 29, 1943, a report will be maintained for each prisoner stating his efficiency in terms of the percentage of the output of a free worker. As far as possible, the work he achieves is to be represented as numbers of pieces. If the prisoner reaches this number or exceeds the minimum quota, then at the end of the week he will receive an efficiency bonus. Anyone who does not complete his work or produces much defective work will receive a penalty of punishment work in his free time or a withdrawal of rations.

2. No prisoner may leave his workplace without reporting to the master, kapo, or foreman. Conversation during work is forbidden. All trips that are made during working hours must be made at double time.

3. Lack of discipline or refusal to work will result in the strictest punishment.

4. Kapos and foremen will be stationed in the halls so that each has a definite work area. All complaints in an area will fall to the supervisors. The presence of any prisoners not belonging to the work detail is also the responsibility of the area supervisors.

5. Work breaks begin with the sounding of the break signal. Each prisoner must end his work before the break signal sounds. After the midday break, a signal will be given three minutes before the start of work. At that time each prisoner must be present at his workplace so that at the sound of the start signal the wheels are ready to turn.

6. Cleanliness of the workplace is a precondition for the orderly accomplishment of work. Kapos and foremen are responsible for this.

7. Whoever does not follow these guidelines will receive a corresponding entry in his efficiency report.

8. Efficiency reports with good and bad comments will be handed in to the labor assignment officer weekly for his evaluation. The result will be communicated to the camp commandant.

9. The attitude and output of each prisoner help determine a decision on release. Industriousness will shorten the period of arrest.

Weimar-Buchenwald, November 26, 1943
The Camp Commandant

135. The Bombing Attack
on August 24, 1944

IN THE AIR RAID of August 24, 1944, the Gustloff Works, which was of great significance to Germany's war production, was almost completely destroyed. The sole responsibility for the unfortunate deaths of several hundred prisoners in this attack falls on the SS, which at the time forbade prisoners to evacuate into camp during an air raid alarm. During an alarm prisoners went into the open air next to the factory grounds but had to remain inside the sentry line. About twenty to twenty-five prisoners remained in the factory buildings to service vital components (the boiler room, transformer station, etc.). Most of the victims were in the SS enterprises at the construction yard and division supplies, where the prisoners were not allowed to leave the rooms at all. In the construction yard alone, more than 100 prisoners died. Only after the air raid was the new regulation imposed that all prisoners immediately move into camp during an air raid alarm.

The attack began with the dropping of high-explosive bombs on the Gustloff Works, which was completely destroyed with the exception of two buildings. At the same time high-explosive bombs were dropped on the forest between the Gustloff Works and the Bismarck Tower, probably because false reports led Allied fliers to presume there was an illegal radio factory there. (We gather this fact from a caption under an aerial photo of the Gustloff Works after the bombardment, which appeared in an illegal number of the *Flugpost* [Airmail] dropped by English pilots.) The radio factory was actually located in Buildings 4 to 7 and was completely destroyed. After the high-explosive bombs, firebombs were dropped, primarily on the railroad yards and the neighboring woods but also on buildings of the German Armament Works. Some departments of the DAW were burned out. Since prisoners tried to save themselves by fleeing into the woods, they suffered greatly from firebombs.

As mentioned before, prisoners were not allowed to cross the sentry line. Since the sentry line was placed as close as possible to the factory, the prisoners had almost no escape from the shower of high explosives and firebombs that fell on all sides. It was an unbearable situation. Frightened men ran back and forth in terror or flattened themselves on the ground. In between there were the horrible cries and groans of the many seriously wounded. To add to the confusion and the madness of the situation, the Ukrainian SS men who made up the sentry line shot at any prisoners who tried to save themselves by running out of the area where the firebombs were falling. At least twenty prisoners were murdered in this way. German SS men, the supervisory personnel at the Gustloff Works, were also shot at as they lay among the prisoners in the forest. These German SS men shot back at the Ukrainian SS men, allegedly killing one.

All production at the Gustloff Works was shut down because of the bombardment. Only Building 13 and the tool building remained standing. In Building 13 parts for the V-2 rocket were to be produced, but production had not yet begun and in fact was never started because the building was completely gutted. A great number of machines in the tool building had indeed survived intact but were deliberately disabled when debris was cleared away.

In addition to the production facilities of the Gustloff Works, the construction yard, and the division supplies, all administrative barracks up to the main entrance of the camp itself were destroyed. All the records of the political department and the photo department went up in flames. The destruction of these barracks, in which so many murders and tortures of prisoners had been decided upon and carried out, excited utter rapture among all the prisoners.

The SS barracks were only lightly damaged in the attack, since unfortunately the bombs aimed at them fell into the stone quarry. But the so-called I Barracks in the Spruce Grove where prominent prisoners were held, was completely destroyed. The Social Democratic Reichstag deputy Rudolf Breitscheid, his wife, and the Princess Mafalda of Hesse met their deaths there. Also killed were about twenty members of the Romanian Iron Guard who were imprisoned there.

No bombs struck the camp itself; only one bomb fell adjacent to the crematorium. The victims of the air raid amounted to 316 prisoners killed, 1,462 wounded, and one missing; eighty SS members killed, 238 wounded, and sixty-five missing; twenty-four civilians killed. The reports spread by the Nazis that the air raid took the life of Ernst Thälmann, the leader of the German KPD, were complete lies. Thälmann was never in Buchenwald.

The air raid of August 24, 1944, showed that these attacks were directed exclusively against the war industry of the Nazis. The Allied pilots in particular did all they could in order not to hit prisoners. The high number of prisoners killed is to be charged exclusively against the debit accounts of the Nazi murderers.

ROBERT LEIBBRAND, Stuttgart

136. The External Details of Buchenwald

Type of Production in These Factories (Status as of March 25, 1945)[4]

Detail, Location	Number of Workers	Type of Production
Gustloff, Weimar [Fritz Sauckel Works]	1,453	Barrels for 8.8-cm cannons, 3.7-cm tank cannons, self-propelled antiaircraft guns, parts and mountings for 7.5-cm antitank cannons, milling of rifle housings, drilling and stamping machines for aircraft parts
Gustloff, Billroda	501	Building of shafts for subterrannean factory at a depth of 1,800 feet; partial installation of machines from Gustloff, Weimar; no production (antiaircraft cannons of 3.7 cm were to be produced)
Mittelbau, Weimar	21	Aiming devices for V-1 and V-2
Erla, Leipzig	1,466	Aircraft production
Hasag, Leipzig	83	Production of hand grenades, antitank grenades
Hasag, Taucha	461	Production of hand grenades, antitank grenades
Hasag, Altenburg	200	Production of hand grenades, antitank grenades
Hasag, Colditz	644	Production of hand grenades, antitank grenades
Hasag, Meuselwitz	328	Production of hand grenades, antitank grenades
Hasag, Schlieben	1,468	Production of hand grenades, antitank grenades
Chr. Mannfeld Biber II,		
Wansleben	1,389	Cannon production
Rothenburg	76	Cannon production
Junkers Works,		
Schönebeck	1,158	Aircraft production
Mühlhausen	569	Aircraft production
Halberstadt	442	Aircraft production
Aschersleben	425	Aircraft production
Niederorschel	527	Aircraft production
Bad Langensalza	1,240	Aircraft production
Westeregeln	560	Aircraft production
Leopoldshall	163	Aircraft production
Malachit AG, Halberstadt	853	Aircraft production, paving
National Radiators, Schönebeck	400	Electrical parts for the V-2

---

4. This list has been checked against the authoritative listing by the International Tracing Service of the Comité International de la Croix-Rouge, *Vorläufiges Verzeichnis der Konzentrationslager und deren Außenkommandos* (Arolsen: Comité International de la Croix-Rouge, 1969), 24–56.

Detail, Location	Number of Workers	Type of Production
Siebenberg GmbH, Hadmersleben	1,154	Aircraft production
Wernig Works, Hasserode	502	Production of armatures
Heinrich Kalb, Dorndorf [Eisenach]	483	Underground factory building, installation of machines for Bavarian Motor Works, no production
Kommando "Laura," b. Saalfeld	684	Tunneling
BMW, Abteroda	226	Motor production
RAW, Jena	909	Renovation of railcars, locomotive repairs
Brabag [Wille], Tröglitz	2,246	Hydration works, gasoline from brown coal
Annen Cast-Steel Works, Annen bei Witten	613	Production of tank armor
Flössberg Metalworks Flössberg	1,185	Production of tank grenades
"Leopard" [Leau] Plömnitz b. Bernburg	1,081	Cannon production
Polte, Magdeburg	585	Production of grenades
G. E. Reinhardt, Sonneberg	469	Wheels for aircraft
Reh, Stassfurt	387	Production of tank parts
G. Wälzer & Co., Stassfurt	235	Production of tank parts
Kalag, Stassfurt	47	Production of tank parts
Ludwig Renntier, Bad Salzungen	720	Preparatory work for arms production by Bavarian Motor Works, 900 feet underground
Stein, Eschershausen	600	Not yet in production
Railcar Factory, Dessau	339	Repair of railcars
Bruns Apparatebau, Bad Gandersheim	524	Armatures for aircraft and tanks
Gazelle, Weferlingen, b. Helmstedt	451	Organisation Todt assignment Highway construction
Hecht, Eschershausen	495	Highway construction
D.-E. St., Berlstedt	211	Brickworks, production of roofing tiles
Construction Office, Hadmersleben	270	Tunneling and construction of underground factories for armaments production
Wansleben	570	Tunneling and construction of underground factories for armaments production
B II, Halberstadt	4,819	Tunneling and construction of underground factories for armaments production
S III, Ohrdruf	9,943	"
Schwalbe V, Berga/Elster	1,781	"
Construction Office, Giessen	77	Building barracks for police and SS officers
Kassel	151	Building barracks for police and SS officers
Sennelager	34	Building barracks for police and SS officers
Tannenwald	31	Underground command center for Reich SS headquarters

Detail, Location	Number of Workers	Type of Production
Construction Office, Göttingen	30	Repair and renovation work for riding school
SS Officers School, Arolsen	126	Restaurant enterprise in the barracks (unloading supplies, shoe repair, tailoring, kitchen work, etc.)
[TOTAL (not given in original)	46,405]	

137. Antifascist Sabotage Actions in Armaments Factories

Up to the great August 24, 1944, air raid on the Buchenwald Works, about 9,000 prisoners worked in the armaments factories. The following factories belonged directly to Buchenwald concentration camp: German Armament Works (DAW), Polte Works, Optical Workshops, Division Supplies, Mittelwerke, Mibau, Gustloff Works II. These factories were for the most part destroyed in the bombardment and were brought back into production only to a limited extent.

The work of the antifascist prisoners set for itself two goals: on the one hand, to make the work conditions for all prisoners as bearable as possible; on the other hand, to contribute to the fall of the Hitler regime through the sabotage of armaments production. How this happened will be shown in detail in the following.

In the Middle German Construction Company (Mibau), for example, the normal output of a civilian production worker pressing coils on the hydraulic presses amounted to 720 pieces in a ten-hour workday. The output of a prisoner in eleven hours was 350 pieces. In the winding and soldering of the coils, the normal output of a civilian worker was twenty to thirty pieces in 9.5 hours; for a prisoner it was eight to sixteen pieces in eleven hours. In mixing the press material for the coils, the prescribed percentage of the various component parts was altered, and ground-up rubber was mixed into it. The soldering of electrical connections was done loosely so that the apparatus was capable of passing quality control. During further use, however, electrical connections would come apart.

Presses, pumps, and washing machines were "repaired" in such a manner that they were repeatedly out of production for days at a time. A few of these cases brought the immediate participants into danger. But it was possible to "excuse" these incidents by the lack of technical qualifications or the laziness of the prisoners. The civilian workers supported us in this struggle by identifying Nazis and Gestapo agents for us. Indeed in many cases there was cooperation between prisoners and civilian employees involving direct sabotage from above.

In Gustloff Works II it was possible to thwart the speedup [*Antreiber*] methods favored by armaments factories in the external camps in order to create bearable working conditions. SS and civilian oversight personnel, both groups corrupt and interested in "organizing," could be played off against each other. SS men prone to

beating prisoners were provoked into attacking at the wrong place so that the civilian factory management was forced to take a stand against it. Of course, this
struggle had to be disguised as intervention on the behalf of valuable manpower
in the interests of war production.

Still more significant, of course, was our sabotage work. Direct sabotage like
the damaging of machines or weapons was possible only in isolated cases. We had
to use forms of sabotage that were difficult to recognize. The first opportunity for
this came in the direction of work assignments. Prisoner functionaries active in
assignment sent good skilled workers off to factories that did not immediately
serve armaments production, while primarily unskilled manpower was sent to armaments factories. Moreover, reliable antifascist specialists were brought into
those positions where they could accomplish systematic sabotage work. German
civilian foremen, masters, engineers, etc. appointed to supervise the prisoners and
organize the production were almost without exception strict Nazis. Accordingly,
their technical and organizational knowledge and capabilities were in general
completely inadequate, so they were dependent upon the skilled manpower
among the prisoners to function in jobs. We took advantage of these weaknesses.
Antifascist kapos, foremen, engineers, technicians, and skilled workers carried
out comprehensive sabotage through many techniques. They used faulty planning and faulty construction; created delays and mistakes in the ordering of machines, tools, and materials; fostered internal disputes over authority in the factory; exaggerated official instructions and examination qualifications; and other
similar methods. As individual examples, the following results of this sabotage activity are presented.

In summer 1942 the assembly of K-98k carbines from individual parts supplied
by outside firms was begun. A monthly production of 60,000 pieces was equipped
and planned for—all individual parts to be produced in Buchenwald by then—
and 1,800 machines with the necessary equipment and training lessons were ordered. But after all that, following nine months of preparation, it was determined
that the project would be impossible to carry out.

Orders for the already canceled project "accidentally" continued for many
months afterward. Several million hours of work were performed in vain. After
two years of operation, assembly of individual parts did not reach even half the
monthly quota. However, despite all the inspections by the SS, civilian workers,
and the Wehrmacht, it was also possible to smuggle weapons and munitions into
camp for the final battle of the prisoners.

Production of carbine barrels was supposed to reach 10,000 pieces per month.
Machines were ordered and delivered; the facilities were sufficient for a [monthly]
output of 15,000 pieces. After a year and a half of production, the maximum output amounted to 8,000 pieces. Use of special tools amounted to four to ten times
the figures prescribed by the Wehrmacht.

Production of carbine stocks was supposed to reach 55,000 pieces a month. But
only 33,000 pieces were fabricated in six months. The tools used in their manufacture should have been sufficient for the production of 280,000 pieces.

For the assembly of the automatic carbine K-43, a monthly quota of 55,000 was set. But from January to July 1944, only 28,000 pieces were delivered. From May onward production fell especially rapidly, so that at the end only 600 pieces per month were produced. Several thousand already produced carbines were returned by the Wehrmacht because of frequent failures. For months, factory committees, engineers, and commissions from the Wehrmacht and the Armaments Office sought in vain for the causes of the failures, which were well known to the specialists among the prisoners.

Planned production of 7.65-mm pistols, set at 10,000 per month, never came into operation at all. For two full years, around 100 prisoners were employed and machines and tools were put into operation, with the result that only 100 faulty test samples were created.

Vehicle construction of infantry vehicles (IF-14s), signal corps vehicles (NF-6s), and gun carriages (AF-18s) reached an average of 50 percent of the delivery quotas. In the last months this production declined sharply; for example, in February 1945 the production of IF-14s reached only one-fourth of the required amount.

The most important assistance for the sabotage work was provided by the tool building, the actual bottleneck of the factory. Here machines, tools, and training for the Buchenwald Works, as well as for the main works in Weimar, were produced. With 150 specialized machines and 300 prisoners and civilian workers, the required amounts ought to have been produced comfortably. In fact, however, only 15 to 20 percent of the orders were filled, so that at the end of 1944, over 2,000 orders were still outstanding.

Tools and machines continued to be manufactured for production lines that had already long been given up. Other tools were unusable because of failure to take into account design changes that had occurred in the meantime. The wrong materials were used, experienced skilled workers created incorrect or inexact drawings, and clever mistakes that were difficult to recognize were made on precisely the most urgently required tools. All these things made the tool building the bottleneck of the whole factory.

In the long run it could no longer be hidden from the upper Gustloff management that something was not quite in order at the Buchenwald Works. There were investigations, accusations of sabotage, etc. It was always possible to counter the accusations. It was constantly pointed out to the factory management that insufficient production was due to poor nutrition and sanitary conditions that were the fault of the SS. Factory managers' demands that the SS camp administration punish prisoners were rendered ineffective by revelations of corruption and incompetence on the part of the factory management.

After the bombardment on August 24, 1944, the new factory director, Tänzer, a typical opportunist, undertook a renewed struggle against sabotage, but in vain. At the last minute the directors sent in chief engineer Saupe, an agent of the Security Service (SD), to restore order, especially in the tool building, and trace the machinations of the prisoners. Without further proof, this Nazi agent had the kapo of the tool building, comrade Falkenberg, arrested on charges of sabotage, taken from his workplace, and locked into the cellblock on April 1, 1945. But now it was too late for an actual investigation. With the approach of the Allied troops, the Gestapo found no more time to follow this track. A few days later the antifascist prisoners released comrade Falkenberg from the cellblock, where he had barely escaped murder at the hands of the Nazi bandits.

The sabotage work in the Gustloff Works and in Mibau will always remain a glorious page in the history of the antifascist prisoners in Buchenwald. They thus did great damage to the Hitler regime and in every way prepared for the liberation of the camp with the help of the antifascist prisoners themselves.

ROBERT LEIBBRAND, Stuttgart

138. Sabotage in the Buchenwald Gustloff Works

In March 1943, after about a year of construction, the Gustloff Works was put into operation. Rifles, pistols, motor vehicles, and cannons were the areas of production in this factory, which employed about 3,600 prisoners.

Buchenwald antifascists now did everything to damage the Nazi armaments industry and sabotage weapons production. From the beginning it was the goal of responsible prisoners who were appointed as kapos, foremen, engineers, and specialists to guide the sabotage work systematically. Individual actions that could lead to easy discovery were rejected.

One of the most essential factors in the organization of sabotage was the technical inferiority of the civilian masters, engineers, and other supervisory personnel. They were not in a position to find the causes of underproduction or faulty production. Through the years the level of production in most workshops of the factory never amounted to more than 40 percent of capacity.

Chief engineer Franz Tänzer functioned as director of the factory for a long time. Originally an enthusiastic fighter for Weimar democracy, he changed his beliefs and became a typical representative of National Socialist boasting and ruthlessness. Professionally, he was a complete zero. He employed a whole series of prisoners in private duties—had lumber, coal, etc. brought to his home for his private use at the cost of the firm and its vehicles—and as a good Nazi naturally forbade other civilians to do likewise.

Tänzer's right-hand man was the "factory engineer" Sidek, former director of testing at the Gustloff Works. His "professional" remarks always called forth the greatest amusement, and not only from the prisoner specialists.

Shortly before the closing of the doors, a "chief engineer" Saupe appeared as director of the tool building. Saupe had the task, as Gestapo agent, of finding the causes of faulty production. After more than two years, it had slowly come to the attention of the upper management (perhaps even the director, Kast) that something was not quite right there. Saupe had the kapo of the tool building arrested for sabotage attempts but was unable to bring his investigation to a close because the American army arrived in the meantime.

Up to the bombardment of the Buchenwald Gustloff Works, Herr Grosse functioned as factory director. It was rumored that he wore his party pin even on his nightshirt. He let himself be advised by prisoner specialists and engineers, since as a former traveling sewing machine salesman he knew nothing. Thanks to his "intelligence," the prisoners were able to obtain the weapons they later used to disarm and capture the remnants of the SS on April 11, 1945.

In this gallery of National Socialist armaments experts, the SS man Bornscheuer—a man who wanted to shoot all prisoners if the Nazis lost the war—also deserves to be mentioned.

The following gives some indication of the success of organized sabotage: By issuing the wrong materials, failure to consider changes in drawings, falsification of time schedules, etc., the prisoners in the tool building achieved a backlog of 2,000 orders involving 155,000 man-hours—and no one could identify a perpetrator. Severe disruptions of production thus occurred in all departments. Of the K-43 automatic carbines, 55,000 pieces per month were to be delivered. However, in March 1944 only 3,000, in April 6,000, in May 9,000, and in June 1944 all of 600 pieces were delivered. By the end of July, after months of systematic preparation, it was possible to render the production practically insignificant.

When a whole series of tools were manufactured out of the wrong material, flaws appeared in the K-43. Because the firms of the armaments industry and even the Supreme Command of the Wehrmacht were unable to find the problems, the army supply depot returned to the factory the entire stock of previously delivered carbines.

In addition to this organized sabotage, hundreds of prisoners engaged in another sabotage activity: the illegal production of commodities for their comrades in camp, all created using the Nazis' material, without requisition slips and during hours when the prisoners actually should have been producing weapons.

HEINZ GROSS, Sühl, Thuringia

139. Sabotage Actions in the DAW Machine Shop

Many qualified craftsmen were employed in the DAW workshops. After hard years of imprisonment, it was often a great joy for these workers to stand once again at the anvil, vice, or lathe. In the early days work was done only for the camp, so the prisoners had a direct interest in what they accomplished. When the doors functioned well or iron boot scrapers were present, when stairs were placed on solid staircases or water and sewage pipes functioned well, then that was good for all prisoners. No one came into conflict with his own political past if he applied his craftsman's skills to the full.

There were also few reservations when in the following period countless chandeliers, decorative fireplace tools, ornate window bars, trunk hinges, desk articles, ashtrays, letter openers, and mailboxes were produced. There were no limits to the creative genius and productive energy of the prisoners, although this work was the greatest possible strategic nonsense in the midst of war. For on the outside there were demands for craftsmen whose talents were senselessly wasted here, and every pound of iron was considered important. But here 200-pound chandeliers that represented weeks of work were placed in a corner because the architect of a boss's villa could tell only by seeing the finished work that he had acted on a wrong idea when he had ordered the piece. Then a new chandelier was begun, to the delight of the grinning prisoners.

After Stalingrad the prisoners became more valuable as manpower. The DAW factories oriented themselves toward war production. They began to install stamping machines and to mass-produce cartridge cases, barracks lockers, the fittings for them, and antitank shells again. Other types of work, such as the conversion of trucks into mobile kitchens, were also carried out, and lathe work was done for aircraft parts.

The conversion of the construction workshop into partial armaments production led to a series of organizational measures. On the whole the technical management was unable to master the work. Again and again they depended on the cooperation of the prisoners, who in the spirit of antifascism knowingly delayed the technical work. The use of incorrect blueprints and placing machines where the electrical connections would have been impossible to make meant that the machines had to be regrouped. The procurement of materials, already difficult due to rationing, was carried out by following to the letter the orders and decrees of the SS Raw Materials Office and the Gau Economic Chamber.

For example, after production of fittings for the Messerschmidt was started, work was not done according to the blueprints of the Vienna Neustadt Aircraft Works. Through feigned activity, more metal and material was cut than monthly deliveries provided for. Planning was thus thrown into confusion and because of the shortage of materials, inexorable sabotage was achieved. Rapid changes in blueprints caused these cut parts to wind up as scrap.

A special chapter was the production of cutting and tailoring tools for mass-production articles like tank munitions [*Mupa*] containers. Hinge and fastener tools were hardened too firm or too soft and thereby stopped the extrusion presses for weeks at a time.

Direct work for the Waffen SS was in the conversion of cargo trucks into mobile kitchens and command trucks. Among others, 100 Opel trucks were provided for such conversion. The construction blueprints were altered in clever fashion so that reinforcements were omitted. This allowed the truck body to loosen so quickly while driving that even during the loading in Weimar, 10 percent of the trucks were sent back because the body slid back and forth during stiff braking.

One form of production in our factories that should not be underestimated was the rebuilding of 2-cm antitank cartridge shells. These were delivered by the millions in trucks and railcars. Since they had already been sorted out, almost 100 percent of the delivered shells should have been recycled. In most cases, however, only 25 to 50 percent went back through the refurbishing process. Improper storage, in part in the open air, and the use of incorrect boring tools had a negative impact on the recycling.

The air raid of August 24, 1944, destroyed all machines, amounting to a value of 750,000 marks. Plant reconstruction occurred under the most forceful measures of the SS. Nevertheless, by April 11, 1945, production still had not resumed.

Trucks of the DAW were repaired so poorly that the regular delivery of construction materials was not possible. Here, too, the activity of the antifascists, some of whom were prisoners of war working in transport, revealed itself in little acts of sabotage. The last attempt to create an armaments factory out of the lathe and milling works likewise brought no success.

ROBERT LEIBBRAND, Stuttgart

140. SS Robs Red Cross Packages

IN SEPTEMBER 1943 I was sent to the post office work detail, to which I belonged until liberation. Until March 1944 all Red Cross packages that arrived at Buchenwald went into camp without inspection via the state customs office in Weimar. In March 1944 this customs office was taken over by the SS under the direction of SS Technical Sergeant Emil Brettschneider of Ullersdorf near Reichenberg (Sudetenland). On that day began the plundering of Red Cross packages. At least two times a week, Brettschneider sent his wife in Ullersdorf express packages that weighed over 30 pounds each. The contents consisted of items stolen from Red Cross and private packages: coffee, chocolate, cocoa, soap, jam, and above all cigarettes. From August 11 to 22, 1944, all packages for the prisoners were seized at Brettschneider's urging. All stolen contents—eggs, bacon, sausages, good preserves, and cigarettes—were distributed among the SS. In this period the SS stole an estimated 5,000 to 6,000 Red Cross packages.

After the air raid on August 24, 1944, Brettschneider transferred his office (the SS customs office) to the Kohlstrasse in Weimar. From this time on, the prisoners could no longer oberve the activities of the SS as closely as before. But plundering went on even more wildly in Weimar, as proven by the arrest of SS Corporal Visser of Emmerich or Kleve at the beginning of March 1945. He had looted packages so openly that the people of Weimar protested. Visser was to my knowledge under arrest for about eight days. What became of him after that I do not know. Since the SS did not notify relatives of prisoners who had died or been murdered by the terror methods in Buchenwald, Red Cross packages continued to come for these prisoners. Brettschneider intentionally held back thousands of Red Cross packages to justify his existence in Weimar. In this manner Brettschneider succeeded in winning an exemption from service at the front.

The second man in this society was SS Sergeant Gustav Ermert of Sauerland, who engaged in all this dirty business with Brettschneider. In mid-February 1945 Ermert became the director of this office. He, too, intentionally held back Red Cross packages in Weimar. How many Red Cross packages ended up in Weimar is not possible to determine, since no records were kept. At the beginning of March 1945, the International Red Cross demanded an accounting report on the packages received. Through SS Private First Class Lauten of Düsseldorf, I found out that seven railcars with Red Cross packages (an estimated 21,000 to 23,000 packages) were missing.

After March 25, 1945, no inmate was allowed in Weimar again. All work, such as the unloading of packages, that was normally carried out by prisoners was now performed by the SS itself. On March 7 SS Sergeant Oswin Hörnig, who did not belong to the customs office, brought the Red Cross packages remaining at the customs office into camp at our request. He informed us that he had found only twenty boxes (each with twenty packages); all the others had been plundered. How many packages were left escapes my memory.

[no signature]

Chapter Ten
The Liberation of the Camp

Because of the transports that were streaming into the camp at the end of 1944, the existing barracks were no longer sufficient. With no more room in the hospital, many sick prisoners had to remain in the blocks. The SS doctors failed to take any initiative as these conditions developed. To have some control over the most seriously ill in the Little Camp, the responsible comrades in the hospital decided to appoint a doctor for each block. In fall 1944 the spread of dysentery in the Little Camp took on a threatening character, but complaints to the SS camp doctor accomplished nothing. The SS camp administration showed absolutely no understanding for the needs of the hospital. In this situation, too, the prisoners took the initiative to help. Through negotiations with the inmate leadership, Block 61 was set up as a sick barracks. This was not an ideal solution, but since nothing else could be done, one at least had to take action to prevent the spread of illness and a possible epidemic. By isolating the ill, primarily those suffering from dysentery, the danger to the entire camp could be eliminated.

The crisis reached its peak in January 1945. Thousands of prisoners came out of Auschwitz, Gross-Rosen, Monowitz, etc. The transports were all in an indescribable condition. The worst transport arrived on January 25, 1945, from Gross-Rosen, bringing two railcars with 398 dead. The prisoners had marched more than 60 miles in the worst imaginable footwear; then they had been loaded into open freight cars in snow and ice and were under way for three weeks without food. The condition of this transport cannot be described: hundreds of cases of heart attacks, hundreds frozen, hundreds starved. The unloading of the transport at the Buchenwald rail station lasted the entire night. The path from the railroad station to the baths was strewn with helpless and dying people. Frostbite was so severe that toes and other bodily parts literally fell off.

There was no room in the camp to house the prisoners. For five days they had to stay in the prisoner baths, in two tents that stood in front of the baths, and in Block 12, which had neither doors nor windows and was impossible to heat. Also used was the unfinished kitchen building that was likewise without windows, doors, or heating. Every day sixty to eighty dead were picked up from these rooms. Day and night one could hear the wails, moans, and cries of these miserable people.

To help these comrades and at least provide a roof over their heads, the prisoners once again took the initiative. From outside the camp thousands of square yards of wood were stolen, brought inside, and used to construct additional shelters in the blocks of the Little Camp.

That was the only possible way of housing these people in camp. No one in the SS administration showed concern for the prisoners' accommodations. The large blocks in the main camp that were intended for 300 people were now occupied by 800 prisoners. Blocks in the Little Camp held 1,200 to 1,400 people.

In the blocks themselves the most catastrophic conditions prevailed. As a consequence of overcrowding, for example, eight prisoners in Block 7 died of suffocation in a single night. Each block in the Little Camp had twenty-five to thirty-five dead every day. Every hour new dead were brought back out of the blocks. Men lay down in their bunks and died there. The appointed block doctors could do nothing to help. Medications were available once a week: twenty or thirty tablets for a block with hundreds of sick prisoners.

To help things a little, the inmate camp leadership had annexes built on Block 51 and Block 57 to accommodate additional sick prisoners. The conditions in the blocks worsened considerably. Still more transports of prisoners in an indescribable condition returned from subsidiary camps. Many moribund cases were taken out of the blocks daily and delivered to Block 61. The prisoners lay almost without clothing, often without blankets. The excretions of the sick dropped from the bunks and spread a horrible stench through the blocks.

Up to this point (January 1945) the SS was no longer giving lethal injections—a consequence of the trial of [Dr.] Hoven, who stood under accusation of murder for the lethal injection of prisoners. Since the proceedings reached a favorable outcome for Hoven and no conviction resulted, the SS resumed lethal injections for the prisoners in Block 61 at the end of January 1945. The SS saw no other solution to the catastrophic conditions. Schiedlausky assigned Sergeant Wilhelm to go into Block 61 every morning. Here Wilhelm examined the patients who had been admitted and gave them lethal injections according to his own judgment.

Under these conditions the prisoners attempted to save what was humanly possible. Since there were many children in these transports, the orderlies gave them special attention. As soon as there was room in the other sick quarters, young people were quickly taken out of Block 61. In Block 61 itself special cubicles were erected to help the sick who still had a chance to live. Prisoners who were to be hanged or executed in another manner were also admitted to Block 61, where they were provided with the personal identification of dead prisoners and their lives thus saved.

In March [1945] a letter came from the SS administration in Berlin stipulating that the sick receive better treatment. Despite this letter, no additional means were put at our disposal to provide better treatment. The letter also contained an order forbidding lethal injections. Thus from this day on no more lethal injections were performed. According to this letter, the Jews, too, were to receive better treatment. They were to be given equality in their treatment with Russian prisoners of war.

OTTO KIPP, Dresden

· 142. HOW IT LOOKED
FROM THE LITTLE CAMP

O N MARCH 11, 1944, I received the assignment to take over Block 53 in the Little Camp since a transport of Poles from Auschwitz was expected. I would like to mention that the blocks in the Little Camp were not residential blocks for humans but horse stables without windows. There was no place in the block to take care of bodily needs. The initial population was 450 comrades, which later climbed to 1,000, 1,400, and even 1,800. There was no running water or sewers; benches and tables were not available and were provided later only to a limited extent. In the middle of the Little Camp, which extended over an area of fifteen blocks, there was a washroom and a room used as a latrine. If we had to go to the bathroom, we had to walk over 300 yards through the muddy streets.

We suggested to the SS several times that it was urgently necessary to provide the water supply and sewage lines to create a bathroom facility. Each time the SS camp administration rejected our requests. Blankets, towels, and soap were available to comrades in very limited quantities at the beginning; later they were not available at all. If at times we received fifty or 100 blankets, it was only through the cooperation of our comrades in the supply room. Since the SS camp administration had refused to provide water and sewer lines or a place for a toilet, we got in touch with our comrades at the DAW and in sanitation. The materials for the above-mentioned facilities were stolen from the German Armament Works, an activity that carried a death penalty if one was caught.

Clothing was so defective that one could see the bare skin of many comrades. At the beginning we received clean clothing every week but in the last year only every three or four weeks. Even then it was only a poor-quality shirt. Underpants and socks were no longer available at all, even in winter. The majority of the comrades had no coat, poor-quality shoes that leaked, no towels, and no soap.

Anyone can see that under these conditions illnesses of every type, as well as vermin—bedbugs, lice, and fleas—would appear in great quantity. The vermin were often so thick that most people could barely sleep at night, and their bodies were eaten alive. Only the initiatives taken by all decent comrades prevented conditions from getting still worse.

The Little Camp had no fixed population; it was a so-called transit camp. Comrades stayed in the blocks for about two to three weeks, were interrogated, and then at the end of the time were transported to an external work detail. Only a small remnant of skilled workers remained behind. In each transport 10 to 15 percent of the prisoners were incapable of working. These comrades were gathered together in three blocks in the Little Camp. The SS frequently sorted out those comrades who were unable to work and sent a portion of them on a transport to be gassed. The SS also drew blood from them to supply field hospitals. The blood donations were not voluntary.

JAKOB RÜDNIGER, Worms

143. BLOCK 61: THE DEATH BLOCK

IN SUMMER 1943 Buchenwald had the special role of providing a collecting point and dispatch center for captured slave workers. Since only strong and healthy prisoners were selected for the [external] work camps, the proportion of the weak, the sick, and invalids in Buchenwald itself grew constantly. The sick barracks, which were already insufficient for a considerably smaller camp, fell far short of what was needed to deal with the flood of prisoners seeking care and treatment. The SS completely denied the problem, which had been urgently and repeatedly put before them by the comrades employed in the prisoners' hospital.

The situation reached a critical point in 1945. A series of horrible death transports arrived from Budapest, Ohrdruf, Czestochowa, Auschwitz, Buna, Blechhammer, Gross-Rosen, etc. As each railcar was opened, dozens of corpses were pulled out; the road from the Buchenwald rail station to the bath was littered with corpses. Then the SS began to liquidate whole transports right at the bathhouse or in a tent erected next to it, which no regular prisoner was allowed to enter at night. At this peak in a situation that had become almost hopeless, the comrades of the hospital were able to obtain a sole concession: a horse stable, Block 61, was handed over for hospital use.

Although this was in itself a rather pitiful result, the comrades of the hospital believed that they at least would be able to bring the weak and sick prisoners under a roof and provide them with treatment for the most serious wounds and diseases. Because the SS did not provide instruments or medications, the block personnel and other comrades stole the items, mainly from the SS infirmary. The population of the sick in the block rose quickly to an unbelievable peak of 816. It was impossible to have additional blocks made available for the sick; the SS murderers coldly rejected every demand.

At the urging of the camp doctor, the SS headquarters in Berlin at this time decided that no more transports be sent to the infamous, shamefully misnamed "convalescent camp" at Bergen-Belsen. Buchenwald concentration camp would have to "solve its overpopulation problem itself."

This "solution" was as follows: In January 1945 the base and camp doctor, SS Captain Dr. Schiedlausky, ordered that all moribund prisoners from incoming mass transports be brought exclusively to Block 61. There they were "sorted" at the entrance steps by the medical corps chief of Buchenwald, SS Master Sergeant Wilhelm. The weak were liquidated there in the antechamber without even arriving in the block proper.[1]

This new bestiality led to a meeting between the more responsible comrades of the hospital and the senior block inmate of Block 61. Allowing due consideration for the circumstances, they drew up the following resolutions.

1. Despite the strict prohibition, immediately upon arrival of a new transport, one of the leading comrades of the hospital would go to the bath. Out of those the SS murderer Wilhelm had selected for death, the comrade would try to bring the greatest possible number of sick into the infirmary illegally.

2. The senior block inmate of Block 61 had the task of exchanging the identities of as many of those destined for liquidation as possible with the names of the hopeless cases from the block.

3. Furthermore, for this exchange, former SS volunteers, SS informers, and traitors in particular should be selected. (Their names were known to their countrymen because Nazi papers had been found among their personal effects.)

4. All those comrades the SS had threatened to shoot or hang would, as far as possible, be taken into Block 61 and their identities exchanged with those of dead prisoners. They would be released the next day with their new names.

5. By holding back official death notifications, food rations would be collected (several thousand in all), which would be distributed among the various national groups, based upon an agreed distribution quota.

The decisions reached at this meeting were efficiently carried out despite all the dangers. In addition, dozens of comrades who were threatened by a death transport to a bad subsidiary work camp were hidden in the two "preference boxes" of the block and supplied with food stolen from the SS. Special consideration was given to young Jews, who were often transported out of eastern camps to Buchenwald in a frighteningly undernourished condition. More than 1,000 comrades were rescued in this manner in the final weeks.

The "normal" number of deaths in this block ran from fifteen to twenty a day; through the murderous activities of the SS, it rose to fifty or sixty. Nevertheless, this number did not satisfy the SS murderers involved. They therefore "suggested" to the senior block inmate that the sixty TB patients in the block "be sent to the other side." Their intended annihilation was avoided by rapidly relocating those threatened to the so-called Little Infirmary.

In March 1945, when SS headquarters ordered better treatment of sick prisoners and criticized the number of deaths as too high—a complete reversal of the or-

---

1. The use of intercardiac injections to kill prisoners in Block 61 after January 1945 was described by a French doctor, Victor Dupont, in testimony at the Nuremberg trials. Dupont was a prisoner at Buchenwald at the time (*IMT,* vol. 6, 245).

der of January 1945—the SS stopped its murderous activities in Block 61. The comrades of the infirmary could not prevent all the murders of the SS, but they did save thousands of lives at the last minute, disregarding all danger to their own lives.

LOUIS GIMNICH, Senior Block Inmate of Block 61

144. RESCUE FROM THE DEATH TRANSPORTS

WITH THE BREAKING UP of the camps in the east, transports streamed almost daily toward Buchenwald. They produced an overcrowding that in the long run would lead to unbearable conditions, particularly in regard to hygiene. In this situation the SS stood by helpless and indifferent. They left it up to the prisoners to make the attempt, even under these horrible circumstances, to create somewhat bearable living conditions. For the SS murderers, there were only two possibilities for survival: One was open liquidation, primarily of the weak. The other was transporting as many as possible to the subsidiary camps with armaments factories. These transports were in most cases death transports, because the living conditions in the subsidiary camps were almost always much worse and more difficult than those in the main camp.

For this reason, the inmate camp leadership set for itself the goal of keeping in camp all those antifascist prisoners from every nation who were capable of fighting. They were not successful in every case because of the tremendous overcrowding of the Little Camp, in which all new admissions were concentrated. It was clearly impossible for a few comrades to find all the valuable antifascist prisoners among the mass transports and the individual admissions (often an additional 300 per day). The various nationality groups therefore had placed experienced, antifascist comrades as room attendants inside the Little Camp.

Although it was not an easy job, the comrades accomplished it, sacrificing themselves in the knowledge that they could contribute to saving the lives of thousands of victims of fascist dictatorship. The room attendants made contact with their countrymen in each newly arriving transport and reported to contact men the names and numbers of the antifascist fighters who had arrived. These contact men then passed on this comprehensive list from all the blocks to a central office in the labor records office. Of course the SS, which had given strict orders for the further transportation of all new arrivals, could not know anything about this. This selection was thus disguised under the heading of "recruitment of skilled workers," although in many cases it actually meant scientists, artists, doctors, etc.

In its own manner the SS also tried to make a selection. On the arrival of mass transports, it often happened that especially hated kapos, "heroes with the whip" [*Prügelhelden*], were beaten to death by their fellow prisoners when they entered the Little Camp at Buchenwald. When the SS learned of a particularly crass example of this, Camp Commandant Pister ordered that all endangered prisoner functionaries be immediately separated from the transports and lodged in isolation. Despite that, not one of the real murderers among the inmates escaped his well-deserved fate.

In the last two months before liberation, more than 2,000 comrades were rescued from the Little Camp and transferred into the large camp in the manner described above.

STEFAN HEYMANN, Mannheim

145. SHOT WHILE ATTEMPTING ESCAPE

ON APRIL 10, 1945, our external detail from S III, consisting of 160 prisoners, received the order to march back to Buchenwald from Ohrdruf. We walked under heavy SS guard and came to Arnstadt by way of Sundorf. At Sundorf we came to a halt by a well—everyone wanted to quench his thirst. While prisoners and SS men crowded around the well, two groups, each consisting of three young Poles, took advantage of the favorable opportunity and ran away in different directions.

No one noticed this until a woman from the village shouted, "The dogs are running across the field!" This attracted the attention of the SS, who immediately opened fire, a few SS men running after the escapees. From one group the comrade Jurek was brought back alive and was shot at the well before our eyes. The other two were able to escape. The second group was caught by the pursuing SS men and two armed civilians and murdered on the spot. We could not help our comrades because the other SS men kept the barrels of their guns constantly aimed at us. But we clenched our weak fists and swore to ourselves, "We will avenge you!"

JAN JAKUBOWSKI, no. 47716

146. SECRET RADIO TRANSMITTER IN BUCHENWALD

MY JOB IN Buchenwald consisted of building and repairing communications equipment, transmitters, teletype machines, and signal apparatus. Access to all offices put me in a position to find out about many important things. As the situation became increasingly tense because of military developments, the camp administration revealed its intention to annihilate the camp by procuring grenades and flamethrowers for use against the prisoners. Thus the prisoners decided to organize for defense, for which the creation of a means of communication with the outside world was needed.

For this purpose, a French military transmitter was built from parts and hidden in the prisoners' cinema. On the 35-meter band attempts at radio contact were made that were very successful. Shortly afterward a secret radio transmitter was discovered in Dora camp. As a result, twenty-nine prisoners were thrown in the cellblock there, eight were shot, and two hanged themselves. Because a search for a transmitter was being made in Buchenwald, too, with heavy hearts we decided to destroy our apparatus.

At the beginning of April, a transmitter allegedly requested weapons for Buchenwald inmates. We determined that it operated at a distance of 20 miles from us on the 42-meter band. Since the situation in the camp was becoming ever more critical, three Polish comrades made a new telegraph transmitter on the night of April 8 and put it into operation.

With well-disguised shortwave receivers, we were regularly able to receive all the news from Allied lands.

On April 11, when the withdrawal of the SS could be observed from the camp, I immediately called all administrative offices on the telephone. No one answered any more. I was also present at the occupation of the gatehouse. In a short time the wrecked public address system was put back into operating condition, and the telephone switchboard and diesel engine center were occupied.

Two calls coming from Weimar long after the occupation show that in Weimar they still had no inkling of the situation in Buchenwald. At 6:00 P.M. the police president of Weimar [SS Colonel Schmidt] tried to reach the commandant— without success, of course. Around 9:00 P.M. a telephone operator from the long-distance office called and asked if it was true that 5,000 prisoners had broken out. We put her mind at rest, to which she replied, "I am so glad that they are still there!"

ARMIN WALTHER, Riesa/Elbe

147. LIST OF THE FORTY-SIX ANTIFASCISTS[2]

Apitz, Bruno	German
Behrens, Paul	German
Berndt, Walter	German
Bokowski, Karl	German

---

2. Original list not alphabetized.

Boulanger, [Jakob]	German
Bräuer, Heinrich	German
Bul, Theo	German
Busse, Ernst	German
Carlebach, Emil	German Jew
Cohn, August	German Jew
Dietzsch, Artur	German
Drewnitzki, Viktor	German
Frenzel, [Adolf]	German
Gadczinski, Artur	Polish
Gärtig, Karl	German
Grosse, Otto	German
Grosskopf, Richard	German
Gründel, Paul	German
Hauptmann, Hein	German
Heilmann, Paul	German
Jellinek, Wilhelm	Czech
Kipp, Otto	German
Kogon, Eugen	Austrian
Kuntz, Albert	German
Leitner, Franz	Austrian
Levit, Achim	German Jew
Lingen, [Dirk van]	Dutch
Löser [Leeser?], Kurt	German
Mühlenstein, Nuchem	Czech
Müller, Alfons	German
Neumeister, Hans	German
Pick [Pieck], Harry	Dutch
Przybolowski, Marian	Polish
Robert, Jan	Dutch
Schalker, Jan	Dutch
Scherlinski, Alfred	German
Schilling, Paul	German
Schulz, Karl	German
Seifert, Willi	German
Senkel [Zenkel], Paul [Peter]	Czech
Siewert, Robert	German
Sitte, Kurt	Czech
Tressor [Tresoor], [Bernhard]	Dutch
Wehle, Willi	German
Wojkowski, Paul	German
Wolf, Ludwig	German

Those listed above should report to signpost 3 on April 6, 1945, at 8:00 A.M.

148. Hidden from the SS

AT 9:30 P.M. ON APRIL 2, 1945, the German prisoner Otto Kipp came to me and asked me whether I was prepared to hide in my block four officers of the British Royal Air Force. I was immediately prepared to do so and hid them from the SS for several days until the danger had passed.

On the following evening all Jews were called to roll call square. I had about 400 Jews in my block, but I brought none of them to the square. The following night the senior block inmates decided to destroy the documents of all Jews since the SS had threatened to force all Jews out of the camp the next morning.

The next morning, the SS carried out roll call. At 6:00 A.M. two SS men came into my block. They ordered all Jews to move to the left wing of the block. I explained to the two SS men that I had no documents to show who was a Jew and who was not. About 200 of the 400 Jews moved to the left wing. As we brought the remaining occupants back into the block, my room attendant and I were able to bring approximately 100 of the 200 Jews into the block again. Then something happened that I would not have considered possible. A Jew approached an SS man and declared that there were still many Jews in the block. The two SS men went back into the block and brought out approximately twenty more Jews.

On the same day we received the information that forty-six German and Dutch comrades should report to the gate. The SS planned to kill them. I immediately declared myself prepared to take nine of these forty-six comrades into my block to hide them. These nine comrades remained hidden in the block for some time.

JAKOB RÜDNIGER, Worms

149. 21,000 Prisoners Liberated

WE PRISONERS had found out from the press and radio that the American army had reached the area around Eisenach [on Sunday, April 1]. That was our Easter present, and we fervently hoped that the liberators would soon appear in Buchenwald.[3]

---

3. The diary of Ernst Thape, an SPD leader and head of the German committee, covers the period from April 1 to May 1, 1945. It is similar to the two accounts given in §149 and §151. See Manfred Overesch, "Ernst Thapes Buchenwalder Tagebuch von 1945," *Vierteljahrshefte für Zeitgeschichte* 29, 4 (1981), 631–672.

On the morning after Easter (April 2), seventeen so-called protective custody prisoners, criminals with long sentences, reported to the gate for a secret work assignment with the SS. Among them were several serving life sentences in prison, so we all began to fear a liquidation detail. At the horse stable, where 8,000 Russian prisoners of war had been murdered by the Nazi bandits, these prisoners had to dig a trench 10 to 15 yards long and 6 feet deep. They worked under constant beatings for three days and three nights, with breaks of only four hours of sleep at a time. Undoubtedly, the horse stables and the men were to be blown up. On the third day the order suddenly came to fill the trench in again. The candidates for death were sent back to the camp under threats to say nothing about their work.

April 3 brought a new sensation. Camp Commandant SS Colonel Pister held a speech in the camp cinema for the so-called rescue squad [*Bergungstrupp*], which was originally composed of Germans only and was employed in cleaning up after bombardments. Pister declared that he had found out that a secret transmitter had requested weapons for Buchenwald. He knew that groups of foreign prisoners wanted to destroy the German prisoners. But [he said] the SS had sufficient means to protect the Germans. Furthermore, he had "the official duty of turning over the camp in an orderly fashion"; the camp would not be evacuated.

During the commandant's speech, an American pilot strafed the camp with light machine gun fire that fell near the kitchen. A truck belonging to a food supply company that was to obtain goods in Gotha had to turn around about 5 miles outside Gotha because there was already fighting in the city. In addition, leaflets that warned against atrocities directed toward Buchenwald prisoners and threatened retribution against the population of Thuringia were dropped on Weimar.

All thinking antifascists saw the commandant's speech as a brazen attempt to lull the prisoners into a false sense of security to defeat any attempt at planned resistance on their part. That the commandant had consciously lied became evident already the following evening. During the entire day of April 4, relative calm prevailed in the camp. Only new arrivals from external details—about 2,700—entered the camp. But about 4:00 P.M. the loudspeakers reverberated with the order, "All Jews report to roll call square!" No Jews appeared, however, and no senior block inmate made an effort to force the Jews of his block to go to the square and thus to their deaths. When the commandant asked the senior camp inmate why no one had appeared, he said that the Jews were afraid that they would be shot. The commandant replied that the Jews would be sent to Theresienstadt to be handed over to the Red Cross.

Obeying command, the entire camp marched into roll call square at 6:00 A.M. on Thursday, April 5. Then came the command, "Jews step forward!" These Jews were then marched to the German Armament Works grounds. Nevertheless, of those Jews who had been in the camp a long time, not one went to the DAW grounds. On this occasion the burning question was already put before the responsible comrades: "How far can we go with our resistance? And if we must be evacuated, which groups should go first?"

To the first question we had to answer that up to this point the power relationship was still too unfavorable for an open struggle. There was still a garrison of about 5,000 to 6,000 heavily armed SS men in the barracks, which we could not match in either numbers or weapons. On the question of priorities in evacuations, we decided that first those who could not be used in the final showdown should be evacuated, especially those who might turn against us. Therefore in response to demands for new transports, no one was taken from the so-called large camp, in which the militant antifascists of all nationalities were held, but only prisoners from the Little Camp.

While the prisoners of the camp were still standing in roll call square, heavily armed SS men came into the camp looking for Jews. Those who seemed suspicious to them were driven into the DAW grounds with beatings. The Jewish interior decorator Kurt Baum had hidden in the cellar of Block 49. When the SS murderers tried to take him along, Baum defended himself and was shot down by the SS. Of the 6,000 Jews in the camp, only 1,500 went to the DAW grounds.

In the afternoon 9,000 prisoners in desperate and starving condition arrived from subsidiary camp S III (Ohrdruf). At roll call square they were immediately sorted into three groups: Germans, foreign Aryans, and Jews of all nations. The Jews were driven to join their fellow victims on the DAW grounds; the others were brought into camp. On the route from Ohrdruf to Buchenwald, hundreds had collapsed from weakness. They were shot without mercy by the SS murderers. In one village a policeman said to the SS bandits who had just shot a victim, "You kill people and leave them lying there. But when the Americans come, *we* must pay the price [*müssen wir das Bad aussaufen*]."

That same evening the records office received a list of the forty-six antifascists whom a Czech named Duda had denounced. The list was sent by the Gestapo in Weimar. The antifascist comrades were ordered to report to the gate the next morning. Since we expected further SS actions during the night, the antifascists of the camp were all in a state of the highest alert.

On Friday, April 6, only one of the antifascists summoned appeared at the gate: the French manufacturer Bloch. Since no one else appeared, he was sent away. The commandant summoned senior camp inmate Eiden and asked him why none of the summoned prisoners had come. Eiden explained that he knew nothing about the list but he would do everything possible to find the missing prisoners. Because at the time an air raid alarm was sounding, the commandant gave him until the all-clear signal to make the men appear at the gate. Of course the comrades had all hidden themselves so well that none of them could be found. And all of them lived to see the day of freedom.

In the afternoon it was announced that a transport 1,500 men strong was to be assembled to be sent to Leitmeritz [Litomerice] in Bohemia to perform earthmoving work. These prisoners were selected from the transport out of S III, which had arrived the day before. At 8:00 P.M. it was announced that on the next day at least 10,000 prisoners would have to leave camp. During the night the doctor would perform examinations to determine those fit for transport. And in fact in the middle of the night the doctors examined about 2,500 prisoners from the large camp.

After all this activity, Saturday, April 7, finally arrived. Because the liberators we so longed for had not yet appeared, it looked as if sufficient time remained for the Nazis to evacuate the camp. First, 3,105 Jews were herded out of the DAW grounds, marching toward Weimar at double time; forty-seven comrades who could not keep up were shot by the murderous beasts. Next came the 1,500 prisoners for Leitmeritz, who were loaded into open freight cars in Weimar. The SS wanted to send still another transport, since the battlefront was drawing ever closer and artillery duels could clearly be heard. With the help of the camp police who had been assigned to guard the grounds, a large number of the prisoners who were taken into the DAW grounds were brought back into camp again. Thus the number of prisoners shut into the DAW grounds was insufficient to make up a third transport.

Since prisoners would not obey orders to appear at roll call square and since the SS was still terribly irate at the disappearance of the forty-six antifascist death candidates, they turned to more brutal methods. Two hundred SS bandits armed with machine guns were placed by the gatehouse facing roll call square. Meanwhile heavily armed block officers stormed into the camp and sought to drive the missing prisoners to the square with beatings and shots. Finally, the required number of 4,500 prisoners was gathered together and marched through the gate.

SS mistrust of the camp functionaries had of course increased greatly because of the events of the last few days. That evening the radio announced that no prisoner, not even those in the camp police, could appear on the camp streets at night. The SS would take over guard of the camp, and any prisoner the SS patrols found outside his block would be shot immediately. The SS men were in a better mood because they had been told the lie that the Americans had been forced to halt and take up defensive positions. To improve morale still more, around 2 million cigarettes were seized from the prisoners' canteen and distributed among the SS bandits. During these last nights, the fascist mass murders celebrated with wild orgies every night at the house of Deputy Camp Commandant Schobert.

Sunday, April 8, began with a great air raid alarm. Around 11 A.M. the senior block inmates were called to the gate, and the deputy commandant announced, "Gentlemen, we must see to it that the camp is empty by 12:00 noon!" But by now the antifascist front was firm enough that the leaders could reply, "We won't go!" This slogan was repeated in every language of Europe.

When the roll call officer ordered over the microphone, "Camp chiefs, march!" no one appeared at roll call square. An hour later a much milder tone was heard: "Anyone who wants to go on a voluntary transport should report to roll call square." But again no one appeared. The camp was in open mutiny against the Nazi bandits.

About 1:00 P.M. the commandant told the senior camp inmate that the camp had until 2:00 P.M. to assemble the transport at roll call square. If no one appeared by 2:00 P.M., the commandant would have to resort to other means. We soon found out what these "other means" were. At 2:00 P.M. 200 armed SS men came from the barracks into the camp and immediately cordoned off roll call square. Thirty block officers with pistols at the ready went into the blocks and drove the prisoners to roll call square. In this action the block officers confined themselves to the evacuation of blocks in the large camp. The camp administration suspected that those who had organized and carried out this mutiny, the antifascists capable of resistance, were to be found in the large camp. The prisoners of the Little Camp, almost exclusively new admissions from external details, were incapable of forming such a strong and united resistance. Of the prisoners who were driven on to roll call square in the manner described above, 4,800 had to march to Weimar the same day to be shipped out.

That night, as the open resistance in camp became visible, the SS patrols were noticeably strengthened. First Deputy Commandant Schobert went into several blocks himself. He threatened the prisoners that "no pig would leave the camp alive" if the camp were not evacuated promptly.

Monday [April 9], too, began with an air raid alarm, during which several bombs fell in the vicinity of the camp. In the meantime it was suggested to the commandant that he evacuate those prisoners who would only rob and plunder if chaos broke out. This justified our holding back all the antifascist fighters from evacuation until further notice, as they represented a guarantee for the maintenance of discipline. But to protect the other prisoners as far as possible, the International Camp Committee decided to continue a tactic of delay and sabotage. At 1:00 P.M. a new transport was to stand ready. But only after a number of block officers appeared in camp once again around 4:00 P.M. was it possible to bring together 4,800 prisoners for this transport by 5:00 P.M. The much-feared canine patrol departed with this transport, along with all the dogs.

The tension in camp reached an almost unbearable level. During the departure of these 4,800 prisoners, six dive-bombers circled and made steep dives while shooting at military targets in the immediate vicinity of the Ettersberg. We knew that in the night between Saturday and Sunday, a shortwave transmitter built by comrades had sent out the message, "SOS, Buchenwald" at regular intervals. We connected the appearance of these planes with the calls for help and assumed that from now on the camp would fall under tighter control by the American air force.

On Tuesday, April 10, the first American reconnaissance planes appeared early in the morning. At 11 A.M. one of these pilots threw into the camp a sack containing two loaves of bread and a can with about a quart of gasoline.

At 9:00 A.M. the commandant informed the senior camp inmate, "The camp will be completely evacuated today! At 11:00 A.M. the Russian prisoners of war will be the first to go, then all the remaining prisoners at intervals of every two hours!" The camp should have been empty already by early Tuesday, according to the original orders, which we were aware of. We had already delayed twelve hours. It was a matter of continuing to delay the evacuations in order to undermine the plan of the Nazi beasts.

Unfortunately, it was not possible to save the Russian prisoners of war from the departing transports. The comrades of the Red Army themselves decided to march off together. At a suitable spot they would overpower their guards and break through to the American army. The military organizations of the Polish and

Czech comrades made a similar resolution. These three groups were equipped with revolvers and a few hand grenades from the existing stocks.

Although enough comrades for this transport stood more or less voluntarily at the disposal of the SS, again the departure was repeatedly postponed. The Russian comrades marched away from the camp in orderly rows of five each at about 2:00 P.M. instead of 11:00 A.M. The Czech and Polish comrades followed them. From radio reports, we heard that this entire transport of 5,000 comrades broke through en masse to the American army and fought alongside the American troops.

During this evacuation the sound of fighting approached ever more closely from the direction of Erfurt. We suspected that the Third U.S. Army was poised for a decisive strike at Weimar. During this last transport five Spitfires [Mustangs] appeared in deep dives and again shot at military targets in our vicinity.

During the night of Tuesday to Wednesday, most comrades slept fully clothed because everyone reckoned with the possibility that it might come to a final show-down with the SS that night. It could be in the form of a mass murder, a bombing by German planes, or a mass evacuation transport. We found out that Erfurt had fallen; thus we were nearing a decisive moment. The SS was already prepared to flee. There was a constant running to and fro in the barracks; each man packed up his booty and threw it into a waiting truck. In this last night the final victims of these mass murderers fell. Sixteen men were hanged in the crematorium, and twenty-four prisoners were brutally slain in the washroom of the cellblock.

We later found out that our suspicions of a bombardment of the camp by German planes were not unjustified. The commander of the district air force head-quarters, Major Staupendahl (in civilian life the owner of a transit firm in Weimar), had ordered that Buchenwald be destroyed with aerial bombs. But the commander of the airfield at Nohra, who received this order, refused.

The last day of our imprisonment, [Wednesday] April 11, 1945, began with an ominous quiet. The tension grew from hour to hour. Around 9:30 A.M. the block officers came into the camp, increasing the prisoners' uneasiness. But these SS bandits had come only to get civilian clothes from the prisoners. They put the clothes on under their uniforms while still in camp, so they could immediately change into civilians for their imminent flight. The artillery fire came ever closer—at times machine gun fire could already be heard; no doubt then, that the lead tanks of the Third Army were swiftly approaching. ...

[The account of the last day has been omitted from this edition because it is essentially the same as the account in § 151 below.]

Thus 21,400 antifascist fighters, among them 900 children, were liberated from the claws of the murderous fascist beasts. On the morning of April 12, a festive freedom roll call took place in Buchenwald, at which the comrades of the individual nations marched by together, singing their national anthems. After addresses by the representatives of the great nations, an American lieutenant greeted the liberated comrades. A new path, toward the rebuilding of Europe in the struggle for an antifascist democratic world, had opened up.

STEFAN HEYMANN, Mannheim

150. THE FIRST ORDER AFTER LIBERATION

THE SENIOR camp inmate, speaking on behalf of the camp committee formed of all nations, announced the following:

1. The SS has left the camp.
2. Representatives of all nations have formed a camp administration. Its orders are to be obeyed unquestioningly.
3. All should remain in their blocks; the barricades should be left standing.
4. All food and all clothing items are the property of the camp inmates. Those who misappropriate them will be treated as looters.
5. All camp functionaries must remain at their posts and carry out their work to maintain order and provide supplies for the camp.

151. APRIL 11, 1945

NOTES MADE by several comrades and the official report of the camp committee served as the basis for this description of the last day of Buchenwald concentration camp, April 11, 1945.[4]

The morning began so quietly that no prisoner could have expected the day would end with such earthshaking events. A few block officers came into the camp to quickly "organize" street clothing to change into. Hundreds of prisoners

---

4. For an official U.S. Army account of the camp's liberation, see Earl F. Ziemke, *The U.S. Army in the Occupation of Germany, 1944–46* (Washington, D.C.: Center of Military History, U.S. Army, 1975) 236–239. A more recent and more complete account based on U.S. Army sources is Robert H. Abzug, *Inside the Vicious Heart: Americans and the Liberation of Nazi Concentration Camps* (New York: Oxford University Press, 1985), chapter 3.

were in the forest section at the northern camp exit and stared nervously in the direction of the Unstrut Valley. Infantry and machine gun fire came steadily closer; artillery fire could be heard ever more clearly, dull thuds following from a distance of about 3 miles. There could be no more doubt that the lead tanks of the Third U.S. Army were moving ever closer.[5]

About 10:15 A.M. there was an air raid alarm. A quarter of an hour later the senior camp inmate was ordered to report to the commandant [Pister], who told him, "I hereby turn the camp over to you. Give me your word of honor that you will not let this fact be known until the Americans are here, to prevent a panic in the camp. From my side nothing will happen to you."

Despite this declaration, SS sentries remained in the guard towers and standing between the towers. The meanness of this last Nazi deceit becomes clear only when one knows that Pister had shortly before demanded that German aircraft bomb or strafe the camp. The commander of the airfield at Nohra, however, rejected the order.

At 11:45 A.M. fighter bombers appeared over the camp. Shortly afterward the new camp alarm—"enemy tanks approaching"—was put into use for the first and last time. SS men ran around anxiously, hoping to salvage a few scattered belongings. Pister, along with a few of his band of criminals, had already fled in automobiles that were packed full of foodstuffs.

At 12:10 P.M. the loathsome voice of an SS man was heard on the camp microphone for the last time. The roll call officer gave the historic command, "All SS men leave the camp immediately!" The next few minutes passed in high tension, as everyone feared that the SS bandits would carry out a bloody atrocity against the prisoners. But all the cowardly dogs had already made a run for it.

An American reconnaissance plane slowly circled over Niederzimmern, Ottstedt, and Ollendorf. Motors growled; machine gun salvos fired unceasingly; grenades exploded intermittently. The sound of battle came ever closer. Around 1:00 P.M. the first American tanks appeared near Hottelstedt. The mill in the valley near Ottmanshausen burst into flames from gunfire. Shortly before 2:00 P.M. an SS reserve company marched into battle at the northwest corner of the forest. It was greeted with heavy machine gun fire from the Americans and immediately beat a hasty retreat. At the same time twelve American tanks penetrated the forest, moving in the direction of the pigsty. The sentries between and on the towers had not yet received orders, but they gradually began to leave their posts and ran with long strides into the forest.

Now it became clear. The cowardly murderers had left the camp, and the prisoners had to take matters into their own hands. The contact men [*Vertrauensmänner*] of all nationalities gathered together and decided to form a camp ad-

---

5. Abzug identifies the unit as Combat Team 9 of the Ninth Armored Infantry Battalion, Sixth Armored Division (*Inside the Vicious Heart*, 49). Another unit that arrived on the first day was the Eleventh Rangers of the Sixth Armored Division.

ministration made up of representatives of all nations. The prisoners' militia [*Stosstruppe*] was brought together in Blocks 3 and 4.[6]

At 2:10 P.M. four American tanks rolled by in an easterly direction toward the sewage treatment plant. By 2:15 they had advanced up to the forest, from which heavy infantry and machine gun fire could be heard, along with the detonation of armor-piercing shells. The tanks that had advanced to the pigsty rolled by at 2:30 in the direction of the SS barracks.

When it became clear that the American tanks had broken through on all sides, the prisoners' military action in support of the approaching American troops began. The first measure was to take control of the command tower at the camp gate. Under the leadership of the senior camp inmate, prisoner shock troops had advanced on this tower, where a heavily armed SS man with a machine gun still stood guard. The SS man was disarmed and taken away as a prisoner, the destroyed camp command center was put back into operation, and the first instructions of the new camp administration were announced. At the same time prisoner shock troops were deployed to secure the weapons in the guard towers. The barbed wire fence was quickly cut in several places, and prisoner troops stormed the guard towers. Quite a few weapons, including antitank grenade launchers, fell into the prisoners' hands. Several SS men who were hiding in the guard towers were also taken prisoner.

A quarter of an hour after the occupation of the command tower, about 3:15 P.M., the white flag flew from the tower. At 3:40 the first tanks broke through on the road by the SS barracks, drove up to the command center without stopping, and continued their advance in the direction of Weimar. The armed prisoner shock troops marched out of the camp and systematically combed the sections of the forest around the camp perimeter assigned to them.[7]

At the same time prisoner troops occupied the camp armory and the SS barracks to seize and distribute the weapons found there. Into their hands fell a rich bounty of weapons, which was immediately distributed among the cadres [*Aktivgruppen*] of the individual nations. Patrols were sent to the neighboring villages and in places made contact with endless streams of American tanks approaching from all directions. At the same time they managed to track down SS bandits hiding in the woods and take them prisoner. In the first assault seventy-six prisoners were taken.

---

6. The official East German doctrine was that the prisoners liberated themselves. For an especially sharp expression of this view, see Günter Kühn and Wolfgang Weber, *Stärker als die Wölfe* (Berlin: Militärverlag der Deutschen Demokratischen Republik, 1976).

7. Two of the first American observers to reach the camp, Edward A. Tenenbaum and Egon W. Fleck, reported, "[We] turned a corner onto a main highway and saw thousands of ragged, hungry looking men marching in orderly formation, marching east. The men were armed and had leaders at their sides. Some platoons carried rifles. Some platoons had *Panzerfausts* [antitank grenade launchers] on their shoulders" (quoted in Ziemke, *U.S. Army,* 236).

Shortly after 4:00 P.M. the first American armored scout car arrived, followed by the first tanks, which drove up in front of the camp. A comrade who had been imprisoned for twelve years greeted the Americans and gave them the directions they asked for. For three hours, without interruption, the tanks, motorized artillery, and motorized infantry rolled by the camp in an easterly direction.

Himmler's heroes, who for years had slaughtered defenseless prisoners, were incapable of putting up any sort of resistance to the Americans. The landscape around the barracks and the eastern edge of the forest was strewn with discarded objects, from letter paper to grenade launchers. Especially numerous were pieces of uniforms, which the cowards had taken off while hiding in the woods. Almost all of them had already put civilian clothes on under their uniforms to escape unnoticed if necessary. Two SS men lay dead upon the road; all the others had fled like cowards. The Americans had not suffered a single casualty in the battle for Buchenwald.

At 4:45 P.M. the camp armed forces were regrouped and assigned to guard the camp and secure its vicinity. The camp committee met at 5:00 and created a camp council with various commissions. The following commissions were created: security, supply, health and sanitation, clothing, camp administration, and information service.

At 5:30 P.M. a car with two American officers arrived at the camp and was greeted by the representatives from all the nations on the camp committee.[8] Captured SS men and even some Wehrmacht soldiers were constantly being brought in. But the command area and the surrounding territory of the camp had already been cleaned up. The battle for Buchenwald concentration camp had been fought and won.

A total of 21,000 prisoners had been rescued: 3,000 French, 2,000 Poles, 2,000 Czechs, 5,000 Russians, 600 Yugoslavs, 200 Italians, 200 Spaniards, 2,200 Germans, and 6,000 other antifascists. They owed it to the U.S. Third Army and their own international collaboration that on April 11, 1945, fascist slavery had ended for them and a new life in freedom had begun.

[no signature]

---

8. The first car was probably that driven by the PWD officers Tenenbaum and Fleck, whose report is cited above. They filed a detailed "preliminary report" (fifteen single-spaced pages) for PWD dated 24 April 1945, circulated in mimeographed form as a classified document with a cover statement from Al Toombs, chief of intelligence (National Archives, SHAEF, G-5, 17.11 Jacket 10).

Chapter Eleven
The Case of Commandant Koch

On March 28, 1939, I arrived in Buchenwald concentration camp and was immediately assigned to the punishment company. There I was not only subjected to the usual abuse by the block officer Schmidt, but I was also often beaten by the room attendant Hans Dender. Dender was later killed for his misdeeds by members of the punishment company. Every day we feared that one of us might be placed in the cellblock, because any member of the punishment company who was placed in jail unfailingly died of a "heart attack" the next day. One of these victims was the Austrian gendarmerie officer Lexer. I worked in the stone quarry, where men were constantly tortured to death before my eyes, as was the Austrian captain Stahl. For members of the punishment company, packages containing clothing were almost synonymous with a death sentence, as criminal prisoners and SS murderers often got rid of the recipients of such packets to come into possession of good clothing. There was a particular type of prisoner—the "prison dandy"—whose concern for appearance led him to take criminal actions.

On May 27, 1940, at the suggestion of SS Sergeant Michael, I became valet for Commandant Koch. Even the smallest offense was subject to exemplary punishment by Koch. For example, I was not allowed to use his toilet. The daily abuse led me to make an attempt to somehow get out of my position. Along with Eglinski, the valet for Adjutant Büngeler, I took two bottles of Bordeaux from the commandant's wine cabinet, which was loaded with booty from France, and drank them. Frau [Ilse] Koch—the "gracious lady" [*gnädige Frau*], as we had to call her—caught us and told her husband. He reported it to the deputy commandant in the following manner: When Deputy Commandant Florstedt reported to the commandant, "All quiet in the camp," Koch added, "But two drunks in my official residence."

When we were called to the gate, we received blows in the face with a whip from Deputy Commandants Florstedt and Schobert. Next we had to crawl or run over two high mounds of road gravel. Then we were strapped to the whipping block, where we received a gag in the mouth and twenty-five lashes on the buttocks with a horsewhip. Finally, I was sent to the cellblock, where I had to do 100 deep knee bends.

But the actual punishment was still to come. Once again the horsewhip played the main role; then we had to stand motionless for hours on a mound of gravel in the glaring heat without caps. My punishment was interrupted only when Sommer hanged me from the steel door of the cellblock, with my arms tied high behind my back, for three hours. The pain can scarcely be imagined; for months afterward I could use my arms only with the greatest caution. Then came the verdict: "life sentence to the punishment company."

We were assigned to the gardening detail, where the murderer Dumböck required stones and dirt to be carried at double time every day. When we could not take it any more, we went into the infirmary to have our injured limbs treated with hot air and massage. Someone informed the SS, and one day we were called into the infirmary, where Florstedt and Schobert, along with the camp doctors Hoven and Eisele, awaited us. We were taken to separate rooms and had to undress. Eglinski received an injection in the arm, became unconscious, and (according to the testimony of witnesses) flailed about furiously. When I met him later, he was quite yellow in the face, and he still had traces of foam around the mouth and was very weak.

The head hospital orderly, Walter Krämer, was supposed to give me the shot. In an unguarded moment he squirted the contents in front of my feet. Of course in order not to endanger Krämer, I had to imitate spasms. The doctors came, looked at me, and said, "It doesn't work." We had narrowly escaped death.

Many weeks later yet another servant girl had suddenly left the Koch household because no one could stand to work for this Fury. I was once again assigned to domestic service in the Koch dwelling. I had to perform all the work in the house. At a prescribed time I had to wake the children, wash and dress them, take them to the toilet, and wipe their bottoms. Then the dog had to be fed and taken for a walk and the coffee made and brought to the "gracious lady" in her bed, in which she often lay shamelessly uncovered. By day the "handsome Waldemar" [Dr. Hoven] frequently came to her; by night, however, Deputy Commandant Florstedt.

It became worse when Koch went as commandant to Lublin. Dr. Hoven was now with "the gracious lady" almost all day. I was locked into the children's room. Despite this I was reproached for not having done my work correctly. As I said before, I was not allowed to use the toilet (my predecessor was sent to the punishment company for a year for doing so). I was not allowed to leave the house because it lay outside the sentry line; any prisoner who went beyond the sentry line was immediately shot. Thus I had to relieve myself in the cellar, hiding among the coals. The conditions became ever more unbearable. "You will end up on the grill [i.e., the crematorium] anyway," Frau Koch would say again and again. Because of Dr. Hoven, I could not go into the infirmary; a change of work detail was out of the question. I was beside myself and decided to put an end to my life. Finally, I used a few hours when I was alone—Frau Koch was at the dressmaker's—to drink myself into unconsciousness.

When I woke up again, I was lying in a cell in the cellblock. At the open door stood Dr. Hoven and Sommer. Hoven said, "Now you can hang yourself!" and Sommer threw me a rope. To this day I still don't know how I managed to stay alive then. The next morning I was led before the new commandant, Pister, who strictly forbade me to talk to anyone about my case. Then I was held in solitary confinement for a long time. Only Hoven visited me often, because he would gladly have gotten rid of me as a witness to his affair with Frau Koch. He would frequently say to me that he was surprised that I was still alive. His surprise was understandable to me, for through the manservant in the cellblock, Hedelmayer, I knew that Hoven had arranged for me to be given poisoned food. Hedelmayer had regularly dumped the food into the toilet and given me the usual camp meals.

After seven weeks in the cellblock, I was interrogated because I was to be sent to another concentration camp. Hoven, however, declared me unfit for transport since I had strong heart palpitations, and he promised me a "tranquilizer." The next meal was handed to me by the cellblock supervisor Jänisch. Despite Hedelmayer's warning, I ate half a spoonful because I was so hungry. Half an hour later Jänisch came to me and said that I could lie down, although that was strictly forbidden. I became very dizzy. The next day my vision was disturbed, and I had severe diarrhea. Of course I received no medication as treatment. After another seven days I was finally sent away in a transport; of course I had not eaten a single bite during this week.

I was transported to Flossenbürg concentration camp, where on admission I was struck with a truncheon by SS Captain Fritsch and immediately sent to the stone quarry. After all attempts at murdering me had failed, they now tried to get rid of me through heavy labor and constant transports. After only three months I was once again pushed out, this time to Gross-Rosen, where the commandant, Rödl, who knew me from Buchenwald, nevertheless made me a valet. But here, too, I remained only a short while, then on January 29, 1943, I went to Sachsenhausen, where I was employed unloading machinery. My normal weight was 135 pounds; now I weighed only 86.

On September 13, 1943, I was brought to Buchenwald in a normal D train [express train] from Berlin to Buchenwald. In the meantime a lot had occurred. Koch, his wife, and Hoven, along with their worst cronies, had been arrested. I was called by Dr. [Konrad] Morgen, who led the investigation, to make a deposition as a witness. Of course I avoided all damaging testimony because I knew that otherwise I myself would be condemned to death. In particular, I was asked whether Frau Koch had satisfied her perverse desires with me (she would use a small stick to beat the penis she forced a prisoner to show her); I could answer no in good conscience. After proceedings that lasted six months, Koch was condemned to death twice; his wife, however, was acquitted. The proceedings against Hoven and Sommer—on charges of murder and attempted murder of prisoners—were dropped because the crimes were no longer punishable during war. Hoven was released, thanks to his high-ranking patrons, but was [later] turned over to the American army as a prisoner. Koch was shot by the SS on the DAW grounds one week before the arrival of the Americans and burned in the crematorium in Buchenwald.

KURT DIETZ, Tiefenau über Riesa

153. Sidelights on the Koch Affair

I T I S H A R D to know which characteristic of the first commandant of Buchenwald, Karl Koch, was the most prominent: his sadism, his brutality, his per-
versity, or his corruption.[1] There are countless incidents that could be used to
prove each of the above characteristics. Prisoners who stood in close proximity to
him (as valets) could say more about them. I want to report only those incidents
that became known to me as an outsider.

One day a repair had to be made in Koch's cellar. Three prisoners were sent
there accompanied by a guard. Upon their arrival Frau Koch herself opened the
cellar door for them. Every few minutes she came down to see that nothing had
been stolen from her supplies. And she certainly had every reason to be concerned! For there lay at least thirty whole hams, about fifty to sixty smoked sausages were hanging on a stick, and several hundred jars of fruits and vegetables
were neatly stacked up. "Last but not least," about 500 to 600 bottles of the finest
wines and champagnes were stored in special cabinets. The sentry's eyes opened
as big as saucers when he saw them, because SS officers in particular snooped
around everywhere looking for forbidden hoarding. It was, after all, wartime, and
all groceries were strictly rationed for normal Germans. The sentry's reports un-
leashed tremendous indignation among the garrison troops. The provisions in
the Kochs' house probably did more to undermine the morale of the troops than
the best Allied propaganda could have done.

The fact that Koch had lamps made of human skin, which of course had to be
decorated with "artistic" tattoos, did not distinguish him from the other SS officers: They had the same "artworks" made for their own family homes. It is more
interesting that Frau Koch had a lady's handbag made out of the same material.
She was just as proud of it as a South Sea island woman would have been about
her cannibal trophies.

Koch did not at all shrink from utilizing the remnants of corpses. The dental
gold that was broken out of dead prisoners was to be handed over to use in replacement teeth for the SS. But since Koch did not have a gold watch fob for his
pocket watch, he requisitioned some gold from corpses and had a beautiful watch
fob fashioned out of it.

How much money flowed into Koch's bottomless pockets can no longer be accurately determined today. He used every occasion to collect money from the
prisoners, almost all of which he appropriated for himself. He constantly

---

1. A biographical description of Karl Koch can be found in Segev, *Soldiers of Evil*, 144–152.

skimmed off profits from the prisoners' canteen through excessive prices. The supply room, too, had to pay him tribute.

A word should be added about Koch's oldest son. In October 1938 the SS lodging construction detail marched off to work, when it had the misfortune to encounter the commandant, who was walking with his son. The boy said to his father, "Father, make the prisoners lie down!" Of course the good "papa" fulfilled his young offspring's wish: He made the prisoners crawl in the mud for a quarter of a mile, to the amusement of the [other] Buchenwalders. This promising offspring was later sent to the music school of the SS and the *Thüringische Gauzeitung* [party newspaper] praised him as "a cultural standard-bearer of the new Germany"!

When as a result of the wartime economy all journeys by automobile for private purposes were forbidden, this "cultural standard-bearer" happened to come home on vacation. Up to then Koch had had no piano in his dwelling. But since the boy wanted to practice the piano, one had to be obtained. The pianos that were to be found in Weimar did not satisfy Frau Koch's refined taste. SS Sergeant Göbler therefore drove to Braunschweig in a truck and picked up a piano from the factory there. But after a few days this, too, was no longer good enough. Göbler again drove the truck to Braunschweig and picked up another brand-new grand piano there.

STEFAN HEYMANN, Mannheim

154. Koch's New Year's Celebration, 1938

Employed in the kitchen of the SS garrison was a prisoner, a former SS noncommissioned officer, who later died in the camp jail. His name unfortunately escapes me. On January 1, 1939, he was caught in a drunken condition and asked where he had got the liquor from. He answered, "I don't know what his name is; I only know what he looks like."

During the evening roll call the prisoner, whose head was covered with blood from blows by the SS, was led past the ranks of all the blocks. He was supposed to identify the supplier of the liquor. Because he could not or would not, at the end of the rounds the infamous Commandant Koch stood in front of the microphone and announced, "Yesterday some prisoners held a New Year's celebration. Today I will put on a New Year's celebration!" This "celebration" was as follows.

The entire detail for the services building, in which the garrison kitchen was housed, had to appear at the gate—200 prisoners. Koch ordered that every second man—thus 100 prisoners—be given ten lashes on the buttocks with the cane. That day the arms of the SS sadists ached from the 1,000 lashes with the cane. During the entire caning scene, the whole camp had to stand at attention despite the icy cold.

As a finale to this "celebration," the entire camp received no food the next day.

[no signature]

155. THE TRIAL OF KOCH

IN THE EARLY YEARS of Buchenwald, thousands of prisoners asked themselves whether there would ever be a court that would uncover the countless disgraceful acts of Commandant Karl Koch and his companions in drinking and murder. This court came, although not in the manner that many had imagined at the time. Nevertheless, it condemned Koch to death, and his SS companions shot the chief murderer shortly before the arrival of the Americans.

How did it come to the trial of Koch? This mass murderer once had the complete confidence of the inspector of all concentration camps at that time, [SS General Theodor] Eicke, for whom he took care of all the dirty work. This confidence began in the early days, soon after the [Nazi] seizure of power, when Koch distinguished himself by particularly bloody conduct in the early Weserland concentration camps. As a reward he was made commandant of the infamous Columbia House in Berlin. The tortures and barbarities practiced in this Gestapo prison in order to force confessions exceed all powers of the human imagination.

For example, prisoners under interrogation were locked by the Gestapo in doghouses in the prison courtyard. There they were chained up by the neck like real dogs. They had to curl up to lie in their huts, and their food was placed in a bowl in front of the huts, so they could only lap it up with their tongues. They had to bark each time an SS man walked by. Anyone who failed to bark immediately received twenty-five lashes with the cane.

The Jewish prisoner Walter Czollek was treated particularly crassly. Not only was he beaten until his entire body was bloody—he suffered a fractured jaw—but these beasts stopped up his anus with hot asphalt and then gave him castor oil to drink.

These and similar horrors sprang from the sadistic brain of Koch, who was chosen as a suitable commandant for Buchenwald camp, which in its early days was considered a special punishment camp.

His misdeeds in Buchenwald have been spoken about extensively in other reports, so it is unnecessary to go into them here. He continued his misconduct until February 1942, when he was transferred to Lublin. The extent of the trust that the higher SS leadership placed in him can be seen in a telegram from Himmler, which ordered that all Jews of Europe be sent to "Koch-Lublin" for extermination. Of course he conducted himself no differently in Lublin than he had in Buchenwald. On the one hand, there was high living in luxuriously appointed rooms, with drinking parties and orgies of all types; on the other, the most brutal barbarities and sadistic tortures. Koch felt so confident that he carried on these excesses quite openly.

But he had many enemies, in particular those who held it against him that all the profits from money stolen from prisoners ended up entirely in the pockets of the commandant himself—likewise the profits from all the robbery campaigns directed against arrested Jews. Even when Koch was still commandant of Buchenwald, there were many SS officers who kept secret notes about his disgraceful conduct, notes that later would play a large role in the trial.

These people felt that their hour had come when Eicke was no longer inspector of concentration camps, after he had been transferred to the front. A charge of incitement to murder was lodged against Koch, to which were later added charges of embezzlement. This was done with the help of SS General Prince von Waldeck-Pyrmont, Koch's longtime superior and his declared enemy.

The grounds for the accusation were Koch's orders to shoot the two German antifascist hospital attendants Walter Krämer and Karl Peix. This order was carried out by the mass murderer Blank, who was arrested in the course of the trial and committed suicide while under arrest.

In glancing over the death list of Buchenwald, Prince von Waldeck had stumbled across the name of Krämer, which he recognized because Krämer had at one time successfully treated him in Buchenwald. The general investigated the case and found out that Koch had ordered both prisoners murdered because they had treated him for syphilis and he feared that it might be discovered. In the course of the investigation, still more of Koch's orders to kill were revealed, as well as embezzlement of property stolen from Jews. By not turning over the property to the Nazi leadership and instead using it himself, Koch had violated Himmler's orders.

In addition to Koch, others were charged: his wife; the camp doctor, Hoven; the earlier deputy commandant, Hackmann; and the supervisor of the cellblock, Sommer.

In preparation for the trial, numerous witnesses out of the ranks of the SS and prisoners were deposed. The presiding SS judge, Dr. Morgen, was extraordinarily feared and hated by all SS officers in Buchenwald. They breathed easier when Morgen moved back to Berlin because they feared that the investigation could also bring to light incriminating material about themselves. And indeed all of them had acted like Koch.

Koch was sentenced to death twice for incitement to two murders. Yet charges relating to killing "prisoners unfit for work" through injections and charges of embezzlement and misappropriation of funds into the millions were dropped. In addition to Koch, only Hackmann was sentenced to death; all the others were acquitted.

Hackmann was shot by the SS at the beginning of March; Koch was shot seven days before the liberation of Buchenwald.

STEFAN HEYMANN, Mannheim

Chapter Twelve
Reports from Other Camps

ON OCTOBER 15, 1942, all Jews in Buchenwald had to report to roll call square. Two hundred comrades who were registered as skilled workers were selected and returned to the blocks. The rest of us were marched off and put into what was then Block 11, where we had to wait for two days for our transport out. On October 17, 1942, we were locked into cattle cars, sixty men in each, and transported to Auschwitz. There were 405 of us comrades, some of whom had been imprisoned in the camp for years, and we knew that we were going to a death camp. The trip was horrible because we received nothing to eat or drink while under way. We were especially plagued by unbearable thirst. Despite that, we all arrived alive at Auschwitz in the middle of the night.

The SS drove us from the infamous unloading ramp into the camp. There the Auschwitz criminal gang—German professional criminals along with Polish fascists and Polish professional criminals—received us. They stripped us naked and robbed us of all the personal belongings we had brought along. After the usual reception ceremonies (showers, disinfection, etc.), we were brought into Block 4A. The Polish room attendant tried to con us. On the first day we received only half a quart of food; bread and margarine rations were arbitrarily shortened, etc.

The next day a delegation of us went to the senior block inmate and said to him something like, "We are longtime prisoners and will not fall for such tricks. We will guarantee you cleanliness in the mess hall and fair distribution of food, but we will do it all ourselves. The Polish room attendant must not set foot in our hall again, or we will throw him out the window!" After a moment of amazed hesitation, the senior block inmate gave in, and from that day on we had order. Nonetheless, the Polish criminals tried several more times to attack our food carrier, but they had to beat a bloody retreat. These incidents gave us Buchenwalders a good name in Auschwitz. They were the reason why, in comparison to other transports of Jews, which were almost totally destroyed, a relatively large number of comrades from our transport remained alive.

Two days after our arrival in Auschwitz, we were sorted out by the roll call officer and the work detail officer. The older comrades and almost all of those who wore glasses were pulled out and sent to Birkenau, where they were gassed the next day, as we later found out. On the sixth day the rest of us were moved to the camp called Monowitz, which belonged to the enormous Buna Works of I. G. Farben, about 5 miles away from Auschwitz. I remained in this camp until the evacuation on January 16, 1945.

When we arrived in Monowitz, the camp was only half finished. Only a few barracks had been crudely erected. Between the barracks there was still a plowed field; the fence consisted of poles without any wire, etc. When a man wanted to go to the toilet, he had to wade in knee-deep mud and call out to the sentry who guarded the toilet; otherwise he would be shot. From the first day on, we were cheated out of food. The cooks were always drawn from the Polish and German professional criminals, who together with the SS skimmed off hundreds of pounds of prisoners' food.

After the rations were further shortened in 1944, the SS men, especially kitchen chef Beiersdorfer, established margarine-free days for the prisoners to stretch the remaining supplies of margarine. It became somewhat better in July 1944 when an Austrian political prisoner, Fiala, took over the kitchen and at least made certain that the prescribed portions were fairly distributed to the prisoners.

The deputy commandant during this whole time was SS Captain Schöttl, who never distinguished himself by any sort of [excessive] cruelties. But he nevertheless faithfully carried out every order, whether it was whipping or hanging, and spent the rest of the time sitting with a bottle of schnapps or sleeping. The commandant who first arrived in Monowitz in July 1944, however, was SS Captain Schwarz, one of the greatest criminals from the early days of Dachau. In Monowitz, too, he distinguished himself by constant whippings and arbitrarily imposed punishments. His hands were somewhat tied, though, because I. G. Farben paid wages only for prisoners who were capable of working.

In addition to the usual punishments imposed in other camps, there was in Monowitz a punishment detail in a mine, which was almost routinely associated with the deaths of the prisoners assigned to it. There were several roll call officers. One was SS Master Sergeant Remmele, who earlier in Dachau had proven himself one of the worst beaters and in Monowitz conducted himself accordingly. There were also SS Master Sergeant Göring; SS Technical Sergeant Hövner, who had four "brides," all of whom he infected with syphilis, for which he was placed under house arrest; and SS Master Sergeant Rackers, the most corrupt SS man that I ever became acquainted with in a camp. He also stole from the prisoners during inspection of the lockers.

The blocks were very primitively constructed. There was sleeping space for only about 170 people, but more than 200 prisoners were squeezed together. The day-room was very small and served as a gathering place for only a handful of "prominents": kapos, foremen, etc. The prisoners therefore spent all their time in the overcrowded sleeping room. The washing facilities were totally unsatisfactory and were located in some buildings adjacent to the living quarters. There were prisoners who, by choice or by circumstances, did not wash themselves for weeks at a time. There was no bathing facility until the end of 1943, so for almost a year the prisoners could not bathe themselves. The distribution of food caused the greatest difficulties because there were not enough bowls for eating. Only in the final months was it possible for nearly every prisoner to have eating utensils, although most were made by the prisoners themselves out of discards from the Buna Works. In the early months in most blocks there were only about fifty sets of dishes for every 200 prisoners. The distribution of meals therefore often took two to three hours, so no one had much left of the very limited free time.

In addition to the poor housing and still worse food, the third enemy of the prisoners was the catastrophic clothing situation. Because of the crimes of the Polish professional criminals in the clothing room, thousands died a miserable death. Often good clothes and shoes arrived at Monowitz. But they were immediately bartered to civilians for geese, hams, butter, and especially schnapps. At times it was so bad that well over half the camp walked around with injured feet. In this case, too, pressure from the German and Austrian political prisoners brought about some improvement later.

The work period consisted of at least eleven hours per day; in the summer it was thirteen hours. The persecutions and punishments usual in other camps, such as punishment exercises and punishment details, were in general dropped. This was because the prisoners were sold as slave workers to I. G. Farben industries and were relatively well paid for. There was a difference between skilled workers and other workers. On average I. G. Farben paid the camp a total of 17,500 marks per month for the slave workers. In the beginning there was only excavation work. Many prisoners of the SS as well as the German professional criminals who at that time were placed over them as kapos were beaten to death or driven into the sentry line. Only gradually did the prisoners come into special work details and workshops. There, for the most part, they had an essentially better life and did not have to work as hard. Prisoners were even employed as bookkeepers in the Buna Works.

The internal organization of the camp was like that in all camps. Even though the senior camp inmate, Kozwarra, a professional criminal from Breslau, appeared from the outside to have power, the actual camp leadership was nevertheless in the hands of the Buchenwald comrades. From their arrival until the last days, they stuck closely together. Because of this, the Monowitz camp came to be known in other Auschwitz camps as "the Jewish Republic." Through our efforts, of the 310 Buchenwald Jews who first came to Monowitz, 110 were still alive at the end. In contrast, for example, out of a transport of 500 Norwegian Jews, only twelve remain alive; and out of a transport of about 1,000 German Jews, at the end only forty-seven were still in the camp. Comradeship and mutual help led to this result.

With time we took over the most important camp positions. The roll call clerk was first Gustav Herzog of Vienna, then Walter Blass of Breslau. The labor service office, which determined the placement of prisoners, was led by Erwin Schulhof of Pilsen. The orderly room of the hospital was led by Stefan Heymann of Mannheim. With the help of the labor assignment office, thousands of comrades were taken out of bad details and placed in the factory buildings or as skilled workers. A special emphasis was placed on the rescue of young Jews, because at times over

1,500 Jewish boys under eighteen were in the camp. Citing the need to train qualified skilled workers, we had special apprenticeship courses or schools set up, financed by I. G. Farben.

The prisoner hospital at first stood under the leadership of Ludwig Wörl, a German antifascist from Munich who put the main emphasis on the struggle to prevent epidemics, especially typhus. This battle was conducted in such exemplary fashion that despite three outbreaks of typhus among the new prisoners, the epidemic was limited to new prisoners; none of the prisoners from the older population became sick. In June 1943 Stefan Budziaszek, a Polish fascist doctor from Auschwitz, became senior block inmate at the hospital. Making common cause with the SS, he expressed his anti-Semitism by sending as many Jews as possible to Birkenau for gassing. The gas chamber was the nightmare that constantly threatened every individual.

At the beginning of the camp, the practice was immediately to transfer all sick prisoners to Auschwitz, where most were sacrificed in the gas chambers. Later, when in addition to the seriously ill, hundreds of prisoners near death from starvation staggered through the camp, these methods were no longer sufficient. The SS doctors assembled all the weak prisoners in transports of about 300 to 400 and sent them to Birkenau for gassing. The SS murderer who raged most viciously was Dr. Endres. But SS Captains Fischer and König also arranged such transports from time to time. Budziaszek, never satisfied with that, always made new proposals for death transports, until finally the prisoner doctors in the hospital unanimously stood up to him. To get around this resistance, Budziaszek one day demanded a list of [those with] bodily infirmities that he said would lead to the granting of supplemental food rations. The prisoner doctors of course put as many names as they could on this list so that as many comrades as possible would receive the supplement. All those on the list were sent away for gassing—387 prisoners as victims of one Polish anti-Semite! Of course this trick could only be used once. Altogether during the twenty-six months that Monowitz existed, approximately 23,000 prisoners were sent to death by gassing.

Our struggle against the SS and its methods of murder was especially difficult because, as antifascist Jews, we had the German professional criminals as well as the Polish fascists against us. From the very beginning we thus sought to establish international links among all antifascist forces, and through patient work we succeeded in doing so. We saw it as our chief task to support and protect all valuable antifascist forces, particularly from the standpoint of their fighting capabilities. With very few exceptions, we were successful. Often at great personal risk, we rescued comrades who were already on the death list and brought them back to life with extra food and a change of work details. An exchange of names with the dead was not possible, since each prisoner, with the exception of Reich Germans, had his number tattooed on his arm. In addition, I could illegally give barracks rest, so that a weakened comrade could be pulled out of work for months at a time. And finally, since I administered the pharmacy, I could help sick comrades with good medication. Through this cooperative work, it was possible to save the lives of thousands.

Thus our antifascist struggle was not just limited to saving endangered comrades. It went beyond that: The eastern European workers employed in the Buna Works and the English prisoners of war, with the help of Polish partisans, tried to take over the camp at the approach of Russian troops and thus save our lives. Unfortunately, it never came to that because the camp was evacuated on January 16, 1945, while the Russian troops were still 50 miles away from Buna. We tried to make contact with the partisans but got no results, as the unfortunate split in Poland had crippled any sort of activity.

Therefore we marched night and day with only a short pause at Gleiwitz. Anyone who fell along the way was mercilessly shot. Nevertheless, many Polish-speaking comrades were able to escape. From Gleiwitz we traveled in open coal cars on a four-day journey through the protectorate [Czechoslovakia] to Buchenwald. When our transport was supplied with food under way, it was only an occasional bowl of soup, a piece of bread, or a swallow of coffee. Most of us were so weakened by the transport and the preceding hardships in camp and on the march that of the 4,500 comrades who were loaded in Gleiwitz, only 3,982 arrived at Buchenwald alive. A total of 470 corpses were unloaded from the cars and several hundred more died in the early weeks at Buchenwald from the consequences of the horrors of the evacuation transport.

It is impossible in this framework to give a precise report of the conditions in Auschwitz and its auxiliary camps. Here it is only a question of showing how the antifascist struggle maintained in the Buchenwald camp was continued under much more difficult conditions by the old Buchenwald prisoners. That is why this report belongs in the overall report on Buchenwald concentration camp.

STEFAN HEYMANN, Mannheim

157. Selections in Birkenau

Selection—that was a terrifying word for every Jew in Auschwitz. It hung like the sword of Damocles over each Jew. All Jews who were injured at work or in bomb attacks, who had wounds (and how many flesh wounds there were!) or skin rashes, who had fever or malaria, who were afflicted by typhus, as well as the great number of undernourished, called the "Muslims" [*Muselmänner*][1]—all, all of them, were murdered.

Selections occurred at irregular intervals, sometimes after two to three months, then after four to five months, then again, as in January 1944, twice within two

---

1. The term *Muselmänner*, or Muslims, was common concentration camp slang for those weakened prisoners near death who were characterized by their vacant expressions. See Des Pres, *Survivor*, 62, 88, 90, 92. Dr. Victor Dupont also mentioned the term in his Nuremberg trial testimony (*IMT*, vol. 6, 245).

weeks. These last selections alone took from the men's camp B II d in Birkenau 1,200 victims each, out of about 4,000 Jews, so around two-thirds of the Jewish prisoners were liquidated. At this time there were in Auschwitz and the immediate vicinity around thirty camps for men and two camps for women with varied numbers of prisoners. A total of 40 percent of the men and 60 to 70 percent of the women were murdered in January [1944].

If the SS doctor came with his staff, the cards had to be quickly altered ("non-Aryans" became "Aryans"). Jews had to undress completely and were quickly observed from front and rear. Then, according to whim, they were sent to the right to record the prisoner number tattooed on the arm; that meant the death sentence. Or they were sent to the left, that is, back to the barracks; that meant a prolongation of life.

When the "action" had been completed in the entire camp, those selected for death by gassing were transferred to gassing barracks. There they were placed under especially strict guard, since they were "condemned to death." Often they remained there for two to three days, usually without food, since they were already considered to be "disposed of" [*abgesetzt*]. They remained in the throes of death, a death only these totally depraved Nazi beasts could think of.

Once a seventeen-year-old boy who was selected for being undernourished said to me, "Hopefully it will go quickly and not cause too much pain. That is the only thing I am afraid of!" For everyone knew that when there was a shortage of gas, too little gas was let in. Then the final suffering, the death by suffocation, lasted three, four, or five minutes, even to the point that many living bodies were shoved into the ovens. Nevertheless, they traveled the road to death not yet broken morally, singing the Internationale, the Hatikvah, and cursing the SS bandits: "Today us, tomorrow you!"

After these two selections in January 1944, there followed at the end of February the liquidation of the second transport of "privileged" Jews from Theresienstadt. It had about 4,000 to 5,000 men, women, and children.

Transports of Jews from Hungary began in March. By August around 400,000 people were gassed and 40,000 were brought into the death camp as work slaves. Today only a few thousand of these are still alive because these [Nazi] criminals viewed the Hungarian Jews in particular as a welcome reserve of manpower for the new armaments works.

WALTER BLASS, Breslau

158. LETHAL INJECTIONS IN AUSCHWITZ

THE DEATH RATE at Auschwitz concentration camp, where I worked in the central records office of the prisoner hospital, stood at 400 to 500 a day. Only a minority died in the beds of the hospital; the majority were those beaten to death by the kapos of work details and, above all, those who were given lethal injections. At Auschwitz the lethal injections went as follows: The prisoner, held down by two men, received an injection of 10 cc phenol directly into the heart. Those who received lethal injections were in part the ill who had reported to the SS doctor, in part working prisoners who were ordered to the prisoner hospital especially for this purpose.

Sick prisoners came in the evening to the outpatient department, where they were hastily examined by a prisoner doctor. If their condition was extremely poor, they were immediately admitted and placed in the so-called reception room. All of the day's patients lay there, mixed together without regard as to whether they had typhus, diarrhea, pneumonia, or a broken leg. Since only the most severely ill were put into this room, many died there every day without ever having been seen by the SS doctor.

If a sick person was fortunate enough to survive the reception room, he was then presented to the SS doctor as a sick call reportee [*Arztvormelder*]. All sick call reportees waited for the SS doctor in the outpatient department of the prisoner hospital. They were stripped naked and arranged in rows by nationalities, not according to their illnesses. The seriously ill patients had to stand on the damp floors and wait for hours until his honor, the camp doctor, had slept his fill. When he finally came, each had to show him a sick card, and the SS doctor sorted them out, one group of cards to the left, another to the right. One group was admitted to the hospital as normal patients; the other was to be given lethal injections. Immediately afterward the records office received the patient's sick card with the note "to be stricken off."

It was my task to invent a diagnosis and cause of death for each of them. In addition we had to write a letter to the camp headquarters for each of the dead. We had a model [letter], which read approximately as follows:

Prisoner No. _____ (last name and first name) died on _____, 194 –, in the hospital at Auschwitz concentration camp. He was admitted on _____ (date at least one week earlier) because of fever and pains on the left side of the chest. A careful clinical examination and an analysis of X-rays resulted in a diagnosis of pneumonia in the left lobe. Despite intensive therapy, attempts to improve the patient's condition were not successful. The illness was complicated by weakness of the heart, which was treated by every cardiac medication. The patient died after prolonged suffering on _____ at _____ o'clock. Cause of death: Heart failure and pneumonia.

Signed, the Camp Doctor

With these letters the SS murderers believed they could cover up their shenanigans in case of a possible investigation. One can easily imagine our feelings in the records office when we had to fill out death certificates, often for acquaintances and comrades who were friends, and when we saw comrades who were often not even sick but merely starving taken away for lethal injections.

It is well known that the prisoners admitted to the hospital were also subjected to frequent "selections" for gassing. I would not like to go into more detail on that but would like to describe the second category, those who received lethal injections although they were still able to work. Newly admitted prisoners, completely naive about the actual situation in Auschwitz, often answered questions about their health by reporting some sort of "complaint" in order to be assigned lighter work. All of these were eventually ordered to report to the hospital building and were poisoned. The largest number were prisoners who were fully capable of working.

At evening roll call came the simple command, "Lift up your pants legs." Then an SS medical corpsman (SDG) or a block officer walked through the rows looking for those who had swollen legs. Those chosen had to step forward and were ordered, "About face, to the hospital! March!" There they were taken directly to the morgue, at the entrance to which a medical corpsman stood with a needle and carried out his murderous handiwork. Maybe hundreds died that way in a day. In addition to the SS doctors, the much-feared corpsman Klähr had thousands of deaths on his conscience.

LEO EITINGER, Drontheim

159. EXPERIENCES OF A FIFTEEN-YEAR-OLD IN BIRKENAU

On May 20, 1944, I arrived at Auschwitz-Birkenau as a fourteen-year-old from the camp at Theresienstadt. The crematorium greeted us with its horrible tongues of flame coming out of its smokestacks. Those of us able to march set out toward the camp on foot and had to carry the sick. Many of the elderly refused to cooperate with the SS, which had taken the last little piece of food from them. They were killed on the spot. After midnight we entered the camp. In the camp we went to join the Czechs; for the first two days we got nothing to eat. In these two days we saw how people who had once been good human beings had turned into ravening wolves. They did not care that we were their countrymen; they beat us to save their own lives.

In the camp it was well known that every transport was gassed after six months. I had been in the camp a month when the oldest transport was gassed. They took us immediately to the selection, at which the strongest men and women were sorted out. The remainder were gassed.

After a lengthy struggle our senior camp inmate was granted 100 strong young people capable of hard work. Out of 1,500 people the camp doctor, SS Captain [Josef] Mengele, selected ninety-eight. I was among the "strong." We immediately went into camp; the rest of the family camp were gassed. In camp I became a helper in the kitchen. I visited the barracks of the Jewish work detail, which worked in the crematorium. These comrades told me about the horrors of the crematorium, where I would later work. After May 19 [1944] the Hungarian transports began arriving, with around 7,000 people daily.

I will now describe the crematoriums and the transports. At the station 2,000 people got off the trains. They had to throw away all their luggage. Afterward the men and women were divided into two groups, at which the larger boys were assigned to the group with the men. Then that great devourer of Jews, Mengele, drove by in a car, seeking out the strongest from each transport. They numbered around thirty out of 2,000. The remainder were led away by SS Technical Sergeant Moll, the officer of the crematorium. The elderly were loaded onto dump trucks and then dumped into burning trenches while still alive. The remainder were led into the gas chambers. Meanwhile new transports were arriving.

In front of the gas chamber was a dressing room. On its walls was written in all languages: "Put shoes into the cubbyholes and tie them together so you will not lose them. After the showers you will receive hot coffee." Here the poor victims undressed themselves and went into the chamber. There were three columns for the ventilators, through which the gas poured in. A special work detail with truncheons drove the people into the chamber. When the room was full, small children were thrown in through a window. Moll grabbed infants by their little legs and smashed their skulls against the wall. Then the gas was let into the chamber. The lungs of the victims slowly burst, and after three minutes a loud clamoring could be heard. Then the chamber was opened, and those who still showed signs of life were beaten to death.

The prisoners of the special work details [*Sonderkommandos*] then pulled the corpses out, took their rings off, and cut their hair, which was gathered up, put in sacks, and shipped to factories. Then they arranged the corpses in piles of ten each. After Moll had counted them, they were taken to the ovens, or if the crematoriums were insufficient, thrown into fire trenches. Once it happened that a victim crawled out of a burning trench. He was beaten to death with truncheons. Once Moll put a naked woman in the trench and shot her in the genitals. Another time Moll found a ring on a member of the special work detail. He ordered naphtha poured over him and had it lighted. On another occasion he arranged twelve women who were lined up behind each other in a row, so that their heads were at the same height. Then he mercilessly shot through them all with a single bullet. He hanged a man up by his hands and shot him until his arms were torn through; then he hanged him up by the feet and repeated the process.

Once an Italian woman, a dancer, was brought to the crematorium. That drunken pig, the roll call officer Schillinger, ordered her to dance naked. She took advantage of a favorable moment, came near him, grabbed his pistol away from him, and shot him down.[2] In the exchange of gunfire that followed, the SS won of

---

2. This incident became one of the more famous stories of resistance to the Holocaust. Because of its ubiquity and the vagueness of its source, Lawrence L. Langer (citing Kogon and Bettelheim) treats it as probably mythical; *Versions of Survival* (Albany: State University of New York Press, 1982), 43. It seems somewhat more credible in this account, as the source was a fifteen-year-old child who reported it even before the war was over and before any published accounts had appeared. See *SSS,* 186; *TPH,* 240; Bettelheim, *Informed Heart,* 259.

course. Once Moll took a family of six. First he shot the youngest in the presence of the rest, then he shot the older ones and finally the father and mother. Thousands of women with shaved heads asked about their children and husbands. I lied to thousands of women, telling them that their loved ones were still alive, even though I knew very well that they were all dead.

JANDA WEISS, Brünn (Brno)

160. Treblinka Extermination Camp

I WAS A MERCHANT, living with my wife and son in Kattowitz [Katowice, Poland]. At the beginning of the war, we fled to Kielce, to my wife's parents. Without any reason, I was arrested by the Gestapo and jailed for four months. Repeated abuse was the order of the day: whippings, kickings, and bites by vicious watchdogs. After bribing a Gestapo agent, I was released.

In July 1942 the ghetto in Kielce was evacuated, and the ghetto residents were brought to Treblinka. We were transported in cattle cars, eighty to 100 persons jammed together in each car. Beatings by truncheons, rifle butts, and countless shootings were part of our treatment. The only luggage we were permitted was hand baggage. I was separated from my wife and never saw her again. Shortly before the evacuation of the ghetto, all sick persons were killed. That included those at home as well as in the hospital, in addition to residents of old people's homes and children in orphanages—a total of 400 to 500 people. The majority were killed through injections, the remainder through shooting.

As a strong, young person I was employed at Kielce in burying corpses in a large trench, inside a spacious garden on the Obrzejgasse on the grounds of a forester's house. About fifty to sixty Jews were occupied with this work. The corpses were thrown into the trenches fully clothed. We had to search through them for jewelry and gold and turn the valuables over to the SS, along with all the money we found. The corpses were covered with potash, the trenches covered over. As we worked, we were beaten and driven on by truncheons. Afterward we were herded into the synagogue, and Gestapo Chief Thomas chose a portion of us to be transported to Treblinka. I was one of those Jews. I know nothing of the fate of those Jews left behind in Kielce.

The transport was horrifying. We were jammed together in railcars; children cried; women became hysterical. Before being loaded onto the railcars, we were robbed of money and jewelry. At first some were shot because they did not immediately turn over their valuables. At the ghetto square we had stood from 4:00 in the morning until 4:00 in the afternoon; then came the transport to the railroad station and the loading onto railcars. The next day, at about 3:00 in the afternoon, we arrived at Treblinka. The railroad station had a large sign with the inscription

"Work Camp Treblinka." From there the train drove onto a siding that went into the forest. I would estimate the distance at 2 to 3 miles.

At this final destination we were presented with a picture of terror and horror. Hundreds of corpses were lying around; in between were pieces of luggage, clothing, suitcases, all jumbled together. We were driven out of the railcars; SS and Ukrainian SS men climbed onto the roofs of the railcars and shot wildly and indiscriminately at the crowd. Men, women, and children wallowed in pools of blood. People screamed and cried. Those who were not struck down were driven over the piles of dead and dying into a square surrounded by barbed wire. Two wooden barracks flanked the open space.

Along with some others, including a certain Gottlieb from Kielce, I was chosen to clean the railcars. As we worked, we could see that all participants in the transport had to squat on the ground. SS and Ukrainian SS men were posted on the roofs of barracks and mowed everyone down with their machine guns. In thirty to forty minutes, thousands of people were killed or wounded. Escape was impossible; only a few individuals managed to jump into an open well, at the bottom of which they were left lying with broken bones and cracked skulls, as I later saw for myself.

Along with several colleagues I had to pick up the corpses from the square and take them to a large trench that had been dug out by bulldozers. Whether dead or merely wounded, all were thrown into the trench. A "mercy shot" for the wounded was a rarity. From time to time the trenches were sprayed by machine gun fire; many corpse carriers lost their lives that way.

We were chased and driven on in our grim work by SS guards who had a drink in one hand and a truncheon or pistol in the other. Trembling from terror and agitation, thirsty, with shaking legs, half crazy from pain and fear, we had to complete our work with the most gruesome images before our eyes. Even now I am horrified by the memory of SS men grabbing small children by the feet and killing them by smashing them against tree trunks, often before the eyes of their sobbing and wailing mothers.

"Willner, bookkeeper with the Orion Firm in Kielce, can't go on; he requests a 'mercy shot' from the SS officer."

"What, with tits like that!" (We worked with bare chests.) "Don't you want to work anymore?" That was his reply, along with punches, beatings, and kicks. The man could not continue; finally the mercy shot came from a drunken Ukrainian.

We got nothing to eat, even though for weeks at a time the special work detail had to perform the same heavy, exhausting work. Two to three transports came in a day. We nourished ourselves with the food that we found in the luggage of the poor victims. We suffered terribly from thirst. At best we were allowed to drink water out of the well from which we had pulled the "escapees." Luggage, clothing, money, and jewels that we had to find and take out of the clothing were piled high in the warehouse. Goods worth millions were taken this way and stolen by SS men. Now and then a child managed to hide between the bundles of clothing and piles of luggage. Freedom did not last long, because by the next day at the latest, the children were punished by being thrown alive into the trenches between the corpses.

Among these came transports of corpses only. I suppose that these people were killed in the wagons by gas; I noticed no wounds. The bodies were twisted together; the skin was blue. Remarkably, it sometimes happened that small children from these transports, three- to five-year-olds, remained alive, though deaf and with glazed-over eyes, incapable of speech. We could not hide them long; after a short time they were discovered by the SS and killed off. There were also transports composed exclusively of children or old people. For hours they squatted on the square, only to be mowed down by machine gun fire.

About our own fate we were clear. We were marked for death. For us there was neither pity nor any sort of favorable treatment. We lived completely cut off in small barracks. We carried the corpses to the trenches in a horse cart; if any of us became tired and sat on the cart, we were driven off by clubs and blows. Shooting, intended as punishment, was seen as liberation from our endless suffering. We were not only corpse carriers, but we also had to burn the corpses in the trenches. Wood was gathered, covered with a fluid, and lighted. The top layer of corpses melted together. I suppose that an exhumation would reveal corpses that were only half charred.

It often happened that I had to throw a wounded comrade into the grave. Their requests for a mercy shot remained unheard; I could not help them.

From time to time groups of 200 to 500 men from Treblinka work camp were driven naked into the woods. In rows and holding hands, as if they were in a circle dance, they were driven to the excavated trenches, where they were lined up on the edge. SS and Ukrainian guards made a sport of giving them the shot in the neck to send them to eternity. After the shootings they kicked the collapsing victims with their boot heels and amidst howls and cries argued over who had kicked a Jew the farthest. Anyone who succeeded in escaping during this sport was no longer granted the mercy of a shot in the neck; he was beaten to death.

In the weeks during which I worked at Treblinka, a small brick building was built on the other side of the forest. On the path to this building, a sign with the inscription "To the baths" was erected. Another sign demanded that all gold, money, currency, and jewelry be left in bundles at the window to the bath. From this time on new arrivals were no longer shot. Inside the enclosure men, women, and children had to take off all their clothes. Shoes had to be tied together in pairs. With clubbings, punches, and kicks, the victims were moved forward to the "baths." Those who were not quick enough were treated horribly. Usually the camp commandant together with his staff were present; he was the one who personally clubbed people to death. No one returned alive; they were gassed in the "baths."

A special work detail like ours took care of the burial or cremation of the corpses. We met people from this work detail because they did not receive food either, and we supplied them from the food we found in the luggage. The thirst that plagued all of us was so horrible that some individuals caught their own urine to at least wet their lips this way. We got the strength to carry out this terri-

ble work from a comrade who constantly encouraged us to do our duty and perform this last service for our dead brothers and sisters, designated as the highest
commandment of our faith.

A number of us made isolated attempts to escape. I belonged to the small number of lucky ones. Between blankets, bundles of clothes, and suitcases that we had
to stack up in railroad cars, I hid together with a thirteen-year-old boy and my
friend Gottlieb of Kielce. We took with us a generous amount of jewelry, gold, and
money, mostly American dollars. Our escape succeeded in September 1942. The
unfortunately too brief period of my freedom I used to inform Jews of the horrors
of Treblinka and to advise them to hide.

I, too, tried to hide, but on January 5, 1943, my friend Gottlieb and I were arrested in Kraków as "partisans." After horrible tortures we had to confess that we
were Jews. We were brought in shackles to the prison of the Jewish ghetto and remained there until March 14, 1943. Then we were taken along with 100 other Jews
in closed vans to Auschwitz concentration camp and from there to Birkenau.
Most were immediately separated out and gassed. Women were sent straightaway
to the left, which meant gassing. But one woman threw herself at the feet of an SS
officer and, as a strong person willing to work, begged to be allowed to remain in
camp and work. She received permission to select some strong women and
brought some with her. For the moment at least, they were saved and put into the
women's camp.

At Birkenau I had the good fortune to be assigned to the clothing room. On
October 26 [1943] most of the prisoners, especially those who had good posts and
working conditions, were sent to Oranienburg. There we spent two weeks in
quarantine in the Heinkel Works, suffering from great hunger and miserable
clothing. We were then forced to go on foot to Sachsenhausen concentration
camp and from there, after another two days, by train to Ohrdruf (Thuringia) to
the infamous S III detail.

First we had to construct the camp. Food and clothing were totally insufficient;
the hygienic conditions were horrible. No wonder that with the heavy work in the
underground bunkers more than half the prisoners lost their lives after a short
time. Anyone who became weak or otherwise incapable of working was chosen in
the selections that occurred at intervals of about eight weeks, to be sent to Bergen-
Belsen near Hannover.

The evacuation of Ohrdruf [in April 1945] in face of the advancing Americans
turned into a death march and further martyrdom. Hundreds of us who were
tired and exhausted, who just wanted to stand still or sit for a moment, were shot
without any previous warning to resume the march. Their corpses lined the roads
to Buchenwald. On the short stretch from Weimar to Buchenwald alone, I loaded
more than 100 corpses on the wagon.

OSCAR BERGER, Kattowitz

161. MASS BURNINGS IN SKARZYSKO KAMIENNA

SINCE 1939 I have lived in ghettos and various work and concentration camps. Buchenwald is my twelfth camp. In my remarks today I will confine myself to a report on Skarzysko Kamienna near Radom [Poland], where it even came to the burning of living people.

On the evening of the Day of Atonement [Yom Kippur], October 1943, Guard Officer Schuhmann came to us in the camp. He entered Barracks 4 and searched for my comrade Mendel Rubin, a well driller from Kraków. He was charged with smuggling a letter to a Pole outside the camp. In the search of his belongings, Mendel Rubin was found to have a cap made of military cloth, similar to a Russian military cap. This discovery was alleged to serve as proof that Rubin had been in touch with Polish partisans and had attempted to provide himself with military clothing. Rubin was led out of the camp; as a rule that meant losing one's life in front of a firing squad. For Rubin it turned out otherwise. We observed that he was not taken to the execution stand but farther away from the camp. After a few days a report came from the Radom Gestapo that he was to be stricken off; he would not return, had been "released."

Jews who were no longer capable of working were "eliminated"; for the most part they met their deaths on the execution stand, which was located at the end of the factory grounds. Thousands were buried there. One day the factory management became uncomfortable with this mass grave. A military commission decided that the corpses had to be removed.

In April 1944 two autos came with German police who requisitioned two wagons of straw that had originally been designated to be spread on our sleeping bunks. The straw was taken to the woods, near Buildings 96 to 97 of C Works. There the straw was woven into matting to surround the site, so that it was impossible to see what happened beyond the straw mats.

Despite this we found out. My friend Mendel Rubin, of whom I spoke earlier, had got information to me and my friends, the content of which was so gruesome and horrible that I just could not grasp it. Rubin was one of those who had worked for four solid weeks inside the straw fence in Skarzysko. The enclosure was always closely guarded by German gendarmes. One day one of these police came over with a piece of soap. He handed it to my comrade Henoch Edelmann of Kraków, who had worked as a sheet-metal worker with the German master Corosta. The soap contained a tiny bottle, and in it was a note with news from Mendel Rubin. He told us that he had some very important news for us and that he would send it as soon as he was certain that a connection had been established. To confirm the receipt of this first report, we should send him pictures of the wife and children he had left behind. He got the pictures and the connection was established.

Reports from Rubin began to arrive; the gendarme turned them over to the two girls working with us, Regina Rabinowicz of Warsaw and Fela of Zamosc. We received four to five letters, one with an attachment from a Polish friend of Rubin's that bore the address "Katyn in the General Government." All these reports were buried; Henoch Edelmann took care of this. The reports went essentially as follows.

For months Mendel Rubin had been a member of a special work detail of sixty-seven men in Radom. It had the terrible task of burning the people the Gestapo had murdered, wiping out any trace of its deeds. He expressly reported that over and over again people who were not completely dead were thrown on the piles and that such people who were still alive when thrown on the piles were even burned. The people had first been dreadfully abused before they were shot and burned. Broken bones and skulls were the order of the day. The number of people dispatched out of this world each day numbered in the hundreds.

We also received a list of prominent personalities whose lives had been taken this way. The special work detail was composed entirely of candidates for death, people already condemned by the Gestapo. They could remain alive only as long as they performed this horrible service. They had to sleep in their clothes, shackled by their hands and feet. They had plenty to eat. Of the money and jewelry they found, they turned over only a portion to the Gestapo. Another portion was given to the gendarmes, who showed their gratitude and performed reciprocal services for the prisoners of the special work detail, providing them with food and drink. The gendarmes—exclusively German, all in the upper ranks—were great consumers of alcoholic drinks, apparently trying to forget the horrors they had witnessed by staying in a drunken stupor.

The connection with Rubin was broken by the death of the gendarme, who fell in a battle with the partisans. From him we had found out that he was a Jew himself, that he had entered into the German gendarme service under false papers. From the reports he had transmitted, we also knew that the men of the special work detail were taken from place to place to perform their tragic tasks.

These men prepared reports in which they described the deeds of the Gestapo and recorded the names of the victims. Some of the reports they had hidden—presumably walled up—in an elementary school building in Brzyn near Skarzysko Kamienna, Radom District. We have no precise details. According to our report, the special work detail had the job of exhuming and burning all the corpses at the execution site during its stay, so that all traces would be wiped out. Even though the mass graves had been covered over, smoothed out, and planted with grass, later we could still find clear traces: pieces of bone, fingers, and melted gold.

In his reports Rubin described for us the horrible work and the pain he had felt when he recognized comrades from work among the murder victims. He could also inform us of the deaths of people, some of them Poles, who disappeared from the factory without a trace and whom he had known from his earlier job in the factory. He also wrote to us that the exhumed bones were not burned but were loaded into a van that supposedly contained a bone mill. As a rule the people of the special work detail were shot and burned after a few weeks; he himself had been in the detail close to seven months. The Pole who had sent us the report with the list of names of murdered Poles had been in it a whole year.

People knew that they would not survive the war, that there was nothing in their lives any more. They had, as they wrote, only one desire that still gave them the strength to prolong their lives. It was to find ways and means of getting out reports that would bring to light the Nazis' bestial acts of murder. This is also the reason I pass along the lines above and hope that my testimony will serve in bringing forth the truth.

MOTEK STRIGLER, Zamosc[3]

162. The Lemberg Ghetto

IMMEDIATELY AFTER German troops penetrated into Lemberg [Lvov], they provoked various anti-Semitic incidents.[4] A Jewish prisoner from a prisoner of war transport of former Soviet soldiers was shot on the street by a German officer. All five Jewish occupants were dragged out of a neighboring house and ordered to dig a grave for him. A crowd gathered, mostly of Ukrainians. The five Jews were beaten bloody; the officer threatened to shoot them if the grave was not finished in an hour.

Another incident: SS men on motorcycles drove a crowd of 100 Jews through the streets. The Jews fell, were run over, then were whipped until they remained lying in the street, completely exhausted and severely wounded. In the streets the Jews were forced to punch and beat each other. Of course no Jew was allowed to step on the sidewalk, insofar as the street in question was not completely off-limits to him.

A few days after the occupation, the Ukrainians were permitted a four-day-long pogrom. The Ukrainian militia carried out arrests, during which everything of value was stolen. Jews who were arrested were dreadfully abused in the prisons. Jewish women were dragged from their homes and forced to clean the toilets of

---

3. Meyer Levin, an American correspondent who entered the camp soon after liberation, reports meeting a prisoner named Mordechai Striegler. The story he told emphasized different experiences than the one related here, but it is almost certainly the same individual. Meyer Levin, *In Search: An Autobiography* (New York: Horizon Press, 1950), 241–244.

4. The German army entered Lemberg (Lvov) on June 30, 1941. Andreas Hillgruber and Gerhard Hümmelchen, *Chronik des Zweiten Weltkrieges* (Frankfurt: Bernard u. Graefe Verlag für Wehrwesen, 1966), 41.

the SS with their bare hands. In addition they had to wash the bodies of those allegedly murdered by the Bolsheviks. Of course all of this work was performed amid the most malicious tortures and abuses. After a few weeks Jews were forced to wear arm bands. Every venture out onto the street became life threatening. Then a cash contribution was demanded from the Jewish population.

Jews also had to set up work details, whose members were exposed to the most malicious abuse. The actual accomplishment of work was of minor importance; the essential thing was to give the sentries an occasion to lash out against defenseless Jews. These persecutions of the first few weeks were followed by the expulsion of Jews from their homes and the seizure of all Jewish property. The homes were given over to Germans or Ukrainians. The Jews had to crowd together in the apartments of acquaintances or even of Jews who were total strangers. These intermediate steps lasted only a short time; then the ghetto was established.

At first the ghetto was in an area that made up no less than one-fifth of the city. (There were about 140,000 Jews—that is, about 30 percent of the population.) Every Jew had to buy his new apartment, Poles as well as Ukrainians taking full advantage of the compulsion that Jews were under. Jews received nothing for the residences they had vacated. They were allowed to take only bedding, kitchenware, and workclothes. Everything else was sacrificed to the mob.

In this ghetto there were a few stores that offered basic necessities, a community hall, two general hospitals, and a hospital for infectious diseases. Life was miserable, everything very expensive. This ghetto lasted from fall 1941 until August 1942, during which time one was exposed to persecutions of the worst kind. It went without saying that when the SS or the Wehrmacht needed something, whether it was furniture, clothing, or other types of consumer articles, they simply demanded it from the ghetto leaders, who had to provide it without compensation.

In August 1942 the "anti-Jewish" actions began. The first lasted about fourteen days, and around 50,000 Jews, mainly the sick, the elderly, and children, were taken to Belzec. It was later rumored that they were gassed there; among them was the entire staff of the hospital for infectious diseases—doctors, orderlies, and nurses. These actions, carried out by the SS Special Service, were repeated every few weeks. The ghetto was relocated to the edge of the city, where almost no walled houses stood. For every Jew they figured 20 square feet [of living space]. There were no stores, the only food was smuggled in. The sanitary conditions beg any sort of description. About 70 percent of the population became ill with typhus. Every day the SS robbed and plundered; at night there were "actions" and murders.

For Jews, work was compulsory, which also meant compulsory beatings. In the meantime a forced labor camp was erected, and young and healthy Jews were delivered there. Old and sick Jews as well as women and children were sent from the ghetto to the camp at Belzec to be gassed. Only a few transports of women were put together for agricultural work; small children were simply taken away from their mothers and frequently murdered in their presence. This condition lasted until fall 1942, when I was arrested.

There were then about 15,000 Jews in the ghetto, into which Jews from the surrounding region had also been delivered, as well as the 12,000 Jews in the work camp. As to the later fate of the ghetto, I found out from reliable sources that the inhabitants survived under the greatest of hardships until March 1943. Then the ghetto was abolished in a final liquidation action of its occupants and the buildings were burned down. The bestial brutality of the actions is very difficult to describe. People were chased with dogs; severely ill patients, often with open wounds from serious operations or broken bones, were dragged out of bed and kicked down the stairs. The limbs of small children were wrenched out, and they were thrown like parcels into transport trucks.

These actions occurred under the direction of the chief of police, SS General [Fritz] Katzmann. A large number of Ukrainians took part in the actions; a former colonel of the [Ukrainian Nationalist] Petlura army, Bisantz, had worked out the "population policy" plan.

The Lemberg compulsory work camp, Weststrasse, was set up as a death camp. On average prisoners lived two weeks and perished of hunger, disease, the knout, or other tortures; others were shot. Sick people were regularly "put behind barbed wire" and murdered. Many reported voluntarily [for death]. A few months after the liquidation of the ghetto, 15,000 occupants of the camp were mowed down with machine gun fire. Since new admissions to the camp were necessarily few because of the exhaustion of the sources of supply [i.e., additional Jews] in the region, the camp closed. A tiny remnant of about 100 Jews, who, remarkably, were well treated later, supposedly existed long after. The camp commandant was SS Lieutenant Colonel Willhaus.

I would like to limit my report on Auschwitz concentration camp, where I was brought myself, to the following observations.

A considerable portion of the Jews delivered were not registered at all but were brought directly out of the railcars into the gas chambers and destroyed. For other transports, a selection was carried out immediately upon arrival. A portion of the men and women who seemed capable of work were then brought into the camp, tattooed, and at the same time registered. Children were for the most part brought immediately to the gas chambers.

Selections of the Jews remaining in camp were carried out every three to six weeks. The weak, the sick, and those prisoners who for very trivial reasons attracted the attention of the SS were brought to Barracks 20, supposedly for "transport." It was actually a matter of transportation to eternity, which was carried out by poisoning with cyanide gas. In the Auschwitz hospital ten to 100 people daily were given carbolic acid injections in the heart, which of course led to death. Concerning the gassing, I would like to note that the condition and placement of the corpses showed that when the gassing was carried out with too weak a dose, a very painful death ensued.

In Barracks 10 various experiments were carried out on Jewish women, in particular sterilization by X-rays or chemical means. These experiments were conducted on specially selected, attractive young Jewish women, mostly Greeks, by the head of the clinic, Professor [Karl] Clauberg (formerly of Auschwitz hospital), who frequently came to Auschwitz.

DR. LUDWIG FLECK, Lemberg[5]

163. MASS MURDERS IN THE RIGA GHETTO

I WAS FORCED to leave school (a technical high school) early, at age fourteen, to find work in a barracks building firm, where I had to perform the most strenuous work for the smallest wages. Then my parents and I were evacuated to Riga on December 7, 1941. The evacuation was announced three weeks in advance by the Cologne Gestapo. At the same time came the order that the sale of any type of goods was strictly forbidden; instead, everything other than furniture was to be packed up. Furthermore, each family involved in the evacuation was ordered to prepare a washtub full of food. With six suitcases, three backpacks, briefcases, and handbags, we appeared at the appointed time at the fairgrounds. It was a so-called NN [*Nacht und Nebel*, Night and Fog] transport, [which left in the middle of the night] to keep the population of Cologne from knowing about the evacuation.

The transport was composed of 1,000 people. Our baggage was searched for objects of value: Watches, wedding rings, as well as all identification papers were taken from the transport participants. After a body search each individual was allowed 10 marks. We were driven into a large hall on the fairgrounds, which were encircled with barbed wire, and had to lie on damp shavings there for the next twenty-four hours.

At 4:00 A.M. on December 8, after we had been limited to only one suitcase for the trip, we were herded under SS guard to the Cologne-Deutz train station. The transport lasted eighty hours and ended in Riga. While under way we received no food, and only a single time did we get water to drink.

At the freight station in Skirotava, we were driven from the railcars by Latvian SS with iron bars and whips. There was no chance even to think of taking our baggage along. Then we had to begin an agonizing march on foot in 24-degree weather. Stragglers who fell behind were driven with kicks into the Riga ghetto two hours later. Forty-eight hours before our arrival, this ghetto had housed 34,500. Now we saw only human limbs and pools of blood, as well as tremendous devastation in all the dwellings. Along with seventeen people, my parents and I

---

5. Ludwig Fleck later had a distinguished career as a scientist and philosopher of science. He is the author of *Genesis and Development of a Scientific Fact* (Chicago: University of Chicago Press, 1979). An overview of his life and work is in Robert S. Cohen and Thomas Schnelle, *Cognition and Fact: Materials on Ludwik Fleck* (Boston: Reidel, 1986).

were herded into a room that was about 140 square feet. Here we were to louse ourselves. In the evening 4,500 Latvian Jews came to look for their relatives but were unable to find any of them. They were the surviving remnant; the 30,000 Jews had been led into a valley and shot down by machine guns. After the mass killing the hills on both sides were blown up and the masses buried under the rubble.

By eating the food we had found in the room, we were able to live for two days. In the meantime another transport of 1,000 Jews from Kassel had arrived. Two days after our arrival, 200 Jews between the ages of eighteen and forty were taken to a camp, Salaspils, 11 miles away from Riga. I was one of those. On the march five comrades were shot by the Latvian SS because they would not give up their boots; among them was a Sally Katz of Kassel. Frozen and hungry, we arrived in an open, snow-covered field where only large wooden barracks without a roof stood. The 4,000 Jews from south Germany who lived there fell upon us like wolves, looking for food and drink. Our hair was cut short. We were assigned bunks that were 18 inches high, 6.5 feet long, and 4.5 feet wide. Each of these bunks housed three camp inmates. We lay there on ice-encrusted planks in the extreme cold. On the third day after our arrival, we saw the first bread and a sleigh full of potato peelings from the SS kitchen in Riga.

SS Technical Sergeant Nickel of Berlin presented himself to us as the commandant, assigned us work, and ordered us to begin work without coats or campfires. The building program involved forty-five barracks in which Latvians and Russians would later be housed. The program was completed except for five barracks; in addition watchtowers had to be built, and the entire rectangle had to be fenced in with barbed wire. In this death camp I starved for seven months; at the end I was covered with lice and weighed only 72 pounds. A small group of Latvian SS men carried out target practice on fourteen arbitrarily chosen comrades, whose bullet-riddled corpses we later had to carry into a nearby forest. The shooting exercise was carried out for the amusement of invited SS officers; among them were SS Major Rudolf Lange, commandant of the security police of the Security Service (SD) in Latvia; SS Second Lieutenant Meiwald; as well as officials of the Gestapo.

On another occasion Lange ordered us to hang sixteen comrades who had worked with their coats on in 30-degree weather. Starved to a skeleton, I was photographed for the [Nazi periodical] *Stürmer.* Thus passed seven months with 6 ounces of bread [per day] and potato peelings. The 15,000 people who eventually went through this camp were almost completely wiped out. Only 192 remained alive; I was one of them. We were brought back into the ghetto on August 2, 1942. Most comrades had died of dysentery, typhus, and exposure to cold (often the bones were visible in their limbs); others were murdered by blows from the whip, on the gallows, or through a shot at the base of the neck.

In regard to the food and the housing in the Riga ghetto, things were not quite so bad. But the atrocities themselves scarcely took a backseat to the severe abuse and the arbitrary acts in the camp. It was common practice to take babies and small children from their mothers, toss them up in the air, and shoot them in front of their mothers. Sometimes the SS shot the mothers or simply left them lying in a faint on the ground. These women often committed suicide a few hours later. My mother, fifty-two years old, was ordered to walk 6 miles with a washtub full of coal fastened to the frame of a pram, and this even though she wore wooden clogs that injured her feet terribly. When she finally collapsed, she was severely beaten and could only drag herself back to the ghetto much later.

Work details of young men were created to dig mass graves of 52 by 13 by 6.5 feet in the Bickernick Forest. These mass graves were destined to be used for transports from Bielefeld, Düsseldorf, Hannover, Berlin, Vienna, Dresden, Leipzig, Kassel, Dortmund, Stuttgart, Nuremberg, and Munich, as well as from Czechoslovakia and Austria. Immediately upon the arrival of a transport, everyone was loaded onto trucks and transported to Bickernick Forest. The transports were driven through the parking lot of the air force, SS, army, and SD. The actions occurred under the direction of Major Arreis of the Latvian SS.

At any given time a work detail of twenty people was lined up in front of the trenches. Groups of about 200 people at a time were led up to the trenches from the arriving truck transports. They were all undressed, without regard to age or sex, and were shot down with machine gun fire. This detail of twenty people had the tragic task of dragging the bodies to the trench. At the end this detail shared the same fate. These atrocities were commonly known. German air force personnel who were eyewitnesses had repeatedly reported them to us.

A group of thirty-eight Jewish comrades, among whom was the father of Kurt Rosenthal of Dortmund, an inmate here [in Buchenwald], was put to work covering up the graves with sand after the executions. This group was kept especially isolated in the central prison in Riga. The father of another prisoner I know, Kurt Donnhart of Cologne, as well as Ernst Kramer of Cologne and Bernard Isaak of Cologne-Deutz belonged to this group. Only sixteen members of this group left the central prison; the others died of madness and hunger. In the cell in which they were housed, a record was played for two hours every day in which the text was repeated over and over: "I must not say anything about what I have seen and done, otherwise I will be shot." Simply making an attempt to pick up one of the photos thrown down by the prisoners who were to be shot was sufficient grounds to be shot oneself. The sixteen surviving prisoners were brought back into the ghetto.

Starting in November 1942 a simpler procedure for getting rid of people was chosen. Closed trucks with trailers into which 200 people could be packed arrived. During the journey a gas apparatus was opened; the journey went to the Bickernick Forest. After about an hour the trucks came back with clothing. These people were interred by the aforementioned thirty-eight-man detail. Later we received whole truck columns full of clothing, suitcases, and prams.

The exchange of letters with the outside world and the possession of money were punished by death. Starving Jews occasionally tried to exchange clothes for a piece of bread and butter. Ghetto inmates who were caught at it first received twenty-five lashes with a cane and then were hanged. Among them was the prisoner Kurt Becher, a nineteen-year-old from Hannover. With him a Heidenheim of Prague was punished for the same offense; another seven occupants of the house were hanged as accomplices. It was not unusual for a few additional room-mates or other people to be arbitrarily accused of failing to make a report to head-quarters; they would [then] be condemned to death as well. SS men frequently raped young women. The commandant was no exception. His name was Krause, an SS first lieutenant from Leipzig who was a former Gestapo official in Berlin. He raped among others Elle Laumann of Krefeld and the beautician Olly Auler of Prague. Krause's preference was to conduct target practice on individual prison-ers, who in many cases were merely wounded; they were then brought into the in-firmary and killed there through injections.

Later the commandant sorted out all people in the ghetto over fifty years of age—2,200 men and women. My parents escaped only by falsifying their dates of birth. All children under thirteen years of age were also part of this selection. Mothers who did not want to be separated from their children were added to this selection. The destination of the transport was identified as Dünamünde, but that was an obvious deception; the transport never reached its destination.

One week later (November 1943) the ghetto was dissolved, then Russian refu-gees were housed there. The 1,500 surviving inhabitants, among them my parents, were sent to Kaiserwald concentration camp near Riga, under the administration of SS Lieutenant Colonel Sauer. A portion went into special quarters in barracks (army quartermaster depot, motor pool, military clothing office, etc.); I was among the latter. On orders from Berlin all women and girls had their heads shaved.

Through a fortunate arrangement, after two months I was able to receive news from my parents, who were suffering horribly from hunger. My work detail per-mitted me to save some of my rations, more than usual, and I found a way to get modest amounts of food to my parents. My parents worked on the Düna. There they had to pull heavy tree trunks from the water and drag them to a sawmill. As a matter of principle, the removal had to be done solely by human power. Xaver Apel, the senior camp inmate of Kaiserwald concentration camp, was a profes-sional criminal from the Berlin Sass band who was under a life sentence; in camp he was called Mr. X. His assistant was another professional criminal, Hannes Dressler of Hamburg. Both were the best of friends with SS Lieutenant Colonel Sauer, who approved and supported all their actions.

It was characteristic of the internal organization of the camp that, for example, Mr. X simply threw into the Düna those prisoners no longer fully capable of working and prevented any attempt to rescue them. They were removed from the rolls, the cause of death given as "heart attack." Another case may serve as an ex-ample of the conditions: A man who was ill from dysentery gave away his meal. Mr. X got word of it and threw him into a kettle of boiling water that was to serve for the preparation of the camp coffee. The comrade was miserably boiled to death; nevertheless, the water was still used in the usual camp coffee. Another comrade named Gustav Haar of Dresden, leader of the so-called camp police, was stabbed and thrown into the latrine.

SS Major Krebsbach of Cologne undertook continuous actions against the weak and the sick. In May my father was chosen in one of these selections because of a minor leg wound. It was again called the Dünamünde transport. My father managed to smuggle a scrap of paper with a last farewell to me. It contained the information that a gas van stood in the immediate vicinity and said he was sending me his last farewell; he appealed to me to stand by my mother to the best of my abilities. In less than an hour he would be beyond all pain.

At the beginning of July 1944, I was taken with 1,350 men and 1,350 women to Stutthof concentration camp [near Danzig]. During the transport many people died of extreme heat, lack of water, and general weakness. Here again the weak and the sick were sorted out and sent to the Stutthof crematorium after they had been killed by means not known to me. My mother was allegedly likewise sent to Stutthof two months later. I was never able to find out more. I myself was soon transported along with other comrades to Buchenwald.

HANS BAERMANN, Cologne

164. THE HEROIC JEWISH STRUGGLE IN WARSAW

THE ENTIRE JEWISH population of Warsaw was registered immediately after the occupation of the city by the Germans [September 1939]. Anyone who failed to register was threatened with a death sentence. Through resettlement a large ghetto was established in Warsaw, cut through by Chlodna Street. A connection between the two halves of the ghetto was created by a bridge over Chlodna Street. A 13-foot-high wall was erected around the ghetto. It was strictly forbidden to stay in the Aryan district [of the city]. In the beginning half a million Jews lived in the ghetto. Through new arrivals from the surrounding region, the number of ghetto inhabitants rose to three-quarters of a million. Crowded together in a small area, many families in a single dwelling, without possibility of employment, without contact to the outside world, these people starved. Only a few dared to leave the walls of the ghetto illegally to procure some food.

Every attempt of the Jewish leaders to get help from abroad was immediately suppressed; leading personalities were arrested. Finally, contact was established with [Morris C.] Tropper, director of the [American Jewish] Joint Distribution Committee (JDC) in Paris. With [German] Governor General [Hans] Frank,[6] Tropper arranged a relief program for Warsaw Jews through the Polish Red Cross. A commission for the ghetto was named and received American support funds,

---

6. Hans Frank was the governor general of German-occupied Poland (the General Government, as it was called) in Kraków from 1939 to 1945. He was tried as a major war criminal at Nuremberg, found guilty, and hanged in 1946.

paying them out to Jews in zloty. Under the leadership of the engineer [Adam] Czerniakow, a Jewish Council [*Judenrat*] was formed. Through JDC aid a people's kitchen was established, along with children's welfare and health facilities; Orthodox circles found help through Rabbi Blumenfeld. After that, conditions improved; possibilities of work were created. After America entered the war, the JDC ended its activities [December 1941]. The Jewish Relief Committee continued its work through self-help. The ghetto was not essentially changed until July 22, 1942, the beginning of the destruction of the Jews.

On July 20, companies of the SS Reinhard Heydrich [battalion] (Lublin extermination detail) under the direction of SS First Lieutenant Tumann arrived in Warsaw. On July 22, 1942, Ukrainian SS men were stationed around the walls of the ghetto. A proclamation was posted: "All Jews—men, women and children—insofar as they are not employed in German businesses, armaments factories, or the ghetto administration, must leave the ghetto!" It said they were to be taken to the east to be employed in the reconstruction of destroyed areas. Only 33 pounds of luggage per person were to be taken along, included in which was to be all jewelry, valuables, money, and a blanket. The Jewish Council would provide for good footwear. The office of the civilian commissar was liquidated; in its place appeared an SS resettlement staff, under the direction of SS Lieutenant Brand, which set up offices in the ghetto at 103 Eisengruberstrasse. The Jewish Council was responsible for the orderly conduct of the resettlement. Every day 10,000 people were to be resettled.

Czerniakow declared that he was not in a position to carry this out. The arrest of Abraham Geppner, Rabbi Schapiro, the editor Eckermann, Dr. Milejkowski, and twenty other Jewish Council members who were held as hostages was intended to force his hand. Czerniakow and his wife committed suicide through poisoning. A baptized Jew, a former colonel of the Polish criminal police, Jakob Sczerinski, became provisional head of the Jewish Council and chief of the ghetto police. The resettlement began. Each day blocks of houses were surrounded; men, women, and children—whoever happened to be seized in the streets or in the houses—were forced to go along, taken to the railroad platform, and shoved into freight cars (up to 120 people per car).

If a total of 10,000 Jews was not reached by 6:00 P.M., the SS and Ukrainian SS intervened, shots were fired, people were killed, and the total of 10,000 was achieved. The ghetto began to empty; hundreds of Jewish corpses covered the streets. A father's attempt to go back and get his children or his clothes was punished on the spot with death. Second Lieutenant Brand claimed to be "humane": Jewish corpses would not be allowed to remain in the street! A Jewish burial squad received arm bands with official stamps from the Gestapo as well as passes so that they would not be hindered in their work or be subject to resettlement. Horses were even assigned to them so that the poor victims could be brought to the cemetery as quickly as possible. Posters encouraged Jews to report voluntarily for transports to the east, as the life there was much easier than in the crowded ghetto. The supply of food in the ghetto was curtailed. For the journey out, 6 pounds of bread and 1 pound of marmalade were issued. To make the Jews more compliant, the water supply to the ghetto was cut off. The campaign was not without success—Jews reported voluntarily.

The SS Property Registration Office [*Werterfassung*] under the direction of SS First Lieutenant Conrad and District Governor Dr. Fischer put 2,000 young Jews into its service and temporarily freed them from the resettlement. All furniture, valuables, clothing, and underclothing left behind were gathered, sorted, and stored in the SS warehouse in 51 Wildstrasse (formerly Dr. Zamenhofa Street). SS members participating in the resettlement action were richly rewarded; the remaining items were given to the National Socialist welfare organization. Jews were pursued day and night; they tried to hide. They suspected what awaited them, despite postcards from Maljinka near Treblinka that said the resettled Jews were doing well. They instinctively felt that these postcards, whose words bore a striking similarity to one another, did not contain the truth but simply represented the only possible way of giving one more sign of life. There would be no escape from the ghetto; the resettlement would continue.

On August 9, 1942, the resettlement was declared officially over. Whoever had not already been resettled, so it was said, would be allowed to remain in the ghetto. The proviso was that all inhabitants of the ghetto had to be newly registered and had to assemble for that purpose at the square formed by Ostrowska, Dr. Zamenhofa, Mila, and Nalewki streets. Capital punishment was threatened for those who did not appear.

A new, quiet hopefulness began to fill and enliven the besieged, frightened Jews. Up to 200,000 men, women, and children obeyed the call and gathered at the required time. In rows of five they marched past SS Second Lieutenant Brand and his staff. This roll call and review lasted six days. Fifty thousand new victims were selected; they departed for the east. The remainder received a pass; they were allowed to return to their homes. The selection was an unnerving plague. Leaving the square was forbidden; day and night people squatted on the pavement. There was nothing to eat, nothing to drink. Many went hungry for almost six full days until the job was completed. SS Second Lieutenant Brand had to "comb through" the Jews.

On August 14 it was our family's turn, too. We passed in front of the lords over life and death. Suddenly, the glance of the second lieutenant fell upon my father. By a wave of the hand he was ordered to step out of the ranks. Before he could extend a hand to me or say anything, an SS corporal gunned him down with two shots from his pistol. I stood for a moment paralyzed, then caught my father in my arms. A minor tumult arose while I dragged the dying man through the gate, accompanied by my mother and two sisters. My father was spared the journey to the east. The selection was over; a further 5,000 Jews were employed by the SS Property Registration Office.

We received no news from those who had left us. We suspected only the worst. In the meantime there came occasional fugitives who had managed to escape Treblinka. One of them was a young Jewish journalist, Jakob Rabinowicz, brother of the chief rabbi of Munkacz. Until his resettlement he had worked with us in the kitchen of the Joint Distribution Center. In a secret meeting of Jewish youth, he reported to us in detail what he had seen and experienced in Treblinka as a member of the rescue detail [*Bergungskommando*]: the mass murder, shooting, and gassing of hundreds of thousands of Jews of Warsaw and other places. He reported on the gruesome deaths our friends and relatives suffered and on his escape in a wagon, concealed by his comrades under bundles of clothes and blankets.

No one believed him. We couldn't imagine it; it was too horrible and gruesome. We held it to be the outgrowth of sick fantasies or at the very least a gross exaggeration. He pleaded with us to believe him and begged us to send a Pole secretly to Kossuv, about 9 miles from Treblinka. The local population knew what was going on—they could smell the burning corpses. We followed his advice and raised funds and established connections with people from the PPS (Polish Socialist party). Several party members, the engineers Tepicin and Landau, Nososki, and Maycharek went to Kossuv and confirmed what we had been told. Polish personnel drove the resettlement trains as far as the gate; no Pole was allowed inside the fences. From a distance one could only see the dense smoke and smell the penetrating odor of burning.

Secret leaflets written in Yiddish reported to the Jews of Warsaw on the "cultural deeds" of our "protectors," this merciless people. The Polish National party spread this knowledge in Polish circles. Under the influence of these horrible reports, there grew a single, unifying thought: to resist the next selection, the next transport to the east. Dr. Isaac Schipper, leader of the Polish Zionists, became the soul of the resistance idea. In a secret meeting of the youth, he said, "If our extermination is determined by fate and by history, then at least we will die in battle. We will not go voluntarily to our deaths in the east!"

With the help of the Polish Socialist party, weapons were obtained; under the Betar [Young Zionist] Leib Leon Rodal of Kielce, a resistance organization was brought to life. Abraham Geppner, a metal manufacturer, donated 1 million zloty for the purchase of weapons; many millions were collected in all. We paid 5,000 zloty for a pistol; a machine gun was 12,000. We had hand grenades. We built bunkers in the cellars. We were able to get older people into Polish Warsaw; remaining behind were predominantly the youth and those women and children who had decided to die side by side with their husbands and fathers. My mother and sister remained in the ghetto. My younger sister, Tolla, went into Aryan Warsaw: She was blonde, blue-eyed, and would not stand out there by her appearance. I never saw her again. We formed small battle groups. Jakob Sczerinski; the lawyer Leikin, the prison chief; Jurek Fürstenberg, chief of the Property Registration Office; and many other Gestapo informers who wanted to save their own lives at the expense of the Jews were assassinated. The assassinations were carried out by fifteen- and sixteen-year-old boys.

January 18, 1943, became a milestone in the history of the sufferings of the ghetto. The German police had to avenge the assassinations of informers. Once again the ghetto was surrounded and the entire population of the ghetto required to report. No one obeyed the order. The word was passed orally to offer no resistance for the time being but simply to hide. The searches lasted four days. Many were caught with weapons in hand; they were immediately shot, along with those dragged out of houses and hiding places. Those who were caught—18,000 men, women, and children—were killed. A proclamation from SS Second Lieutenant Brand announced that he had had to defeat the bandits who had carried out the assassinations. These 18,000 "bandits" had been killed, the Property Registration Office had new territory to work, and the Jewish Council would have to provide for the burial of the "bandits."

In the ghetto we now numbered about 40,000, mostly youth, organized in small battle groups of the Jewish youth organization. We knew what stood before us. We did not want to go down without a struggle; we believed that we could avenge the deaths of those who fell without resistance as victims of the Nazi terror and lust for murder. We wanted to encourage and give an example to those Jews we hoped were still alive outside Warsaw. Our battle would call the public opinion of the world to our defense, for the total defeat of the Nazi lust for power, which did not shrink from murdering defenseless human beings and robbing them of their possessions. The Zionist leader Dr. Schipper remained with us in the ghetto.

Passover, April 19, 1943, was approaching. Through friends from the Polish side we found out that in Praga, a suburb of Warsaw, a few companies of Black SS (Reinhard Heydrich Battalion) had arrived. At 4:00 A.M. on the second day of Passover, the SS surrounded the ghetto. Our young men went from house to house, announcing mobilization for battle. Everyone rushed to the cellars, taking along their weapons and food. Platoons of SS moved into the ghetto. At the corner of 42 Nalewki Street (the Hermann Brauer Clothing Factory), a young man stepped out of the entrance and spoke to a group of twenty-five SS men led by a platoon leader. He pointed to the third courtyard and said that a group of ten Jews were hidden there. The SS platoon followed him. Scarcely had they arrived in the third courtyard when the youth pulled out his pistol and shot down the platoon leader.

The signal for battle was given. Shots were fired from windows; hand grenades exploded; there was deafening noise. The young man who had fired the first shot was Mordechai Nutkowicz of Ripin. He fell down dead, but not one of the SS men left the courtyard alive. The entire district arose in an uproar. Battle sounds came from all quarters; the SS had not expected such a reception. They hastily left the ghetto. All was quiet until the next day.

On the following day tanks moved into the ghetto, shooting houses until they burst into flame. We tried to extinguish the fires and battle the tanks with grenades, but we were powerless. We crawled into the bunkers; SS infantry moved into the ghetto. They were greeted with a hail of bullets and grenades. We were fired upon from airplanes; the ghetto burned in every corner. The fire lasted four days. The bunkers were searched with listening devices then were blown up with mines and grenades. Anyone found with a weapon was shot on the spot. The cleansing action lasted fourteen days. The survivors were taken to Lublin concentration camp [Maidanek].

I myself went with my mother and sister. The transport offered the usual picture: people squeezed together in cattle cars, 100 to 120 at a time, no food, no water. At Maidanek the cars were unloaded, women and children to the left, men to the right. I saw my mother and sister led with the others between Fields 1 and 2. A little house received them; they were never seen again. They died by gassing. Dr. Schipper died after one month. I remained at Maidanek until June 24 [1943]; from there I was taken to Auschwitz.

A new picture of horror: thousands of French, Dutch, Greek, and Hungarian Jews, including women and children, were brought to the infamous gas chambers. I myself fell sick with hives, a harmless skin disease, and was nevertheless selected, brought to Block 20, and was to be gassed the next day. I owe my survival to Jusek Kenner, who was able to obtain a diamond ring and give it to the senior camp inmate. He took me out of the block during the night. From Auschwitz I went to Thuringia, to the infamous camp S III (Ohrdruf), and on April 5 [1945] to Buchenwald. From there we were to be evacuated again. I then went into hiding and held out until the Americans liberated us.

VLADIMIR BLUMENFELD, Warsaw

165. THE "HEAVENLY CHARIOT" OF DACHAU

AT DACHAU the Reich SS leadership constantly carried out experiments on healthy human beings. One of their showplaces was doubtless the Luftwaffe experimental station, which was directed by a personal friend of Himmler's, Dr. [Sigmund] Rascher, a Luftwaffe captain. The experimental station was housed in Block 5 of the prisoner hospital at Dachau concentration camp. In the street between Block 5 and the adjoining barracks, an experimental van was placed. The street isolated it from the rest of the hospital and from the view of unauthorized persons. The experimental van was a tall, closed box on wheels, with built-in instruments for measuring atmospheric pressure, temperature, and altitude. With the help of this apparatus, one could subject a human guinea pig to the physical conditions of flight above 32,000 feet and from there plunge him into a vertical dive toward the earth.

From the behavior of the experimental subject during these procedures, the effects of a vertical dive on the human organism could be determined. The experimental subject, clad in a waterproof suit and equipped with a life preserver, was then plunged into a swimming pool of water at 33 to 35 degrees. The subject had to survive in there for at least two hours but in most cases until physical exhaustion, thus until death. Anyone who had the rare good fortune to come out alive was put into bed with a prostitute, whose bodily warmth was supposed to bring back to life the by then almost completely stiffened body. These prostitutes were housed at Dachau concentration camp—Station RF (Reich leadership), as it was officially named—especially for this purpose. This latter procedure was introduced only later, after a series of deaths.

Dr. Rascher was not satisfied with observing the external behavior of his victims during the experiments; in his medical zeal he wanted to determine what went on in the brains of his victims immediately after the high-altitude flight. The skull of a Jew who was fully conscious was split open after the high altitude flight and his brain examined. An eyewitness to this misdeed is the prisoner Willi Oppel of Karlsruhe.

The "heavenly chariot," as the van was named, spread horror throughout the entire concentration camp. The first victims were recruited by the labor assignment office as special details offering supplemental rations. Volunteers innocently reported. But after a few days, dark rumors filtered through the camp. No longer did anyone volunteer. The victims were then simply taken from the prisoner barracks under the most varied pretexts. Unsuspecting new arrivals were preferred. The director of the station himself, the "captain," as people in the camp named him in horror, went on the searches for new victims.

After about three months, Himmler visited the captain's station. There he met three survivors of the experiments: Two of them he personally released from camp and transferred to the Luftwaffe in Berlin. The third he sent back to the station with a wave of the hand. The "heavenly chariot" was removed from the camp after six months. The camp breathed a sigh of relief. At the same time a prisoner who was employed in the station brought to the labor assignment office the death certificates of eight prisoners who had been sent to heaven the evening before the end of the experiments.

After the removal of the van, only the water experiments were continued. Later all experiments were stopped.

HERMANN HALLER, Bohndorf, Württemberg

166. Malaria Experiments at Dachau

In German concentration camps the health of thousands was destroyed in the name of allegedly scientific research. In a "special unit" were placed those "greens" who were examined in January 1942 by SS Captain Prachtel. Only those in the best of health between twenty and forty-five years of age were considered suitable. In March 1942 the first five men had to report to the infirmary. Thereafter twenty more reported each week.

Professor Dr. Klaus Schilling carried the responsibility for all the experiments; his collaborator was the previously mentioned Captain Prachtel. Captain Plöttner later took his place.

The experiments proceeded in the following manner: Anopheles mosquitoes infected with malaria were needed to carry the disease to healthy humans. Disease-carrying insects from the tropics—from Madagascar, the Crimea, and other regions—were acquired and used to infect the bodies of the experimental subjects. The behavior of various human blood groups under the disease was also studied. The first onset of the disease occurred as a rule three weeks after infection. At this point the patient was brought back to the hospital. Whereas at first the patient had bouts of fever every two or three days, in the more advanced stages attacks came two to three times a day. Damage to the heart, jaundice, severe diarrhea, and often even inflammations of the lung were "side effects."

With the first onset of fever, the observation of the disease began. Heartbeat and behavior of other bodily organs were recorded on charts. At the same time the professor tried to heal what he had previously infected, but a complete cure was achieved in only a very few cases. After their release most subjects still complained of heart pains and digestive problems.

Of 200 human subjects, seventeen died. Later the ratio of cases of sickness to numbers of deaths increased considerably, as the initial screening examinations and the age limits fell by the wayside. Especially high were the losses suffered by Polish clergymen. It is not possible for me to give an approximate total number of deaths, but the prisoner orderly August Vieweg could provide precise statistical material. At the end of 1943 he told me that he had around 1,500 patient's folders in his archive. Nevertheless, the experiments were scheduled to continue for another two years.

Reich SS Leader Heinrich Himmler visited the experimental facility, accompanied by Reich Medical Leader Conti. He declared in a pathetic tone after the visit, "Boys, you have done the fatherland as great a service as that accomplished by our soldiers at the front. I will not forget you at the next release!" It should be noted that none of them was released.

HELMUT ABLEITER, Stuttgart

167. NATZWEILER CONCENTRATION CAMP

Along with twenty orderlies I was brought from Dachau concentration camp to Natzweiler [France] to work in the infirmary. At that time there existed only a position in a so-called external work detail that was assigned to the building and expansion of the camp. This detail, composed of eighty prisoners, was assigned to road building, which—as soon became clear—meant that of us twenty orderlies, only three survived the extreme exertion.

At the end of the first year of the existence of the camp, four primitive barracks and a kitchen had been erected under the most inhuman working and living conditions. Of the 900 prisoners housed there over the course of time, no less than 330 "died." More correctly put, they were murdered, either slowly or quickly. A further 300 camp inmates were returned to Dachau as invalids, since they were incapable of further work.

The camp commandant was SS Major [Egon] Zill of Plauen; the deputy commandant was Captain [Joseph] Kramer of Augsburg. The leadership of the camp inmates was in the hands of the "greens," that is, the criminal prisoners. The SS bandits welcomed these antisocial elements as tools to use against the other prisoners. The camp doctor, SS First Lieutenant Eisele, supported the greens by every means available. SS First Lieutenant Blanke carried on this gruesome office after him, although only for a short time.

The method of construction and arrangement of the barracks, in terraced steps on the side of a mountain, was so primitive that it was impossible even to think of proper hygiene.

The most feared work detail was the stone quarry. Every day 200 men had to move out to work. Of the 600 inmates of the camp, only about 100 were capable of work, and those were the greens, the camp VIPs. Of the remaining prisoners perhaps 100 at most could be considered capable of limited work. Many were so worn down by abuse, overexertion, and privation that they could no longer walk. But since the stone quarry detail had to consist of 200 men, anyone who could no longer walk had to be driven to the work site in wheelbarrows, etc.

The food was totally insufficient, the midday meal completely inedible. Sixty percent of all inmates weighed less than 110 pounds. The hunger was so great that the weakest inmates were killed by their dehumanized fellow prisoners to obtain their meager daily rations. In a single night no less than thirty murdered inmates were delivered to the camp infirmary.

The method of treatment in the infirmary defied all description. The kapo was a professional criminal who was in league with the senior camp inmate, Rosch; with the criminals Käseberg, Hösel, and Liese; and with the kitchen kapo Pollmann (a repulsive homosexual). They had countless murders on their consciences.

On July 8, 1942, I was witness to a terrifying event that will never fade from my memory. In the corridor of the infirmary stood six coffins in a stack. They were crates hammered together of rough boards, out of which blood seeped through the joints. Suddenly a knocking could be heard from the bottom coffin. A weak voice quavered, "Open up! Open up! I am still alive!" The greens pulled out the bottom coffin and opened it. A Polish prisoner with an injured head and broken legs stared out at us from the coffin, in which he was lying with a dead man. I wanted to intervene, to free him from his terrifying situation, but I was immediately pushed aside by one of the professional criminals. A few dull thuds, then the coffin was nailed shut again and sent to the crematorium.

The work details for the stone quarry and road construction received the assignment to build a new road. The work force was made up of Russian civilians and prisoners of war. They had to perform their forced labor on rocky, sharp-edged stones without shoes on their feet. SS and criminal malefactors tried to outdo each other in mutual incitement and horrors. The infamous kapo Sametinger, who on his release from the camp was personally conducted to the Wehrmacht by the commandant, played a major role. Especially popular was the method of chasing prisoners into the sentry line. Fifty percent of the prisoners employed in road construction met their deaths this way.

For years the greens occupied all camp offices. A small improvement in conditions first appeared when political prisoners who were energetic, but above all were determined antifascists, arrived from other camps. Through their activity it became possible to force out the most infamous of the professional criminals. A few of them were killed by their own cronies in the punishment company; others were transferred back to Dachau.

In the youth block the former Wehrmacht soldier Hans Müller became the senior block inmate. He beat young men unconscious with a truncheon if they did not obey him like dogs. Another criminal was the camp kapo Christian Knoll of Nuremberg. In his narrow-minded boasting he named himself "the hangman of Natzweiler." On the ledger of this inhuman creature must be placed among others the painful death of a young Russian who, along with some other comrades, attempted escape. Unfortunately, he was caught and beaten to death on roll call square before the eyes of all the prisoners. From Müller and Knoll he received no fewer than 154 lashes with the whip on the naked buttocks. The tortured prisoner had long since lost consciousness, yet the beasts continued to beat him.

One day 120 NN [*Nacht und Nebel*, Night and Fog] prisoners arrived at Natzweiler. This designation can be traced back to an order of Himmler that declared that a certain group of French and Dutch opponents of Nazism were outlaws. Among them were a number of prominent French personalities, higher officers, governmental officials, and doctors. Even during admission into the camp by the political department, they received beating after beating. The camp functionaries received strict instructions that the NN prisoners could be seen in public only while engaged in the most strenuous work. After the first three hours of work, eighty of them had already collapsed. Within six days twenty prisoners were driven into the sentry line and were shot "while attempting escape."

While working on the steep mountain slope, a swift kick from an SS man or a green foreman would cause the prisoner to fall outside the sentry line, where he was shot down. The SS sentries received three days leave for each execution, as well as a supplemental ration of food and tobacco. An Alsatian SS man, Fuchs, in particular profited from this policy. The SS man van der Mühlen was appointed especially to undertake abuse and shootings. The camp doctor, SS Captain Schiedlausky, forbade the prisoner orderlies, under threat of severe punishment, to treat the badly injured prisoners. The political prisoners in the infirmary nevertheless treated their NN comrades at night under extremely difficult conditions.

Prisoners who escaped the hell of Natzweiler—Cichosz, a Polish captain and Spanish civil war fighter; a German officer named Haas; a French officer named Civon; a Czech named Mautner—will certainly confirm the conditions described in this sketch.

ROBERT LEIBBRAND, Stuttgart

168. SS Special Camp Hintzert

T HE SS special camp Hintzert near Trier was actually to have been a labor disciplinary camp for shirkers [*Arbeitscheue*], with a maximum sentence of eight weeks. But in summer 1940 it became a special punishment camp for political prisoners from Luxemburg. The camp held only 600 to 800 prisoners, making it possible for the SS to observe closely all events in the camp, to recognize even the most trifling offenses against camp regulations, and to punish them strictly. So, for example, smoking a cigarette, which was strictly forbidden, could mean death for the prisoner caught at it.

The reception of new prisoners occurred as follows. The new prisoner had to make a so-called honor round: He had to circle through the courtyard, enduring blows from sticks, insults, kicks, and douses of water, which continued until he fell down. Some remained lying on the square—already dead on the spot. Old people and invalids who were not capable of running had to stand while holding heavy iron bars straight out in front of them. The undressing, haircutting, and shaving that followed occurred under constant shouting, accompanied by blows from sticks and kicks. All bodily parts covered with hair were shaved by the most primitive means, blood flowing in streams as a result. The soap and razor blades that were saved this way were traded for food on the black market by the quartermaster, SS Master Sergeant Schattner.

Camp life began in the early morning with the so-called morning calisthenics, administered by SS men Tammer and Schaaf. The exercises consisted of long-distance running, crawling, tumbling, and knee bends, during which the prisoners were constantly abused with kicks and blows. Once when a prisoner had to spit during morning calisthenics, Sergeant Schaaf used kicks and blows to force him to lick up his own spittle.

After the morning exercises came washing, dressing, bed making, and cleaning of the rooms. Usually only about five minutes remained for the distribution of coffee and bread, including eating and drinking. Afterward all rushed to morning roll call, after which the distribution of work assignments followed. The work details were difficult without exception. The Pleurig work detail described below serves as an example.

Prisoners ran at double time from the camp to the Rheinsfeld train station, which was 2.5 miles away. From there they went by train to Pleurig, after which they marched 5 miles to Pellingen, mostly up a steep hill and under constant abuse. Then the work on the water line began. It was the most difficult trench digging, during which the SS watched closely to make sure that no prisoner straightened his back for even a minute. During this heavy labor, with its long marches, the prisoners received for lunch only a piece of bread and a soup made from unground grain and turnip leaves. The work details Thalfang and Nonnweiler were similar. Every evening on their return, the work details pulled a small wagon behind them on which were piled the softly groaning prisoners who had collapsed from the exertions and beatings. In front of the infirmary building, the wagon was tipped over by the block officer so that the patients simply fell out onto the ground.

Especially feared was the interrogation of new prisoners, during which a horse-whip and a noose for hanging played major roles. The interrogating Gestapo officials were named Ratke, Rockel, Moritz, Suder, Schmitt, Klöcker, Butzke, and Dörstel. Especially stubborn prisoners were put in the so-called dark cell, where they sometimes remained more than four weeks. These cells remained locked the entire day, so prisoners had to urinate in a drinking cup. No opportunity was given to clean the cup.

The general level of camp rations was so bad that even after only four weeks many prisoners died of undernourishment. And at every occasion prisoners were punished by the withdrawal of rations.

The camp doctor was SS Master Sergeant Brendel, by trade a brick mason. His "treatment" consisted of blows with a cane or fireplace poker on the naked chest. He was a notorious drunkard. One night Brendel came into Sick Room 5 totally drunk and, amid the howls of patients, overturned all the hospital beds. He used a stick to smash all the lamps, glasses, and bottles in the room. Then he forced the prisoners who were lying on the floor, among them Pastor Keup of Berdorf, to scurry through the room picking up the splinters and pieces of broken glass.

After December 1942, when it was permitted to receive parcels of food, a splendid time began for the SS. Under the pretext that the packages were too heavy, they were regularly plundered or simply not distributed at all. Among the robbers of parcels, the most active were the roll call officers Kleinhenn and Kertel. Camp Commandant Sporenberg definitely knew all about these crimes but did nothing to stop them. On the contrary, he continued to stir up the SS men against the prisoners. In addition to the block officers mentioned, the sergeants Vieth, Windig, Trinkaus, and Klein were especially infamous.

Unfortunately, there were a few prisoners who took care of the business of abuse for the SS. First to be named should be the senior camp inmate, Eugen Wipf of Switzerland, who beat many prisoners to death or crippled them. The few Jews who were brought into camp were considered fair game and were murdered after a short time. The French who were brought into camp were designated with large white letters, *H.N.* [*Hunde Nation*, nation of dogs].

This report is only preliminary and can therefore say only a little about the horrible beatings and deaths that were part of the daily routine at Hintzert.

ALBERT BEFFORT, Bech, Luxemburg

Letter of Transmission

HEADQUARTERS
THIRD UNITED STATES ARMY
PSYCHOLOGICAL WARFARE BRANCH
APO 403

11 May 1945

(G-2)

SUBJECT: Report on Buchenwald Concentration Camp

TO: Lt. Col. Louis Huot, Psychological Warfare Officer, Third United States Army

1. This team, consisting of the undersigned officer, T/3 Max M. Kimenthal, T/4 Richard Akselrad, and T/5 Ernst Biberfeld, arrived at the Buchenwald Concentration Camp (near Weimar, Germany) on April 16th.

The team's mission was to make a thorough investigation of the concentration camp, its organizational setup, and of what had happened there from the time of its establishment until its liberation by Allied troops on April 11th, 1945.

2. In making this report the team was greatly assisted by a number of liberated inmates of the concentration camp. Especially the work of Dr. Eugen Kogon of Vienna contributed essentially to the successful completion of the team's mission.

3. The nature of the mission and the fact that a number of the men working on this report do not speak English made it necessary that the report be written in German. In view of the importance of this document it is suggested that PWD, SHAEF arrange to have same translated into English. This officer discussed this question with Mr. Crossman of PWD SHAEF, and the latter agreed that this would be possible.

4. It is suggested that this document be made available to interested agencies of the Allied Governments and also to the participants of the San Francisco Conference now in session.

ALBERT G. ROSENBERG
2nd Lt. Inf.
C.O. Det. B. 4th MRB Co.
PWD, SHAEF

Glossary

action: [*Aktion*] A planned SS or Gestapo raid to round up prisoners of a particular category.

antisocials: [*Asozialen*] A category of prisoners that included the homeless, street people, "idlers," and drifters.

Aryan: Term used in Nazi racial ideology for Nordic race; non-Jews.

block: A barracks building. Dormitory blocks were usually divided into two separate wings.

block officer: An SS noncommissioned officer in charge of a barracks. An inmate leader, the senior block inmate, exercised day-to-day control over the block.

caracho: Double time in camp slang; term originally from Spanish.

cellblock: Cells at the camp main gate that the SS used as a jail and for special punishments.

Center: [*Zentrum*] Official name of the Catholic political party in Germany from 1871 to 1933.

commandant: Camp commander. At Buchenwald Karl Koch was commandant until early 1942, Hermann Pister until April 1945. See *deputy commandant.*

concentration camp: [*Konzentrationslager*] Abbreviated in German as KL (official) or KZ (prisoner slang). Established by the SA or SS beginning in 1933 to house political prisoners or opponents of the regime.

Death's-Head SS: [*Totenkopfverbände*] Special SS units trained at Sachsenhausen to serve as concentration camp guards.

deputy commandant: [*Lagerführer*] Literally, camp leader. The deputy commandant exercised day-to-day control over the camp, assisted by other staff officers such as the roll call officer.

Dora: Concentration camp near Nordhausen, used for underground assembly of V-2 rockets; originally a branch camp of Buchenwald.

Ettersberg: Forested mountain near Weimar, Thuringia; site of Buchenwald.

extermination camp: A camp whose main purpose was mass extermination of Jews and others targeted for death by Nazi ideology, such as Auschwitz, Treblinka, and Maidanek. These camps had gas chambers, unlike Buchenwald.

gate: [*Tor*] Gatehouse that served as the main entrance to the camp grounds and SS control center for the camp and that housed the camp jail.

General Government: [*General Gouvernement*] German occupation government in Poland after October 1939, headed by Hans Frank. The eastern third of Poland was occupied by the Soviets between September 1939 and June 1941.

German Armament Works: [Deutsche Ausrüstungswerke, or DAW] SS-owned industrial enterprise located on the grounds of Buchenwald; originally produced wood and metal products, later munitions.

German Earth and Stone Works: [Deutsche Erd- und Steinwerke] SS-owned clay mine and pottery works at Berlstedt, manned by Buchenwald prisoners.

378

Gestapo: [Geheimes Staatspolizei] Literally, secret state police. Political police under Reich SS Leader Heinrich Himmler that controlled admission and release of prisoners at Buchenwald through the political department in camp.

ghetto: During World War II, walled or fenced sections of East European cities where Jews were concentrated as the first step toward their liquidation.

Gustloff Works: Large SS-owned munitions factory located on the grounds of Buchenwald.

I Barracks: Isolation Barracks; the section of Buchenwald outside the fence where celebrity prisoners were held as hostages.

Judenrat: Literally, Jewish Council. Units set up in ghettos by German occupation forces for self-administration.

kapo: Prisoner leader of a work detail or other administrative unit. From the Italian *capo*, meaning head or chief.

KPD: [Kommunistische Partei Deutschlands] Acronym for the Communist party of Germany.

labor records office: [Arbeitsstatistik] Controlled assignment of prisoner labor from Buchenwald, including branch camps and external details. Prisoner clerks made the actual assignments.

Landtag: German state parliaments from 1871 to 1933. See *Reichstag*.

Little Camp: Small section of camp separated by barbed wire where new prisoners were quarantined. In spring 1945 filled to overflowing with starving and diseased prisoners.

Main Economic and Administrative Office: [SS Wirtschafts- und Verwaltungs-Hauptamt, or WVHA] Head economic office of the SS in Berlin, commanded by Oswald Pohl. Section D under Reinhard Glücks administered concentration camps; prisoner labor fell under WVHA control.

Muslim: Prisoner slang for an inmate in a catatonic state near death. Possibly from a Hindu or Muslim ascetic known as a fakir.

Nationalist: [Deutsch-Nationale Volkspartei, or DNVP] A conservative political party in the Weimar Republic. Once allies of Hitler, some of its members were jailed later in the Third Reich.

Night and Fog: [*Nacht und Nebel,* or NN] Term used in Nazi documents referring to secret deportation of prisoners, usually late at night, from occupied territories; applied in particular to French and Dutch prisoners as per Hitler's order of December 7, 1941.

NSDAP: [Nationalsozialistische Deutsche Arbeiterpartei; National Socialist German Workers party] Acronym for the official name of the Nazi party.

Nuremberg laws: German racial laws of September and November 1935 under which Jews lost rights of citizenship. Persons were categorized as Jews if they had at least two Jewish grandparents, as non-Aryans if they had one Jewish grandparent or a Jewish spouse.

Organisation Todt (OT): State-owned construction enterprise engaged in priority civilian and military projects, headed by Albert Speer. A large employer of prisoner labor.

organize: Prisoner slang for obtaining food or other necessities illegally.

Personal Property Room: [*Effektenkammer*] Room where prisoners' personal belongings were kept until death or release.

politicals: Political prisoners, also called reds, after the identifying triangles they wore on their uniforms.

professional criminals: [*Berufsverbrecher*] From Gestapo terminology for prisoners convicted of violations of the criminal code; called greens in camp slang, after their identifying triangles.

protectorate: [*Protektorat*] German occupation government of Bohemia and Moravia (previously Czechoslovakia) after March 1939. Headed by Reinhard Heydrich until his assassination in May 1942.

Rath action: [Also known as *Kristallnacht*] The Nazi attack on Jewish stores, homes, and synagogues on November 9, 1938, allegedly in reprisal for the assassination of Paris embassy secretary Ernst vom Rath. Many Jewish prisoners were brought to Buchenwald thereafter.

Reich Security Main Office: [Reichssicherheits Hauptamt, or RSHA] SS headquarters in Berlin under Heinrich Himmler; Section 5 (Gestapo) controlled all concentration camps.

Reichstag: German national parliament in Berlin from 1871 to 1933, stripped of its powers under the Nazis.

Reichswehr: Official name of the German regular army until March 1935. See *Wehrmacht.*

roll call square: [*Appellplatz*] Paved square near the gate where prisoners reported for daily roll calls.

room attendant: [*Stubendienst*] Prisoner orderly in charge of the room where prisoners slept; his principal duty was distribution of food rations.

SA: [Sturmabteilung] Storm troopers; Nazi paramilitary organization founded in 1919, often called Brownshirts because of their uniforms. They played a role in creating the first concentration camps after Nazi seizure of power in 1933.

Security Service: [Sicherheitsdienst, or SD] A special SS secret police unit, separate from the Gestapo, commanded first by Reinhard Heydrich, then Ernst Kaltenbrunner.

senior block inmate: [*Blockältester*] Literally, block elder; inmate leader in charge of a barracks.

senior camp inmate: [*Lagerältester*] Literally, camp elder; inmate leader appointed by the SS to head camp self-administration.

sentry line: [*Postenkette*] SS armed sentries used to guard details of prisoners working outside the camp. Many prisoners were shot for crossing this invisible line.

SPD: [Sozialdemokratische Partei Deutschlands] The Social Democratic party of Germany, a moderate socialist party in the Weimar Republic.

SS: [Schutzstaffel] Unit originally formed as Hitler's bodyguards, identified by black uniforms. By 1939 a mass organization under Heinrich Himmler that controlled the police and penal systems, economic enterprises, and military units (Waffen SS).

submerge: To disappear, usually by changing identity with a dead prisoner.

subsidiary camp: [*Aussenlager*] A forced labor branch camp under control of Buchenwald, usually located at a mine or factory too far away for prisoners to return to camp daily.

V-1 and V-2: [*Vergeltungswaffen*] Literally, revenge weapons; German rocket weapons built in secret underground factories by prisoner labor. See *Dora.*

Waffen SS: Military units under direct SS control, distinguished from the regular army. See *Wehrmacht.*

Wehrmacht: Official name for the regular Germany army after March 1935. See *Reichswehr.*

whipping block: [*Bock*] A wooden trestle on which prisoners were strapped during whippings.

work detail: [*Kommando*] SS terminology for a squad of prisoners assigned to labor duties. Some (external details) were assigned work outside camp grounds but returned at night.

work detail officer: An SS noncommissioned officer in charge of a work detail. Actual daily control was in the hands of a prisoner kapo.

Notes to the Introduction

1. The most valuable introduction on the liberation of the camps is Robert H. Abzug, *Inside the Vicious Heart: Americans and the Liberation of Nazi Concentration Camps* (New York: Oxford University Press, 1985). See also Jon Bridgman, *The End of the Holocaust: The Liberation of the Camps* (Portland, Ore.: Areopagitica Press, 1990).

2. Eugen Kogon, *The Theory and Practice of Hell: The German Concentration Camps and the System Behind Them*, trans. Heinz Norden (New York: Berkley 1980), x–xi.

3. At least one other copy survived until recently. It was still in Kogon's hands at the time his revised edition appeared in 1974. His copy was reportedly destroyed in a basement flood at his home some years later.

4. Kogon's book appeared as *Der SS-Staat* (Munich: Karl Alber Verlag, 1946). The English translation by Heinz Norden first appeared in 1950 and was based on the 1949 German edition.

5. In addition to the references to the Buchenwald Report, see Manfred Overesch, "Ernst Thapes Buchenwalder Tagebuch von 1945," *Vierteljahrshefte für Zeitgeschichte* 29, 4 (1981), 631–672. See also Christopher Burney, *The Dungeon Democracy* (New York: Duell, Sloan and Pearce, 1946), 117–139.

6. Egon W. Fleck and First Lieutenant Edward A. Tenenbaum, "Buchenwald, a Preliminary Report," Headquarters Twelfth Army Group, Publicity and Psychological Warfare, 24 April 1945, 12, National Archives (NA), Record Group (RG) 331, SHAEF, G-5, 17.11, jacket 10; "Testimony of Captain Robert Dinolt, Medical Corps," 19 June 1945, 5, NA, RG 338, case 000-50-9, box 446.

7. Telegram Berne to Foreign Office [London], 28 April 1945, copy to SHAEF, NA, RG 331, SHAEF, G-1, 254 PW Camps.

8. Fleck and Tenenbaum, "Report," 2.

9. Overesch, "Ernst Thapes Buchenwalder Tagebuch," 651.

10. Fleck and Tenenbaum, "Report," 6.

11. Interview with Peter de Wetter, January 18, 1994.

12. Brigadier General Eric F. Wood, "Report on Inspection of German Concentration Camp at Buchenwald," dated 25 April 1945, of visit on 16 April, NA, RG 331, SHAEF, G-5, 105.

13. "Testimony of Captain Robert Dinolt," 3.

14. Major General Warren F. Draper, "Report of Visit to Buchenwald Concentration Camp," 30 April 1945, NA, RG 331, SHAEF, G-5, DP 2711, 7, 1.

15. "Testimony of Captain Robert Dinolt," 3.

16. Wood, "Report," 4.

17. Lieutenant Colonel F. van Wyck Mason, "Report on German Concentration Camp for Political Prisoners at Buchenwald," 4 May 1945, 1, NA, RG 331, SHAEF, G-5, 60, jacket 3.

18. Fleck and Tenenbaum, "Report," 14.

19. Draper, "Report," 3.

20. Wood, "Report," 1.

21. "Testimony of Captain Robert Dinolt," 5.

22. "The Victims Speak: Children of Buchenwald," PWD Weekly Intelligence Summary, 16 May 1945, NA, RG 331, SHAEF, G-5, 7.32, rel. with G-2; Lieutenant C. I. Schottland and M. Macdonald, "Report on Field Trip to Buchenwald," 12 June 1945, NA, RG 331, SHAEF, G-5, 2711, 7.21.

23. *Nachrichten* 6, 21 April 1945; 7, 22 April 1945, Archiv Buchenwald, 77 2–62; address by Herschel Schacter in Brewster Chamberlain and Marcia Feldman, eds., *The Liberation of the Nazi Concentration Camps 1945* (Washington, D.C.: United States Holocaust Memorial Council, 1987), 35–39.

24. *Nachrichten* 10, 25 April 1945; 17, 3 May 1945, Archiv Buchenwald.

25. "Final After Action Report," Twelfth Army Group, vol. 7; "Report on Operations, G-5 Section," 83, NA, RG 331.

26. Alfred D. Chandler Jr. and Stephen Ambrose, eds., *Papers of Dwight David Eisenhower, The War Years* (Baltimore: Johns Hopkins University Press, 1976), vol. 4, 2615–2616, and vol. 5, 187–188 (chronology); Harry C. Butcher, *My Three Years with Eisenhower: The Personal Diary of Harry C. Butcher, USNR, Naval Aide to General Eisenhower* (New York: Simon and Schuster, 1946), 803–805; David Eisenhower, *Eisenhower at War* (New York: Random House, 1986), 765–766.

27. Eisenhower, *Eisenhower at War*, 765–766.

28. Butcher, *My Three Years*, 803–805; Martin Gilbert, *Winston S. Churchill: The Road to Victory*, vol. 7 (Boston: Houghton Mifflin, 1986), 1305.

29. John Colville, *The Fringes of Power: 10 Downing Street Diaries, 1939–45* (New York: Norton, 1985), 591. Entry dated 19 April 1945.

30. Robert Rhodes James, *Winston S. Churchill: His Complete Speeches, 1897–1963*, vol. 7 (New York: Chelsea House, 1974), 7145.

31. "Buchenwald Camp, The Report of a Parliamentary Delegation," Cmd. 6626 (London: His Majesty's Stationery Office, 1945). Copy in NA, RG 338, box 444.

32. Ibid., 7.

33. Chandler and Ambrose, *Eisenhower Papers*, vol. 4, 2623.

34. "Atrocities and Other Conditions in the Concentration Camps in Germany; Report of the Committee Requested by Gen. Dwight D. Eisenhower through the Chief of Staff, Gen. George C. Marshall," 79th Cong., 1st sess., S. Doc. 47, presented by Mr. Barkley, May 15, 1945. Copy in NA, RG 338, box 444.

35. Ibid., 16.

36. Butcher, *My Three Years*, 816.

37. Telegram to AGWAR from SHAEF Main dated 1 May 1945, NA, RG 331, SHAEF, AG, 000.5-2, #11.

38. NA, RG 331, SHAEF, G-5, 17.11, 8929/263.

39. Chandler and Ambrose, *Eisenhower Papers*, vol. 4, 2679.

40. United Nations War Crimes Commission, "Visit of Delegation to Buchenwald Concentration Camp in Germany, Report," NA, RG 338, box 444; Richard Thompson, "Report of Special French Mission Trip to Germany," 27 April 1945, NA, RG 331, SHAEF, G-5, 2711, 7.21.

41. Telegram, Twelfth Army Group to ETOUSA, Secret, Priority, 9 May 1945, signed Bradley, NA, RG 331, SHAEF, G-5, 2711, 7.21.

42. Commanding General, Seventh Army to Headquarters, Sixth Army Group, copy to SHAEF Main, 10 May 1945, NA, RG 331, SHAEF, G-1, 254–263; Memo from SHAEF to Chiefs of all General and Special Divisions, 14 May 1945, signed Colonel H. H. Newman, AGD, NA, RG 331, SHAEF, PWD, 353.02.

43. Percy Knauth, *Germany in Defeat* (New York: Alfred A. Knopf, 1946), chapter 2; Margaret Bourke-White, *Dear Fatherland, Rest Quietly* (New York: Simon and Schuster, 1946), 73–75; Edward R. Murrow broadcast reprinted in Louis L. Snyder, *Encyclopedia of the Third Reich* (New York: McGraw-Hill, 1976), 44–45.

44. Meyer Levin, *In Search: An Autobiography* (New York: Horizon Press, 1950), 241–244.

45. Civil Affairs and Military Government Summary No. 348, 20 May 1945, NA, RG 331, SHAEF, G-5, 17.16, jacket 11.

46. Letter to Leonard Ingrams, PID, London, from Duncan Wilson, Assistant to Deputy Chief of Operations (PWD), 21 May 1945, NA, RG 331, SHAEF, PWD, 319.1, 15901; *Deutsche Konzentrations- und Gefangenenlager, was die amerikanischen und britischen Armeen vorfanden, April 1945*, Archiv Buchenwald, Sig. 32-0-2; PWD, Weekly Intelligence Summary #35, 31 May 1945, NA, RG 331, SHAEF, PWD, 350.9.

47. "Guilt of the German People: Reaction of Ps/W," PWD, Weekly Intelligence Summary #35, 31 May 1945, NA, RG 331, SHAEF, PWD, 350.9, 1.

48. "How Much Do the Germans Know?" PWD, Weekly Intelligence Summary #31, 2 May 1945, NA, RG 331, SHAEF, PWD, 350.9, 7.

49. "Report of Investigation of Alleged War Crime," to the Commanding General, Third U.S. Army, 3 June 1945, signed Raymond Givens, NA, RG 338, case 000-50-9, box 446.

50. These are incomplete figures based on numbers for fifty-four of the seventy-seven camps liberated. Letter to SHAEF, G-5, DP from Colonel A. H. Moffitt, Jr., 29 June 1945, NA, RG 331, SHAEF, G-5, DP 2711/7.

51. Order to Commander, P & P.W. Div., Twelfth Army Group, Attn. Al Toombs, 29 March 1945, NA, RG 331, SHAEF, PWD, 201.

52. "Namensliste der bei der PWD beschäftigten Personen," original document from April 1945 in the possession of Albert G. Rosenberg.

53. Short biographical sketches in *Der Spiegel* 42, 1 (January 4, 1988), 156; Joachim Kaiser, "Chronist, Mahner und Helfer," *Süddeutsche Zeitung*, December 29, 1987, 11; "Streitbarer Mahner," *Frankfurter Allgemeine*, December 29, 1987, 23; Peter Glotz, "Der streitbare Linkskatholik," *Frankfurter Allgemeine*, December 30, 1987, 19; Anton Andreas Guha, "Eugen Kogon gestorben," *Frankfurter Rundschau*, December 29, 1987, 4; *Wer ist Wer?* vol. 12 (Berlin: Arani, 1955), 623. See also Lutz Lemhöfer, "Eugen Kogon als Faschismus-Forscher," *Die Neue Gesellschaft/Frankfurter Hefte* 12 (1988), 1106; Peter Graf Kielmannsegg, "Abschied von Eugen Kogon," *Merkur* 42, 3 (March 1988), 252.

54. Lemhöfer, "Eugen Kogon," 1106.

55. On Othmar Spann, see Herman Lebovics, *Social Conservatism and the Middle Classes in Germany, 1914–1933* (Princeton: Princeton University Press, 1969), especially chapter 4, "Corporatism in Industrial Society."

56. Glotz, "Linkskatholik."

57. Letter to SHAEF, PWD, Intelligence Section, to Colonel Paley from Second Lieutenant Albert G. Rosenberg, 28 May 1945. This letter dates Kogon's arrival in Buchenwald as fall 1938, though in the preface to the revised edition of *Der SS-Staat* (x), Kogon stated that he arrived in September 1939.

58. Glotz, "Linkskatholik."

59. Affidavit of sworn testimony by Dr. Eugen Kogon, September 24, 1946, doc. 281, NA, RG 338, case 000-50-9, box 447.

60. The handwritten notes, in German script, were probably those of Kogon. In any case he used identical terms indicating the party affiliations of the fifteen German and Austrian informants in the preface to the 1946 edition of his book (xii–xiii).

61. Kogon, *Der SS-Staat* (1946 ed.), xi–xv.

62. Ibid., xiii.

63. "Erinnerungsblätter," *Nachrichten* 6, 21 April 1945, 2, Archiv Buchenwald.

64. Archiv Buchenwald has two such collections: the *Einzelberichte*, also labeled as *Erlebnisberichte*, identified as the material of Otto Halle; and another collection identified as the material of Stefan Heymann. Both sets show about a 70 percent duplication of material from the report translated here.

65. Semi-Monthly Progress Report, PWD Main, 7 June 1945, NA, RG 331, SHAEF, PW 319.1.

66. "Catalog of Documentary Evidence Relating to Buchenwald Concentration Camp," NA, RG 338, case 000-50-9, box 439.

67. "Einzelbeispiele von Folterungen und Grausamkeiten," NA, RG 338, case 000-50-9, *United States v. Prince Josias zu Waldeck et al.,* box 446. One item of supporting, untranslated evidence, listed as B-7, is described as section 4 of an interrogation report, dated 14 May 1945, and is probably from the Buchenwald Report. Givens, "Report," 3.

68. NA, RG 331, SHAEF, PWD, 370.5, Troop Movements, cable dated 11 June 1945.

69. Kogon, *Der SS-Staat* (1946 ed.), xiv.

70. Interview with Albert G. Rosenberg, May 1988.

71. *L'Enfer organisé: le système des camps de concentration* (Paris: La Jeune Parque, 1947); *Sociología de los campos de concentración* (Madrid: Taurus, 1965).

72. Eugen Kogon, *Der SS-Staat* (Munich: Kindler Verlag, 1974); paperback reprint edition (Munich: Heyne, 1989). The last chapter first appeared as "Das Gewissen der Deutschen und die Konzentrationslager" in *Die Neue Rundschau* (Stockholm), no. 4 (July 1946).

73. Kogon, *Theory and Practice of Hell,* 111–112.

74. Ibid., 182–183.

75. Ibid., 192–197.

76. On Kogon's biography, see note 53 above.

77. See footnotes 120, 126, 135, 142, 148, and 150 from Kogon plus others from Rousset and Bettelheim in Hannah Arendt, *Totalitarianism* (New York: Harcourt, Brace and World, 1968), 133ff.

78. Konnilyn G. Feig, *Hitler's Death Camps: The Sanity of Madness* (New York: Holmes and Meier, 1981). On Buchenwald, see especially 85–115.

79. Knauth, *Germany,* 67.

80. Elie Wiesel, *Night,* trans. Stella Rodway (New York: Bantam Books, 1982), 61–62.

81. See, for example, Eberhard Jäckel, *Hitler's World View* (Cambridge: Harvard University Press, 1981; originally published in German, 1969), chapter 3; Lucy Dawidowicz, *The War Against the Jews, 1933–1945* (New York: Holt, Rinehart and Winston, 1975); Robert Edwin Herzstein, *The War That Hitler Won* (New York: Putnam's, 1978).

82. Christopher R. Browning, *Ordinary Men: Reserve Police Battalion 101 and the Final Solution in Poland* (New York: HarperCollins, 1992), 160.

83. Ibid., 161.

84. Letter to Bishop Mandell from J.E.E. Dalberg, Lord Acton, 3 April 1887, in Alan Palmer and Veronica Palmer, *Quotations in History* (New York: Barnes and Noble, 1976), 1.

85. Milan Kundera, *The Book of Laughter and Forgetting*, trans. Michael Henry Heim (New York: Penguin, 1981), 3.

Selected Bibliography

General Works

Abzug, Robert H. *Inside the Vicious Heart: Americans and the Liberation of the Nazi Concentration Camps.* New York: Oxford University Press, 1985.

Bauer, Yehuda. *A History of the Holocaust.* New York: Franklin Watts, 1982.

Bridgman, Jon. *The End of the Holocaust: The Liberation of the Camps.* Portland, Ore.: Areopagitica Press, 1990.

Browning, Christopher R. *Ordinary Men: Reserve Police Battalion 101 and the Final Solution in Poland.* New York: HarperCollins, 1992.

Buscher, Frank M. *The U.S. War Crimes Trial Program in Germany, 1946–1955.* New York: Greenwood, 1989.

Cohen, Elie A. *Human Behavior in the Concentration Camp.* London: Free Association Books, 1988.

Dawidowicz, Lucy. *The War Against the Jews, 1939–1945.* New York: Holt, Rinehart and Winston, 1975.

Des Pres, Terrence. *The Survivor: An Anatomy of Life in the Death Camps.* New York: Oxford University Press, 1976.

Feig, Konnilyn G. *Hitler's Death Camps: The Sanity of Madness.* New York: Holmes and Meier, 1981.

Gilbert, Martin. *The Holocaust: A History of the Jews of Europe During the Second World War.* New York: Holt, Rinehart and Winston, 1985.

Kempowski, Walter. *Haben Sie davon gewußt? Deutsche Antworten.* Afterword by Eugen Kogon. Hamburg: Albrecht Knaus Verlag, 1979.

Krausnick, Helmut; Buchheim, Hans; Broszat, Martin; and Jacobsen, Hans-Adolf. *Anatomy of the SS State.* New York: Walker and Company, 1968.

Langbehn, Hermann. *... Nicht wie die Schafe zur Schlachtbank; Widerstand in den nationalsozialistischen Konzentrationslagern.* Frankfurt: Fischer Taschenbuch, 1980.

Lerner, Daniel. *Psychological Warfare Against Nazi Germany.* Cambridge: MIT Press, 1971.

Levi, Primo. *Survival in Auschwitz.* New York: Collier Books, 1961.

Lipstadt, Deborah E. *Beyond Belief: The American Press and the Coming of the Holocaust, 1933–1945.* New York: Free Press, 1986.

Marrus, Michael R. *The Holocaust in History.* Hanover, N.H.: University Press of New England, 1987.

Müller-Hill, Benno. *Murderous Science: Elimination by Scientific Selection of Jews, Gypsies, and Others, Germany, 1933–1945.* New York: Oxford University Press, 1988.

Segev, Tom. *Soldiers of Evil: The Commandants of the Nazi Concentration Camps.* New York: Berkley Books, 1991.

Snyder, Louis L. *Encyclopedia of the Third Reich.* New York: McGraw-Hill, 1976.

Yahil, Leni. *The Holocaust: The Fate of European Jewry, 1932–1945.* New York: Oxford University Press, 1990.

Works Relating to Buchenwald

Bartel, Walter, ed. *Buchenwald: Mahnung und Verpflichtung.* Berlin: Kongress Verlag, 1960.

Bettelheim, Bruno. *Surviving and Other Essays.* New York: Vintage Books, 1980.

Burney, Christopher. *The Dungeon Democracy.* New York: Duell, Sloan and Pearce, 1946.

Carlebach, Emil. *Buchenwald: Ein Konzentrationslager.* Frankfurt: Röderberg Verlag, 1984.

d'Harcourt, Pierre. *The Real Enemy.* New York: Scribner's, 1967.

Dietmar, Udo. *Häftling X in der Hölle auf Erden.* Weimar: Thüringer Volksverlag, 1946.

Fein, Erich, and Flanner, Karl. *Rot-weiß-rot in Buchenwald.* Vienna: Europaverlag, 1987.

Jahn, Rudi, ed. *Das War Buchenwald! Ein Tatsachenbericht.* Published by the Communist party of Germany, city and district of Leipzig. Leipzig: Verlag für Wissenschaft und Literatur, 1945.

Julitte, Pierre. *Block 26: Sabotage at Buchenwald.* Garden City, N.Y.: Doubleday, 1971.

KL Bu: Bericht des internationalen Lagerkomitees Buchenwald. Weimar: Thüringer Volksverlag, 1946.

Knauth, Percy. *Germany in Defeat.* New York: Alfred A. Knopf, 1946.

Kogon, Eugen. *Der SS-Staat: Das System der deutschen Konzentrationslager.* Munich: Karl Alber Verlag, 1946.

———. *Der SS-Staat: Das System der deutschen Konzentrationslager.* New ed. Munich: Kindler Verlag, 1974. Reprint, Munich: Wilhelm Heyne Verlag, 1989.

———. *The Theory and Practice of Hell.* Translated by Heinz Norden. New York: Berkley Books, 1980. First English ed. 1950.

Konzentrationslager Buchenwald; Geschildert von Häftlingen. Vienna: Stern Verlag, 1946.

Levin, Meyer. *In Search: An Autobiography.* New York: Horizon Press, 1950.

Mermelstein, Mel. *By Bread Alone—The Story of A-4685.* Los Angeles: Auschwitz Study Foundation, 1979.

Michel, Jean, and Noucera, Louis. *Dora.* New York: Holt, Rinehart and Winston, 1980.

Poller, Walter. *Medical Block Buchenwald: The Personal Testimony of Inmate 996, Block 36.* New York: Lyle Stuart, 1961.

Robertson, E. H., ed. *Paul Schneider, the Pastor of Buchenwald.* London: SCM Press, 1956.

Rousset, David. *The Other Kingdom.* New York: Howard Fertig, 1982.

Fiction

Apitz, Bruno. *Nackt unter Wölfen.* Illustrated by Fritz Cremer. Halle: Mitteldeutscher Verlag, 1958.

Remarque, Erich Maria. *The Spark of Life.* New York: Appleton-Century-Crofts, 1952.

Semprun, Jorge. *What a Beautiful Sunday! (Quel beau dimanche).* Translated by Alan Sheridan. San Diego: Harcourt, Brace, Jovanovich, 1982.

Wiechert, Ernst. *The Forest of the Dead.* New York: Greenberg, 1947.

Wiesel, Elie. *Night.* Translated by Stella Rodway. New York: Bantam Books, 1982.

Index